LANGUAGE, CHILDREN AND SOCIETY

The Effect of Social Factors on Children Learning to Communicate

International Series in Psychobiology and Learning

Editor: Samuel A. Corson

In Preparation

V. RENTEL and S. A. CORSON
Psychobiological Aspects of Reading

Other Titles of Interest

B. ASHEM and E. G. POSER
Adaptive Learning

ERON et al.
Learning of Aggression in Children

A. M. GRAZIANO
Child Without Tomorrow

L. A. HERSOV, M. BERGER, D. SHAFFER
Aggression and Antisocial Behaviour
in Childhood and Adolescence

LEFKOWITZ et al.
Growing up to be Violent

R. LYNN
Personality and National Character

C. E. RENFREW
Speech Disorders in Children

LANGUAGE, CHILDREN AND SOCIETY

The Effect of Social Factors on Children Learning to Communicate

Edited by

OLGA K. GARNICA

Assistant Professor
Department of Linguistics
The Ohio State University

and

MARTHA L. KING

Professor
Early and Middle Childhood Education
The Ohio State University

PERGAMON PRESS

OXFORD · NEW YORK · TORONTO · SYDNEY · PARIS · FRANKFURT

U.K. Pergamon Press Ltd., Headington Hill Hall, Oxford OX3 0BW, England

U.S.A. Pergamon Press Inc., Maxwell House, Fairview Park, Elmsford, New York 10523, U.S.A.

CANADA Pergamon of Canada, Suite 104, 150 Consumers Road, Willowdale, Ontario M2J 1P9, Canada

AUSTRALIA Pergamon Press (Aust.) Pty. Ltd., P.O. Box 544, Potts Point, N.S.W. 2011, Australia

FRANCE Pergamon Press SARL, 24 rue des Ecoles, 75240 Paris, Cedex 05, France

FEDERAL REPUBLIC OF GERMANY Pergamon Press GmbH, 6242 Kronberg-Taunus, Pferdstrasse 1, Federal Republic of Germany

First edition 1979

British Library Cataloguing in Publication Data

Language, children and society. - (International series in psychobiology and learning).
1. Children - Language 2. Language arts
I. Garnica, Olga K II. King, Martha L
III. Series
401'.9 LB1139.L3 78-41153
ISBN 0-08-023716-9

In order to make this volume available as economically and as rapidly as possible the author's typescript has been reproduced in its original form. This method unfortunately has its typographical limitations but it is hoped that they in no way distract the reader.

Printed and bound at William Clowes & Sons Limited Beccles and London

Contents

Contributors

JANET BLACK
Department of Early and Middle Childhood Education
College of Education
The Ohio State University
Columbus, Ohio 43210

AKKE DE BLAUW
Institute for General Linguistics
University of Amsterdam
Amsterdam, The Netherlands

BARBARA BOKUS
Psycholinguistics Unit
Institute of Psychology
Warsaw University
Warsaw, Poland

KATHRYN MATEY BORMAN
Department of Learning, Development and Social Foundations
College of Education
University of Cincinnati
Cincinnati, Ohio 45221

LOUISE CHERRY
Department of Educational Psychology
University of Wisconsin-Madison
Madison, Wisconsin 53706

CLARA DUBBER
Institute for General Linguistics
University of Amsterdam
Amsterdam, The Netherlands

OLGA K. GARNICA
Department of Linguistics
The Ohio State University
Columbus, Ohio 43210

JEAN BERKO GLEASON
Department of Psychology
Boston University
Boston, Massachusetts 02215

CHERYL A. GRACEY
Department of Linguistics
University of Michigan
Ann Arbor, Michigan 48109

JUDITH GREEN
Department of Early Childhood Education
Kent State University
Kent, Ohio 44242

DELL HYMES
Graduate School of Education
University of Pennsylvania
Philadelphis, Pennsylvania 19174

PARTRICIA IRVINE
Department of Educational Foundations
College of Education
University of New Mexico
Albuquerque, New Mexico 87131

VERA JOHN-STEINER
Department of Educational Foundations
College of Education
University of New Mexico
Albuquerque, New Mexico 87131

DEBORAH KELLER-COHEN
Department of Linguistics
University of Michigan
Ann Arbor, Michigan 48109

MARY RITCHIE KEY
Department of Linguistics
University of California-Irvine
Irvine, California 92664

ELLIOT G. MISHLER
Department of Psychiatry
Harvard Medical School
Boston, Massachusetts 02115

HELGI OSTERREICH
Department of Educational Foundations
College of Education
University of New Mexico
Albuquerque, New Mexico 87131

GHISLAINE VAN ROOSMALEN
Institute for General Linguistics
University of Amsterdam
Amsterdam, The Netherlands

JEFFREY SHULTZ
Department of Learning, Development and Social Foundations
College of Education
University of Cincinnati
Cincinnati, Ohio 45221

MAUREEN SHIELDS
Department of Child Development and Educational Psychology
Institute of Education
University of London
London, England WC1H 0AA

GRACE SHUGAR
Psycholinguistics Unit
Institute of Psychology
Warsaw University
Warsaw, Poland

ROGER SHUY
Center for Applied Linguistics
1611 North Kent Street
Arlington, Virginia 22209

CATHERINE SNOW
Institute for General Linguistics
University of Amsterdam
Amsterdam, The Netherlands

CYNTHIA WALLAT
Department of Early Childhood Education
Kent State University
Kent, Ohio 44242

General Editor's Preface

One of many anecdotes circulated about the distinguished American physiologist, Anton J. Carlson, relates to his custom of confronting fledgling scientists, after the first presentation of their research, with the question: "Why did you do it?" This is a sensible question to ask regarding any new project, including the introduction of a new series of Monographs on Psychobiology and Learning.

Psychobiology represents an integrated holistic approach to learning, behavior, and physical, mental, and emotional health. Psychobiology is based on a unitary concept of mind-brain and nature-nurture interrelationship. It rests on the assumption that the central nervous system represents the physico-chemical basis of learning, emotion, and behavior. As figuratively expressed by Ralph W. Gerard, one of America's outstanding neurophysiologists, "For every crooked thought, there must be a crooked molecule." Similarly, the various configurations of molecules in a living organism, and especially in humans, are, in turn, influenced by a variety of physico-chemical, as well as psychosocial stimuli, thus justifying the Bard of Avon's expression: "We are such stuff as dreams are made of."

In the light of the foregoing, the object of this series of Monographs on Psychobiology and Learning will be:

1. to incorporate into learning theory and practice, principles and methods derived from recent remarkable developments in psychobiology and studies on mechanisms of psychobiologic integration of perceptual, behavioral, and physiologic functions;

2. to elucidate the relationship of recent discoveries regarding the right-left structural and functional asymmetries in the brain to rational-verbal and intuitive-nonverbal types of learning and communication and the problems of creativity, esthetics, and ethics;

3. to clarify the interactions between genetics and psychosocial, cultural, and emotional factors in the differential abilities of students to learn various concepts and skills and to develop independent functioning abilities and wholesome social interactions;

4. to elucidate the effects of stress and anxiety (in students and teachers) on learning, social communication, and adaptive behavior;

5. to bring to the attention of teachers and students, studies on the development of adaptive coping mechanisms in meeting stressful situations and improving learning skills.

Samuel A. Corson

Department of Psychiatry
The Ohio State University
Columbus, Ohio 43210 USA

Preface

This volume represents a broad and comprehensive effort to consider the processes involved in the development of communicative skills in the young child, in particular as these unfold during the child's participation in social interactions in a variety of everyday, educational situations. For a fuller understanding of these processes, through which the child learns the vast array of communicative skills necessary to function effectively in social contexts, it is necessary to consider the broad range of situations in which the communicative exchanges are embedded--school, home, community, etc. The chapters in this book reflect a wide range of interests and the authors represent a diverse set of disciplines. They are linked together by an underlying theme--the social genesis of communication and its inextricable interrelationship (ties) with the contexts in which it develops.

Some of the chapters in this volume are based on papers presented and discussed at an invited interdisciplinary conference on social interaction and language development held at The Ohio State University in May 1976. The conference was conducted under the auspices and with the financial support of the following units: The Graduate School, College of Education, College of Humanities, Department of Linguistics, and the Department of Early and Middle Childhood Education. The participants in the conference were Drs. Louise Cherry, Jean Berko Gleason, Dell Hymes, Vera John-Steiner, Elinor Keenan, Deborah Keller-Cohen, Mary Ritchie Key, Elliot G. Mishler, and Roger Shuy. Dean Hymes and Dr. Shuy were the keynote speakers. In addition, the following nine Ohio State University faculty members participated as discussion leaders or chairpersons: Virgina Allen, Sharon Fox, Olga Garnica, Martha King, Maia Mertz, Gay Pinnell, Victor Rentel, Kevin Ryan, and Johanna de Stefano.

We owe thanks to many who helped to make the conference and this book possible. We are, of course, indebted to the various authorities of The Ohio State University for generously supporting the conference. We thank Mary Kuhner for her original efforts in arousing interest in holding a co-sponsored conference on this topic, to Ilse Lehiste for her early support of the idea, and to the many colleagues and students who gave their time and encouragement without which the conference could not have taken place. We thank the conference participants for their fine presentations and all the authors who contributed papers to the volume. We acknowledge with pleasure the assistance and advice given to us by the series editor, Dr. Samuel Corson, and the publishers.

We are also grateful to Marlene Payha and Barbara Fincher for performing the many secretarial tasks that were thrust upon them as a result of the conference and subsequent manuscript preparation. We are especially indebted to Linda Weiss whose accurate and efficient work in typing the manuscripts in final form made the task of preparing the volume manageable. Our thanks also to Nancy Ensign who assisted in checking the manuscript and to David Borker who assisted in the final stages of preparing the indexes. Without their efforts this book would not have been possible.

Olga K. Garnica
Martha L. King

Columbus, Ohio
May 1978

Introduction

There has been a slow but steady, ever growing trend in the last half decade for some linguists and some educators to come together to explore how children learn and use language to communicate in a set of social settings, what could be termed educational contexts--both formal and informal. This is a critical undertaking for both sides. It is an important venture for educational researchers and teachers whose need is to understand the educational setting and convert this understanding into a form that can be acted upon directly. It is an equally important venture for the linguist, especially the developmental psycholinguist, who seeks to understand how language functions for the child in his/her social world and also sees the need to make such research efforts relevant to the urgent social problems that surround us.

Past associations between these two fields have a long standing but often rocky history filled all too often with false promises, unrealistic demands and a certain amount of pettiness and distrust from both sides. The papers in this book are written from the shared broad perspective that language is to be viewed within the dynamics of the wider social context in which it is embedded, that it not only created and shaped by the situation but shares in creating the context itself. The focus is on the social interaction that takes place between child and adult (or another child). This interaction occurs in a variety of situations--home and other informal teaching contexts to the formal classroom.

The papers in this volume cover many facets of language use, but throughout there is a general theme of understanding how social goals are achieved in educational situations through the use of communicative skills. This theme is addressed from many perspectives. Some of the papers identify pervasive global problems in the communicative process. Others present an analysis of relevant and essential information accumulated in some aspect of linguistics. Still other present detailed micro-analyses of very specific interactional protocols. Traditional views on some issues, such as those related to sex differences and those dealing with egocentric speech, are reconsidered. Many current practices in education, e.g., those regarding traditional methods of assessing language skills, are questioned. In all, many challenges to current research methodologies and actual practices are presented.

The first paper by Dell Hymes sets the scene for those to follow by painting a vivid picture of human discrimination and prejudice which touches every child involved in the education process in our country, a result he links to language ignorance. He admonishes linguists for failing to give more attention to the needs of society and calls for educators to become more aware of the critical role of language in all kinds of learning situations. From a somewhat different perspective, Roger Shuy sketches some of the contributions of linguistics to education and delineates some of the problems involved in reaching greater cooperation between linguists and educators. He stresses that a greater understanding of language functions in the learning process is dependent upon studying language within that learning context. In many instances, however, linguists have difficulty getting access to such environments, partly because teachers are often wary of the potential value of this research for them and partly because professional relationships between the researcher and the teacher have not always been adequately established. Other factors, such as the complexity of the entire formal education complex and the increasing concern of the public, especially parents, about the use of children as objects of investigation have served to limit investigations.

Despite these problems and restrictions, the papers that follow show that considerable work is currently underway and that the problems and issues addressed by such research have important implications for the education of children. There are six major issues or themes which are addressed by the authors:

1. The interplay of environmental versus biological factors in the acquisition of communicative skills.
2. The role of sex as a variable in the acquisition and use of communicative skills.
3. The importance of considering the notion of both communicative competence and interactional competence and the different approaches available to study.
4. The problems and effects of the bilingual experience on the child's communicative abilities.
5. The effect of informal versus variously structured formal educational experiences on the child's communicative output.
6. The need to consider the expressive aspects of communication in conjunction with studying the referential aspects of children's communication.

In the discussion that follows no attempt is made to comprehensively examine these broadly defined areas of concern. Many of these issues have been discussed to one degree or another in the Hymes and Shuy articles, in previous articles by these authors, and by others. In any case, a full and detailed discussion of each would take up considerably more space than is available here.

ENVIRONMENTAL VERSUS BIOLOGICAL FACTORS

The nature versus nurture controversy seems to be with us as much as ever, albeit in a different form. The current general consensus among psychologists, linguists, etc., seems to be that both biological and social factors are present as forces in the developmental process and that they interact to produce adult behavior. The difficulty lies in the identification of factors belonging to one or the other category and in the problem of how to characterize this interaction. These difficulties and the futility of approaching development from the interactionist perspective is discussed very effectively and in great detail by M. P. M. Richards in "Interaction and the concept of development: the biological and social revisited" (in M. Lewis and L. A. Rosenblum, eds., Interaction, Conversation and the Development of Language, 1977). The issue of the role of biological versus social factors is raised in the articles by Gleason, Key and Cherry. In the Gleason and Key articles the issue is discussed in terms of its relevance to discussions of the ontogeny of sex differences in language (and to some extent non-language related) behaviors. Cherry advocates what she terms a comprehensive model, called the sociocognitive approach to communicative development, which calls for the integration of various factors contributing to the developmental process.

SEX DIFFERENCES AND COMMUNICATIVE SKILLS

The study of sex differences and the development of communicative skills is again currently receiving widespread attention both in terms of studies pointing to the differing usage patterns exhibited by the sexes and others indicating the differential linguistic treatment of males and females in a wide range of educational situations--home, nursery school, grade school, etc. As mentioned above, the articles by Gleason and Key discuss sex differences in this realm, mostly from a theoretical perspective which includes (in both papers) a summary of existing research. The de Blauw et al and Garnica papers address the issue of sex differences and communicative behavior in the early years of a child's life, infancy and the toddler period. The role of the mother/caregiver is emphasized.

COMMUNICATIVE COMPETENCE AND INTERACTIONAL COMPETENCE

It has been clear to many for a number of years now that to understand the processes involved in the child's learning of communicative skills it is necessary to expand the idea of competence beyond Noam Chomsky's rather limited vision of what is involved in this process (as what he termed linguistic competence) to include factors related to language use. The notion of communicative competence, first proposed by Dell Hymes, and of interactional competence, proposed by Aaron Cicourel, provide a broader view of what the child must learn in the developmental process. The meaning of the term communicative competence is discussed in the paper by Dell Hymes. The two terms together are also presented in the paper by Janet Black. Some fundamental questions arise out of these two notions: What new avenues of research are most appropriate and necessary for study? What new methodological and procedural approaches must be developed to go along with these new theoretical constructs? The papers by Keller-Cohen and Gracey, Mishler, Cherry, Garnica, Shields, Bokus and Shugar, and Borman explore various aspects of these questions. Although they focus on different research topics, different social contexts (home, school, etc.), and different interactive dyads (adult-child, child-child) they all ultimately rely heavily on the micro-analysis of conversational interaction sequences to establish what rules are in effect if we look beyond linguistic competence to characterize the abilities that must be learned to function satisfactorily in everyday face-to-face interactions.

BILINGUALISM AND THE DEVELOPMENT OF COMMUNICATIVE SKILLS

The ever growing recognition that this nation is not a homogeneous monolingual state has begun to have a powerful impact on public policy and formal education in the United States. The details and consequences of this fact are detailed in Hymes and receive further attention in subsequent sections of this introduction. Some of the major questions associated with this issue are: What is the effect of simultaneous membership in several distinct speech communities on the learning and display of communicative skills in a variety of educational situations? What strategies are used by bilingual/bicultural children in learning such skills? Are these strategies alike or different when compared to the development in children from a more homogeneous linguistic background? The paper by John-Steiner et al, Osterreich and John-Steiner, and Keller-Cohen and Gracey address such issues in school aged (John-Steiner, et al, Osterreich and John-Steiner) and preschool children (Keller-Cohen and Gracey). The former studies investigate children who form one of the major bilingual groups in the country--the Native Americans; the latter deals with children learning to be bilingual by incorporating English into their language repetoire. All three studies have as much to contribute to our general understanding of the process of learning to communicate as they do to our general understanding of bilingual functioning.

THE FORMAL VERSUS INFORMAL EDUCATIONAL PROCESS

Every young child begins the process of learning communicative skills in an informal educational context, that of the home and the neighborhood. By the same token, virtually every child at some point enters a formal educational system of some sort, be it a traditionally oriented classroom or an open classroom situation, which then parallels the continuing informal education that the child receives. Researchers who have studied the school situation all seem to agree that the transition to the formal learning situation puts a formidable demand on the young child to learn new social rules of behavior, to find new ways of using his/her already developed communicative skills and to learn new ones appropriate to the new social environment. The child's adjustment to the formal learning (school) context and the differential effect of different types of learning environments on children with differing informal education backgrounds is discussed in the papers by Shultz and Borman. The paper by Green and Wallat addresses another issue closely related to this one--the problem of how to go about segmenting the seemingly continuous stream of behavior that constitutes the classroom experience into discernable units so that it may become possible to identify the social rules (and appropriate language use rules) that the child must learn in order to function effectively in the classroom.

EXPRESSIVE VERSUS REFERENTIAL ASPECTS OF COMMUNICATION

One of the most pervasive trends in the study of the development of communicative skills is the almost exclusive attention paid to the referential use of language to the exclusion of the expressive function. If this trend were somewhat reversed we might be surprised to find that our current views on the process through which children achieve social goals through the exercising of communicative skills might undergo extensive revision. This point is touched upon in the Hymes article, more so than elsewhere, and it is an important point indeed. Focus on the expressive function of communicative behavior is one of the interesting features of the Vera John-Steiner et al paper on children's imagery. It deserves more attention by researchers.

The need to continue along such lines of research is great for American communities throughout the United States. Never before has the need to understand the development of communicative skills in educational contexts been so crucial. Today the traditional focus of formal education has been challenged as inappropriate for large segments of the pupil population--children from a great variety of minority speech communities that exist in our culture. Children of the poor, minority racial and ethnic groups have in the past been segregated in ghetto schools, subjected to inferior and often demeaning instruction, and all too easily allowed to drop out of school. Recent interpretations of the Constitution by The Supreme Court have determined that such past practices must be eliminated. The courts have mandated that all children in the United States have the right to a truly educationally sound learning environment in which they can have equal opportunity to learn and maintain dignity and self-respect. It is all too unfortunate that it is by court order and not by mandate of the majority that such changes are ordered. Change imposed from outside unfortunately results in little or no truly effective change at all.

In the 19th century the children of immigrants were expected to learn English and associated customs of established Americans. Today the situation has changed. Ethnic groups throughout the country insist on maintaining their own identity, their own language and customs. At the same time, they insist that their children learn in school those concepts and skills that are necessary for social and economic advancement and power. All too often children of widely varying speech communities are found inside the same classroom, a classroom with a single teacher. There is little evidence that either judges or educators understand the complex nature of the social setting that is created. And this situation is now found not only on the east and west coasts where it receives the most publicity, but throughout the land--in the rural heartland and in the cities. Often the urgency of the demand to achieve educational equality brings about simplistic solutions from schools, for example, the introduction of a rigid skills-centered curriculum, which restricts rather than enhances the development of the kind of environment in which individuals from different experience background could coexist in harmony. To quote H. L. Mencken, "For every complex problem there is a simple solution, and it is wrong." So it is in this case. There are no simple solutions, but there is a complex problem, a complex problem that needs to be researched through cooperative efforts from a wide variety of perspectives by individuals sensitive to and aware of the issues involved. The papers in this volume represent a step in this direction. May there be many more.

Olga K. Garnica
Martha L. King

Language in Education: Forward to Fundamentals

DELL H. HYMES
Graduate School of Education, University of Pennsylvania

In this paper I would like to speak to the issue of imperatives for change--change in the current university settings, and change in schooling in general. I believe profoundly in the need for change in the way we understand language, and in what we do with language in schools. In fact, I personally agreed to become Dean of the School of Education at the University of Pennsylvania on the strength of that belief. But let me pause here and address myself to those of you who might suspect that you are about to hear yet another lecture from a self-appointed bearer of light to the benighted. This is not so. Part of what we need to know in order to change is not now known by anyone. No one who gives priority in the study of language to the needs of education could consider present linguistics a region of the already saved, toward which educators must look for missionaries and redemption. Teachers are in fact closer to part of it than most linguists. I have argued against the mainstream in linguistics for years, precisely because it has been inadequate to study the role of language in human life. It has made assumptions, adopted methods, accepted priorities that prevent the contribution to education that serious study of language should make.

There are important scholarly reasons for critique of the mainstream in linguistics, reasons that draw on traditions of thought with roots in the anthropology of Sapir, the sociology of Marx, the linguistics and poetics of Jakobson, the literary criticism and rhetoric of Burke. The contribution of each of these men, and something of my debt to them appears in a number of my other writings (see Hymes 1970, 1974, ch. 8 for Sapir; Hymes 1974:85-86, 121-122, 204, for Marx; 1975, for Jakobson; 1974, ch. 7, for Burke.) There are scientific problems internal to linguistics that cannot be solved without change in the foundations from which they are approached. But there are civic reasons for critique as well. One by one some of us find it intolerable to continue defining the field of linguistics in a way that divorces it from the needs of the society which supports it. The number of students of language sharing this outlook is growing rapidly. The time is ripe for a relation between the study of language and the study of education that is one of partnership, not preaching as has so often been the case in the past.

Please do not misunderstand me, however. To criticize linguistics is not to absolve education. The ability of schools to deal with the linguistic situation in the United States is severely limited. One often hears it said, that it is important to start with where the child is and develop the child's full potential. To do this, linguistically, one must have knowledge of the ways of speaking of the community of which the child is part. Too little knowledge of this sort is available. Each of us has some insight into these things--

some command of the ways of speaking, but each of us is a poor judge as well. Just because language is basic to so many other things, so presupposed, much of our speaking is out of awareness. We may be ignorant of much of it, or even in good faith confidently misreport it. Things we are sure we never say may turn up on someone's audio tape recorder. Matters of more or less may be assimilated to a sense of all-or-nothing. Our impressions of the speech of others may be remarkably accurate for placing them, without our being able to say accurately on what the impression was based, and without our being aware that our own speech may contain some of the same features. Recently a linguist and anthropologist in Montreal recorded the speech of two friends, a man and a woman, each speaking sometimes in formal situations, sometimes in informal situations in which the colloquial French known as Joual was appropriate. She played samples to a distinguished Montreal audience. The audience heard four people, not two. It could not be convinced that there were only two, so strong were its preconceptions as to the categorical difference (Gillian Sankoff, personal communication).

If we are to know objectively what speaking is like, there must be ethnographies of speaking. We must be open to the discovery of facts that may turn out to be inconsistent with or contrasts to our present assumption about grammar, pedagogy, or social life. Educators and linguists alike have been remiss in not thinking of such knowledge as needed. Where linguists have pursued intuitions and universal models that ignore the realities of speech communities and language use, many educators have pursued notions of language and correctness that have had the same effect. Why strive for more knowledge about something one already knew was not really 'language'? that one knew was 'wrong'?

All this leads me to believe that there are three primary imperatives for change: (1) to acknowledge the need for knowledge of the language situations of our country, (2) to support training and research to obtain such knowledge, and (3) to change the relations between linguistics and education.

To elaborate on this last imperative, let me say that a new relation between linguistics and education may be basic to all the rest. The essential point is that the nature of the change that is needed is not one-sided or one way. Linguists and educators should work together and change together. Only then can research on language be relevant to the situations faced by schools. I shall return to the topic of the relation between linguistics and education. Now let me turn the discussion to the need for knowledge.

WHAT DO WE NEED TO KNOW?

Certain goals on which we would probably all agree should govern imperatives for change. The treatment of language in schools should help, not harm those involved. It should help children, and through them their families and communities, to maintain and foster self-respect. It should be consonant with respect for diversity of background and aspirations. It should contribute to equality rather than inequality. It is probably hard to keep from nodding at words like these. Such words are familiar and accepted. Yet we face assumptions and ignorance about language that contradict and work against such goals.

Consider a school in a community. What would you want to know, if you were responsible for the linguistic aspect of the schooling there? There are many who would not think that there was much that they needed to know, even how to use the language of the children. To take an example from my own experience, most teachers in Madras, Oregon, the school which children from the Warm Springs Indian Reservation attend, do not think they need to know anything about the Indian languages used in the children's homes or the etiquette of rules of speaking taught these children in the home environment. Recently I was asked to a meeting at the Philadelphia School Board to help resist pressure to remove the requirement that a teacher in a TESOL class know the language of the children being taught English, that is, be able to communicate with them. Indeed, by and large, knowing languages and knowing about language is little valued in our country, if it involves acceptance of diversity. To take another example, you and I may have no difficulty in understanding standard West Indian English, may even admire it (I think it, myself, the most lovely English I have heard) but a Jamaican student who was recently admitted to a state-affiliated university in Philadelphia was required to take a course in English for foreign students because of her "poor" English. Have you not often heard educated middle-class whites say in exasperation to a cab-driver or voice on the phone, "Oh, I can't understand you", although the speaker's variety of Black English or English with a Spanish accent was entirely intelligible? Having identified the difference, the listener closed his ears.

When educated, concerned people want to know about language, what is it they are likely to want to know? A graduate student at my university reports that when she recently spoke to a group that supports her studies, the serious, well-intentioned questions they posed to her made assumptions about languages and their relations to human groups that a linguistics student could not even have imagined entertaining. Recently I was asked by a cultured voice on the phone to help with a program being planned for the Canadian Broadcasting System, to view French in Montreal in the light of similar situations in the United States and the Caribbean. I began helpfully providing names of persons who might have been of assistance, but as the conversation progressed it became increasingly clear that the premise of the program was that the French-speaking lower classes of Montreal could not think right because they could not speak right. You can imagine the haste and confusion with which I withdrew the information I had provided and tried to dissociate myself entirely from the project.

These are merely recent instances that have impinged upon me in the course of a month or two. It is almost too painful to be a student of language attentive to such things. Examples of prejudice, discrimination, ignorance bound up with language accumulate so readily, it makes one wonder if discrimination connected with language is not so pervasive as to be almost impervious to change, so deeply rooted as to almost preclude support for the asking of questions that might lead to change. To be sure, some may be sure that children would be fine if left alone, and be glad to learn what is wrong with schools. Others may be sure that schools are doing what is right, and be glad to learn what is wrong with children and the homes from which they come. It is hard to find people who sense a need to understand objectively the school child's communicative world. It is a world seriated into a multiplicity of contexts of situation and ways of speaking suitable to each. A world of a plurality of norms for selecting and grouping together features of verbal style, and a plurality of situation-sensitive ways of interacting and interpreting meaning in terms of styles, such that a type of situation such as classroom interaction with a teacher or formal test-taking has meaning in terms of its relation to the rest. Such that each involves a spoken or written genre that has a place in a series of such, a possibility of performance dependent on particular rules for commitment to performance. To understand the part of a verbal repertoire that appears in educational settings, one needs to be able to compare choices of communicative device and meaning, displays of communicative and cognitive ability, across a range of settings. To understand the part of a child's (and also teacher's) ways of speaking one sees in school, one needs to understand the whole. One needs to do or to draw on linguistic ethnography. (This is a point which I have elaborated on in my Introduction Cazden et.al. (1972) and have reiterated on other occasions.)

As you know, very little has been done and there is little to draw upon. What I have sketched in very general terms is what one might reasonably ask about if one is concerned with the role of language in schooling in another culture or country. In a sense, we need to be able to stand back from our own situation so as to see it as strange and understand that we need to know many things about it.

THE LITTLE WE ALREADY KNOW: BLACK AMERICAN, NATIVE AMERICAN AND SPANISH-SPEAKING AMERICAN

By my statements in the previous section I do not mean to suggest that nothing at all is known or being done. Certainly there has been a good deal of attention in recent years to patterns of speech associated with some of the major groups that make up this diverse country. Yet the research is scattered and spotty with regard to both geography and class. The case of 'Black English' is instructive. In the 1960's, the way of speaking of Black Americans attracted a good deal of attention. The research has been important in demonstrating the systematic, rule-governed nature of the vernacular spoken by many blacks, as against notions of it as an incoherent corruption. Notions of black children practically without language were shown to be a function of intimidating formal situations in schools, i.e., to be situational, not general (see e.g., Labov, 1972; Kochman, 1977). Some of this work helped as well to highlight the respects in which distinctive features of the vernacular point to the wider spectrum of Caribbean creoles and their West African elements (Rickford, 1977). Awareness grew of the place of the vernacular in peer group interaction against the background of Caribbean and African traditions of spoken artistry. Still, research focused mostly on the variety of speech most strikingly different from the public standard, the vernacular of adolescent urban males. Much less analytic attention was given to the speech of black women, of preachers and ministers, of established upper-class families, or to the Caribbean and African background of elaborated 'talking sweet' and public oratory (see Wright, 1975).

Some explanations of the material that became known were so partial as to be false. Some linguists wished to treat the vernacular as only superficially different and formally derivative from standard English, for reasons having to do in part with convenient simplicity of a grammatical model. Others wished to treat the vernacular as so distinct that it might require its own textbooks. There are indeed places where people want their variety maintained independently in print from a closely related one (in Czechoslovakia, for example, Slovaks feel this way about the relation of their variety to Czech). In the United States, such a conception fails to take into account the actual attitudes of many black people who want the variety of

English in the classroom, especially the written variety, to be the common standard. Still others drew from this isolated fact the inference that blacks deprecated the vernacular, even speaking of 'self-hatred'. In point of fact, there is widespread acceptance of the vernacular variety at home and in informal situations generally (see Hoover, 1975). Yet sympathetic interpretations of black speech can be inadequate too. Many come to know black terms for uses of language, such as 'shucking' and 'jiving', and regard them entirely as an Afro-American ethnic heritage. Yet analogous genres of language use can be found among lower class white youths and such ways of coping verbally may have their origin in subordinate social status as well as in ethnic tradition.

The relation between varieties and uses of English, on the one hand, and being black, on the other, is complex and only beginning to be adequately known. The situation is little better with regard to other major groups. We think of Native Americans in terms of the many languages lost, and of efforts to maintain or revive those that remain. The relation of schools to these efforts is of the greatest importance. My own anger about the treatment of language in schools comes largely from experience of local schools and educational research institutions that affect Indian people at Warm Springs reservation in Oregon. But these situations must not be oversimplified. Indian Americans themselves may differ in their views as to what is best in terms of language, and aspects of language that are crucial to the success of Indian children may not involve the traditional Indian language at all. What the Indian children speak and understand may not be an Indian language, but an Indian variety of English. There are probably several dozen such Indian varieties of English in the United States. They play a significant social role. Someone who has been away from a local community and who returns to it, must take up the local variety of English or be judged a snob by the members of that community. Features of children's speech that may seem to be individual errors may in fact reflect a community norm. They may reflect a carryover into English of patterns from an Indian language. In the English of Indians at Isleta pueblo, south of Albuquerque, New Mexico, a double negative contrasts with a single negative as a carryover of a contrast between two types of negation in the Isleta language. There are doubtless other such examples, but the fact is that Isleta English is the first form of Indian English carefully studied and reported on in print, and that only in the last few years (Leap, 1974).

The language situation of an Indian community will be more complex, in having a standard as well as a local vernacular English present, and a vernacular (perhaps even reduced) variety of an Indian language as well as or even replacing the 'classic' language form. In the Southwest, Spanish may be a factor as well. Yet we have hardly more than a few sketches of such cases. In research with the language patterns of Indians as with Blacks, we have not attempted to provide systematic knowledge of the language situation of the communities experience by the children who speak these varieties. Research has focused not on social reality, but on the exotic elements of the varieties. To say this is not to condemn study of traditional Indian language. Much of my work continues to be devoted to the study of one group of languages, now nearing extinction. I and a colleague are the last to work intensively with fully fluent speakers, and like others in such a situation, we have obligations both to those who have shared their knowledge with us and to those who later will want access to it. The work has its contribution to make to respect and self-respect for Indian people. The disproportion between what most linguists do and what most needs to be done is not here. There have never been enough trained scholars, and much has been lost unrecorded in consequence. With all its wealth our country has sparsely supported knowledge of the languages that first named the continent. The fact is telling. We have barely managed to study languages that fit our image of the noble Redman, let alone begun to notice the actual linguistic makeup of Indian communities.

The knowledge we need in order to begin to understand the linguistic situation of Indian children, goes beyond studying the formal characteristics of the varieties of language to studying patterns of language in their speech communities, i.e., customary community ways of answering questions, calling upon others, taking turns in conversation, speaking or remaining silent, giving instruction by verbal precept of observed example--all the ways in which etiquette of speaking and value of language may take distinctive shape. Many Indian children come to school speaking only English yet encounter difficulty, not because of language difference, but because of difference in patterns for the use of language (Philips, 1972). Children found 'shy' and non-talkative in class may be as talkative as any, if observed in situations where the rights and duties of speaking are those of the community from which they come. In such a case one needs to know, not a language, but a community way of speaking.

The issue and language most prominent today, both politically and socially, is bilingual education for Spanish/English speaking children. I cannot attempt to comprehensively discuss this complex situation here, except to note that the general difficulty is the same as with the two other groups discussed above. Too little is known to provide a basis for forming policies and developing practical programs in schools. The widespread resistence to such an endeavor may indeed cause bilingual education to be seen as having failed before it will ever have a chance to be understood and given a fair trial period. Efforts to provide equal educational opportunity to Spanish-speaking children proceed with a minimum of information as to the Spanish the children speak, in relation to the varieties and uses of Spanish in the community from which they come. No simple general answer can be laid down in advance. There are several national and regional standards, Cuban, Puerto Rican, northern Mexican, Columbian, etc. In many communities there is a range of varieties from a standard to colloquial vernacular and an argot, as well as ways of intermixing Spanish and English in conversation that can count as a special variety among intimates. The attitudes of Spanish-speakers toward the elements of this complex language situation are themselves complex. Clearly it is not enough to advocate the teaching of "Spanish." It is possible to have Anglo children doing well in a Spanish class in a school, with Spanish-speaking children doing poorly. There are problems with the degree of fit between (a) the Spanish spoken by the children and the Spanish being taught, (b) the attitudes of the teacher, and (c) the language-linked aspirations of cultural traditionalists and the job-linked aspirations of some of the working class. The desire of some speakers to institutionalize Spanish as a language of higher education and professional activity may not match the needs of children for whom Spanish is primarily a vernacular of the home and community. There exist problems of children educated in Puerto Rico coming to the mainland with inadequate English and problems of children educated on the mainland going to Puerto Rico with inadequate Spanish.

There are difficulties in assessing the language abilities of children, both for assignment to classes and for evaluation of problems. Assignment to classes is sometimes being done under mandate of law in a begrudging rough-and-ready fashion minimizing the number of children to be assigned. Sometimes the availability of funds in a school district prompts forced assignment to special classes of bilingual children who have no English problem at all. Valid assessments of language ability require naturalistic observation across a range of settings, but such methods have been little developed in explicit form.

Formative evaluation of programs in bilingual situations needs ethnographic knowledge of the community language situation, and summative evaluation needs ethnographic monitoring of the process by which a program comes to have particular meanings and outcomes for participants and community. (The concept of ethnographic monitoring is discussed further in Hymes (MS)). Such success as bilingual programs have, will be best attested in the debates which lie ahead, not by test scores, but by case-history accounts that show convincingly the benefits to children and communities, and how they were achieved.

ETHNIC HERITAGE AND USAGES OF LANGUAGE

The situations of Black Americans, Native Americans, Spanish-speaking Americans are salient but not unique. Bilingual education is an issue for communities of Chinese, Japanese, Filipino, and other ethnic groups. Many European languages in addition to Spanish are maintained in the United States to a significant extent. Immigration renews some of these communities. All of them participate in a climate of opinion that is world-wide. The general truth would seem to be that about twenty years ago, when those who spoke in the limelight foresaw an end to ideology, and an endless technocratic future whose chief problem would be leisure, many ordinary people around the world were drawing a different lesson from their experience. They had been caught up in such a vision of the post-war future for a while, only to begin to find that their place in it was not worth the giving up of all that they had been. Progress came more and more to seem the 'dirty word' that Kenneth Burke called it--less an engine carrying them onward and upward, more a juggernaut about to run over them, their place, their customs, their speech.

This general revival of concern with ethnic heritage is not merely a part of the annual tourist laundry ring around the world, with each countryside emptying out in summer to take in someone else's carefully staged culture while on vacation. It is a shift in outlook that has to do with what one is for oneself, as a member of a family with a certain name, as part of a particular history, as a knowledge of certain places, as certain ways of meeting sorrow and sharing joy. Many of you may know personally the price that can be exacted in acquiring a lingua franca at the cost of a language of the home.

Some repudiate concern of this kind as nostalgia and sentimentality, even as a dangerous refusal to face present realities. I think that something quite profound is involved. Although any one concern may seem particularistic and limiting, when all such concerns are considered together, one sees something general, a deep-running tide. It is a vision limited to national lingua franca that begins to appear old-fashioned, limited, sectarian.

The deep-running tide seems to me a shift in what is regarded as the dominant obstacle to a way of life in balance with human needs. A century, even a generation ago, it was common to think that the dominant obstacle consisted of traditional ideas and customs. Except when compartmentalized in diminished form, as objects of intermittent piety and curiosity, specific cultural traditions, beliefs, conventions, identities, seemed brakes from the past on progress. The future lay with a science and mode of production that could realize the control of nature, and the plenty, of which mankind was capable. Now we are far less sure. Some critics of contemporary society consider the very idea of incessant technological change to be itself the dominant obstacle to a way of life in balance with human needs. Not that material progress is irrelevant, but that the quality of life is seen more clearly to depend on other things as well. What seemed a policy in the interest of all has come to seem an instrument of profit to some at the expense of others in many cases. Uncontrolled, it threatens community today and even sustenance tomorrow. There is an essential linguistic dimension to this. It is hard to specify, but necessary to address. Let me try to suggest something of its nature.

The internal structures of language and the structures of use to which languages are shaped alike show two fundamental, complementary general kinds of function, of meaning, at work. They are intertwined in reality, but our way of thinking about language has separated and opposed them.

Let me stress that I do not mean to suggest that every aspect of language structure and use can simply be assigned to one or the other of the two generalized types of function. They are not either-or catch-alls. They are interdependent. Their nature is not quite the same at one level of language as at another. Their manifestations enter into a variety of relationships as between levels of language. The essential point is that an adequate study of language cannot be built on attention to just one of them. I speak of generalized types of function because there is no agreement on the specific set required in a model of language structure (and a good many specific functions may need to be recognized); some of these are universal and some local. I do think, however, that at any one level there are fundamentally just two kinds of means, and an organization of these means, roughly a 'what' and a 'how'. The principle of contrastive relevance within a frame that is basic to linguistics applies to both: the 'same thing' can be said in a set of contrasting ways, and the 'same way' can be used for a set of contrasting 'things'. A key to the organization of language in a particular culture or period is restriction of free combination of 'whats' and 'hows', the things that must be said in certain ways, the ways that can be used only for certain things. The admissible relations comprise the admissible styles. In effect, the study of language is fundamentally a study of styles. (There is further discussion in my Introduction to Cazden, et.al., 1972; and Hymes, 1974).

One function can be roughly indicated as concerned with naming, reference, sheer statement, the technical, analytic, propositional, logical uses of language. Modern linguistics has built its models on this aspect of language. Modern science, technology, and rationalized bureaucracy give it preeminence. For a time the uses of language characteristic of literature, religion, personal expression, were neglected and on the defensive. For a time the pinnacle of knowledge appeared to many to be a single logical language to which all science and legitimate knowledge might be reduced. That ideal has been largely given up and replaced by recognition of a plurality of legitimate uses of language. The seminal figures in philosophy of course were Cassirer and Wittgenstein, and there have been related developments in poetics, anthropology, sociology.

The other function is concerned with interpersonal, expressive, aesthetic uses of language. In part it is because an ideal of language that seemed the touchstone of progress, of the advance of reason, has been too often traduced. The idioms of objective knowledge, of science, mathematics, logic, experiment, statistics, contract, regulation and control were once seen as common bases for progress for us all. We have too often seen claims to authority, couched in such idioms, turn out to be rationalizations of special interests, elite excuses, outright deceptions, as was the rhetoric surrounding the events of the Vietnamese war. Idioms of moral concern and personal knowledge that had at first no standing came to be seen as more accurate guides than the trappings of elaborate studies and reports. A little later it was the discovery of the personal voice of the President (Nixon) in the transcripts of audio tapes that decided, I think, the public verdict on a president. I could not prove the point, but I think that these two experiences have had complementary, decisive effect on our sense of validity in the use of language.

I sense a more general drift as well. Increasingly we are concerned to have a place for things that cannot be said without distortion, or even said at all, in the idioms of elaborated, formal, purportedly rational and referential speech that take pride of place in public science, public government, linguistic and pedagogical grammars. There are things we know and need to be that have no standing there. A sense of this is a reflection of the central problem of the role of language in modern society, the crisis of language, namely, what the balance is to be between modes of use of language. The old dichotomies--correct vs. incorrect, rational vs. emotional, referential vs. expressive, fail to capture the nature and complexity of the problem, for it is not a matter of mutually exclusive opposites, but of the interweaving of mutually indispensable functions.

EDUCATION AND ITS LINGUISTIC FOUNDATIONS

To be more precise, concrete and clear about these issues would require far more than this short paper. To explain the ramifications of these points for the study of language, to trace the implications at different levels of the organization of language, to appraise the efforts that are being made now to devise an adequate general model necessitates extensive discussion. In this context I can only try to say clearly what this complex situation means for the future of language in education. It is this. Linguistics developed out of a situation in which the study of language was loosely distributed across a variety of disciplines. It became the central discipline by development of general methods for the formal study of language structure. The methods and the associated conception of language structure focused on an essential, but partial, aspect of the organization of language. Other aspects remained secondary or eschewed. The first focus of attention was phonology, and proceeded through morphology and syntax, and has now reached semantics and even 'pragmatics', the interpretation of meaning in context of use. It is becoming increasingly clear that linguistics as we have known it is inevitably part of a larger field (Hymes, 1968).

At the first, the study of language structure was divorced from consideration of language use. Now language use is included along with language structure by most. Eventually it will be generally recognized that it is not language use that is a derivative of structure, but structure that is dependent on use. It will become clear that one can never solve the problems of the organization of language in social life without starting from social life, i.e., from the patterns of activity and meaning within which linguistic features are organized into styles and ways of speaking. A linguistics that is truly the science of language, a linguistics that is truly a foundation for education, will be a linguistics that is part of the study of communicative interaction. It will understand linguistic competence as part of communicative competence. It will understand the character of competence in relation to the social history and social structure that shape it in a given case.

Such a linguistics, should the day arrive, will have an essential property. Its practice and theory will be adequate to all the means employed in speech and all the meanings that speaking (or another use of language) has. The theory of English phonology will attend not only to the features that make a consonant /p/ instead of /b/, but also to how adding aspiration to these sounds can make the word containing such a sound appear angry. The theory of syntax will attend to isolated grammatical sentences as but a special case among the intelligible, acceptable sequences of discourse. The theory of meaning will attend not only to words and constructions, but also to the meanings inherent in choice of dialect or variety, conversation or narrative genre, or the occasion to speak or be silent. Theory of competence will go beyond the study of the innate and universal abilities of man to study the kinds of competence valued and permitted in a given society, and to the study of opportunities and obstacles of access to kinds of competence. It will recognize that the very role of speaking, of language and use of language, is not the same in every society. Societies differ in their ideals of language and ability in language. It will be recognized that language, like sex and eating, is a universal possibility and necessity of society, but without power to determine its place or meaning. The relative importance of language among other modes of communication and its role as resource or danger, art or tool, depends on what is made of it. The latter point seems obvious, yet so difficult for many to grasp, so deeply engrained is the contrary assumption. (For further discussion of the above point of view see Hymes, 1961a; 1962b; 1964a, b; 1966, 1974).

Two things follow from the previous discussion. First, the relation between education and linguistics cannot be a matter simply of joining the two together as they now exist. We do not yet have the kind of linguistics just described. Second, we are not likely to get it if linguistics is left to itself. The prestige of formal models as against empirical inquiry remains strong. The pull to continue to concentrate on familiar ground will be great. To get the linguistics we need will necessitate pressure from outside the field of linguistics. Educators ought to be in the forefront. If you remember just one point from this paper, remember this: Do ask yourself what linguistics can do for you, but demand of linguistics that what it can do <u>be</u> done. Do not be apologetic for making this demand, or assuming that it diverts the study of language from pure science to murky application. The fact is that the study of language does not now have the knowledge on which much of application should be based, and cannot get it without new theoretical, methodological, and empirical work. To attract attention to the needs of education is not a demand for applied linguistics. It is a demand for change in the foundations of linguistics. The struggle for educational change with regard to language, and the struggle for scientific adequacy in the study of language, are interdependent.

I have used the word 'struggle' advisedly. I would be misleading to suggest that the kind of linguistics we need is an apple almost ripe, ready to drop at a tweak of the stem. There is indeed a diffuse slow drift in the right direction, but there are two great difficulties. One is the hierarchy of prestige. Many scholars view work entwined with practical problems as having low status. The more abstract and remote from practical problems the investigation, the higher its status. Some leading linguists (such as William Labov) want to reverse this polarity. Educators can help and the current academic crisis in finding conventional positions for PhDs may provide some leverage. The fact that linguistics itself is evolving in a direction that makes work in educational settings germane is of help, the fact, just mentioned, that new theory is part of what is needed. A second, even greater, difficulty remains. This is the difficulty of seeing language in education in the context of American society, steadily and whole.

SEEING OUR LANGUAGE SITUATION

The history of attention to language situations within the country points up this great difficulty. The use of English by Blacks has been evolving into a new system in the United States since before the Revolution, but we have only begun to adequately study this phenomenon as a consequence of the civil rights movement and the federal attention and funding that responded to it. Spanish-speaking Americans have been in this country for centuries, also, but Spanish bilingualism and language situations have begun to be studied only as a result of the socio-political mobilization of Spanish speakers. American Indian communities have been multilingual for decades and new and distinctive ways of speaking have been developing for generations without much attention from scholars and researchers. The interest of many Indian people in maintaining and reviving traditional languages fits into the traditional approach to the study of Indian languages, but it has taken the Native American mobilization of recent years to make academic scholars think about what they could do for the preparation of materials useful in education. Indian English and ways of speaking still remain relatively little studied.

In general, educationally significant aspects of different language situations have come into focus only after the community in question has been defined as a social problem, and, more especially, as a social force. Previous attention to the languages involved focusing upon what seemed most exotic and remote. Immigrant languages and Native American Indian languages alike have been viewed mostly as something lingering from the past.

We need to begin to think of the linguistic heterogeneity currently existing in our country as continuously present. The United States <u>is</u> a multilingual country, with great numbers of users of many languages. American multilingualism is not an aberration or a residue. If anything, it has increased in recent years, especially with regard to increased use of Spanish, Vietnamese and perhaps a few other languages. We need to address the linguistic heterogeneity of our country as a permanent feature of its character, to discuss what shape it will and should have, and anticipate the future. To do so, we have to address the linguistic ethnography of the United States as a sustained, central scientific task. Ad hoc responses after the fact of social mobilization connected with language come too late and provide too little help. And ad hoc responses are too easily distorted by the immediate terms of social and political issues. Members of language communities themselves may have only a partial view. We need sustained work that provides both knowledge of language situations and an independent, critical assessment of language problems.

Educators have a stake in the mounting of such a program of study, since mobilization around issues of language so commonly turns attention to schools. Educators have a special stake in making sure that a sustained program of study includes independent, critical attention to the nature of language problems. That attention should include study of the process by which something having to do with languages does (or does not) become defined as a problem in our country in the first place. It is not to be assumed that there is a fit between public recognition of problems and actual language situation. As I have stated above, teacher failure to recognize the structure and role of Black English vernacular still handicaps many Black children, and did even more before it became recognized as a 'problem' in the 1960's. Some of those who resist such recognition continue to be of Black origin themselves.

There are four kinds of situations that we must consider. First, there are indeed situations recognized as problems that are genuinely problems, e.g., bilingual education. Second, there may well be situations not defined as problems that can be left alone. But I suspect that there is a third set of situations not now defined as problems that ought to be so defined--situations taken for granted but at possible cost. For example, very little has been done to study communication in medical settings, especially between professional personnel and patients (Shuy, 1974). What are the effects of difference in idiom, terminology, semantic system? or even of difference in native language, there being so many medical personnel of foreign origin? and in some regions so many patients with little command of English? Perhaps there is no recognized problem because those affected have little visibility or consciousness of common concern. Yet a series of articles in the New York Times might make this situation, itself unchanged, suddenly a 'problem'. Finally, there may be situations defined as problems that ought not to be, the issue being falsely or superficially posed, e.g., the supposed problem of children with practically 'no language'. Any of us may be subject to cultural blinders and public fashions. We need comparative, critical, historical perspective to transcend them.

In short, we need to be able to see our country in terms of language, steadily and whole. To do so is to go beyond questions of diversity of languages and language varieties. Black English, Navajo, Hopi, Zuni, Spanish, Italian, German, Slovenian, the many, many languages of this country are salient and important. The diversity they comprise is so great, so neglected, as to be almost overwhelming by itself. Yet there is something further. There is a unity that has also escaped us. I do not mean political and social unity. That is not in question. To be sure, the drive for homogeneity has been so great that even today the thought of diversity being accepted can frighten some. Street signs in Spanish, even in a Spanish-speaking neighborhood, can attract ire. A telephone company may refuse to hire a Spanish-speaking operator to answer emergency calls in an area with many Spanish-dominant speakers. To argue for recognition of ethnolinguistic diversity seems troubling to many, as if the ties between us were so fragile as to break beneath a crumb of difference. But the forces making for integration, for the economic and communicative ties of the country, are irreversibly dominant. To argue the right to diversity is to argue only for breathing space within the hive.

The unity in terms of which we need to see our country is the unity in its dominant groups and institutions that gives it a certain cut and pattern, regarding language, regarding the value placed on language, the way in which language enters into life. We need to be able to imagine the United States sociologically as if it were a small country, a Belgium or Switzerland, a single entity of which one could ask, as one can ask of any society: what are the basic patterns of the use of language? what are the values, rights, responsibilities, associated with language? what is the outlook of the culture with regard to language? how did it come to be that way? how does it seem likely to change?

We are able to think of the Navajo or the French in this way. We need to be able to imagine ourselves this way as well, to find, through comparative, historical and descriptive study, a mirror in which to see the United States as possessed throughout its history of language policies, of predominant attitudes towards language and its role, that give it one place among many possible places in the roster of the world's cultures.

The unity to be seen is not simple. Imagine that the only language in the country was English, even Standard American English. Situations, roles, activities, personal characteristics such as age and sex would still affect and shape ways of using language. The occupational and class structure of the society would still be present as a source of heterogeneity, on the one hand, and hedgemony, on the other. Let us consider heterogeneity first.

Inherent heterogeneity. Even if everyone used some form of Standard American English, all the manifold ways of talking as a person of a certain kind, of using language to do a certain kind of thing, would be present. This would still need to be discerned and described and the consequences considered. Many of the judgments made of persons in everyday life, many of the opportunities one has or does not have, involve command or lack of command of these styles and genres and of being able to talk like an X or being able to use language to do some activity. Such diversity is inherent in social life. Research has barely begun to address these issues adequately and relating linguistic devices and patterns to social meanings and roles. It is the same here as with differences of whole language or language variety. Research mostly follows the lead of social mobilization. The study of sex-related differences in language appeared for the first time only a few years ago. Yet until recently, if one attended only to the published literature, one would have had to conclude that men and women talked alike in every society except for a few American Indian tribes, the Chukchee of Siberia, and some scattered other groups. Again, status-related differences in language are hardly the monopoly of the Japanese, Koreans and Javanese, yet until recently linguistic theory treated them as fascinatingly special.

There is a general lesson to be drawn from this discussion. A linguistics that starts from grammar can see socially relevant features only when they intrude into the grammar. If the very units of phonology or morphology cannot be stated without reference to the sex or status of a participant in speech, then the social fact is taken into account. Indeed, the case may become celebrated as an instance of "men's and women's speech" or special concern with the expression of status. Yet sexual roles and status differences are universal in society and assuredly come into play when people speak to each other. Starting from grammar, one does not see how they come into play. One has to start from the social feature itself and look at the use of language from this vantage point. Only then can the features of language that are selected and grouped together as characteristics of speaking like a woman, speaking like an elder, and the like, be seen clearly.

Allow me a final example. Many studies have brought to our attention the interesting way in which choice of second person pronoun in French (tu : vous), German (Du : Sie), Russian (ty : vy), etc., can signal greater or lesser social distance between participants in a speech event. Much has been written on these pronouns and related forms of salutation and greeting (e.g., Bates and Benigni, 1975; Paulston, 1976; for two recent and valuable studies). Yet it is a safe assumption that variation in social distance is universal, and universally expressed in one way or another in the use of language. Management of social distance may well be one of the most pervasive dimensions of language use. One has to start from recognition of social distance to begin to see thoroughly and accurately how it is accomplished as a function of language.

Even if only standard English were found in the United States, then there would be many socially shaped patterns of language use to discover and consider. Still, the diversity would have a certain unity. It would not be the "English" language, but the history, values and social structure of the United States that would give a characteristic configuration to these patterns.

Hidden Hegemony. Even if the situation were now as we were imagining it above, schools would not find their language-related problems resolved. The concern to develop the full potential of each child would lead to recognition of language as involving more than learning the forms of a standard language. For example, I suspect that there is a pervasive dominant attitude that discourages verbal fluence and expressiveness in white males. It ought to be more widely recognized that in most known societies it is men who are considered the masters of verbal style, and indeed often trained in its ways, whereas women are subordinated and even disparaged. In our own country, as we know, it is commonly girls who show most verbal ability, who learn or retain foreign languages, etc. Men in public life whose work depends on use of language may be heard to disclaim any special knowledge or command of it. Again, I suspect that many persons spend much of their lives in what might be called 'verbal passing', the maintenance of a public verbal face that is not chosen, but imposed. And what is the fate of narrative skill in our society? There is some reason to believe, I think, that the expressivity of traditional narrative styles has often been disapproved by the upwardly mobile persons and the middle-class more generally. One sees a loss observing over several generations of a vital narrative style in some people of Indian communities. People continue to relate accounts and narratives, of course, but are we storying more and enjoying it less?

The most serious problem of all, and the most difficult one for schools to accept perhaps, is that our culture is so oriented toward discrimination among persons on the basis of language that even a society of 200 million speakers of Standard American English would show a class and occupational structure much like the present one, matched by a hierarchy of fine verbal discriminations. In other words, we must consider the possibility that schools, along with other institutions, have as a latent function the maintenance and reproduction of the present social order on the apparently impartial ground of language. Given the inherent variability in language and language use, even a society of Standard American English speakers would show detectible differences in pronunciation, diction, preferred syntactic constructions, and the like. Are we so convinced that language change is language decline (as many of our educated elite appear to be), so predisposed to correctness and correction, that most of that society of standard English speakers would still leave school with a feeling of linguistic insecurity and inferiority?

THE CALL FOR CHANGE: EDUCATIONAL LINGUISTICS

Perhaps our society can never come closer to equality of opportunity, to a treatment of language in schooling that starts where the child is, that develops the fullest linguistic potential of the child. Still, those are the goals in terms of which one often speaks. It is only that the change required to come closer to them is so pervasive--change in knowledge, change in attitude, ultimately change in social structure itself. Change in what we know can never be enough, yet without it the other changes are impossible. One sees some change in the treatment of Black English Vernacular that would not have come about without the research of the past decade or so. Knowledge of other situations can have their effect also, especially in the context of a view of the history and direction of the role of language in the society as a whole.

My call for such knowledge in relation to schools amounts to a call for an educational linguistics, as a major thrust in schools of education, departments of linguistics. It is addressed to all concerned with language and with education. Let me add, however, that it should be shaped not only by educators and linguistics, but also by members of the communities as well--teachers and parents both. Inherent in an adequate study of language is that one must draw on knowledge that members of a community already tacitly possess. The same is true for ethnography, which seeks knowledge of ways of speaking in relation to cultural contexts. Insofar as the work to be done involves the making of policies and the seeking of goals, members of the communities that are affected must necessarily play a part in the process of change. The educational linguistics envisioned here is in part a community science.

Such an educational linguistics entails change in both linguistics and education. In a sense, its goal must be to fill what might be called a 'competency' gap. There is a gap in the sense of a lack of persons able to do the kind of research that is needed. The gap exists because the need to fill it has not been recognized, and recognition of the need depends on overcoming a 'competency' gap in another, theoretical sense. Both linguists and educators may use the term 'competence'. The gap between their uses of this term is at the heart of what needs to be changed.

In linguistics the term 'competence' was introduced by Chomsky a decade or so ago. Its ordinary meaning suggested a linguistics that would go beyond language structure to the linguistic abilities of people. The promise proved a bit of hyperbole. The term was used in a reduced sense as equivalent to just that portion of competence involving knowledge of a grammar, and grammar itself was defined in terms of an ideal potentiality, cut off from any actual ability or person. Grammar was to explain the potential knowledge of an amalgamated "everyone in general," and of no one in particular. Social considerations were wholly absent from such a notion of competence. The result has been conceptual confusion that has led some to abandon the term altogether. Others have attempted to modify it. Still others denounce its use. In Chomskyan linguistics, in short, 'competence' meant an abstract grammatical potential, whose true character and whose relation to realized behavior alike remain quite uncertain. The image of the language acquiring child has been one of an immaculate innate schemata, capable of generating structures unconstrained and unshaped by social life.

In education the terms 'competence' and 'competency-based' have become associated with a quite different conception. The emphasis is upon specific, demonstrable, socially relevant skills. No one can be against demonstrable skills, but there is fear that the notion reduces education to a very limited conception of ability and potential. It suggests an image of an externally shaped repertoire of traits that does not allow for going beyond what is already given. It suggests that success in transmitting basic skills is something that was once in hand, was subsequently lost, and must now be restored.

Each of these notions of 'competence' treats as basic something that is derivative. The simple linguistic notion treats formal grammar as basic, and consequently the use of language as unconnected, or dependent, whereas in fact the opposite is the case. What we conceive as 'grammar' is a precipitate, of a normative selection from among the ways of speaking, the true verbal repertoire, the full organization of means of speech. 'Grammar' began this way in the service of Hellenistic cultural hegemony and continues that way in the service of a certain conception of science. A valid notion of verbal competence reaches out to include the full organization of means and meanings of speech, and becomes part of a notion of communicative competence.

The notion of 'competence' that has gained currence in education treats distinguishable skills as elementary and underived, whereas any prescribed set of skills is a precipitate of a complex of assumptions and understandings as to the nature of society, its present and future opportunities, and the probable or prescribed relation of a group of students to it. There is a tendency to focus on instrumental, vocational ingredients of verbal skill, perhaps at the expense of the full range of verbal abilities valued and possible. In both cases the limited notions of competence is bound up with a limited ability to see the nature of the language situations and verbal practices in the United States. That limitation is endemic.

I want to suggest that the problem of language in education is not to go back to basics, but to go forward to fundamentals. We must consider questions such as: (a) how does language come organized for use in the communities from which children come to schools? (b) what are the meanings and values associated with use of language in the many different sectors and strata of the society? (c) what are the actual verbal abilities of children and others across the range of settings they naturally engage? (d) what is the fit (and misfit) between abilities and settings--where is an ability frustrated for lack of a setting, a setting unentered for lack of an ability, in what ways are patterns of personal verbal ability shaped by restrictions of access to settings, on the one hand, culturally supported aspirations, on the other?

When we consider where a child is in his/her development and what his/her potential is, we are considering abilities for which 'competence' is an excellent word. The point is to understand the term 'competence' as something close to its ordinary sense, mastery of the use of language. To use the notion in education, we need to know its nature in the many speech communities that make up the country, and we need to be able to relate these characteristics to the larger historical and social factors that constrain them. Ethnolinguistic description can at least enable us to see where we truly stand with regard to linguistic competence in the United States. The knowledge it provides is indispensable for those who wish to change where we stand.

To see the need for knowledge of the language situations and practices of our country, to support training and research to obtain such knowledge, and to change the relations between linguistics and education so as to bring into being an educational linguistics that can foster all this is imperative for change. These are the fundamentals to which we must move forward.

The key to implementing such changes is, I think, primarily in the hands of Schools of Education. There is little chance of success, little chance of results relevant to schools, if educators do not play a principal role in shaping the growing concern of students of language with the social aspects of language. At the University of Pennsylvania we are expanding a Reading and Language Arts program into a general program of Language in Education, and including in it a specialization in Educational Linguistics as a foundational field. The purpose is both to train researchers and to influence the training and outlook of those in other parts of the School. The new program is possible partly because it has the cooperation and support of linguists outside the School of Education. Each School of Education may find its own particular way to incorporate the objectives I have outlined above, but a successful pattern ought to have these three ingredients mentioned: training of research specialists, influence on the training and outlook of others, cooperation between educators and linguists.

The greatest challenge to research, the research of greatest benefit to schools now, will be to domesticate and direct the skills of ethnography and descriptive linguistics, of sociolinguistics or ethnolinguistics in broad senses of those terms. We need programs of research that can function within a limited frame of time, say a year, and provide through linguistic ethnography a usable sketch of the ways of speaking of a community or district served by a school. For the most part linguistic ethnography has flourished abroad with studies of cultural uses of language in Mexico, Africa, Panama, the Philippines. We need to bring it home to Pittsburgh and Philadelphia, to Cleveland and Columbus, as well. The support of Schools of Education will be essential for this. The models of research that are needed are not wholly ready to hand. Practical relevance and research development must grow together.

It is not too much to imagine, indeed, that language in education can be an integrating focus for many areas of study. The ties with Reading and Language Arts, developmental psychology and English Studies, are obvious. When, one considers the way in which problems of language are shaped by cultural assumptions and attitudes, it becomes apparent that there are ties with the historical, sociological and anthropological foundations of education. There is a complex of spurious and genuine problems of language diversity in relation to special education and school counselling. Issues of curriculum and instruction arise as well. With a bit of luck and a lot of initiative, education might find itself a major force in shaping the study of language in the United States.

BIBLIOGRAPHY

Bates, E. and Benigni, L. (1975) Rules of address in Italy: A sociological survey. Language in Society, 4(3):271-288.

Bauman, R., and Sherzer, J. (eds.). (1974) Explorations in the Ethnography of Speaking, New York: Cambridge University Press.

Cazden, C., John-Steiner, V., and Hymes, D.(eds.). (1972) Functions of Language in the Classroom, New York: Teachers College Press.

Hoover, M. E. R. (1975) Appropriate uses of Black English as rated by parents. Stanford University, School of Education, Stanford Center for Research and Development in Teaching, Technical Report No. 46.

Hymes, D. (1961a) Functions of speech: An evolutionary approach. In F. C. Gruber (ed.), Anthropology and Education, Philadelphia: University of Pennsylvania, pp. 55-83. Reprinted in Yehudi A. Cohen (ed.), Man in Adaptation, Chicago: Aldine, pp. 247-259.

Hymes, D. (1961b) Linguistic aspects of cross-cultural personality study. In B. Kaplan (ed.), Studying Personality Cross-culturally, Evanston: Row, Peterson (later: New York: Harper and Row), pp. 313-359.

Hymes, D. (1962) The ethnography of speaking. In T. Gladwin and W. Sturtevant (eds.), Anthropology and Human Behavior, Washington, D.C.: Anthropological Society of Washington, pp. 15-53.

Hymes, D. (1964a) Directions in (ethno-)linguistic theory. In A. K. Romney and R. G. D'Andrade (eds.), Transcultural Studies of Cognition, Washington, D.C.: American Anthropological Association, pp. 6-56.

Hymes, D. (1964b) Introduction: Toward ethnographies of communication. In J. J. Gumperz and D. Hymes (eds.), The Ethnography of Communication, Washington, D.C.: American Anthropological Association, pp. 1-34.

Hymes, D. (1966) Two types of linguistic relativity. In W. Bright (ed.), Sociolinguistics, The Hague: Mouton, pp. 114-158.

Hymes, D. (1968) Linguistics--the field. International Encyclopedia of the Social Sciences, 9, New York: Macmillan, pp. 351-371.

Hymes, D. (1970) Linguistic method of ethnography. In P. Garvin (ed.), Method and Theory in Linguistics, The Hague: Mouton, pp. 249-325.

Hymes, D. (1974) Foundations in Sociolinguistics, Philadelphia: University of Pennsylvania Press.

Hymes, D. (1975) Pre-war Prague School and post-war American anthropological linguistics. In E. F. K. Koerner (ed.), The Transformational-generative Paradigm and Modern Linguistic Theory, (Amsterdam Studies in the Theory and History of Linguistic Science, IV; Current Issues in Linguistic Theory, I), Amsterdam: John Benjamins B. V., pp. 359-380.

Hymes, D. (MS) Language development in a bilingual setting. Paper presented at Symposium at the Multilingual/Multicultural Materials Development Center of California State Polytechnic University, March 19-21, 1976.

Kochman, T. (1977) Review of language in its social setting. In W. W. Gage (ed.), Language in Society, 6, pp. 49-64.

Labov, W. (1972) Language in the Inner City: Studies in the Black English Vernacular, Philadelphia: University of Pennsylvania Press.

Leap, W. (1974) On grammaticality in Native American English: The evidence from Isleta. International Journal of the Sociology of Language, 2, pp. 79-89.

Paulston, C. B. (1976) Pronouns of address in Swedish: Social class semantics and a changing system. Language in Society, 5(3), pp. 359-386.

Philips, S. U. (1972) Participant Structures and Communicative Competence: One Springs Children in Community and Classroom. In C. Cazden, V. John-Steiner, and D. Hymes (eds.), Functions of Language in the Classroom, New York: Teachers College Press.

Rickford, J. R. (1977) Processes of pidginization and creolization. In A. Valdman (ed.), Pidgin and Creole Linguistics, Bloomington: Indiana University Press, pp. 190-221.

Shuy, R. W. (1974) Problems of communication in the cross-cultural medical interview. Working Papers in Sociolinguistics, Austin, Texas: Southwest Educational Research Laboratory.

Wright, R. (1975) Review of English in black and white, by R. Burling; and Language in the inner city, by W. Labov. Language in Society, 4(2), pp. 185-198.

On the Relevance of Recent Developments in Sociolinguistics to the Study of Language Learning and Early Education

ROGER W. SHUY

Georgetown University and Center for Applied Linguistics

INTRODUCTION: THE SAN FRANCISCO EXAMPLE

Recent events in educational legislation are instructive about the process of change in American schooling. In January of 1974, after four years of litigation and appeals, the U. S. Supreme Court ruled in favor of a San Francisco Chinese family named Lau who claimed that the local school system had violated their constitutional right to access to education by providing that education in a language which was foreign to the learner, English. By ruling in favor of Lau, the Supreme Court said, in effect, that it is an American citizen's right to expect the strong and the educated to construct learning in such a way as to adjust to the beginning points of the weak and the uneducated. Interestingly enough, education has been claiming this as a basic tenet for years, usually expressed as "starting with the child where he is." Although this principle is widely proclaimed, the reality of the principle is widely absent, for major American educational policy follows a self-proclaimed compensatory education model which places little value on diversity and much emphasis on making the child as much like the main-stream as possible as soon as it can be done. Lau vs. Nichols suddenly changed all this and, with one stroke of legislation, brought legislative power to what had been almost empty verbiage in teaching and learning.

The Process Leading up to Sociolinguistic Research

It will not be our purpose here to evaluate the strengths or weaknesses of this particular Supreme Court decision but, rather, to examine the process which has led to current developments in sociolinguistics and the study of language learning in early education.

This bilingual education legislation, like much of educational legislation is really an expression of a moral value derived from a great deal of intuition and from very little empirical research. Social scientists had not provided Congress with a clear data base for bilingual education any more than they had offered ample evidence that busing would lead to better learning for the educationally disadvantaged. In fact, when confronted with the assertion that bilingual legislation preceded the knowledge upon which it could be based, the lawyers for both Lau and Aspira [the Aspira Consent Decree is a similar piece of legislation relating to New York City Puerto Rican children,] readily admitted that such was the case, noting further that without such legislation, the knowledge base might never be started. [These assertions were made at the TESOL meeting in Los Angeles in March, 1975.] This is not to say that <u>no</u> knowledge base existed prior to legislation rather that it was far from adequate and convincing. Nor is this to cast criticism on the legislation, for it was undoubtedly well motivated and much needed. It is called to attention, in this case, as a rather humbling reminder that educational research here, and in many other instances, tends to follow the legislation rather than precede it.

In fact, the developmental model might be said to look something like the following:

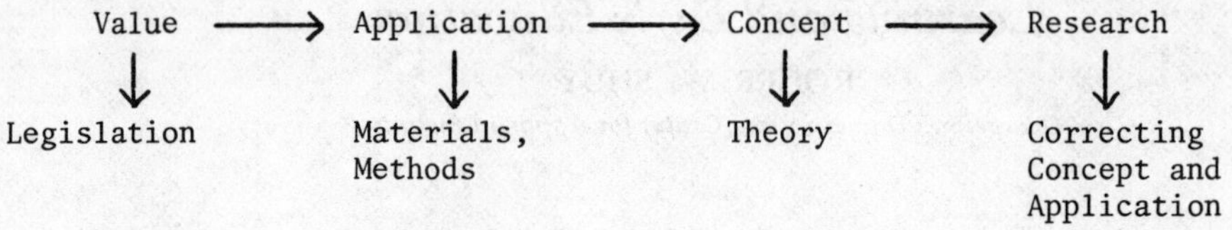

Fig. 1

In San Francisco, the city school system faced the need to develop a master plan by which Lau vs. Nichols could be carried out in the schools. It was at this time, months after the value system had been legislated that a concept and application became foremost in the minds of the schools. In developing this master plan, it became evident that the legislation had left a great deal which was unclear. In order to develop a plan for seven thousand from Chinese, Spanish, Japanese and Tagalog speaking homes, it was necessary to answer the following questions:

1. Which children can best benefit from bilingual education?
2. Which communities want bilingual education?
3. What do the communities understand bilingual education to be?
4. What are the goals and objectives of bilingual education?
5. What resources are available to implement these goals and objectives?
6. What new resources are needed?
7. What staff training is necessary for successful implementation of these goals?
8. What evaluation procedures can best determine how successful the individuals and programs have been?

ISSUES FOR SOCIOLINGUISTIC APPLICATION

Although each of these questions appears, on the surface, to be an educational question, in reality each involves sociolinguistic knowledge and assistance. Today, the eventual success or failure of bilingual education will heavily depend on the extent to which sociolinguistic knowledge is called upon or developed in response to questions involving:

Needs assessment. Linguists call this sociolinguistic survey work. They have assessed language knowledge and attitudes in other countries but they have not begun to address the sociolinguistic fieldwork questions involved in U. S. bilingual education.

Goals and objectives. Linguists have asserted sociolinguistic theory but they have not yet developed bilingual education theory. Until they have clearly specified the parameters of language maintenance, transitional bilingualism or some intermediate theories, they will not have contributed maximally to bilingual education.

Materials and resources. Sociolinguistics has made singular contributions in language variability as it relates to phonology and grammar, but not as it relates to functional language. The latter may prove to be the most useful contribution of all.

Teacher education. Sociolinguistics has contributed the concepts of variability and continuum to education but it has still not impacted clearly enough on either pre-service or in-service education.

Evaluation. Recent Office of Civil Rights (OCR) guidelines for implementing Lau vs. Nichols have clearly specified that assessment of individual language abilities must go far beyond anything currently in existence. Most language testing, in fact, is discrete point testing. That is, it isolates a given feature for analysis on the assumption that the correct representation of that feature will reflect a more global understanding than that (or any other) feature might be expected to provide. For example, if a child fails to discriminate between shoes and choose, he can be said to be not an effective speaker of English. The recent OCR guidelines indicate that such discrete point testing distorts the reality of language usage and must be avoided in the future. The guidelines argue, instead, for an assessment of spoken language in, of all things, a realistic social context. They say, in effect, that to measure language effectively, one must hear it spoken continuously in contexts and settings in which the natural use of such language might be expected, both in and out of school. The implications of these guidelines for sociolinguists are exciting. They support most of the known critical measurement points of sociolinguistics: the legitimate existence of variation, the need for realistic contextual concerns when analyzing language, the possibility of a language continuum rather than discrete point polarities and the extreme importance of ethnographic observation and analysis.

The Need for Revamping Sociolinguistic Strategies

The point of this lengthy introduction is to set the stage for an analysis of three barriers to sociolinguistic relevance to early education. By examining a real, recent event in educational history, I hope to have made it clear that one should take lightly any claim that either linguistics or education can take any credit for the institution of the value to be developed. In the case of bilingual education, the awareness of the problem came about as a result of legislation. Likewise in the sixties, it was Civil Rights legislation which opened the door to the study of various English vernaculars. Linguists and educators had ignored the problem for decades. From the precedents set in recent years, it also appears that the application phase tends to precede the concept phase and that it is not until we get ourselves into a terrible muddle that research is called upon to correct the concept or to improve the application. It is difficult to determine exactly at which point the legislation should take place but one would hope that supportive research would be called upon before legislation takes place. Theoretically, the process noted in fig. 1 should probably be reversed as follows:

Value ⟶ Research ⟶ Concept ⟶ Application

with legislation entering at the point at which research shows the idea to be viable. At least part of the reason why sociolinguistic knowledge has not preceded the legislation stems from the fact that appropriate research was not conceived of or carried out in time to be useful to the legislators. A second reason is that research has been isolated from the school setting. Third is that educators, especially classroom teachers, have built a defense against research, terming it irrelevant, impractical and not related to the real problems of teaching. This situation, coupled with the growing hostility of minorities toward researchers, has tended to cut off research which could serve the questions posed by the Lau vs. Nichols decision and by educators concerned with falling SAT scores, writing ability, reading and other language arts areas.

The remainder of this paper will describe recent efforts that have been made to overcome barriers to the successful implementation of sociolinguistics in early education. These are barriers to getting into the schools, barriers to getting to the teachers and barriers of getting to the children.

BARRIERS OF GETTING INTO THE SCHOOLS

Linguists, psychologists and educationists alike have found it increasingly difficult to elicit sympathy for their requests to do research in the schools. School administrators have grown weary of what one of them refers to as "...interruption of class routine, disruption of the curriculum, pulling children out of class, inordinate testing and hair-brained hypothesis testing, all in the name of educational progress." They further complain that after the research has been completed and the researcher gets his publication or advanced degree, the classroom is no better for the experiment, for the results are never presented in terms that can be understood, or, worse still, they are not presented at all. Small wonder that school systems are getting more and more hostile to the miscellaneous graduate students, psychologists, and other researchers who invade their classrooms looking for "feedback factors," "process determinants" and doing "ipsative analyses" on their subjects.

Meanwhile, these same schools have been plotting almost monthly in-service education programs, some geared to college credit and some simply for enrichment. It was in the context of such a situation that the Center for Applied Linguistics approached a nearby school with a unique suggestion for the interrelationship of research to the classroom.

What CAL wanted was a setting in which to study the acquisition of functional language by children in the early grades. Such research would necessarily disturb normal classroom routines, for it was thought necessary to video tape a number of classrooms throughout the school year. The very presence of video tape equipment, to say nothing of the two or three additional adults in each classroom, was assumed to be disruptive. In addition, CAL anticipated that it would be necessary to tape individual interactions of student to student, student to research, teacher to student, and teacher to researcher. This too was expected to be disruptive.

CAL expected to have to give up something of value in order to obtain the rights to such a privilege. Two such services were developed. For the entire school year, monthly in-service education was provided the teachers at that school by the CAL research staff. This service grew out of the research itself but was not limited to it. Secondly, any teacher who wished was encouraged to select a CAL staff member to work within the development of classroom teaching materials, articles for teacher journals or other possible topics. In addition to these two services, general and individualized, CAL contributed some of the video taping equipment to the school upon completion of the project, along with a training program for its use. Since a considerable amount of time was necessary for coordinating this effort, CAL also contributed to the salary of the vice-principal for performing this service.

It can be expected that a great deal of negotiation went on between the school personnel, parent-board and parents. Specific releases were secured from the parents of all the children who were to be video taped and from the school personnel as well. Assurances of anonymity were made. The right to final review of any potential distributable product was secured. Children whose parents did not choose to sign release forms were carefully avoided and, if such were inadvertently recorded, the tapes were erased.

The point here should be clear. The answer to the common complaint of the rape of the school by the researcher is to negotiate a fair deal and build it into the proposal. This takes time but it is essential if we are to get into the schools at all. The advantages, by the way, do not accrue only to the schools in such an arrangement. Many research insights about the language of children have developed out of discussions with and observations of the teachers.

Having given the school tangible evidence of trade-off value, it was then possible for the CAL staff to go about the research which might not be viewed as immediately useful to the schools but which, in the long run, will far outweigh the values of the in-service training or the television equipment. The research question, in fact, grows directly out of the sort of legislation described earlier.

The Aspira Consent Decree in New York specifies that the school system should determine in which language, English or Spanish, the child can most effectively participate in the classroom. The school system's department of research pursued the question by devising two discrete point tests, one in Spanish and one in English, made up largely of phonological and grammatical items. The assumption was that such test questions will yield an answer related to the child's ability to participate in the classroom in one language better than the other. It is not our purpose here to catalogue all the absurdities of this procedure but it should be stated that it is not likely that any test of grammar or phonology will adequately reveal the potential for effective participation in the classroom.

It did not occur to the test developers that to determine such participation one might observe the languages in use in the classroom, to define what "effective participation" really means and to seek out subjective judgments of such effectiveness on the part of teachers or even peers. Instead they found some surface level measurements of language ability, measured them and pretended that they were important. What the legislation calls for is a clear statement of what really matters in terms of effective language functioning in the classroom.

If the schools had only stopped to consider the matter, they might have concluded that it is far more important to be able to seek clarification than to produce appropriate sounding vowels or grammar. Empirical evidence is abundant that one can become Secretary of State in this country without producing American sounding English speech. On the other hand, if one cannot use language to clarify, promise, assert, request, command, refuse, get invited, open, close, continue, interrupt, etc., one will not get very far at all. The CAL research project was set up to describe the developmental aspects of some of these language functions. The results of such research will get at the heart of what it means to effectively participate in the classroom.

As a product of this New York City experience, the schools are even more hostile to research than ever before. Teachers resented the intrusion of the task of measuring every Puerto Rican child's reading, writing, speaking and listening abilities. A whole week of school was lost in hundreds of schools. Perhaps such an effort would have been tolerable if some good could be seen to have come out of it, but the research was not sociolinguistically oriented and the results are, at best, suspicious, and more realistically, untrustworthy. Incidents such as this contrast sharply with CAL's careful efforts to avoid intrusion and to "pay back" the school for the opportunity to do the research. It is the contention of this paper that sociolinguistic research in the schools will need to continue to develop creative, immediate "pay-offs" for the schools in order to justify the existence of their presence.

BARRIERS TO GETTING TO THE TEACHERS

The educational system has devised many ways to keep information away from teachers. If one trains teachers that methodologies of various sorts are important and that the knowledge base being methodologized is not, one will get passive and unthinking teachers. In the field of reading, for example, teachers are most frequently trained in a few comparative methodologies for teaching reading rather than in the contents involved in the reading process, the assumption being that methods are more practical than underlying knowledge. In the crowded curriculum there is thought to be no room for irrelevant information or abstraction. What is needed is practical, hard-hitting, result-getting strategies.

It is difficult to imagine anything more debasing to a field than to assert that what is known is not important as long as one behaves adequately. Yet we seem to have done this to reading teachers, who have been taught methods of teaching reading but have little knowledge about the linguistics of reading, the psychology of reading or the sociology of reading, all of which could contribute to the critical teacher tasks of accurate diagnosis, effective prescription and an understanding of the dynamic, complex phenomenon that we call reading.

Much of what linguistics has to offer the field of reading is not necessarily associated with sociolinguistics. Phonology, lexicon, and grammar, for example, have been long recognized as units of decoding or word analysis by reading people. What has been wrongly assumed, however, is that such units are methods in themselves rather than part of a gestalt. Of course, children can decode by using letter-sound correspondences, syllables, affixes and words, but they also process syntax and larger units of semantic and pragmatic discourse, an activity little studied or understood by the reading researchers. Naturally, all of this occurs in a social context (or in varying social contexts) and is therefore subject to all of the constraints which are currently being investigated by sociolinguists for spoken language. Elsewhere, I have hypothesized that from the onset of reading to well-developed reading, the child has a repertoire of language accesses available to him and that these accesses vary in cruciality to the reader as he becomes a better and better reader. This hypothesis is illustrated below:

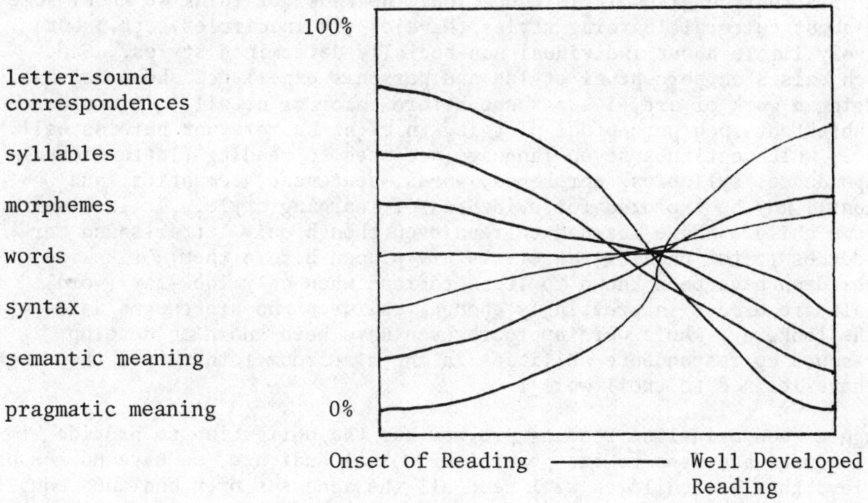

Fig. 2. Language accesses.

This figure can be thought to represent a theory of reading in which the various language accesses to reading (letter-sound correspondence, syllables, etc.) are of different cruciality to the process of learning to read at different stages in the acquisitional process. That is, letter-sound correspondence seems to be of high cruciality at the onset of reading (as a rather behavioral "starting" skill) but grows less critical to a given reader as he becomes more and more proficient. Good readers do not read letter by letter; they process by larger and larger language units, up to and including contextual meaning units. Such a theory argues for moving immediately toward meaning in reading and for all learning to take place in realistic meaning contexts (no study of letters in isolation from meaning units). There has been some disagreement among reputable scholars on exactly how this movement toward meaning and realistic meaning context is to be carried out. Some argue that it is better to start to read whole sentences, for meaning is thought to be most significant at the syntactic level. I have argued that meaning exists as far down as the morpheme level, and although I would agree that it is important to develop materials which are found in realistic language contexts, I disagree with those who would totally abandon decoding. Learning theory has long held that different kinds of learning can take place at different stages of learning. Thus behavioral, skill-focused learning can be adequate in the early stages of reading but should be replaced as soon as possible by more cognitive strategies (thus involving meaning). For some critics, this means sentences. I would argue that for the typical cooperative child who will accept the fact that certain dull or odd things must be done in order to get to later more interesting things, almost any reading approach can be successful. Some children may be ready to accept such behavioral (letter-sound type) instruction earlier or later than others. Some sort of diagnostic instrument should be able to predict who such children are. It seems likely that one type of prediction will be based on the child's personality more than on the reading tasks or on the language accesses themselves.

Relatively little is known about learning style, despite the rather large amount of attention given it in education. We know (or think we know) some things about cultural learning styles (Navajos sit in circles, etc.) but relatively little about individual non-socially determined styles. Some research exists on perceptual styles and personal experience shows me that, in judging a work of art, I see shape before color or detail. It would seem reasonable that such perceptual plugging-in might be relevant here as well. Figure 2, which outlines seven language accesses to reading (letter-sound correspondence, syllables, morphemes, words, sentences, semantics, and functions), may be explored for evidences of learning style. It is clear that some children have learned to read even though only letter-sound correspondences (often phonics) materials are placed before them. Likewise, some children have been known to learn to read when only look-say (word) materials are used. Interestingly enough, children who are taught using only the look-say, whole word approach even have been known to develop letter-sound correspondence abilities in the classroom (otherwise, they might never have learned to spell well).

Although a good main-line reading program has the obligation to provide multi-language accesses to its general or normal audience, we have no reason to believe that all children will need all the accesses or techniques equally or in the same proportion presented in the teacher's manual or, for that matter, at all. It would seem reasonable to me, for example, that one child's learning style might involve a combination of letter-sound correspondence and syntax, completely ignoring the whole word and syllables accesses. Other children may have similarly idiosyncratic learning styles. This does not mean that main line program is in error for presenting it all. What this suggests, instead, is that it would be efficient if we could figure out what amounts of the language accesses best suit the learning styles of each child.

In order to do this efficiently, it is first necessary to clarify what we mean by efficiency. What I mean by efficiency is getting to the right-hand side of Fig. 2 as soon and as well as possible. This means that I am not very concerned that the child who gets there maintains his ability to hold in focus the component skills which get him there. I regard letter-sound correspondence, syllables, morphemes, and, to a certain extent, words as component skills in the gestalt of reading for meaning via sentences, paragraphs, pages or books. As such, they are beginning skills, primarily useful as stages in the acquisition of the real skill. The real skill of reading involves getting various kinds of meaning from the printed page.

The theory of reading depicted in the following figures contrasts with other theories which are represented by stages 1 or by flow chart 2. These latter theories posit discrete stages or positions which children pass through in their learning to read. If sociolinguistics has taught us anything, it has instructed that variability is common, that a continuum describes language better than discrete stages and that diagnosis or evaluation should be preceded by observation. Much of reading theory ignores these tenets and assumes that a reader passes through some sort of stages or flow chart. A sociolinguistic view of reading allows for the possibility of a continuum rather than discrete stages, permits a high degree of variability in the production of reading, accounts for social factors as influences on the reading process and attempts to develop an inventory of individualizing features which can be observed by the teacher in order to diagnose, evaluate and prescribe.

It is reasonable to believe, for example, that one particular child's representation of Fig. 2 might look like this:

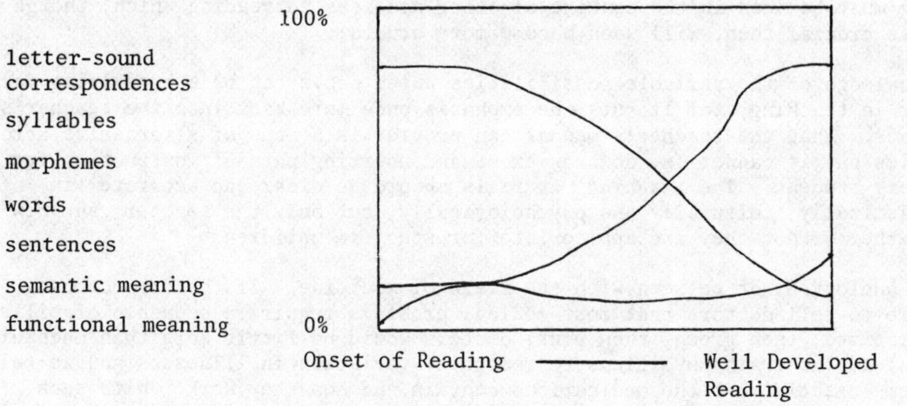

Fig. 3. Language Accesses

Another child's language access configuration might look like this:

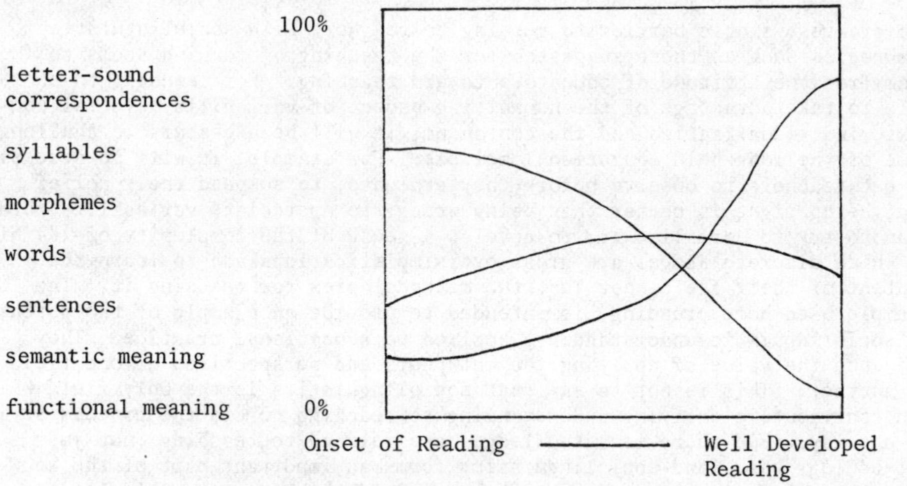

Fig. 4. Language Accesses

Such a view of reading says, in essence, that teaching is not a rote, mechanical process like turning a bolt on an assembly line. There is not a single best method of teaching reading which, once mastered, will make classroom efforts easier. All children do not progress similarly and they do not move from one stage to another in an orderly fashion. The environment in which reading is learned is not constant and may turn out to be a decisive factor in the child's learning.

What sociolinguistic view of reading does assert is that there are many language accesses to reading and that these accesses are, in themselves, not methods. That letter-sound correspondences are useful at the onset of reading must be seen in the context of other accesses to reading which, though less crucial then, will soon become more crucial.

Knowledge of the variable possibilities noted above can be a humanizing factor in teaching, for it puts the emphasis once more back into the teacher's hands. What the teacher's manual can provide is a menu of alternative strategies but it cannot lay down an exact and unerring path of instruction for every student. The teaching materials should be clear and accurate linguistically, culturally and psychologically, but only the teacher can know whether or not they are appropriate for specific children.

An analogy might be seen with the field of medicine. If the drug company were to tell doctors that most medical problems require a sequence of pills, first red, then green, then pink, doctors would be little more than mechanics. Instead, we train physicians to recognize variation in illnesses and we tell them exactly what the medications contain and how they work. With such training, doctors can vary the sequence of pills to suit specific diagnoses which their training permits. But until the physician learns what the various illnesses are, what typical healing sequences are like and what the medications can do, he cannot exercise creative diagnosis or prescription.

The greatest single barrier to getting to teachers with sociolinguistic strategies such as those suggested for the teaching of reading seems to stem from the attitude of educators toward teaching. For teaching to be able to take advantage of the humanizing aspect of variability, social context, individualization and the continuum, it will be necessary to challenge some of the long-held educational beliefs. For example, it will be necessary to get teachers to observe before they evaluate, to suspend their belief that being right is better than being wrong, to appreciate variability rather than to try to normalize it, to develop a sense of the complexity of learning in which discrete stages are gross oversimplifications and to learn the content of their field, not just the methodologies for teaching it. The example used here, reading, is intended to provide an example of the potential of sociolinguistic understandings applied to educational practice. They evidence the value of applying the metaphors and perspectives of one field to another. This is not to say that sociolinguistics is the only field which can contribute clarifying understanding to teaching nor is the process strictly one way. But there is a knowledge base related to teaching, not just a methodology base, and sociolinguistics forms an important part of the knowledge base. Curiously enough, such knowledge has been systematically excluded from the teacher training process. Recent efforts to connect sociolinguistic knowledge to the reading process have developed from the inside out rather than as applied sociolinguistics. That is, theories of reading have developed which incorporate sociolinguistic principles, whether stated as sociolinguistic principles or not. Teachers who fear the unknown have had little solace from the apparent complexities of linguistic terminology and concepts. But they do understand reading. It is up to the sociolinguist to continue to "do reading", rather than linguistics, at least as far as the teachers are concerned. This is one way to overcome the barrier of getting to the teachers.

If sociolinguistic information is to get to the children for whom it is intended, it will be necessary to cut through a number of barriers which currently serve as impediments.

THE CHILD'S NEED TO BE PREPARED

There seems to be a predisposition in education toward child repair. Recently, when I was addressing a combined group of reading researchers, administrators, and teachers, I described some current developments in functional language theory and research and was astounded at the assumed implications which the research seemed to have for these people. It had somehow not occurred to me that our work in determining the developmental stages of functional language would be taken to mean that we advocate the teaching of these functions to children who have not yet acquired them.

My surprise that our descriptions would be used in this way is simply a lack of foresight on my part. It also illustrates one of the dangers of cross-disciplinary study, namely, that the assumptions and presuppositions of one field are not necessarily those of the second. On the other hand, it is exactly this sort of misunderstanding which can lead to useful insights. It had apparently not occurred to some people that there are other ways to use developmental data than to repair the child with it. Since this particular research is being carried out on upper middle class children from language rich backgrounds, it is possible that the results could be misused as normative or base line data for all other children. The principle which underlies such an assumption grows out of the educator's belief that children need to be repaired. When stated bluntly in these terms, the assumption is easy to deny, yet a lack of sociolinguistic sophistication in American classrooms is clearly evident. Stages of normal language development, like normal language variation, seem difficult to accept. There is no reason to believe that all children will learn to request, clarify, refuse, promise, correct, warn, praise, apologize, suggest or hedge at the same time or at the same rate. Most adults, in fact, never learn to condole and some never even learn to deny very effectively. If there is a predictable pattern for the acquisition of language functions (and there is every reason to believe that such a pattern exists), this knowledge need not be used to teach five year old normalcy to four year olds. It is useful, instead, to understand the child in terms of what he is able to produce, to distinguish his language use from his attitudes or presumed misbehavior and to tell whether he has a learning problem or a language difference.

In short, it is difficult for a teacher to sit by and let an undeveloped form go unrepaired. The viewpoint espoused by sociolinguists is that many such forms are normal acquisitional stages. The evidence of these forms and functions can be used positively to plot the child's progress on the development of language abilities--to know where he is now and where he will be going next rather than to serve as evidence against his lack of perfection.

This problem is endemic to education largely because teaching puts such great emphasis on evaluation. Our recent work in teacher education points out the difficulty teachers have with dispassionate observation. Invariably when we play a video tape of a classroom to a group of teachers we have to force the teachers to keep from evaluating the instruction, the children, the facilities, and other matters. To observe without necessarily evaluating is a difficult task for a teacher. One classroom, in fact, produced the following exchange:

> Teacher: What's your name?
> Girl: Mary Jane.
> Teacher: Very good!

What, I ask you, can be so very good about happening to know one's own name? If a teacher is going to assess the child's language effectively, however, it will be necessary to learn to avoid the instant evaluation that now seems to characterize the field. There will be little progress in the tendency to repair faulty children until teachers learn to observe child language without necessarily evaluating it. The staff of the Detroit Dialect Study learned this lesson a few years ago when we hired several teachers to typescript oral tape recordings of Detroit Child speech. The results were disasterous. In many instances, the teachers apparently did not hear what was actually on the tape. They wrote down, no doubt, what they thought they heard, but this was often a far cry from accuracy. The same problem obtains with the reading method called the language experiences approach. Teachers are to write down what the child says, then let the child read it, the assumption being that the child will read his own language more effectively than textbook prose. This is all well and good except for the fact that the teacher does not write down exactly what the child says. Instead the teacher records what the child should have said or what the teacher wishes the child had said. Neither the Detroit teachers nor the language experience approach people were maliciously attempting to divert reality. They were simply doing what came naturally to them, editing what they heard in much the same way that we all subconsciously edit what we hear to make it fit what we think is right.

This sort of repair is done on the micro level, with individual children, and on the macro level, with entire classes. Sociolinguistics will need to continue to develop strategies for overcoming the barrier of the compensatory education syndrome if it is to be maximally effective. Essentially all public attitudes, at least as they are expressed by federal educational policy, treat the child as though he or she needs to be repaired. Even bilingual education legislation is set up to overcome presumed language handicap, but precious little is said about the advantage of developing or preserving two communication systems rather than one. If any area of study could counterbalance compensatory education models, sociolinguistics should be the one to do it, since its basic premises include a respect for variability, even to the extent of recognizing such variability as an essential humanizing factor. Although sociolinguistic research has pointed out the validity, logic, systematicity and even the beauty of language variation, whether based on age, sex, race, socioeconomic status or geography, the predisposition toward normalized behavior still dominates the field of education and sociolinguists have not yet effectively neutralized it.

One of the curiosities of American education grows out of the strange inconsistencies with which various precepts are held. Perhaps no field of study is more elitist than that of literary criticism, yet scholars in this area hold language diversity, at least one type of language diversity, in very high esteem. Likewise American journalists and media commentators have made the most conservative statements about language (Edwin Newman's _Strictly Speaking_ is a current example) yet journalists have long recognized the need to vary one's style to suit one's audience. Literary critics also have recognized the need of good writers to establish their own style and the generally accepted rules of poetry writing permit the stretching of natural language usage to the tortured syntax of e. e. cummings and Wallace Stevens.

Somehow these insights into the value of language variability have never been generalized beyond the somewhat narrow scope of their inception and specified domains. Today, the same English department which expects writers to difersify their language in order to establish an individual literary identity, tends to reject variation in spoken or written language which attempts to establish a personal or social identity.

One of the more interesting paradoxes of humanity is our need to be like each other, which is juxtaposed on our simultaneous need to be different from each other. Such paradoxes seem harsh at first glimpse but it does not take a long time to realize that it is out of such paradoxes that our humanity is defined. Suppose, for a minute, that everybody was exactly alike. Try to imagine what our language would be if there were no variability at all. The first thing to go would be poetry, which was defined by Alexander Pope, the eighteenth century poet as "What oft' was thought but ne'r so well expressed." What Pope meant was simply that there are not really very many new ideas in the world ("what oft' was thought") but that greatness comes in the way these ideas are uttered ("but ne'r so well expressed.")

THE CHILD'S NEED TO UNDERSTAND

For sociolinguistics to contribute to the ability of children to understand their environment, particularly the environment of the school, the field will need to overcome barriers imposed largely by its own doing. The focus of much of early sociolinguistic research was on phonological and grammatical features, particularly as such features "interfered with" school success as measured by reading, writing and speaking. The result of such research impacted primarily in the social aspects of language use rather than on language functions or comprehension. Consequently, the major contribution of sociolinguistics to reading was in the decoding or skills area, with concerns over whether or not dialect differences were sufficient to interfere with reading skills. In the areas of writing and speaking, the concerns were more in affect than in cognition, with particular attention being given to the social acceptability of certain non-standard realizations. As useful as such research might be, it speaks less to the more crucial concerns of children's language learning than to the acceptance of a child's language by others, especially teachers.

More recently sociolinguists have become concerned with how children acquire functional language competence, the underlying knowledge that people have which allows them to use their language to make utterances in order to accomplish goals and to understand the utterances of others in terms of their goals. It includes a knowledge of what kinds of goals language can accomplish (the function of language) and what are permissible utterances to accomplish each function (language strategies). An example of such functions, strategies and utterances in noted is Fig. 5.

Function	Strategy	Utterance
Giving an order	Performance	I hereby order you to come home.
	Direct imperative	Give Jane some milk.
	Wh- imperative	Won't you please buy me a bike?
	Statement	Mr. Green, I need some more paper.
Promising	Performative	I hereby promise you that I will be home by ten-thirty.
	Future statement	I'll be home by ten-thirty.
	Conditional statement	If you give me a dollar, I'll be home by ten-thirty.
	Question	Will you let me take care of my own affairs?

Fig. 5

This figure is in no way complete. There are many more functions, many other strategies for each function and, of course, many other utterances which could be used for each strategy. More important, the figure is incomplete since the context of each utterance needs to be specified to insure that the utterance is permissible to accomplish the function. For example, the sentence, "If you give me a dollar, I'll be home by ten-thirty" is a promise only if the context shows that the addressee desires that the speaker come home at that time, and if the speaker believes that a dollar is valuable incentive. It could also be a threat if the context shows that the addressee desires the speaker to stay away and the speaker either considers receiving money to be inappropriate or considers a dollar to be too little money to be an incentive.

Functional language competence also accounts for knowing what utterances cannot do. In English, the statement, "You are fired" works to fire the addressee but the utterance, "you are a frog", does not work to turn the addresse into a frog. In the U. S., at least, uttering the words, "I divorce you" does not constitute the completion of divorce proceedings but "I christen you John" does work to christen a child. Likewise if a teacher tells a student, "you have one minute to get over here," the utterance can act as an order but if the student says the same thing to the teacher such a meaning is, at best, far fetched.

This very sketch and incomplete discussion of some aspects of functional language competence shows that a speaker's underlying knowledge must be extensive and complex. In the literature of linguistics, sociolinguistics and philosophy three other terms are also used to refer to functional language competence: communicative competence, pragmatics of natural language and speech act competence. All who have studied this phenomenon agree that language users cannot possibly learn and store in memory all of the complexities of functions, strategies and utterances as item lists any more than they can store phonological or grammatical language as item lists. This knowledge must be learned and stored according to organizational principles. These principles may be considered constitutive rules which account for the successes and failures in the utterances meant as promises, for example, but they also separate promises from orders, requests for information, etc. In a similar manner, the constitutive rules of football not only account for the successes or failures of particular plays but also account for football and not baseball or soccer.

In terms of the mismatch between child language and school language, a great deal needs to be learned about functional language. It is my opinion that mismatches in this area offer considerably greater interference than anything researched in the past. We have ample evidence that phonological interference is not very important. Grammatical interference seems to be possibly important, but no where nearly as much as functional language interference.

It is fortuitous that sociolinguistic interest in language functions developed at the same time that educators, particularly reading specialists, have received interest in comprehension. The contribution of linguistics to reading in the past has been almost entirely at the level of early decoding, especially at the letter-sound level. Sociolinguists added very little to this knowledge, stressing primarily the potential effect of interference of the vernacular spoken language on the reading of written textbook prose. Part of the failure of linguists to impact in the field of reading resulted from the linguists own predisposition to analyze language features which contribute more in the skills area of reading, writing and speaking than in the cognitive areas. With the more recent focus on meaning, both semantic and pragmatic, sociolinguists have stumbled into an area which holds high promise of pay-off in education.

Functional language competence is relevant to beginning reading instruction in three ways: first, in terms of teacher education; second, in terms of the fit between the child's developing functional language competence and the schools curricula and materials; and third, in terms of the current issues of the education of culturally and linguistically different children.

To say that more emphasis should be placed on training teachers about how language works in order that they can better understand, appreciate and diagnose problems in their students is a gross understatement. It has been shown in various studies in the past that teachers are not trained adequately to diagnose relevant student problems related to language (Shuy, 1970). Reading teachers, in particular, suffer from being given only information on methods of teaching reading without being given the knowledge of linguistics which will enable them to diagnose a pronunciation problem from a grammatical miscue, the knowledge of psychology which will enable them to differentiate and evaluate the gestalt of reading from its component parts, and the knowledge of the cultural aspects of reading which will enable them to distinguish reading problems from sex-role fulfillment or group membership pressures.

Applications of knowledge of how language functions work can enable a teacher to interpret apparent misreadings appropriately. The most prominent occasions in which such diagnoses might be made concern comprehension questions. If teacher requests are made, for example, with strategies which have not yet been acquired, confusion is apt to result. The meaning of the teacher's utterance, regardless of how well intentioned it might be, must be expressed in terms of both the semantic and pragmatic (functional) meaning system of the child. There is insufficient material provided to teachers regarding any kind of language competence and problems in the educational setting arise from a failure to apply information about a teacher's and a child's functional language competence.

Although baseline normative data on functional language acquisition still do not exist, some of the ways in which curricula and materials can conflict or support the development can be noted. The material of many reading primers that use a playground for a setting while having a range of ages and statuses in their characters often present language which is undifferentiated for these distinctions. There is an obvious effort to have the setting relate to the actual elements in the child's universe but the questions by the characters, the requests made, the orders given do not relate to the actual functional language rules related to politeness and relative status of the addressee and the speaker. Such samples of language give little assistance to the child developing these distinctions and are potentially in conflict with his development.

Likewise, curricula can also conflict with functional language development.

For younger children, a major curriculum objective is for the children to learn cooperative social organization. In a recent incident in which two children had agreed upon a turn taking arrangement in play, one teacher perceived the resulting argument, actually caused by violation in turn taking, as the unwillingness of one child to share. This incident illustrates that the cooperative social organization, which was the goal of both the curriculum and the children's language in conflict, can be easily misconstrued or narrowly defined.

Much about functional language appears to be very culture specific. What remains to be researched are specifics concerning the functional language competence necessary for effective interaction in an educational setting and a comparison of the realization of such competence across cultures. What appears to American teachers to be defiance in Vietnamese refugee children (arms folded in front of them) is actually a stance of submissiveness in that culture. We need to know what functional language performance by children is judged necessary or desireable by teachers even though it may not be necessary for effective interaction. We need to obtain data on the differences in functional language competence across cultures and languages and what the demands of the school setting are on such functions. Such research has hardly begun but it offers a much richer source of explanatory power concerning the mismatch of child language and school language than has heretofor been conceived.

CONCLUSION

In this paper I have argued that recent developments in sociolinguistics have led us closer to an effective contribution to the study of language learning in early education. In doing so, sociolinguists have made progress toward overcoming certain barriers which in the past have served to slow down the implementation of linguistics in the schools. Though still far from efficiently, sociolinguists have begun to consider ways of combating the anti-research bias of many schools. By focusing on the teacher's goals rather than on our own, sociolinguists are also beginning to make a contribution to the field of reading. Finally, by turning research attention from phonology and grammar to meaning, sociolinguistics is on the verge of saying something crucial to language arts in general. Whether or not the field of sociolinguistics ever gets to the position in which values and research go hand in hand, preceding theory and application remains to be seen. But the gap seems a bit narrower than it was a few years ago.

BIBLIOGRAPHY

Shuy, R. (1970) Teacher Training and Urban Language Problems. In R. Fasold and R. Shuy (eds.), Teaching Standard English in the Inner City, Washington: Center for Applied Linguistics, pp. 120-141.

Assessing Kindergarten Children's Communicative Competence

JANET K. BLACK
Ohio State University,
Department of Early and Middle Childhood Education

INTRODUCTION

The importance attached to the development of oral language skills is evident in the numerous programs and special personnel in schools that focus on this one aspect of education. As programs are created, new personnel employed, and resources allocated to the identified task, evaluation becomes a crucial responsibility. Further allocation of resources or revision in the curriculum often rests on evaluation of the language development program which in turn is usually measured by the evaluation of children's oral language. The assessment of children's oral language ability has presented many problems due to (1) the nature of the assessment instruments, (2) certain problems in eliciting children's true language competence, and (3) the somewhat narrow view of oral language competence. One method which could take these problems into account is teacher observation of children's spontaneous oral language within the social context of the natural classroom environment. Patton (1975, p. 26) says, "Given the state of the art, standardized tests are no substitute for your [the teacher's] own carefully considered observations about children you [they] personally know."

A major criticism of standardized tests concerns their inherent biases. In a more natural setting, children would be free to use their own vocabulary and styles of speech reflecting their knowledge of life, associations and values. Children would not be discriminated against because of diversity in thinking patterns or expression. Observation of children's oral language over a period of time would not penalize those who mature later in verbal skills. This method of assessment provides children with time and experience in which language can be practiced and learned naturally while giving the teacher an idea of the child's progression. Because observations would be conducted at a variety of times, there is not the rigid time bias against children as is seen in a more formal testing situation. Furthermore, children speaking in the social context of the natural classroom environment would be relatively free of the emotional and social pressures of a more structured evaluation. Finally, this method would not penalize children who are learning in a variety of ways as it takes into account the language from the natural setting and not the oral language produced in certain skill task areas.

Other criticisms of standardized language tests concern the artificiality of the standardized testing situation and their failure to take into account recent research findings in relation to the appropriate indicators of communicative competence. As a result of her own classroom experience with second graders while on leave from Harvard, Courtney Cazden (1975, p. 345) says, "Tests seem inevitably to elicit a more monitored form of speech...

even when the tester is a familiar teacher." Labov (1972) has also documented this phenomenon of "hypercorrection." It seems that when in doubt about speech and when in a situation where speech is of great concern (such as the standardized testing environment), individuals use speech forms that are more prestigious as in the case of dialects, or more rule governed as in the case of development (Cazden, 1975). In other words, young children in a more formal situation, such as the standardized testing environment, are more prone to follow the regular rules, i.e., for forming plurals and the past tense of verbs.

COMMUNICATIVE COMPETENCE

Communicative competence is generally considered to have two integrated aspects: grammatical and interactional. While respected measures of oral language presently include an analysis of children's grammatical competence (that is, syntactic complexity, vocabulary diversity, and use of morphological rules), the nature of the standardized testing situation limits their ability to demonstrate actual competence as it occurs in more natural situations. Moreover, tests neglect completely the equally important aspect of language--interactional competence.

INTERACTIONAL COMPETENCE

The literature suggests that both language and the various functions of language are learned, practiced, and used from birth in the social or interactive context with family and significant others (Doughty, 1972; Lewis and Cherry, 1975; Strauss, 1962). As the child attends to this social interaction and participates in it, he/she learns what Hymes (1971) has referred to as "communicative competence." Communicative competence underlies our language, social, and cognitive behavior in face to face interaction situations. Hymes (1971) contends that normal children acquire knowledge of sentence structure not only as grammatical, but also as appropriate. This phenomenon is not explained in transformational grammar which separates linguistic theory into two parts, linguistic competence and linguistic performance. Linguistic competence refers to the speaker's knowledge of grammar "thus severing it at once both from knowledge and from whatever else besides knowledge (e.g. motivation, identification, experience) may be involved in using knowledge" (Hymes, 1972, p. XXXV). On the other hand, linguistic performance is seen as an imperfect manifestation of an underlying system essentially concerned with psychological byproducts of grammar (Hymes, 1971). Hence, Hymes says that a speaker's competence is in itself a matter of adequate performance in that the speaker demonstrates his/her ability to select and use appropriate communicative means in appropriate contexts (Hymes, 1974).

According to Cazden (1972) communicative competence has two aspects:

> It includes both knowledge of language (in the more usual and narrow sense of syntax, phonology, and semantics) and knowledge of the social world and of rules for using language in that world so that speech is appropriate as well as grammatical and creative within both linguistic and sociolinguistic rules. Together, these aspects of communicative competence are realized in the child's actual speech behavior or performance. This performance

> includes both speaking and comprehending. (Cazden, 1972, p. 3)

Cicourel (1972) refers to this same phenomenon, but calls it "interactional competence," which he defines as the "ability to recognize, receive, process, and generate communicational procedures (which are at the same time informational resources) while simultaneously integrating and elaborating our thinking and reaction to these activities in the act of production and comprehension." (p. 213) The ethnography of speaking, according to Cicourel,

> ...implies that the social setting is an integral part of semantic processing, and that ideal normative conversational rules (Sacks, 1970; Schlegloff, 1969) exist whereby participants trade on implicit socialization experiences for deciding when and how the selection and generation of different lexical items or strings will occur. (Cicourel, 1972, p. 216)

Cicourel describes seven properties which provide a link between sociolinguistic and cognitive properties which appear to be basically relevant for the kind of interactional competence necessary for production of everyday social structures. In order to achieve adult interactional competence, children must acquire a facility with these seven properties (see Fig. 1).

Mishler (1976) suggests that young children, and particularly, first graders are "conversationally competent." He concluded from his research, that first grade children and adults do not differ significantly in the length of their utterances including their questions. He found that first grade children have the ability to vary speech style, and to use features of adult conversation such as turn taking, repair and recycling as well as appropriate stress, intonation, and terminal politeness exchanges.

Black's (1977) study based upon the analysis of video and audio tapes of twelve kindergarten children in the sociodramatic area of the classroom indicates that young children's interactional competence can be observed and documented. The oral language samples were analyzed according to the Interactional Competency Checklist based upon the following criteria: (1) the view that oral language develops, is practiced, and utilized in the social or interactive context (Strauss, 1962; Hymes, 1971; and Lewis and Cherry, 1975); (2) Hymes' (1964) idea that a speaker's competence is in itself a matter of adequate performance in that the speaker demonstrates his/her ability to select and use appropriate means of communicating within particular contexts; and (3) Cicourel's (1972) seven properties of interactional competence which were adapted to the context of the sociodramatic environment. The Checklist is shown in Fig. 1. The discussion of data derived from applying the Checklist follows and demonstrates that young children do indeed possess interactional competence.

I. <u>Ability to Adapt to Changes in the Setting</u>

This category is based on Cicourel's second and fourth properties of interactional competence and attempts to assess whether young children can "behave as if they share the same social setting and are receiving and processing the same information," and "can normalize discrepancies to sustain social interaction" (Cicourel, 1972, pp. 217-218). These properties were adapted to the sociodramatic environment under the following subcategories.

A. Adjusts to the various themes of play
B. Extends the organization of the plot
C. Extends character development

II. <u>Nonverbal Appropriateness</u>

Based on Cicourel's fourth property of interactional competence, this category assesses whether young children possess "normal form repertoires" of possible appearances, behaviors, and utterances that can be understood when emergent in contextually organized settings (Cicourel, 1972, pp. 217-218). This property was adapted to the sociodramatic environment under the subcategories of gestures, facial expressions and body movements. In addition, two other subcategories of nonverbal behavior, vocal intonation and stress, were included based upon Mishler's (1976) research which indicated first graders use of appropriate stress and intonation.

A. Uses appropriate gestures
B. Uses appropriate facial expression
C. Uses appropriate body movement
D. Uses appropriate vocal intonation
E. Uses appropriate stress

III. <u>Familiarity with Normal Constraints and Conditions</u>

This category is based upon Cicourel's third property of interactional competence which concerns such items as a knowledge of who can speak first or next, what topics are considered socially relevant, how to terminate an exchange, repair, recycling, and repeating (Cicourel, 1972, pp. 217-218). These subcategories have been investigated in adults (Schegloff and Sacks, 1973, 1974) and in children (Mishler, 1976).

A. Knows when to speak first or next
B. Discusses topics socially relevant to the situation
C. Knows how to terminate a conversation
D. Repairs (corrects) oral language
E. Recycles (rephrases) oral language
F. Repeats oral language

IV. <u>Sequencing</u>

Cicourel's first and sixth properties of interactional competence are included in this category which assesses whether young children demonstrate the ability to think back or reflect upon previous experiences with present and possible future informational events, objects, and resources with the communicative setting (Cicourel, 1972, pp. 217-218.

A. Links past experience with present informational events
B. Links past experience with possible future informational events.

Fig. 1. Interactional Competency Checklist

ABILITY TO ADAPT TO CHANGES IN THE SETTING

The first category in the Interactional Competency Checklist is the ability to adapt to changes in the setting which refers to the child's ability to adjust to the various themes of play, extend the organization of the plot, and character development within the sociodramatic area. The following sequences provide documentation for this particular category.

In this sequence selected for analysis Tai (T) cooks while Mike (M) and Mikey (Mi) play doctor. M throws the medicine bottle into T's cooking bowl. This evolves into the theme of M and Mi throwing props into the waste basket. T cooks pudding, tea, and sets the table for Mi and M to eat.

(1)	T-M&Mi:	OK, I set the table.	T walks back to Mi and M at the waste basket.
(2)	M-Mi:	Oh boy! Hey, look what I did.	M, Mi and T look in the waste basket full of props.
(3)	Mi-M:	Telephone!	
	M&Mi:	(Laughter)	
(4)	T-M&Mi:	Quit it.	Mi walks to the telphone table, picks up the phone and throws it to M. M puts it into the waste basket.
(5)	M-Mi:	I got it! (the telephone)	
(6)	T-M&Mi:	You guys are always causing me trouble. So please don't.	T has her arms folded. Mi stops and looks at T.
(7)	M-Mi:	Sit, sit, down.	M and Mi walk toward the kitchen table. T thinks M and Mi are coming to eat.
(8)	Mi-M:	Sit down. Which way now?	
(9)	T-M&Mi:	OK	T seems to indicate to M and Mi that they should begin to eat.
(10)	Mi-M:	Ok, now let me have it.	M takes the cup that Mi wants. Mi takes the tablecloth off the table. Most of the dishes fall on the floor.
(11)	T-M:	OK. Not yet.	M starts for the waste basket.
(12)	M-Mi:	Oh, I got it.	M puts the cup in the waste basket.
(13)	Mi-M:	Look at those cups from the table.	
(14)	T-M&Mi:	Thanks.	
(15)	M-Mi:	Pudding's all gone.	M takes the pudding and throws it in the waste basket. Mi

		follows M. T returns to the stove.
(16) Mi-M:	Look what you have. You have a lot of trash.	Mi points at the dishes and tablecloth lying on the floor.
(17) M-Mi:	Oh boy! I'll throw it in the trash can. We're throwin' everything in the trash can.	M picks up the tablecloth and throws it into the waste basket. Mi picks up a saucer and throws it into the waste basket.
(18) T-M:	How about the broom, after I sweep?	T lifts up the broom. Mi looks at T.
(19) M-T:	Yah, let me have it.	M turns and walks toward T.
(20) T-M:	After I sweep.	T begins to sweep. Mi picks up a wooden spoon and throws it into the waste basket.

In this particular sequence, Mi and M have created a theme of play which focuses upon throwing props from the sociodramatic area into the trash can. Initially T does not contribute to this theme and attempts to stop behavior (4,6). Then T sets the table but does not want M or Mi to put the cups and plates into the trash just yet (11). Here there is a slight shift in T's attitude. It is now OK if M and Mi <u>eventually</u> dump the cups into the trash. Nevertheless, they do dump the cups into the trash (12,13), and T responds (14) with a sarcastic, "Thanks." The very next time T speaks (18), she says to M, "How about the broom, after I sweep?" She has decided M can have the broom to dump into the trash after she is finished sweeping. T is now supporting the on-going theme, that of dumping props into the trash. She then combines her "mothering-housewife" role (character extension) with the extension and organization of the plot, throwing props into the trash can. The following transcriptions and descriptions extracted from this episode demonstrate T's ability to adapt to changes in the setting:

> Then throw that (tool kit) in the trash.
> Throw that stove in the trash.
> Put the whole house in the waste basket.
> You have to take everything out to do that (put the high chair in the trash).
> Now we can get my stuff just about in (the waste basket).
> Here's something (a dish for the trash).
> Here's an apple (for the trash can).
> You guys better clean up. You know what? He's coming for dinner. I'm going shopping.

NONVERBAL APPROPRIATENESS

Nonverbal appropriateness is the second category of the Interactional Competency Checklist and refers to the child's use of gestures, facial expressions, body movements, intonation and stress.

In the following sequences of T and G, the transcription and description of behavior will occur in the left hand column. Documentation and explanation of the underlined behavior will be presented in the right hand column.

(1)	T-M:	Yes we do! [have a dog] (T nods affirmatively while continuing to cook.)	(intonation and stress, body movements)
(2)	T-M:	There's no more [milk] left. They used it all for the cake.	(intonation and stress)
(3)	T-M&Mi:	You guys are always causing me trouble, so please don't. (T folds her arms.)	(intonation and stress, body movement)
(4)	T-M:	Thanks. (T has just set the table. M has removed a cup from the table and thrown it into the trash.)	(sarcastic intonation and facial expression of disgust
(5)	T-M:	She wants, she doesn't want to sit down, and she wants to sit there. (T motions to the high chair.)	(gesture)
(6)	G-C:	Is the baby sick? (G takes the baby and uses the stethescope to examine her.)	(intonation and stress, body movement)
(7)	G-C:	No! No! No! (G does not want C to put on the band aid.)	(intonation and stress)
(8)	G-M:	Smell this Megan. (G holds out the perfume ring and points to it.)	(gesture and body movement)
(9)	G-C:	Ouch! (C and G bump heads.)	(body movement, intonation and stress, facial expression)

The above episodes indicate that young children do use appropriate nonverbal behavior, that it is possible to document this behavior and assess its appropriateness within the communicative context.

FAMILIARITY WITH NORMAL CONSTRAINTS AND CONDITIONS

Familiarity with normal constraints and conditions, the third category of the Interactional Competency Checklist, refers to the child's knowledge of such items as who can speak first or next, topics socially relevant, how to terminate an exchange, repair, recycling, repeating, and interrogatives.

(1) Who Can Speak First or Next?

Following are some examples of the types of interactions which indicate that young children have a knowledge of who can speak first or next.

(1) C-G: Is she all right? Is she all right?
(2) G-C: No, we're gonna have to give her medicine.
(3) C-G: Is that all right?
(4) G-C: That's all right, but she needs her medicine right away.

(5) G-M&C: Well, time to go trick or treating. Now where's that mask at? Where's the mask at? Where did that mask disappear to? Where's the mask?
(6) M-G: What mask?
(7) G-M: That, this mask. (the one that goes with his costume)
(8) M-G: Look around the house and find it. Maybe it's behind that table.
(9) G-M: It was behind that table. That's where it was.

(10) T-M&Mi: You guys want pudding or cake?
(11) M-T: Pudding <u>and</u> cake.
(12) T-M: I can only make one.
(13) M-T: Uh, hum pu-pudding. Ugh!
(14) T-M: OK.
(15) Mi-T: Pudding, yah!
(16) T-M&Mi: All right pudding.

These three episodes demonstrate that young children do facilitate the interactive process in that they appear to possess the knowledge of turn taking in conversation. In the sequence (10-16), T begins by asking a question involving a choice (10). M's response is not quite what T requested in that she asked if M and Mi wanted pudding <u>or</u> cake (10). She then takes her turn and makes the clarifying response (12). M and Mi then respond to her statement of clarification (13,15). T again demonstrates her knowledge of turn taking in her response to both M (14) and Mi (16) after M and Mi have provided the information which T had requested. G and M also demonstrate an understanding of the appropriate time to respond in a conversational setting (5-9). G begins by asking a question (5). M indicates a knowledge of turn taking by responding with a question (6) which requests further information from G. G understands that it is his turn to respond and provides the requested additional information (7). M then takes her turn and provides G with a plan of action and some information (8). G then follows M's suggestion which answered his initial question (5). He then takes his turn to acknowledge M's suggestion and to announce that he has found the mask (9). Much of turn taking involves the use of questions (1,3,5,6, and 10), responses, and clarifying questions. The use of interrogatives is the second subcategory under the category of familiarity with normal constraints and conditions.

(2) Interrogatives

Questions are catalysts for continued conversation and interaction. Following are examples of several of the children's facility in the use of interrogatives.

(1) T-M&Mi: You guys want pudding or cake?
(2) M-T: Pudding <u>and</u> cake.

(3) M-G&C: What's the matter kids?
(4) C-M: I ain't no kid. I'm the mother.

(5) C-G: I'll, I'll be the nurse, OK?
(6) G-C: Okeedoekee and I'll be the doctor. Don't forget.

The children demonstrate they can use questions and to evoke appropriate responses from the individual or individuals with whom they are interacting. In episode (1,2), T asks M and Mi a specific question (1) and she is able to evoke a response which is appropriate. M asks a question (3) which prompts a response from C (4) which provided information to M. In episode (5-6), C asks G a tag question which evokes an appropriate response from G (6).

(3) Repair, Recycling, and Repeating

These three conditions serve the purpose of soliciting attention to the speaker and the content of the speaker's language. Documentation of the children's facility with these conditions follows.

(1) M-T: Here baby, I'm gonna throw your little baby in the trash can. Good little baby.
(2) T-M: She wants, she doesn't want to sit down, and she wants to sit there.
(3) M-Mi&T: Hey where's something else?

(4) G-M: Now where's that mask at? Where's that mask at? Where did that mask disappear to? Where's the mask?
(5) M-G: What mask?
(6) G-M: That, this mask.

(7) E-J: Yah, well we, Jonathan, why don't you decorate the tree and then you can help. Dec, decorate the tree and then you can cut. Then you can cut. (J is cutting wrapping paper. E wants him to decorate the tree first.)
(8) J-E: I'll get some jewelry. This is to put on the tree.

In episode (1-3) T responds to M's threat to put her baby in the trash (2). In this response she recycles and repairs adding emphasis that the baby does not want to be thrown in the trash. The next time M responds he wants to know where something else is that he can throw in the trash (3). Evidently the recycling and repairing in T's response have convinced him that the baby is not to be thrown in the trash and that he had best look elsewhere for more items to put in the waste basket. G's initial question (4) in the episode (4-6) contains repetition and recycling which draw attention to G and his problem of finding the mask. In (5) M responds appropriately to G's question. Again demonstrating G's effective use of the techniques of repetition and recycling. In episode (7-8), E (7) repeats, recycles, and repairs in her attempt to stop J from wrapping presents and begin decorating the tree. She is obviously effective in knowing how to get her message to J as he stops wrapping presents and begins to decorate the tree (8).

(4) Topics Socially Relevant

In T's case, most of the topics pertained to her two contributions to the theme of play through "mothering" and through throwing props in the trash can. The first items listed pertain to the roles of housewife and mother while the second list concerns the filling of the trash can.

Housewife, mothering topics:

There's no more butter. I need the eggs.
You guys want pudding or cake?
I'm gonna clean the refrigerator.
You guys better clean up. You know what? He's coming for dinner.
I'm going shopping.

Topics pertaining to filling the trash can:

Throw the stove in the waste basket.
Don't throw the spoons in.
Those are women's shoes.
How about the baby's chair?

For G, most of the topics concerned the two themes of doctoring and Halloween. Following is a list of items socially relevant to the role of doctor, and a second list containing items socially relevant to Halloween.

Doctor topics:

What's wrong and what's the problem?
Is the baby sick?
No, we're gonna have to give her medicine.
I hurt her a little. Gotta put the band aid on.
She's all right now...Let me put on a bandage.

Halloween topics:

Well, time to go trick or treating.
Now where's that mask at? Where's that mask at?
Yah, I'm going (to the Halloween party) on a witch's broom.
Somebody's going to lose their britches. That's a trick.

For J, most of the topics concerned the theme of Christmas. Following is a list of items socially relevant to preparations for Christmas.

Christmas topics:

This is to put on the tree.
Rudolph the red nosed reindeer had a very...(J is singing)
Hey's where's my list? Where's my list?
How do you spell Merry Christmas?
I'm Santa Claus and I'm writing. That says Merry Christmas and to all a good night.
I'm planning a surprise for the mothers.
This is the present that goes under the Christmas tree.
I don't know how to wrap presents.
I wish somebody would help me wrap this present.

(5) How to Terminate an Exchange

Knowledge of how to conclude conversation or interaction is observed in the following episodes.

(1) T-M&Mi: I'm going shopping.
(2) Mi-T: Bye.
(3) T-MI: Bye, bye.

(4) M-G: Are you going on a date?
(5) G-M: Yea, I'm going on a witch's broom. You, you too? Up we go. Yea, Halloween!
(6) M-G: Halloween's so fun!
(7) G: Shoom!
(8) M-G: Bye.
(9) G-M: Bye.

(10) M-B&G: We made a mess of the playhouse.
(11) G-M: Ooo, Ben did it.
(12) M-G&B: And we've been breakin' stuff in the playhouse.
(13) B-M&G: We've been breakin' stuff. We've been breakin' stuff.
(14) G-B: Ben, don't.
(15) B-G&M: Good bye. I'm going off to King's Island.

In episode (4-9) G takes off on his broom (7). M responds by terminating their exchange (8) and then G also responds with a terminating exchange (9). They both mutually understand that G is leaving and appropriately terminate the conversation. Peer pressure evidently causes B to terminate a conversation in episode (10-15). According to G (11), B has been the major cause in creating a mess in the sociodramatic area. B finally responds to the accusation by terminating the conversation (15). How to terminate an exchange when someone's talk is insulting is one of the abilities described in Cicourel's third property of interactional competence (Cicourel, 1972, pp. 217-218).

SEQUENCING

Sequencing, the fourth category in the Checklist, refers to the child's ability to think back or reflect upon previous experiences from multiple sources including those in the setting and to link past experiences with present and possible future informational events, objects and resources within the communicative setting. Following are documentations of several children's ability to draw on past experiences and relate them appropriately to the on-going interaction in the sociodramatic area.

(1)	That's OK. I'm making it for the dog.	(T knows dogs need food and has some idea of how to prepare their food.)
(2)	There's no more butter. They used it all for the cake.	(T has knowledge of the ingredients used to bake a cake.)
(3)	You guys are always causing me trouble, so please don't.	(M and Mi have been taking T's cooking props. T has a prior understanding of "trouble.")
(4)	I'm gonna clean the refrigerator.	(T indicates that she knows that refrigerators need cleaning from time to time.)
(5)	Those are women's shoes.	(This statement suggests that T has knowledge of differentiation

		between men's and women's shoes.)
(6)	How about the baby's chair?	(T appears to know that babies' chairs are unique to other chairs.)
(7)	You guys better clean up. You know what? He's coming to dinner.	(T is aware that it is socially appropriate to clean up before having guests.)
(8)	What's wrong and what's the problem?	(G demonstrates a knowledge of a doctor's examining procedure.)
(9)	No, we're gonna have to give her medicine.	(G knows that if someone is sick, medicine is often part of the treatment.)
(10)	I hurt her a little. Gotta put a band aid on.	(G knows that the appropriate procedure for protecting wounds includes application of a band aid.)
(11)	I'm gonna braid her hair. Where's the rubber band?	(G indicates an awareness of the function of combs and rubber bands in keeping hair in place.)
(12)	You look like a real witch.	(G is aware of those aspects of appearance which makes someone look like a witch.)
(13)	Now where's that mask at?	(G knows that a mask is an appropriate part of a Halloween costume.)
(14)	Someone's gonna lose their britches. That's a trick.	(G appears to know about Halloween tricks and pranks.)
(15)	Yah, well we, Jonathan why don't you decorate the tree and then you can cut. Then you can cut (the wrapping paper.)	(E knows that the tree should be decorated first before presents are placed under it.)
(16)	We have tinsel out in Tuscon to decorate our tree only my dad decorates it.	(E knows that tinsel is for decorating the Christmas tree and relates a past experience when tinsel was used.)
(17)	Looks like we'll have to get some right up here.	(E seems to be aware that the proper procedure for decorating a Christmas tree involves a fairly even distribution of ornaments.)
(18)	I betcha my presents gonna be wrapped right.	(E knows there is a proper way to wrap presents.)

It appears that young children are able to think back or reflect upon previous experiences from multiple sources and to link or use them with present and possible future informational events, objects and resources within the communicative setting. In (8,9, and 10) G brings information from past experiences of his own visits to the doctor. He uses this prior knowledge to carry out his portrayal of the doctor which facilitates the interactive process in the sociodramatic environment. Similarly, E's direction to J to decorate the tree first (15) refocused his attention on interaction with the others in the group decorating the tree. E's observation (17) of the bare spot and what should be done about it also prompted interaction involving getting a chair to reach it and discussion about who was going to use it. In (18) E's indication of a proper procedure for wrapping presents stimulated interaction concerning how to wrap presents. Thus, it would appear that young children do use past information in the present interactive context and that this process facilitates the interactive process.

SUMMARY

The presentation of data involving the Interactional Competency Checklist indicates that it is possible to observe and document young children's interactional competency. From this analysis, it would appear that young children do indeed demonstrate interactional competence in familiar environments over which they exercise control. These findings lend support to the body of research indicating that young children are virtually competent in their communicative abilities.

IMPLICATIONS

The results of this investigation pose some implications for oral language evaluation procedures and for teaching strategies. Assessment of communicative competence, if it is to be comprehensive, must include interactional as well as grammatical competence for it is ultimately the child's ability to use appropriate language in particular communicative settings which determines his/her communicative competence.

Because of the deficit model inferred by standardized testing, teachers have been conditioned to view the detection of disabilities within children as part of their teaching responsibility. Consequently, the teacher becomes involved in testing and diagnosing behavior in a manner that focuses on what the child cannot do. Thus, there is little attention given to what the child can do. The research indicates that children have virtually obtained communicative competence by the time they enter school. That is, they are for the most part competent both grammatically and interactionally. Therefore, if children are given the opportunity to interact in environments over which they exercise some control, their response tends to be more natural and reflective of their true communicative competence. Thus, the immediate need is for researchers and teachers to discover and extend such competencies rather than dwelling on alleged language deficits.

Teachers, however, appear to have little confidence in their observational judgments and subjective data. Too often, teachers rely too much on data obtained from standardized testing situations and fail to be adequately sensitive to the richness of information contained in more informal environments. Teachers need to become better observers and documenters of behavior in a variety of situations over an extended period of time so that patterns of behavior and development can be seen in an emerging process. Certain techniques of analyses used in this investigation could be readily applied in the assessment of kindergarten and preschool children either as observational guidelines or for funding purposes.

This study also contains some implications for programming for language instruction. Often teachers administer a standardized test to detect areas of weakness and then prepare lessons which concentrate on the mastery of skills found on the standardized instruments or adopt a formal program to eradicate these "deficiencies." Unfortunately, as has been indicated in the research, the information obtained is often based on misanalysis caused by inaccurate diagnosis. The subsequent result is that children are often subjected to remedial programs which are often unnecessary and a waste of time, money, and energy. Furthermore, language programs often require the teaching of specific skills which involve much talking done primarily by the teacher. Thus, students respond in a rote manner dependent upon memory and the collection of information rather than the acquisition of language through natural social interaction with others and the ultimate integration of knowledge.

The data imply the importance of opportunities for children to talk to each other as they go about their work and play in the natural classroom environment. Thus, teachers, rather than maintaining quiet classrooms with many teacher directed activities often involving prescribed language skills, should provide numerous experiences and opportunities for children to interact and use their language with each other. It would appear that this opportunity to practice and use language with peers in the natural classroom environment could be the most effective language program.

BIBLIOGRAPHY

Berko, J. (1958) The child's learning of English morphology. Word, 14, 150-177.

Bernstein, B.B. (1972) A critique of the concept of compensatory education. In C. Cazden, V. John and D. Hymes (eds.), Functions of Language in the Classroom. New York: Teachers College Press.

Black, J. K. (1977) Informal and formal means of assessing kindergarten children's communicative competence. Unpublished Dissertation, The Ohio State University.

Carroll, J. B. (1968) Development of Native Language Skills Beyond the Early Years, Princeton, New Jersey: Educational Testing Service.

Cazden, C. (1975) Hypercorrection in test responses. Theory into Practice, 14, 343-346.

Chomsky, C. (1969) The acquisition of syntax in children from five to ten. Research Monograph Series, 57, Cambridge, Mass.: M.I.T. Press.

Cicourel, A. V. (1972) Cross modal communication: The representational context of sociolinguistic information processing. In R. Shuy (ed.), Monograph Series on Language and Linguistics, Twenty-third Annual Round Table, Washington: Georgetown University Press.

Fisher, M. S. (1934) Language Patterns of Preschool Children, New York: Columbia University.

Hymes, D. (1971) Competence and performance in linguistic theory. In R. Huxley and E. Ingram, (eds.), Language Acquisition: Models and Methods, 5-28, London: Academic Press.

Hymes, D. (1973) Introduction. In C. Cazden, V. John and D. Hymes (eds.), Functions of Language in the Classroom, New York: Teachers College Press.

Hymes, D. (1964) Language in Culture and Society; A Reader in Linguistics and Anthropology, New York: Harper & Row.

Labov, W. (1972) Sociolinguistic Patterns, Philadelphia: University of Pennsylvania Press.

Lewis, M and Cherry, L. (1975) Social behavior and language acquisition. Paper presented at a conference, The Origins of Behavior: Communication and Language, Princeton, New Jersey.

McNeill, D. (1970) The development of language. In P. H. Mussen (ed.), Carmichael's Manual of Child Psychology, I, 1061-1062, New York: Wiley & Sons.

Meier, D. (1975) Another look at what's wrong with reading tests. In Testing and Evaluation: New Views, Washington, D.C: ACEI, 32-36.

Meier, D. (1973a) Reading failure and the tests. City College Workshop Center, an occasional paper.

Meier, D. (1973b) What's wrong with the tests? Notes from City College Advisory Service to Open Corridors.

Menyuk, P. (1963) Syntactic structures in the language of children. Child Development, 34, 407-422.

Menyuk, P. (1964) Syntactic rules used by children from preschool through first grade. Child Development, 35, 533-546.

Mishler, E. G. (1976) Conversational competence among first graders. Paper presented at the Conference on Language, Children and Society, Ohio State University.

Patton, M. Q. (1975) Understanding the gobble-dy-gook: A people's guide to standardized test results and statistics. In Testing and Evaluation: New Views, Washington, D.C.: ACEI, 18-26.

Sacks, H., Schegloff, E. A., and Jefferson, G. A. (1974) Simplest systematics for the organization of turn-taking for conversation. Language, 606-735.

Schegloff, E. A., and Sacks, H. (1973) Opening up closings. Semiotica, 8, 289-327.

Strauss, L. (1962) The Savage Mind, Chicago: University of Chicago Press.

Sex and Social Class Differences in Early Mother-Child Interaction

AKKE de BLAUW, CLARA DUBBER, GHISLAINE van ROOSMALEN and CATHERINE E. SNOW
Institute for General Linguistics, University of Amsterdam

INTRODUCTION

The role of early social interaction in influencing later cognitive and social development is well attested. Ainsworth (1969), for example, identified the following five variables as crucial to normal development: frequent physical contact, sensitive responses to the baby's signals, freedom to explore, an environment in which the baby derives a sense of consequences for his own actions, and mutual delight of the baby and the mother in their transactions with each other. Indications are accumulating that certain aspects of the early interaction between a baby and its caretakers may also contribute in crucial and specific ways to the development of communication and language (see Snow, 1977b). For example, Clarke-Stewart (1973) found a relationship between aspects of maternal verbal behavior at nine months and children's verbal ability one year later. Elardo, Bradley and Caldwell (1977) found a high correlation between the variable 'emotional and verbal responsivity of the mother' at six months, and the language ability of the child at three years.

If aspects of the interaction between child and caretaker as early as six months can affect language ability two and a half years later, it is important to collect information concerning differences among various cultures and social groups, and between male and female caretakers and children, in the form and frequency of the early social interaction engaged in. It is the purpose of this paper to present data on (1) the nature of mother-infant interaction between three and six months, (2) changes in the interaction during that period, and (3) sex and social class differences in certain aspects of the interaction. The observations to be reported on were collected in the course of a longer-term study of the same group of babies (see also Snow, de Blauw and van Roosmalen, in press).

PROCEDURE

Sixteen Dutch mother-infant pairs living in Amsterdam were observed at home when the babies were 3, 4.5 and 6 months old (± one week). The observation sessions, which lasted one hour, were carried out by two observers (AdB and CD or GvR). The mothers were contacted via an infant health clinic which served both a middle class and a lower class neighborhood. Eight of the families studied were identified as middle class (MC) and eight as lower class (LC) on the basis of the mothers' schooling and the fathers' occupations. Four of the children in each group were boys and four were girls.

All the babies observed were second children, with an older sibling aged 18 months to four years, except one third-born whose immediately older sibling fell into this age range. The older child was always present during the observation session.

The mothers were told that the purpose of the observations was to study the development of infant vocalizations, especially the social vocalizations most likely to occur if both the mother and the older sibling were present. All the observation sessions included a feed, which took about 20 minutes, and the caretaking and play activities immediately preceding and following the feed.

Scoring and Analysis

The observation sessions were tape-recorded and the observers noted the occurrence of certain predetermined maternal and infant behaviors using a checklist. The checklist was filled in 8 times per minute, by the two observers alternately. Each observed for 7½ seconds, then filled in the list while the other observed for 7½ seconds. The infant behaviors noted on the list were: gaze direction (to mother, to observer, to sibling, to object, active), arm and leg movements, play with object, smile and vocalization. The vocalizations were categorized as positive (clearly happy noises, often associated with laughter), negative (crying, fretting, fussing), or neutral (soft vocalizations, neither clearly positive nor negative). The maternal behaviors noted were: vocalization to baby, to older child, to other, smile at baby, looking at baby, holding baby, touching baby, playing with baby, and various caretaking activities (feeding, bathing, dressing, changing). Details of the situation (room, position of mother and infant, important objects present, etc.) and interesting aspects of the interaction not captured by the checklist (e.g., details of the games played, which objects the infants were looking at or playing with, etc.) were noted as well.

Because relatively little social interaction occurred during the portions of the observation sessions devoted to feeding, and because these took varying amounts of time for different babies, these portions were omitted from the analysis of social interaction. Forty minutes of potential social interaction were thus analyzed per session (for the few cases in which less than forty minutes was available, the figures were adjusted to equal forty minutes.)

RESULTS

Mother-Infant Interaction between Three and Six Months

Infant smiles and vocalizations. Infant smiles and vocalizations are important behaviors in establishing social interaction. They are behaviors which mothers respond to reliably (Snow, 1977a) and go to a great deal of trouble to elicit (Snow, de Blauw, and van Roosmalen, in press). At three months, the babies studied vocalized in 30.9% of the possible scoring intervals, a result which agrees remarkably well with the findings of Rebelsky and Abeles (1969) for Dutch babies (33.4%) and Lewis and Freedle (1973) for American babies (25%, not including crying). A significant ($p < .005$) decrease occurred in the amount of vocalization between three and six months, to 18% of the possible intervals (this and all other age differences were tested with a one-way analysis of variance). This decrease is primarily accounted for by the decrease in neutral vocalizations (see Fig. 1), which is the only subcategory of vocalizations for which the decrease was significant ($p < .005$).

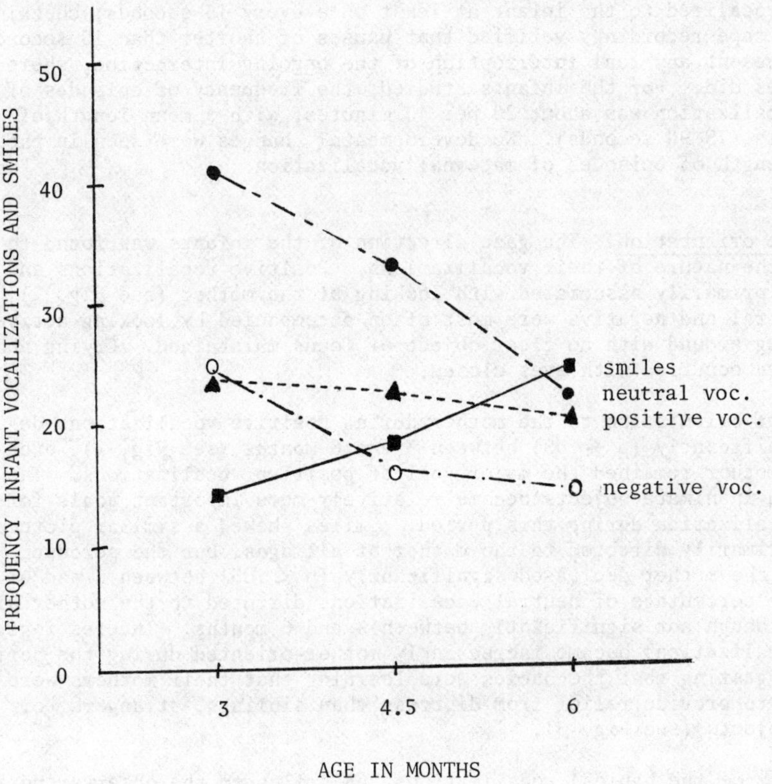

Fig. 1. The mean frequency with which the infants produced positive vocalizations, neutral vocalizations, negative vocalizations, and smiles at 3, 4.5 and 6 months.

There is, then, a clear tendency for infant vocalizations to become more interpretable, more clearly positive or negative, during the period under study.

The decrease in vocalizations contrasts with a steady increase in the amount of smiling between 3 and 6 months (see Fig. 1). Landau, (1977), who looked at smiling frequency at 2, 4, 7 and 11 months, found an increase between 2 and 4 but a decrease by 7 months. She postulated a smiling peak sometime before 7 months. Our results suggest that this peak lies fairly close to 6 months.

Maternal vocalizations. Two aspects of maternal vocalizations to the infants are of interest: how much the mothers talk to the babies, and how they pattern their talking. The frequency of the maternal vocalizations was measured as the percentage of 15 second intervals during which the mothers vocalized to the baby. This remained at a level of close to 60% at all three ages studied. Patterning of vocalization is reflected by the number of episodes of talking to the infants and the mean length of those episodes. An episode of maternal vocalization was defined as a period during which the mother vocalized to the infant at least once every 15 seconds; checking against the tape recordings verified that pauses of shorter than 15 seconds did not represent any real interruption of the ongoing interaction, whereas longer pauses did. For the infants studied, the frequency of episodes of maternal vocalization was about 20 per 40 minutes, with a mean length of 5-6 intervals (75-90 seconds). No developmental changes were seen in the number or length of episodes of maternal vocalization.

Babies' gaze orientation. The gaze direction of the infants was found to be related to the nature of their vocalizations. Positive vocalizations and smiles were primarily associated with looking at the mother (see Fig. 2), whereas neutral and negative were most often accompanied by looking actively, i.e., looking around with no clear object of focus maintained. Crying and fussing often occurred with eyes closed.

The degree of orientation to the mother during positive vocalizations decreased significantly ($p < .05$) between 3 and 6 months (see Fig. 2), even though the mother remained the major goal of positive vocalizations. The observer and inanimate objects became relatively more important goals for positive vocalization during this period. Smiles showed a similar picture; they were primarily directed to the mother at all ages, but the percent directed to the mother decreased significantly ($p < .05$) between 3 and 6 months. The percentage of neutral vocalizations directed to the mother also decreased, though not significantly between 3 and 6 months. Interestingly, negative vocalizations became increasingly mother-oriented during the period studied, suggesting that the babies were learning that their mothers were more likely to provide relief from distress than siblings, strangers, or inanimate objects (see Fig. 3).

The frequency of the babies' vocalizations and smiles to the observer peaked at 4.5 months. This result agrees with other findings (see Landau, 1977, for review) that smiling to any representation of the human face reaches a peak at about 4 months, and then declines, presumably because of a growing ability to recognize the face as strange.

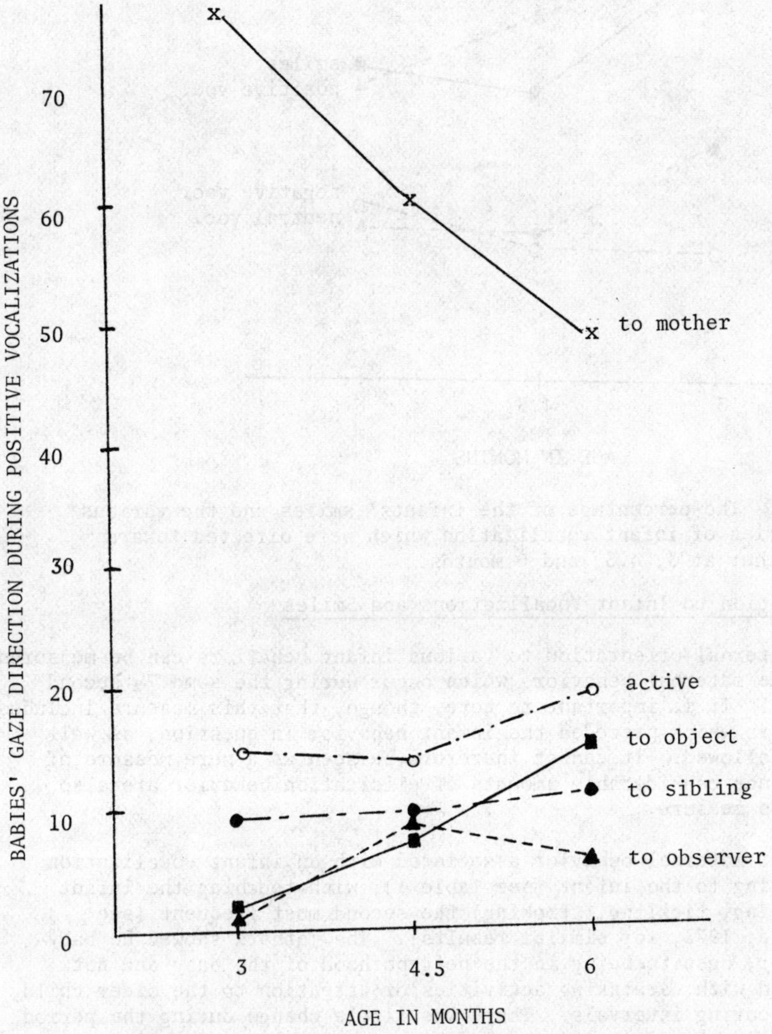

Fig. 2. The percentage of the infants' positive vocalizations which were directed to mother, sibling, object, observer, or activity at 3, 4.5 and 6 months.

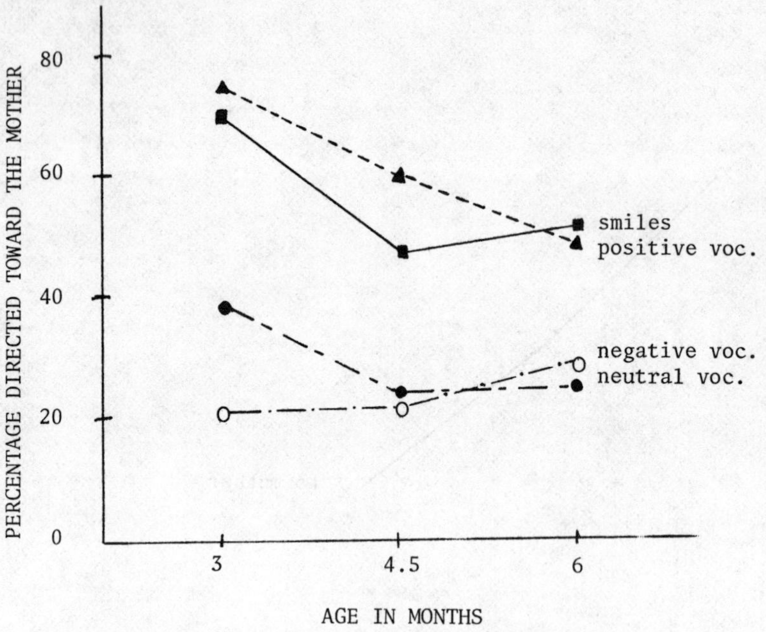

Fig. 3. The percentage of the infants' smiles and the various categories of infant vocalization which were directed toward the mother at 3, 4.5, and 6 months.

Maternal Orientation to Infant Vocalizations and Smiles

The degree of maternal orientation to various infant behaviors can be measured by looking at the maternal behaviors which occur during the same 7½ second scoring interval. It is important to note, though, that this measure includes maternal behaviors which preceded the infant behavior in question, as well as those which followed. It cannot therefore be seen as a pure measure of responsivity, since considerable amounts of elicitation behavior are also reflected in this measure.

The most frequent maternal behavior associated with an infant vocalization or smile is talking to the infant (see Table 1), with touching the infant (primarily cuddling, tickling, stroking) the second most frequent (see Lewis and Freedle, 1973, for similar results). The mothers showed no baby-oriented behavior, despite being in the neighborhood of the baby and not being preoccupied with caretaking activities or attention to the older child, in 6-7% of the scoring intervals. There was little change during the period 3-6 months in maternal orientation to infant vocalizations and smiles, except that touching declined sharply between 4.5 and 6 months (see Table 1).

Analysis of maternal orientation to the different categories of infant vocalizations shows a clear differentiation; mothers showed greater orientation to positive vocalizations and smiles than to neutral or negative vocalizations (see Table 2). Maternal vocalizations were higher and instances of no baby-oriented behavior were lower to positive vocalizations and to smiles than to neutral or negative vocalizations. Touching the baby was especially associated with infant smiling, a finding accounted for by the mothers' tendency to use tickling and other physical contact to elicit smiling and laughing (see also Landau, 1977). There is no evidence for any developmental change in the patterning of these maternal behaviors, suggesting that elicitation and response sequences may be fairly well established by 3 months.

TABLE 1 Mean percentage of the intervals during which the infant was smiling or vocalizing in which various maternal behaviors occurred

MATERNAL BEHAVIOR	AGE IN MONTHS 3	4.5	6
Vocalize to baby	59.7	58.5	61.7
Touch baby	13.5	12.6	6.1
No baby-oriented behavior	6.4	7.5	6.6
Occupied with other activities	20.3	21.4	25.5

TABLE 2 Mean percentage of the intervals during which the infant was producing specific sorts of vocalizations in which various maternal behaviors occurred

MATERNAL BEHAVIOR	INFANT VOCALIZATION	AGE IN MONTHS 3	4.5	6
Vocalize to infant	Positive	69.4	69.8	67.5
	Neutral	53.7	46.9	47.9
	Negative	59.4	63.2	63.9
	Smile	68.5	60.9	70.1
Touch infant	Positive	12.9	12.0	4.8
	Neutral	16.7	7.9	2.8
	Negative	12.1	7.9	5.9
	Smile	19.4	14.9	8.9
No baby-oriented behavior	Positive	1.2	2.6	3.0
	Neutral	7.9	13.9	10.5
	Negative	10.0	8.2	9.0
	Smile	4.6	6.2	2.2

Relationship between maternal and infant behavior. Lewis and Freedle (1973) found a high positive correlation between frequency of infant vocalization and of maternal vocalization to the infant. We found no clear correlation at any age between frequency of maternal vocalization and infant vocalization, either for the total frequency of infant vocalizations or for any subcategory of infant vocalizations. There was, however, a pattern of high correlations between measures of maternal orientation toward the infant and of infant orientation toward the mother (see Table 3).

TABLE 3 Correlations between the frequency of various sorts of infant vocalizations directed to the mother and maternal orientation to those vocalizations

	AGE IN MONTHS		
CATEGORY OF INFANT VOCALIZATION	3	4.5	6
Positive	.70***	.76***	.29
Neutral	.16	.41*	.47*
Negative	.29*	.00	-.18
Smile	.56*	.88***	.53*

*Correlation significant p < .05
***Correlation significant p < .005

There were two factors which seemed to contribute to maternal orientation toward the infant: the nature of the infant vocalization and the infant's gaze direction. First, frequency of mothers' vocalizations to the infant correlated more highly with frequency of infant positive vocalizations and smiling than with frequency of neutral or negative vocalizations. In fact, for crying there was no correlation at all after 3 months. Second, maternal vocalizations correlated more highly with infant behaviors directed toward the mother than with the same behaviors directed toward the sibling, observer, or an object (see Table 4).

TABLE 4 Correlations between the maternal behavior vocalization to infant and the infant behaviors positive vocalization and smile directed to various goals at 3, 4.5 and 6 months

	INFANT GAZE	AGE IN MONTHS		
INFANT BEHAVIOR	DIRECTION	3	4.5	6
	Mother	.70***	.76***	.29
	Sibling	-.41*	-.59**	-.54*
	Object	-.28	-.22	-.10
Positive	Active	-.40	-.30	-.16
Vocalization	Observer	-.46	.04	-.31
	Mother	.56*	.88***	.53*
	Sibling	-.42*	-.16	-.17
	Object	.69	-.02	-.43*
Smile	Active	-.30	.00	-.26
	Observer	.21	-.81***	-.31

Note: Since some babies did not produce some combinations of behavior and gaze direction, the n for some correlations was smaller than 16.

*Correlation significant p < .05
**Correlation significant p < .01
***Correlation significant p < .005

Thus, the mothers who talked the most to their infants has infants who smiled and vocalized positively toward the mother.

The absence of a correlation between frequency of maternal vocalization to the infant and the frequency of infant vocalizations, taken together with the pattern of correlations between maternal vocalization to the infant and infant orientation toward the mother, suggest very strongly that the mothers were responding to a constellation of cues in these social interactions, all of which were crucial to their interpretation of the infant's behavior. This result makes clear why mothers find it difficult to engage in communicative interactions with infants who do not establish eye contant, such as blind or Mongoloid babies.

Sex and Social Class Differences

Infant vocalizations and smiles. No consistently significant sex or social class differences were found in frequency of infant vocalizations or smiles. LC babies vocalized more than MC babies, but this difference was significant only for 4.5 months ($p < .01$; this and all other sex and social class differences were tested with a two-way analysis of variance). This result agrees with the findings of Lewis and Freedle (1973), who found that 3 month old LC babies vocalized more.

Boys produced consistently more negative vocalizations and more smiles than girls, but the difference was significant only for negative vocalizations at 6 months ($p < .05$). This result agrees with the findings of Moss and Robson (1970) for 3 month olds; Rebelsky and Abeles (1969), however, found the opposite.

Maternal vocalizations. MC mothers vocalized significantly more to their babies at 3 and 4.5 months than LC mothers, a result which confirms Tulkin and Kagan's (1972) findings, though Lewis and Freedle (1973) found no social class difference in maternal vocalization. By 6 months, LC mothers talked more, though not significantly, to their babies than MC mothers.

There were neither sex nor social class differences in the number of episodes of maternal vocalization to the babies, nor in the mean length of the episodes, at any age. There was, however, a significant ($p < .05$) interaction for both number of episodes and mean length of episode at 6 months; MC girls received more, shorter episodes of maternal vocalization than LC girls, whereas MC boys received fewer, longer episodes than LC boys.

Babies' gaze orientation. No social class differences were found in infants' gaze direction during vocalization or smiling. Nor were there any significant sex differences in orientation toward the mother during vocalization or smiling, though there was a strong tendency for boys to vocalize positively and smile more toward their mothers than girls. Girls, on the other hand, vocalized positively and smiled more toward the older sibling (significant for 4.5 and 6 months, $p < .05$).

Maternal Orientation to Infant Vocalization and Smiles

There was a strong tendency for mothers to be more oriented toward boys' vocalizations and smiles than toward girls' vocalizations. This difference reached significance only for positive vocalization at 4.5 months and neutral vocalization at 6 months ($p < .05$). Mothers were, however, less oriented toward boys' than girls' negative vocalizations, though this difference was not significant. Mothers also touched boys more during the same interval as a vocalization or smile, though this difference was significant only for neutral vocalizations at 3 months ($p < .05$). Lewis and Freedle (1973) found that mothers were more likely to respond to girls with talking and to boys with physical contact. Our results, on the other hand, suggest that mothers produce all sorts of baby-oriented behaviors more to boys than to girls. Only during crying or fussing were the girls more likely to receive maternal attention.

No significant social class differences were found in the mothers' orientation toward their babies, except that at 3 months MC mothers talked more to their babies during negative vocalizations than LC mothers ($p < .05$). The MC mothers talked more to their babies during smiles and all categories of vocalization at 3 and 4.5 months, but at 6 months this difference has reversed. No social class differences in touching were found. In general, then, social class differences in maternal orientation toward infant smiling and vocalization were small, and any tendency for the MC mothers to be more baby-oriented had disappeared by 6 months. This result disagrees with the findings of Tulkin and Kagan (1972), who found greater responsivity among MC mothers at 10 months. However, the social class groups studied by Tulkin and Kagan were probably considerably more different from one another economically, educationally, and culturally than the Dutch groups we studied.

DISCUSSION

In this study of mother-infant interaction, we have directed our attention to some quantitative aspects of the way mothers and infants talk to one another. It is important to point out that the qualitative aspects of mother-infant interaction are equally worthy of study. Semantic and functional characteristics of the maternal, the child's development of conversational skills, and the introduction and development of games are all crucial features in a full description of mother-infant interaction.

We found that infant vocalizations occurred about 30% of the time at 3 months and 18% of the time at 6 months, and that LC babies vocalized more than MC babies. Mothers' vocalizations to their babies, on the other hand, occurred about 60% of the time at all ages, and MC mothers talked to their babies more than LC mothers. These results, and the lack of correlation between the two measures, make clear that frequency of maternal and of infant vocalization have little direct relationship to one another.

A much stronger relationship can be seen between mothers' vocalizations to their babies and specific sorts of infant vocalization directed toward the mother. Smiles and happy vocalizations produced by the baby while looking at his mother were almost sure to be associated with baby-oriented behavior on the part of the mother. Neutral or negative vocalizations, however, or vocalizations directed toward someone or something else, were much less likely to be associated with baby-oriented behavior from the mother. This relationship explains the finding that boys were more mother-oriented than girls, and mothers of boys were more baby-oriented than mothers of girls. Girls directed more of their smiles and vocalizations to their older siblings, and therefore received less maternal response.

Although social class differences in the degree to which mothers talked to their babies and were baby-oriented were found at 3 and 4.5 months, by 6 months these had all disappeared. This suggests that, though there might be social class differences in beliefs about the importance of talking to babies, babies' ability to understand what is said and to communicate with the adult, etc., these belief systems can be influenced by the experience of interaction with a baby. Because of their attendance at the same infant health clinic, and their consequent exposure to the same advice concerning how to care for infants, the mothers in the study were remarkably homogeneous in their caretaking practices. Thus, their opportunities for interaction with their infants, and for observing how the infant reacted to various behaviors, were also quite similar. This fact may explain why the social class differences present at 3 months disappeared by 6 months (see Goldberg, 1977, for a discussion of how infant behaviors reinforce specific parental behaviors).

It is clear that all the babies studied had by 6 months the opportunity to learn a great deal about the nature of communication. They had experienced countless occasions of response to their spontaneous smiles and vocalizations. They had learned that mothers are more likely than siblings or strangers to respond to crying and fussing. They had participated in hundreds of sequences in which adults attempted to elicit specific behaviors, and expressed glee when the attempt was successful. Considering the nature of what a baby could learn about communication from interaction with his caretakers in the period before 6 months of age, it is not surprising that researchers have found relationships between aspects of early mother-child interaction and the child's language ability several years later.

BIBLIOGRAPHY

Ainsworth, M. D. S. (1969) Object relations, dependency, and attachment: A theoretical review of infant-mother relationships. Child Development, 40, 969-1025.

Clarke-Stewart, K. A. (1973) Interactions between mothers and their young children: Characteristics and consequences. Monograph of the S.R.C.D., 38, No. 6-7.

Elardo, R., Bradley, R., and Caldwell, B. M. (1977) A longitudinal study of the relation of infants' home environments to language development at age three. Child Development, 48, 595-603.

Goldberg, S. (1977) Social competence in infancy: A model of parent-infant interaction. Merrill-Palmer Quarterly, 23(3).

Landau, R. (1977) Spontaneous and elicited smiles and vocalizations of infants in four Israeli environments. Developmental Psychology, 13, 389-400.

Lewis, M., and Freedle, R. (1973) Mother-infant dyad: The cradle of meaning. In M. Lewis and R. Freedle (eds.), Communication and Affect: Language and Thought, New York: Academic Press.

Moss, H. A. and Robson, K. S. (1970) The relation between the amount of time infants spend in various states and the development of visual behavior. Child Development, 41, 509-517.

Rebelsky, F. and Abeles, G. (1969) Infancy in Holland and the United States. Paper presented at the S.R.C.D. meeting, Santa Monica, California.

Snow, C. E. (1977a) The development of conversation between mothers and babies. Journal of Child Language, 4, 1-22.

Snow, C. E. (1977b) The role of social interaction in language acquisition. Paper presented to Minnesota Symposium on Child Development. November, 1977.

Snow, C. E., de Blauw, A. and van Roosmalen, G. (in press) Talking and playing with babies: The role of ideology of child rearing. In M. Bullowa (ed.), Before Speech, Cambridge University Press.

Tulkin, S. and Kagan, J. (1972) Mother-child interaction in the first year of life. Child Development, 43, 31-41.

What Will a Three-year-old Say?: An Experimental Study of Situational Variation

BARBARA BOKUS and GRACE WALES SHUGAR
Institute of Psychology, University of Warsaw

Ever since William Labov posed the 'fundamental' sociolinguistic questions--Why does anyone say anything? Under what conditions will they say it to us?--the investigators of adult and child language have been finding many differences in the way the same speaker (or type of speaker) talks to various listeners. In his investigation, Labov found that it made a difference whether a strange adult conversing with a boy sat with him behind a desk or sat on the floor eating peanuts with him and another boy. In the former case the boy said little and could not be induced to say more; in the latter, he indulged freely in lively and meaningful conversation. Clearly the two situational variants had radically different eliciting properties from the standpoint of the child. Diverse studies of effects of gross situational variables on child language characteristics were first summarized by Cazden (1970). Much more research, however, is needed to deal with the questions such as: What configurational changes in basic social situations are decisive in producing the important differences in a child's speech? Can we discover through experimental manipulation the minimal and manipulable factors in a conversational situation which will produce reliable changes in the way a child will talk to a listener? A positive answer to the latter question holds important implications both for theoretical and practical issues.

In this paper, we report on an experimental study which examined one situational contrast for effects upon child discourse.* In this study the same children talked to the same adults in a standard natural setting about a standardized set of pictures. In one experimental situation both child and adult had perceptual access to the picture; in the other, the child had sole access. The results revealed that there were significant differences in what the child said, how much verbalization he produced and how he constructed his discourse, and that these differences varied systematically according to the experiment conditions.

THE PROBLEM

If we, as researchers on child language and educators, believe that the child must himself experience the uses of language through his own efforts and actions in order to attain competence as a user of language (as argued by Cazden [1974] and others) then we ought to give profound thought to the ways

*This research was conducted by Barbara Bokus for a Master's degree in Psychology under the supervision of Professor Tadeusz Tomaszewski, University of Warsaw, 1977.

in which we can provide occasions for the child to develop this particular type of experience. Plainly, to develop the uses of language, the child needs to test out their value in his own terms within social situations that demonstrate their degree of effectiveness. Whatever list or classification of language functions we wish to subscribe to, there remains one functional dichotomy which ought to receive our closest attention, and this pertains to the use of language to impart knowledge to a listener who does not already possess that knowledge. The informative function has been regarded as the one inherent function of language (Halliday, 1975), marking it off from other communication systems. This function concerns the passage of symbolic content, by linguistic means, from mental source to mental destination.

Once the inherent function emerges in the infant's language (which Halliday's 1975 study of Nigel dates at about 22-24 months; see also Shugar, 1975b) we can pose the following question: Under what conditions will the child display readiness and willingness to impart to someone information having such characteristics? One may posit at least three necessary conditions internal to the child. First, the child must have some information to impart, knowable to himself and retrievable by himself (coded experiences, future intentions, associations and hypotheses about states of affairs). Second, the child must believe that the interlocutor does not already have this particular knowledge, i.e., he must recognize the existence of certain discrepancies in the states of knowledge between himself and the other. Third, the child must be motivated, by an urge to communicate, to impart this knowledge to the particular interlocutor. For these conditions to exist in the child, the experiential prerequisites unquestionably include exposure to and participation in diverse interpersonal situations involving communicative exchange. What essential experience must such situations provide? On the one hand, such experience must promote the development of a strong communicative urge. To cite Cazden (1974) "everything we know about language development suggests that it develops best, in function as well as structure, when motivated by powerful communicative intent" (p. 218). The crucial feature of the situation in this respect is likely to be the display of readiness by the adult interlocutor to receive the child's information and to accredit him as its source.

On the other hand, such experience must provide the child with the opportunities to develop ways of discriminating what is and is not perceptible to (and therefore knowable by) self as separate from the other. Following the reasoning in Shields (1976), we agree that the communicative process depends upon both "what is common and what is distinct in the interlocutors' experience, the common or presupposed constituting a field across which differentiated messages pass" (p. 4). The child basically expects the field to be shared roughly in the same way. Such knowledge, derived from earliest mother-infant interactions, is the sine qua non for the next steps of making adjustments to the viewpoint of another (Shields, 1975).

If we accept this view we need to learn more about the shaping of the communicative process from the point of view of how the language inherent function operates, i.e., the points of departure, activization of sources of information, the building of informationally differentiated messages, negotiations for a common understanding of messages, etc.

One way in which we may attempt to examine the interpersonal communicative process as envisaged above is to compare discourse structure and content as produced by the same children in situational variants where access to the source of basic information is the one discriminating variable. Discourse organization may predictably reveal the child's differentiated selections of information sources. Its description may lead us to interpretations of reasons behind the selective process. We hypothesized that, in a properly motivated task situation, the child will be strongly influenced in the amount, complexity and manner of selection of informational content he brings to that task by the single variable of shared or nonshared source of basic perceptual information.

METHOD

Subjects

The subjects were 52 children between three and four years (mean age 3 years 6 months). All attended a nursery school in Warsaw, Poland, and were monolingual native speakers of Polish. They were randomly selected from four schools, and were from various socioeconomic backgrounds. Their parents were skilled and unskilled workers, white collar workers and professionals.

Materials

The stimuli selected for presentation were two pictures selected from a book entitled Pod kasztanem (Under the Chestnut Tree) written by Irena Geiling (Berlin: Rudolf Arnold) with illustrations by Ilse Hefster. The storybook was intended for children age three to five years. The two pictures are reproduced in Appendix A.

Procedure

The basic situation was a story-telling episode which was incorporated into the morning activities of each child's school activities. Each child told a story about each of the two pictures. There was a two week interval between story telling session #1 and story telling session #2 for each child. Two experimental conditions were included in the study. In one condition the child told a story while viewing the picture with the adult--the joint perception condition (henceforth JP). In the other condition the child told a story while having sole perceptual access to the picture--the sole perception condition (SP). The experimental conditions were counterbalanced and the sessions were conducted according to the design presented in Fig. 1.

Nursery School Group

Story telling session	1	2	3	4
I	Stimulus Picture A JP Condition	Stimulus Picture A SP Condition	Stimulus Picture B JP Condition	Stimulus Picture B SP Condition
two week interval				
II	Stimulus Picture B SP Condition	Stimulus Picture B JP Condition	Stimulus Picture A SP Condition	Stimulus Picture A JP Condition

Fig. 1. Testing sessions

Thus, for example, children from nursery school group 1 told a story about Picture A in the first story telling session while jointly viewing this picture with the adult listener (JP condition). Two dren told a story about Picture B to the same adult listener with sole perceptual access to the picture (SP condition).

The general procedure for the story telling sessions was uniform across children. Each child first received a picture and joined a "train" (a chain of marching children). The child then "got off at this station," escorted by the experimenter, which was a story-telling nook where the classroom teacher was sitting. In the JP condition the experimenter sat the child at a right angle to where the teacher was seated and requested that the child open the envelope. E said: 'Put the picture down on the table so that Mrs. (name of teacher) can see what's in the picture too.' The teacher initiated the ensuing dialogue with the basic request: 'Tell me about this picture.' In the SP condition, the experimenter helped the child remove his picture from the envelope and place it on a stand by the table between the child and the adult. The child was then seated in similar proxemic position. E said: 'Put the picture on the stand so that Mrs. (name of teacher) can't see what's in the picture.' The teacher initiated the dialogue with the same request: 'Tell me about your picture.' In both variants the experimenter returned to the 'train' game. After the story-telling episode ended, the child returned to join the train, and another child was let off to engage in the next story-telling episode with the teacher. To ensure normalcy and naturalness of setting conditions, all children present participated and more pictures were used; however, only the experimental children and pictures were analyzed.

Adult participation in the dialogue was predetermined and kept uniform but some leeway was allowed for natural responses within a range of utterance types at recognized points in the flow of the child's discourse. Apart from the initiating and terminating routine, the teacher's role was primarily to sustain the flow of speech from the child and to encourage speech forward by displaying interest and curiosity in what the child was saying. At no time did the adult attempt to take the initiative in the dialogue. The role therefore was strictly pragmatic in the sense of controlling speaker-hearer relations in terms of the task at hand. No substantive contribution to the discourse was made by the teacher.

The activity context was also preset in such a way as to allow for the consideration that child-adult conversation arises with highest naturalness and frequency in a context of other activity which forms a favorable 'enclosure' for it (Shugar, 1972). The adult was engaged in her own line of activity (knitting) while listening. In both situations she looked intermittently at the child, always at moments when she addressed the child. In the SP condition her eyes rested solely upon her knitting. In the JP condition she frequently looked at the picture.

The story telling sessions were audio taped, and the experimenter made notes of gross nonverbal behavior from a distant observation point. The material was transcribed and forms the basis of the data analysis. Sample stories told by the children appear in Appendix B.

Utterance sequences produced by the child within the dialogue were treated as a discourse unit and subjected to various analyses.

DATA ANALYSIS

Formal analyses included a word count to establish discourse length and calculations of the ratio of compound and complex sentences to simple clauses and juxtaposed word sequences (procedures developed by Przetacznikowa, 1968, for analysis of early speech in Polish children).

Discourse content and structure were analyzed by procedures developed for text analysis of adult-child dialogues in children 18 to 36 months (Shugar, 1975a). Briefly, the basic concepts underlying such an analysis are as follows. In line with Halliday (1970), text is understood as a semantic organization of information, whose structure is dependent upon the situation in which the text is built up. Two kinds of situation are distinguished in terms of the text building process. One kind is the interlocutors' situation, which gives rise to text and to which the text contributes informationally. The other is the situation to which reference is made, about which information is coded by linguistic means. Whereas the former provides the pragmatic demands upon language for text construction, the latter provides the sources of information for the text-constructing process.

In the study by Shugar cited above, children under three years of age were shown to contribute new information mainly by shifts either to different focal elements in the reference situation or to a new reference situation. The latter constitutes a major shift since it required the child to locate a new source of information. The evidence showed that at this age studied reference situations could be shifted with ease and versatility within a restricted range that was accessible cognitively. Characteristic of this study was the fact that the adult carried the main burden of text building, with the child's utterances contributing by means of various simple linguistic operations upon that text.

In the present study, in contrast to the study cited above, the three-year-old child carried the entire burden of text construction, the adult contributing nothing in the way of referential material. We expected that the child would be able to show the same ease and innovativeness in selecting and shifting his reference situations, and at the same time command an extended and enriched range of possible reference situations. A set of empirical categories of reference situations was extracted from the raw data, by use of certain criterial features, to be reported in the result section below.

It must be stated explicitly that this system of interpreting the child's intended meanings is based on an assumption that the child will map his meanings onto text by lexicogrammatical means commonly used by both himself and his interlocutor, as well as by the analyzer, thus rendering his meaning graspable by the adult. But if the child means something other than what is mapped onto text, that meaning is not to be captured from the text, and the child will be misinterpreted. Interpretations of the child's intended reference situations are obviously our own, and we must concede a margin of error in the area of nontransparency to the child's meaning.

Critical features for discriminating reference situation shifts were indicated by lexicogrammatical changes (sentence subject, predicate, and verb tense). A reliability check was conducted of the replicability of this procedure. Three independent judges analyzed all the material. Inter-judge agreement was 96.73%.

RESULTS

Control of Adult Performance

Failure to meet role requirements by the various adult listeners within and across situational variants would obviously contaminate the discourse product. An analysis of the number and type of adult utterances produced in the story telling sessions showed no statistically significant differences between the adult listener ($x = 5.67$ and 5.44 for the JP and SP conditions respectively, $t = 0.724$). Two utterance categories differed in frequency. These were (a) expressions of curiosity and interest, e.g., "Oh! Is that so!" ($z = 2.716$, $p < 0.01$) in favor of the SP condition and (b) probes, e.g., "What else?" ($z = 1.707$, $p < 0.05$, one-tailed test) in favor of JP condition. These differences, as indicated below, are a function of the contrasting characteristics of the variant discourses which call for differential responses from the adult. That is, expressions of interest and curiosity were responses to information from absent sources (more numerous in SP condition) and probes for further discourse were responses to silences (more numerous in JP condition). Despite a significantly greater number of probes, however, the child has significantly less to say in the JP condition. Therefore there was no difference in the fulfillment of pragmatic functions dependent on differences in adult performances.

Discourse Length and Complexity

Discourse was significantly longer in the SP condition than in the joint perception condition. Average length of the stories (in words) was 43.6 as compared to 37.6 respectively ($t = 1.8$, $p < 0.05$). Furthermore, discourse was grammatically more complex in the SP condition than in the JP condition. The ratios of complexity (as defined above) were 1:2 in the JP condition and 1:1 in the SP condition. These frequency differences are statistically significant ($z = 2.4$, $p < 0.01$).

Discourse Text Analysis

Discourse text produced in the SP condition was comprised of a longer chain of reference situation units ($\bar{X} = 9.25$) than that produced in the JP condition ($\bar{X} = 7.98$). This is a significant difference by the T test version of Cochran and Cox ($t = 2.49$, $p < 0.01$).

Choice of Reference Situation

The choice of reference situations are defined as a unit by identifying the 'subject' or element in terms of which the situation takes on a given configuration at a given moment in time (see Tomaszewski, 1975). These were categorized according to the following criteria: (1) element selected as reference situation shifts (RSs) subject (self, pictorial element, other element in setting, element outside of setting); (2) spatiotemporal localization of RS in relation to communicative setting. A frequency count of occurrences of the above categories are presented in Table 1.

TABLE 1 Frequency of occurrence of Reference Situation categories in child discourse units produced in each experimental situation (in absolute numbers and percents)

Spatial relation of RS to communicative setting		Selection of RS subject	Temporal feature of RS: present JP	present SP	absent JP	absent SP	Total JP	Total SP
	Present	child speaker	72 17.3%	45 9.4%	12 2.9%	34 7.1%	84 20.3%	79 16.4%
		pictorial element	208 50.2%	149 31.0%	94 22.6%	166 34.5%	302 72.8%	315 65.5%
		other element in setting	18 4.4%	3 0.6%	2 0.5%	3 0.6%	20 4.8%	6 1.2%
	Remote	element outside setting	3 0.7%	28 5.8%	6 1.4%	53 11.0%	9 2.2%	81 16.8%
		TOTAL	301 72.5%	225 46.8%	114 27.5%	256 53.2%	415 100.0%	481 100.0%

The child selected self as RS subject with equal frequency in the two experimental conditions (84 and 79 choices). In both situations, the child chose self most often as RS subject located in the temporal present as against absent. This predominance, however, is much greater in JP condition (72 as compared to 12) than in SP condition (45 as compared to 34). When we compare the frequency dominance in JP and SP conditions for temporally present RSs, we observe that the child selects self with a statistically significant predominance in the joint perception condition, i.e., 17.3% as compared to 9.4% respectively, ($z = 3.57$, $p < 0.001$). This means that the child much more often expressed what he is doing at the moment and what he is experiencing (seeing, liking/disliking). On the other hand, when we compare the frequencies of choices of self as absent RS subject, we see that the frequency is much higher in the SP than JP condition, i.e., 7.1% as compared to 2.9% respectively, ($z = 2.98$, $p < 0.002$). This indicates that the child with greater frequency expresses what he has done or will do, has experienced or will experience, in the SP condition.

The most frequent choice of RS subject, as is to be expected by the nature of the task, is a pictorial element; but this particular choice occurred more often in JP (72.8%) than in SP (65.5%). Further differences will be indicated presently. Other elements in the communicative setting were selected to a far greater extent in the JP ($z = 4.5$) while elements beyond the setting were overwhelmingly more often selected in SP ($z = 11.5$).

Secondly, the major source of reference situations in the joint perception condition lay in the perceptual field of the child, either in the picture or in the communicative setting. Of these (71.8% of the total), pictorial sources accounted for 50.1%. On the other hand, the major source of RSs in the isolated perception condition (59.0%) was internal to the child. Internally derived RSs were variously displaced from the communicative setting. Primarily they were only temporally displaced (42.2%); and least often were spatially remote only (5.8%). In 11.0% of the cases they were both temporally and spatially absent. The difference of frequency of present versus displaced reference situations between the JP and SP conditions is statistically significant ($z = 2.46$, $p < 0.01$). Further, the pictorially based choices of reference situations in the SP condition were located in present on nonpresent time with about the same frequency (31.0% as compared to 34.5% respectively).

The above results show that, depending on which situational variant the child finds himself in, he constructs his discourse text with predominantly different referential material, drawn from different sources. Further, he relates himself to the text content in different ways and to different extents. In the JP condition, he is more situation-bound; while in the SP condition he shows more freedom from the immediate context and tends to assume more of a reportative or observer stance to the situations to which he refers.

The Sequential Organization of Discourse

How the child organizes his discourse will be shown by establishing the starting point(s), the ending point(s), and the major shifts in sources of reference situations. Sequential analyses are portrayed in the graphs of fig. 2.

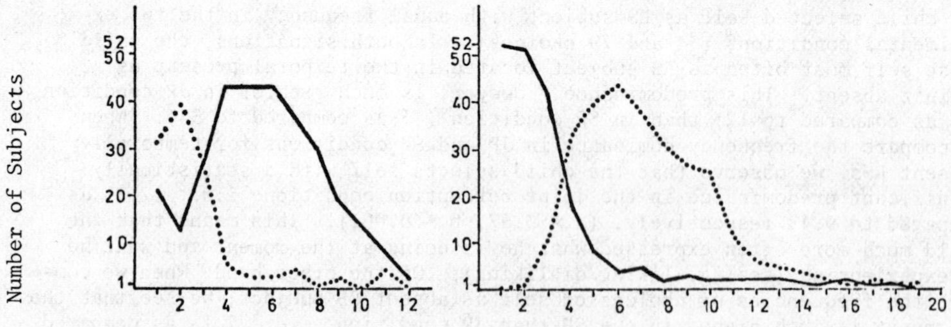

RS chains
JP Condition

RS chains
SP Condition

Fig. 2. Successive choices of present or absent reference situations in RS chains of discourse units based on frequency of occurrences in discourse units of all subjects.

Figure 2 presents two profiles of discourse organization, i.e., successive choices of either temporally present or absent reference situations making up the RS chain, based on frequency of occurrences in all the stories. There is a contrast of prevailing order. For the joint perception condition, the majority of children start from spatiotemporally remote reference situations, and move rapidly, at the second shift of reference situation, to the perceptually present type. On the other hand, for the SP conditions it is evident the children (without exception) start from the perceptually given type and then move, at the second or third shift of reference situation, to the absent, internally derived type. In either condition, by the fourth RS shift, 40 or more are constructing discourse with referential material of different derivation: perceptual in JP and internal in SP. After the seventh shift there is a descending trend in both cases. In both conditions, the prevalence of one or the other tendency is maintained throughout following the initial major shift.

DISCUSSION

On the stength of the preceding evidence one is tempted to postulate the working of two opposing strategies applied by our subjects in the organization of discourse. One could view the child's position as follows. Encountering the conditions of JP the child selects as a starting point for his discourse some information that is not shared, i.e., not a straightforward description of the picture visible by both interlocutors, but indirectly related to it, therefore new to the interlocutor. But since the adult's line of regard is mainly directed to the picture, the child is drawn back to the perceptually obvious, and does not depart again from the pictorial realia. At best he may add the novelty of referring to his own present activity and states, but he tends to run out of material upon which to construct his text.

The same children encountering the SP condition in which they control the basic source of information, choose a different point of departure. They start by sharing the perceptually given information (describing the picture) until the major shift to the new source of information, the internal store of coded and recreated experiences, such as, associations with the picture content, imaginings of what preceded observed states, hypotheses as to further courses of events. The greater length of their discourse indicates the desire to communicate everything that links up with the picture. The tendency to refer to self in the immediate gives way to a tendency to assume an external and reportative stance to situations about which they talk.

How are we to understand why the same reasonably representative sample of children of the same age and presumably similar overall stages of language development display such basic differences in speech performance in response to the same standard task? The differences are clearly attributable to the features of the situation. Joint adult-child perception of a picture source apparently acts to dampen the referential domain of a discourse, while the condition under which the child has independent control over the perceptual source acts to broaden out and open up that domain along dimensions of time, space and imagery. While the former has constrained discourse and led to early closure, the latter has impelled it forward and activized to a greater degree the cognitive-semantic processes in the child.

Two accounts suggest themselves concerning how the child interprets the situation as he encounters it, and the nature of the interpersonal relations it sets up. The first account concerns authority relations and competence superiority as affects the informativeness feature of the child's discourse.

In one variant, the child functioned as one of two sources of information about the picture content, and the less direct source as compared to direct visual intake. The adult, therefore, already in possession of the basic information, acted as a control over the child's information in terms of correctness. In this configuration of relationships, the child renounces early after his initial impulse to impart something 'new' to that which is given from his internal store, and falls into a presumably old pattern of the examination type of question-answer routine. Here the knowledgeable adult is seen in the role of corroborator or corrector. In point of fact, on numerous occasions the child bluntly ended his discourse with a statement like "You can see it all for yourself." In the SP condition the child had sole access to all sources of information, his opportunities for transmitting information were correspondingly greater and his role in the exchange weightier and more challenging. Differences in situational opportunity, and differential responses to them, can be understood in the light of behavior stream studies of early speech functions (Shugar, 1975b) which document the claim for an early emergence of a drive in the child to assert himself as a competent source of information, a drive akin to the more general urge to acquire competence in all fields of agency.

The other account concerns the degree of interpersonal cognition that we must accredit the child in terms of estimating what the adult can know and cannot know and, in turn, his awareness of adult expectancies. In our formulation of the problem at the beginning of this paper, three conditions internal to the child were postulated as prerequisites for the active use of the inherent function of language: (1) possession of information; (2) belief that the other does not already have this information and (3) motivation to impart the information to the other. The situation present in the SP condition could lead to the obtained results if and only if these conditions were satisfied in the child. The child did in fact adjust the kind of information he provided to the adult's actual state of knowledge, by first sharing the perceptual data, and only then drawing on inner and private sources of information. In the JP, the child clearly assumed that the adult is taking in the given information directly and commences with other information. Our conclusion is therefore that the factor altering the child's entire activity in constructing discourse is his recognition of the adult's position in the situational configuration and his adjustment to this recognition. This claim is supported by other studies (Maratsos, 1973; Shields, 1975). Instead of accepting the Piagetian view of the basic egocentric character of early child speech, we might make more progress by accepting the postulate argued by Shields (1975) that the child develops schemata of persons differently from object schemata due to the nature of early interpersonal experience, as a result of which the child's grasp of the standpoint and information held by others is similar basically to that of adults, being only more primitive, more imperfect.

In the above discussion we have tried to give two accounts for the differential responses in discourse construction studied in two situations. Quite evidently these accounts are not mutually exclusive but each affect the other. Furthermore, they do not exhaust the possible ways of interpreting the findings. One thing, however, is clearly evident: the manifestation of communicative competence is situationally dependent. We may employ Bernstein's (1966) concepts in stating that if the communicative situation is limiting, the code employed by the child will tend to be restricted; if that situation is open, the code will tend to be elaborated.

BIBLIOGRAPHY

Bernstein, B. (1972) Social class, language and socialization. In P. P. Giglioli (ed.), Language and Social Context, Harmondsworth: Penguin Education.

Cazden, C. B. (1970) The neglected situation in child language research and education. In F. Williams (ed.), Language and Poverty, Chicago: Markham.

Cazden, C. B. (1974) Two paradoxes in the acquisition of language structure and functions. In K. Connolly and J. Brunner (eds.), The Growth of Competence, London: Academic Press.

Halliday, M. A. K. (1970) Language structure and function. In J. Lyons (ed) New Horizons in Linguistics, Harmondsworth: Penguin Education.

Halliday, M. A. K. (1975) Learning How to Mean: Explorations in the Development of Language, London: Edward Arnold.

Maratsos, M. P. (1973) Nonegocentric communication abilities in preschool abilities. Child Development, 44 (3), 697-700.

Piaget, J. (1955) Language and Thought in the Child, New York: Meridian Books.

Przetacznikowa, M. (1968) Rozwoj struktury i funkcji zdan w mowie dziecka (Development of sentence structure and function in child speech). In S. Szuman (ed.), O rozwoju jezyka i myslenia (Development of Language and Thought), Warsaw: PWN.

Shields, M. (1975) Cognition and communication in the acquisition of language. Paper delivered to the Third International Child Language Symposium, London.

Shields, M. (1976) Some communicational skills of young children--a study of dialogue in the nursery school. Paper delivered to the Psychology of Language Conference, Stirling.

Shugar, G. W. (1972) Relations of language structure and activity structure in the early developmental period. PhD dissertation. University of Warsaw.

Shugar, G. W. (1975a) Text analysis as an approach to the study of early linguistic operations. Paper delivered to the Third International Child Language Symposium, London. [To appear in proceedings]

Shugar, G. W. (1975b) Child's intent: Functional development of early utterances. Paper presented at AILA Fourth International Congress, Stuttgart. [To appear in proceedings]

Tomaszewski, T. (1975) Czlowiek i otoczenie (Man and his Surroundings). In T. Tomaszewski (ed.), Psychologia, Warsaw: PWN.

APPENDIX A: Stimulus Pictures for Stories

Picture A

Appendix A: Stimulus Pictures for Stories
Picture B

APPENDIX B: Sample Transcripts

Samples of story telling discourse units produced by two different children in each of the situational variants. They are translated into English from the Polish originals, with some Polish syntactic features retained.

Sample #1
Krysia, girl, aged 3;3
Picture B, JP condition

Teacher: Krysiu, tell me about this picture.
Child: That bee (points to picture) wanted to fight with the flies and the butterflies...he didn't fight.
Teacher: No? Why not?
Child: Coz he's flying.
Teacher: Mhm.
Child: He's got wings now...see...(shows picture)
Teacher: Oh, why?
Child: He's flying.
Teacher: Mhm.
Child: He flies good. He's flying.
Teacher: Really?...And what else? What else in your story, Krysiu?
Child: Nothing. You can see for yourself.
Teacher: That was a very interesting story, you know.
Child: I know (pushes picture away slowly and turns head toward the window).

Sample #2
Krysia, girl, aged 3;3
Picture A, SP condition

Teacher: Krysiu, tell me about your picture.
Child: A tree is standing, and children are standing. The children feel very good. They feel good.
Teacher: Yes? Why?
Child: At school the children thought--they want to make mushrooms out of chestnuts.
Teacher: Mhm.
Child: The children ran to the park in the morning. Tomorrow they're coming to get chestnuts, the next day too.
Teacher: Yes?
Child: They'll bring a basket for the leaves coz lots of leaves flew off the tree. The wind threw the leaves down, silly, lots of leaves it threw down, and chestnuts it threw down.
Teacher: Aha.
Child: The children are going to make a GREAT big forest at school. They'll play...they'll play how the squirrel ran away with the chestnuts into a hole. I saw...the bear chased her at the zoo. I saw.
Teacher: You did?
Child: Yeh...
Teacher: Are you going to tell some more, Krysiu?
Child: It's nice. (shows picture to teacher)
Teacher: Very nice, and your story was very interesting, too.

Sample #3
Mariusz, boy, aged 3;8
Picture B, SP condition

Teacher: Mariuszku, tell me about your picture.
Child: Mariuszek sees some sky and some flowers. The flowers are growing on the meadow big and red. The flowers are standing high. They're sad...
Teacher: Oh, why?
Child: Coz they heard about the beetle.
Teacher: Aha.
Child: The beetle eats flowers just like these flowers. In the country it eats in the garden. Flowers and stems and grass it eats in the country near Warsaw.
Teacher: Really, why?
Child: Coz over there the stems are good and a lot of beetles underneath. These tiny flowers are going to have good stems too. The tiny flowers will grow up a little more.
Teacher: Mhm.
Child: A lot will grow up. There's going to be a whole lot of little flowers.
Teacher: Yes?
Child: Uhhuh. They'll be that big (shows picture to teacher) These ones will be great big flowers.
Teacher: Is that so?
Child: Uhhuh...I saw flowers like that. I'll show Barbara the picture, okay?
Teacher: Okay, Mariuszku.
Child: (goes to E with picture)

Sample #4
Mariusz, boy, aged 3;8
Picture A, JP condition

Teacher: Mariuszku, tell me now about this picture.
Child: The chestnuts wanted to spend the winter on the tree but they fell off.
Teacher: Yes, why?
Child: They didn't hold on with their paws to the tree too hard in the night. Now they're laying under the tree. On the grass they're laying on the grass under the tree they're laying.
Teacher: Mhm.
Child: The children are picking up the chestnuts. Lots of chestnuts they're picking up. They've got lots, look! (shows picture)
Teacher: Aha...what else is there in your story, Mariuszku?
Child: That's all. You can see. You know everything already.
Teacher: That was a very interesting story, Mariuszku.

*Children's Situational Competence: Two Studies**

KATHRYN M. BORMAN
School of Education, University of Cincinnati

INTRODUCTION

The ability to communicate has been considered a yardstick of children's underlying social competence. Further, specific social skills such as the child's capacity to take the role of others (Piaget and Inhelder, 1966; Flavell, Botkin, Fry, Wright and Jarvis, 1968), and to recognize feelings (Izard, 1971) are competencies which increase with age. The expression of these skills in conversational interchange has been measured by children's sensitivity to turn-taking rules in conversation (Mueller, 1971; Garvey and Hogan, 1973) and their ability to employ verbal strategies and appeals of increasing social-cognitive complexity (Cook-Gumperz, 1973; Garvey, 1975).

In addition to understanding the psychological landscape, the child must also be capable of interpreting the social environment. The socially adept individual implicitly communicates an understanding of commonly accepted group norms and practices. This skill reflects the child's capacity to interpret the requirements of the particular situation in which the child is involved as a participant in conversation. A school child's repeated chant of a nonsense rhyme will no doubt provoke his teacher's censure if this behavior occurs during a classroom reading group activity. The same behavior in another context might be tolerated by the teacher as a legitimate form of tension release. Knowing the difference between the two situations and acting upon that knowledge constitute an aspect of the child's social competence. All in all, a complex network comprising an understanding of group norms, social roles, personality theory, etc. constitute the constellation of social and interpersonal skills required in conversation (Gumperz, 1971).

By the time the young child enters kindergarten, practice of communication skills in contexts of shared family activity has allowed mastery of many

---

*This project was partially supported by grants from the University of Minnesota Computer Center, the University of Minnesota Graduate School, and the University of Cincinnati Research Council. Portions of this paper were presented by the author in the symposium "Social Competence in the Classroom" at the annual meeting of the American Anthropological Association, Houston, Texas, December, 1977. The author acknowledges the assistance of Sara M. McMullen, David Doth, Joyce S. Walker, Catherine R. Wagner, Sara Burstein and Bev Lazar in carrying out Study One and the assistance of Dan McKee, Nancy Shapiro, Sandra Bauman, LeeAnn Franz, and Jane Shreve in conducting Study Two. The author also thanks Jeffrey Shultz and Christopher M. Matey for comments on earlier drafts of this paper.

aspects of vocabulary, grammar, intonation and gesture. When "speech is embedded in a context of shared activity" (Wells, 1975:115) and such activity is experienced with frequency, the child cultivates at least rudimentary "situational competence." Situational competence can be seen as a summary term descriptive of the full set of linguistic, interpersonal, and social knowledge skills required by the demands of communication in a specific context such as dinner times, trips to the grocery store, and others. Within the classroom, children will experience variable opportunities to develop additional competencies. In part, the variation in experience will depend upon individual differences such as the child's sex (Flapan, 1969). In part, the variation will depend upon family background features, such as the child's birth order (Wells, 1975). Differential acquisition of situational competence reflects differences in classroom process encountered by children. Children in an open classroom will probably experience more occasions in which interaction is intentionally planned by the teacher (Shapiro, 1973). Children in traditional school programs will be more likely to play a passive role in the classroom and, as a consequence, might be less likely to initiate or maintain conversational interaction than children in an open classroom.

Not only are the skills necessary to understand and produce speech complexly ordered but speech itself functions as an interconnected set of variables. Though constituted of individual utterances, conversation is socially constructed speech. Dell Hymes suggests three levels of generality which order the conversational context. First, speech acts are "the key and minimal units mediating immediately between the usual levels of grammar and the rest of a speech event or situation in that ... (they) implicate both linguistic form and social norms." (Hymes, 1972:56-57; Florio, 1976:11). Next the speech event is the set of utterances bounded by a socially mediated beginning and end such as the round of introductions that precedes a meeting at which several members are newcomers. Finally, the speech situation is the gathering of people with a "right" to be there at a place regularly associated with such interaction and with the communicative roles and purposes at least broadly defined, e.g., a cocktail party.

Jerome Bruner (1975) has argued for the study of the "ontogenesis of speech acts" in children's communicative behavior, and some research has begun to study the work accomplished by children in producing speech acts. For example, Catherine Garvey (1975) has investigated the strategies used by Halloween trick or treaters. It seems clear that research investigating children's speech act production should be carried out in natural settings in which the conversational interaction of participants has social meaning. In such arenas the situational competence of participants can be assessed in terms of features of their conversational exchanges.

The acquisition of the set of skills necessary to generate effective communicative behavior seems dependent upon processes of socialization by which the developing child learns to master conversational skills first in the family and later in the classroom. These skills are the part of personality taken into account by the knowledge one must have to deal successfully with question as to who talks first in a conversation and who is expected to respond. Within a given conversation context it is necessary to know what is it appropriate to talk about and under what circumstances can conversation express an imaginative (or regulative, etc.) purpose. These are the sorts of questions that must be implicitly addressed by the individual in the context of a specific speech event. By analyzing the individual utterances of children who are systematically observed in conversational interaction while engaged in a specific activity or speech event, an assessment of children's situational competence can be carried out.

ASSESSING CHILDREN'S SITUATIONAL COMPETENCE

If situational competence is seen as dependent upon the socialization process it becomes crucial to examine the ecological environment surrounding that process as it occurs in an agency of socializagion - for example, the school. In considering the development of situational competence two studies were designed. Study One examined processes of socialization in two kindergarten classrooms of different curricular format or program design. Study Two was undertaken at a later time in a third kindergarten classroom (in another city) and was designed to examine the impact of different aspects of that classroom's curriculum upon the same group of children.

The concept of the speech act was central to procedures followed in analyzing children's naturally occurring conversation in both studies. For purposes of conversation analysis in the present research, acts were considered to be collections of utterances termed CONVERSATION GROUPINGS which (1) focus upon an identifiable subject, (2) may be bounded by pauses of three seconds or more either signaling a change in conversation focus or serving to "allow" a conversation participant to enter the interaction, and (3) perform a function or set of functions in the social context in which they occur.* (cf. Sacks, Schegloff and Jefferson, 1974; West and Zimmerman, 1974, 1977 for elaboration and some illustrations.)

The speech situation was the daily round of activity engaging a group of kindergarten children and their teacher. Most simply, a situation was the school program experienced by a particular group of kindergarten children. Classroom events were the set of regularly, generally daily-occurring, classroom activities scheduled by the teacher, i.e., snack time, story time, etc. In both studies, activities were the major independent variables since transcriptions of conversations were obtained with reference to the event the child was participating in at the time recordings were made. In Study One, activities are summarized as school programs (open classroom versus traditional classroom) in the report of findings. In Study Two the complete event was documented on tape, i.e., a specific activity was recorded from its beginning through its conclusion.

In both studies two sets of independent variables measuring qualities of recorded classroom interaction were taped in the course of two separate analyses of the same transcribed data. (See figure 1) Coding procedures at Level I isolated and grouped utterances into CONVERSATION GROUPINGS. In Study One utterances were categorized within groupings with reference to ALL CHILDREN/ OR TEACHER or FOCAL CHILD (the child targeted for tape recording). In Study Two ALL CHILDREN and TEACHER constituted separate categories in addition to the FOCAL CHILD category. Level II coding tapped the often implicit functional work accomplished by all utterances contained in a specific conversation grouping. The identity of the initiator of each conversation grouping was coded as TEACHER <u>or</u> CHILD <u>and/or</u> FOCAL CHILD.

*See also Barker (1965) and Barker and Wright (1955) whose work organizes behavior into verbal behavior episodes very much like speech acts.

Level 1	Level II
All Children & Adults Participating In the Recorded Interaction	All Children Participating in the Recorded Interaction
Utterance Units Initiated and Responded to (I)	Child Initiated Conversation Units (I) or (CU) Innovative Imaginative Expressive Regulative Interpersonal Instructional
Utterance Units Initiated but not Responded to (NI)	Child Initiated Non Conversation Units (NI) Innovative Imaginative Expressive Regulative Interpersonal Instructional
Response Utterance Units Verbal Responses (R) Non Verbal Responses (NVR) Choral Responses (CR)	
Child or Teacher Under Observation	Child and/or Teacher Under Observation
Utterance Units Initiated by Child/Teacher (I)	Conversation Units Initiated by Child and/or Teacher (I) Innovative Imaginative Expressive Regulative Interpersonal Instructional
Utterance Units Initiated by Child/Teacher (NI)	Conversation... (NI) Innovative Imaginative Expressive Regulative Interpersonal Instructional
Response Utterance Verbal Responses (R) Non Verbal Response (NVR)	

Fig. 1. Order of Analysis

Level I Analysis Procedures

The smallest unit of analysis is the utterance unit. The utterance is seen as either an initiating utterance (I or NI) or as a responding utterance (R or RU). The utterance unit is comparable to the t-unit (Cazden, 1977) and is, most simply, a main clause and any subordinate clauses which may attach to it.

The largest unit of conversation is the conversation grouping. It is comprised of an initiating utterance and the responses to the utterance which may follow. Conversation groupings are of two types. The first is the conversation unit (CU). It includes the initiating utterance (I) and all verbal responses or nonverbal responses (R or NVR) from conversation participants which attach to the initiating utterance. The nonconversation unit (NI) is an initiating utterance that is not responded to appropriately or receives no response at all. It is for practical, conversational purposes an utterance without communicative value.

Level II Analysis Procedures

All conversation groupings (CU/I) identified as either conversation (I) or non-conversation (NI) units, along with any attached responses, (R or NVR) were grouped according to interpersonal purpose of communication (Halliday, 1973; Bernstein, 1971; Wells, 1973). Groupings were classified according to one of four purposes as follows: (1) Regulative in which the primary thrust of the interaction is toward formulating rules, negotiating about their enforcement, and regulating the behavior (ongoing or future) of the participants; (2) Instructional in which the primary thrust of the interaction is toward the "school" learning of the participants in the interaction and centers on construction or reconstruction of knowledge; (3) Interpersonal in which the primary thrust of the interaction is either toward the development of individual identity and differentiation from the group or toward the development of interpersonal skills and abilities (including "good manners"); (4) Innovative-imaginative-expressive in which the primary thrust of the interaction is toward spontaneous or creative experssion of feelings.

A subgroup of nonconversation units was regarded as speech inappropriate to conversation analysis. An interpersonal purpose of such speech is highly questionable; rather, children appear to utilize some nonconversational language as speech for self in task situations demanding highly focused attention to detail (Kohlberg, Yaeger and Hjertholm, 1968). The following categories of egocentric speech (adapted from Wells, 1974) were used in analyzing data recorded in the present research. (1) Commentary utterances are those which either comment on ongoing activity or plan future action and act as a form of control or monitor of nonverbal behavior in the execution of larger complex tasks; (2) Expressive are utterances, most frequently exclamations, which are expressions of an affective reaction to a situation; (3) Heuristic are utterances in which the child is verbalizing his experience in order to organize it from the point of view of his existing knowledge (e.g., "and the water goes down here, and in a pipe and out to sea"). Since relatively few utterances fell into these categories, the set was collapsed into a single classification for nonsocial speech (initiations not responded to - cognitive egocentric speech) utilized in subsequent data analysis.

STUDY ONE

RESEARCH HYPOTHESES

Level I

Children in the open program were expected both to initiate and to respond to more conversation units (I) and response units (R) than children in the traditional program. In contrast, traditional classroom children were expected to initiate more nonconversation units (NI) than their open classroom peers.

Level II

Children in the open classroom were expected to initiate more conversation units (I) which displayed in interpersonal function. Less likely to occur in the open classroom milieu would be the instructional and regulative purposes of speech.

SAMPLE

The sample consisted of 93 ten-minute audio taped transcripts recorded during two six week observation periods in two kindergarten classrooms. The classrooms were located in different public elementary school buildings. The schools were situated in a predominantly white middle class neighborhood in a large midwestern city. As part of a federally funded public alternative school project, parents of children in the neighborhood were enabled to select either the "open" or "traditional" program of schools observed in the study or to choose a "continuous progress" or "free" school option. Schools in the present study were found not to vary along background or input variables such as (a) socioeconomic status (SES) as measured by number of families receiving Aid for Dependent Children, and racial composition, or (b) along outcome variables dimensionalized as either school achievement measures or (c) school "climate" measures such as average daily attendance or pupil mobility (rate of transfer).

A set of control variables regulated the collection of the 93 audio taped records. First, all of the transcripts were exactly ten minutes in length. Second, in order to allow comparisons to be made across season (fall vs. winter), sets of transcripts were gathered in each kindergarten setting of six "focal" children. After an initial observation period, three boys and three girls in each classroom were selected as focal children. In all but two cases in which three transcripts were taken, a set of four transcripts was compiled for each child during each observation period. Focal children were chosen on the basis of sex and their initially observed classroom situational competence. Third, all records were taken during daily occurring one hour intervals in each classroom during which children were allowed to initiate their own activities in the classroom. These intervals were established in the curricula of both teachers prior to the planning of the research and were not added to the classroom agendas for the convenience of the researcher. These events, in other words, were naturally and regularly occurring classroom activities. The set of transcripts were characterized by the attributes summarized in Table 1.

TABLE 1 Number of Transcripts by School, Sex, and Season

	FALL		WINTER	
	Boys	Girls	Boys	Girls
"Open" Kindergarten	12	12	12	12
"Traditional" Kindergarten	11	11	11	12

Mean age of open program boys was 5;7 Mean IQ = 125
Mean age of open program girls was 5;9 Mean IQ = 111
Mean age of traditional program boys was 6;0 Mean IQ = 122
Mean age of traditional program girls was 5;7 Mean IQ = 113

METHOD

A Sony BM-11 Secutive 100 tape recorder was used to collect all of the audio taped data of classroom interaction. The Sony is a relatively unobtrusive, compact (4.5" x 6.5"), battery operated tape recorder that has a built-in microphone. The recorder was placed close to the target or focal child during recording. It soon became a taken-for-granted appendage of research activity and, therefore, an accepted part of their environment for all of the children most of the time. Children, especially during the first recording sessions of the fall, would occasionally notice the presence of the investigators and address us. The standard response to children's questions was that we were watchers and not talkers. Children accepted our status as mute observers. They did not see us as adult supervisors, however else they may have perceived us. "Deviant" behavior, for example block throwing, was begun in our presence, only to be discontinued at the approach of the teacher.

In addition to tape recording the conversation, the two and occasionally three observers kept field notes for each ten minute segment. Shifts in the location of the focal child frequently demanded the removal of the recorder from one spot to another by one of the observers.

RESULTS

The results reported here are for the 48 transcripts recorded in the open classroom during Activity Time and the 45 transcripts recorded in the traditional classroom during a similar segment of the school day. The identity of each transcript corresponded to one of the six focal children who has served as a conversation marker for classroom interaction patterns in each school milieu. The two analyses reported here involved (1) identifying conversation groupings, generally utterances, and (2) tagging the speech domain of these conversation groupings.

At both levels of analysis, individual transcripts were (1) analyzed independently by two coders and (2) data were analyzed by at least one and most often by two of the investigators who had been present at the time of taping the transcript in question (See Fig. 1). Hoyt (1941) intraclass correlations indicate an overall reliability coefficient of .92 for Level I categories. An 87 percent agreement was determined for Level II categories.

Level I

A set of t-tests were computed for each dependent variable, i.e., classroom production of conversation units (I), nonconversation units (NI), and response units (R). These comparisons indicate differences in production of conversation components by (1) all children and adults, (2) focal children only such that a "composite child" was constructed from all the data for focals in each classroom setting. In addition, a "composite" girl and boy from each classroom also were projected from the data for purposes of separate analyses by sex.

There were several significant results obtained when data were grouped in the manner described above (Table 1). However, because results were combined for all other children and the teacher recorded on transcripts of focal children, the relative contributions of each of these two groups cannot be ascertained.

If results for this set of individuals are seen as a measure of the focal child's conversational climate, the findings of all children and teacher reported in Table 1 portray the open classroom as the more sustaining environment.

Other results suggest that the open classroom operates on the basis of an interaction imperative that impelled open classroom children to engage in more successful conversation-making as reflected in their production of both more I- and R-units. In contrast, children in the traditional program, more tightly controlled by their teacher, experienced fewer initiating utterances receiving appropriate response as reflected in a greater number of NI units. Though patterns of conversation recorded in the two classrooms reflected these expectations, only the latter comparison was significant (Table 2).

TABLE 2 Statistically Significant Level I for Focal Children by Type of Program

Focal Children	Open Program	Traditional Program	
Initiations not responded to (NI units)	$\overline{X} = 6.5$	$\overline{X} = 11.0$	t = 3.47*

* p value $< .002$

When data were grouped by sex of focal child, a significant difference emerged between girls in the two schools in production of unsuccessful conversation. Over both observation periods, traditional program girls initiated significantly more conversation that did not receive appropriate response than did their same sex counterparts in the open program ($t = 2.507$, $p < .02$). Also contributing to the overall effect reported in Table 2 were observed differences between boys in the two classrooms. During the second observation period, traditional program focal boys were observed to engage in more failed conversation than open classroom boys ($t = 2.599$, $p < .02$).

Level II

A set of t-tests were performed for each dependent variable measuring conversation purpose (i.e., Regulative, Innovative-imaginative-expressive, Interpersonal, and Instructional) within each of two conversation dimensions (I and NI) analyzed at Level I. Statistical contrasts were also made between schools as to domain expressed in a given set of conversation groupings (e.g., traditional focal boys NI units.)

The analyses reported in Table 3 refine those results reported above (Level I) because they specify which conversation domains or purposes are associated with utterances made by all children and the focal child as distinct from the teacher in both classroom milieux.

Children in the open classroom context utilized conversation expressing an Interpersonal purpose as had been anticipated. It had not been predicted that the open classroom would also provide a context for significantly more Instructional interaction than the traditional classroom. However, data for all children indicate that this is so. The traditional classroom is the scene of more conversation denoting both a Regulative and an Imaginative-innovative-expressive function.

TABLE 3 Significant Level II Contrasts by School Program

	Open Classroom	Traditional Classroom
All Children Conversation Units (I/CU Units)	Mean	Mean
Regulative Units	9.1	11.8*
Interpersonal Units	2.6**	1.3
Instructional Units	4.3**	2.5
Nonconversation Units (NI Units)		
Regulative Units	7.1	14.7**
Focal Children Only - Nonconversation Units (NI Units)		
Regulative Units	2.0	5.7**
Imaginative-innovative-expressive Units	0.8	2.2**

*p value < .01
**p value < .05

In summary, both sets of analyses provided a clear picture of differences in classroom conversational life. The open classroom can be portrayed as a sustaining conversational environment in contrast to the traditional setting. Children in the open program initiated more successful, i.e., completed conversation, and were enjoined to respond to more conversation bids than their traditional kindergarten classroom counterparts. Moreover, the conversation was likely to express an Instructional or Interpersonal purpose. In contrast, traditional classroom children produced more unsuccessful or incomplete conversation. Additionally, the conversation produced by traditional classroom children was significantly more often in the Regulative or Imaginative-innovative-expressive domains than conversation of open classroom children.

DISCUSSION

The language of young, preschool-aged children typically exhibits an Imaginative-innovative-expressive function. Because they are not much older than this group, kindergarten children in a free play situation in their classrooms could be expected to utilize this speech domain with some frequency. Likewise, the production of substantial amounts of regulative speech by school children is not surprising (Rosen and Rosen, 1973:72). The important finding of variability among same age children along these conversation dimensions seems attributable to differences in the amount of active organization by teachers of children's activities in the two classrooms observed. That is, children's communicative behavior was strongly influenced by situational constraints.

Traditional classroom children most often were involved in activities supervised in a most perfunctory manner by their teacher. Play in the blockroom was characterized by active construction and demolition of structures. The room itself was a narrow space separated from the classroom by a wall and entered through a doorway. Play in these circumstances was usually quite noisy, and children, apparently unable to comprehend verbal messages, often did not respond to each other's verbal initiations. If conversation were undertaken, it was often disruptive of interpersonal relations as in the following exchange involving three boys and a girl in the blockroom. All of the children at the time this transcript was taken were engaged in building a large house with blocks. Becky, the female participant, was one of only two girls observed to be accepted in the blockroom on a regular basis by the boys whose almost exclusive use of the room had been established by the winter period when the transcript was made. [Transcripts follow conventions developed by Sacks, Schegloff and Jefferson (1974) which presents a description of the markings used to indicate pauses, interruptions, etc. in the conversational texts of transcripts.]

Rick: Just first ((made)).
(two second pause)
Becky: (in reference to some blocks) Tom, do you need these ((little ones))?
Tom: (screaming) YES
(four second pause)
Becky: These little ones?
Tom: (to boys who are building the house) No, <u>not</u> like this ... put it <u>straight</u>.
(two second pause)
Becky: Do you need these little ones, Tom?
Tom: YES
Becky: I think we're gonna have a [problem].
Tom: [What] are you deaf?
Becky: What are <u>yoooooou</u> yelling?
Sam: Oh Becky.
Tom: (to Becky) Goll, you're deaf.
Sam: Is she?
Tom: No, she's not deaf. But she never hears anything, what when my mom says something.
Rick: Yeah, so is my sister
(three second pause)
Just like my sister,
(ten second pause) (Becky leaves the blockroom).

Becky's next recorded utterance "You got bad breath (( ))." was made to a girl who had been observed in the classroom to be quite passive and who had been described by her teacher as "a perfect little lady." Though Becky's motives cannot be known, it appeared that she had looked for and found an ideal scapegoat in Barbara, "the perfect little lady."

These traditional classroom children were observed to be capable of sustained, mutually engaging conversation, though in all situations observed in this classroom, relationships between boys and girls appeared strained. A context in which girls and some of the boys could be observed to play in relative harmony was the playhouse. However, in this context, play was dominated by themes and motifs provided by the girls; boys' roles in play were modified by girls' concerns. Indeed, just as the blockroom in time became fixed as a masculine province, so the playhouse became established as a feminized preserve.

Play recorded in the following transcript was centered in the playhouse and involved Becky, Ted, Charles and Barbara. This excerpt comprised approximately eight of the ten recorded minutes of the transcript.

Becky: (at the stove) Oh, I'm making supper...I'm making supper. (ten second pause)
Ted: (plumbing the sink) That's a (( )).
Becky: (pushing Ted away from the sink) Get over there. (Ted leaves) (36 second pause)
Barbara: (to Becky as Barbara and Charles approach) Mother...
Charles: Pretend I'm...Pretend...And, Becky, pretend you called the police ((because)) I was dead. And a ambulance. (Charles moves to assume a dead position outside the kitchen)
Charles: (to Barbara) You gotta call. Until you please call (( )). Someone's dead.
Barbara: He looks drunk.
(eleven second pause) (Barbara moves to the phone in a corner of the kitchen while Becky continues to prepare the meal)
Barbara: (to the phone) (( ))
(five second pause) Hello.
(three second pause) Hello. I'd like to uhmmmmmm...
I would like to...I would like the ambulance to come over here [(( ))]1
Charles: [Pretend the ambulance and police are coming.]1
Barbara: (to the phone) You are? [(( ))]2
Charles: [Right Now. Pretend the ambulance and police are coming]2 right now because I was dead.
Barbara: Yeh I know. (to phone) (Four-twelve Fifth Avenue Southeast. (places receiver down and makes ambulance sounds)
(nineteen second pause)
(Becky and Barbara place a doll under a tent devised from a small blanket)
Becky: Baby should be all right.
Barbara: Is baby under there?
Becky: Yeh.
(five second pause)
I wonder what (( ))
(five second pause) (Ted returns and places a hat on his head)
Becky: Hey, you (( )) are the police
(Charles enters the kitchen)
Charles: (to Ted) Ok. You can be the police and you're gonna get me (( )).
(Charles returns to his dead position)
Ted: (approaching Becky at the stove) Hi, what's cookin'?
Becky: Well, (( ))'s sittin right out there in the backyard. (thirty-six second pause) (Ted remains in the house with Becky who cooks and does other housework)

(Charles is still prostrate)
Ted: The kid in the backyard looks dead
(fourteen second pause) (Charles gets up and enters the kitchen)
Charles: (( )) Becky, pretend I was already at the hospital already.
Becky: Ok.
(fifteen second pause) (Charles goes to the hospital, a space under the window across the room. Ted removes his hat and pulls out the doll bed from a corner in the playhouse) (Finally Charles gets up and enters the kitchen)
Charles: (approaching Becky) Pretend you had to go (( )) me. Pretend you were gonna visit me.
Becky: Ok. Not now.
(fifty second pause) (Charles returns to the hospital. Becky's work continues as a solitary activity. Ted's solitary play takes him in and out of the playhouse. Finally, Charles returns to the kitchen)
Charles: (approaching Becky) Pretend you asked me ((what was wrong)) when you were coming to visit me, Ok?
(four second pause) (Charles returns to the hospital. Becky leaves to visit him)
Becky: Oh. poor son, I...
Charles: Pretend I had a broken leg.
(Charles is interrupted by the crash of the large calendar which he has accidentally knocked to the ground)
Becky: Oh gosh.
Patricia: (seated nearby) Hey, put that back up.
Becky: It falled down by itself...

In this episode, a narrative was enacted and sustained by the children, though with frequent and lengthy pauses. In fact, mutually constructed and focused interaction is limited throughout the activity. Charles may have experienced frustration in his role as the neglected "dead" man. Even when it appeared that help was on its way in the form of the ambulance and driver, he received only cursory attention from the others who remained in the kitchen. After a period of eighty-four seconds during which his role in play was not acknowledged by the children, Charles, apparently having given up hope that Ted will haul him off, came forward to announce that he had already gone to the hospital. And there he must wait for more than a full minute for Becky to acknowledge him by a visit. It may be that children do not actually experience frustration in such pretend play encounters. In fact, no protest was made by any of the boys, even by the stranded victim. Nonetheless, it is certainly true that if speech production is seen as important in the practice and development of social skills, interaction in the playhouse and the blockroom inhibits such skill acquisition.

The contexts in this classroom which appeared to provide most listener and speaker sensitivity to conversational needs of participants were those focused upon small group activity engaging all group members. Boys more often than girls in this traditional classroom centered their attention upon Lego or Lincoln Log projects and the like and often expressly excluded girls from their play. The boys Sam, Bob and James recorded in the following interaction were by January a comfortable trio. The following recorded activity at the Lego table had been underway for the two minutes of the free play period which had elapsed. Though Sam appeared to take the lead in the design and construction of the ship, the project engaged the attention of each boy for the duration of the activity.

James: Want to make some flashlights.
Sam: Sure, in the front.
James: I'll put//this will be a flashlight (( )) okay?
Bob: How come it can't be (( ))?
Bob: Let's have it in the middle.
Sam: This is the emergency (( ))//We need high lights.
Bob: Yeah.
Sam: In case...//in case an emergency...// In case another army ship is in trouble.
Bob: We'll come to [the rescue] [1]
Sam: [We're almost][1] ready.
James: [Yeah][2]
Bob: [We're almost][2] ready
James: We're ready to shoot up, right?
Bob: Right.
Sam: We just need a few more legos on.
Bob: And we need safety things.
Sam: Naw. We only need one.
Bob: In case the storm comes
Sam: We only need one and they can all run under her cus there's that much men and we don't need that.
Bob: Noo there's more men.
James: Hey, we need steering wheels. Hey, we need steering wheels.
Sam: We don't want it now. It's going to wreck everything if you do that.
James: Hey, why don't'// We want steering wheels.
Sam: Well, where's some holes? Some hole ones. Look for some holes. (Bob begins to look for lego blocks that have holes to insert wheels)
Sam: One of the legos with the hole in it.
Bob: Where's some holes?
James: Hey, we want one of these (He holds up a plastic building piece) We want one of these, huh.
Bob: Right.
Sam: Where are the hole// We need...
(four second pause)
Sam: Maybe there's a hole one in here. (Begins to dig in box) One of those ones with a little hole in it.
James: These are our sleeping bags. There are our tents, okay? (James had constructed tents from non-lego materials)
(seven second pause)
James: You been camping before?
Bob: Yeah, I have.
Sam: Me too.
James: I have
Bob: So have I.
James: At California
Sam: You want to see...// These are safety things in case a man fall//
Bob: I'll tell you which lake I went to.
James: Where?
Bob: Gun Lake
James: Where's Gun Lake?

Sam:	Gun Lake?
Bob:	For real. It's not a for real gun, it's just for real water. But that's the name of the lake, Gun Lake. (two second pause)
Sam:	(displaying circular legos to be used as life preservers) Do you want to say these are fakey things in case a man falls overboard and throw these in the water?
Bob:	Yeah.
James:	(indicating small structures he has made) These are our sleeping bags.
Bob:	Yeah. Those are our tents.
Sam:	Ready to// Ready to launch. (James has meanwhile gone to look for more materials so does not participate in the "launch")
Bob:	(Pretending to be a man overboard) Help Help.
Sam:	One man's drowning. Throw it overboard. Plahhhhh (water sounds)
James:	(Returning) Hey, I found some more.
Sam:	Good...

The boys' conversation in this context displays features which indicate mutuality and cooperation - building the ship is a socially shared experience. James' assertion..."we need steering wheels..." is interjected three times into the conversation, the third time in the form "We want steering wheels," and ultimately prompts an alteration in the ship's construction. (He actually means life preservers and his intended meaning is correctly interpreted by Sam.) The building operation is modified to accommodate James' demands to include construction of circular life preservers which are attached to the ship by Sam. Bob's sensitivity to paralinguistic cues, specifically both the stress on the word "gun" in Sam's question "Gun lake?" and the utterance's form as an inquiry, enable Bob to clarify his meaning: "For real. It's nota for real gun, it's just for real water. But that's the name of the lake, Gun Lake."

The consistent practice in the open school of allowing children to select options which focused their activity upon projects such as poster construction or paper-bag penguins accounted for most of the perceived differences between the two classrooms. Nonetheless, when children in either classroom were engaged in a task which involved them in interaction with three or four others and when the task itself had a clear and mutually agreed upon purpose, children in both settings were observed to participate in conversation that was itself both mutually engaging and purposeful. It appears, then, that the particular classroom speech event, blockroom play, Lego construction, playhouse pretend play and the rest, to varying degrees "allow" a situational competence to be generated in peer interactions. Children's situational competence, therefore, is strongly influenced by classroom environmental features.

STUDY TWO

INTRODUCTION

Study One had been useful in pointing out differences in aspects of children's communication patterns which are influenced by variations in school program. These pattern differences seemed to be dependent upon aspects of the social context. However, dimensions of this study's design presented problems in understanding which specific aspects of the school program on the one hand and which properties of children's groups on the other influenced communication. The difficulty in interpreting results of the first study arose from the global manner in which classroom activities had been investigated. The analysis had really been conducted on the level of the speech situation or classroom (open versus traditional) program. However, when transcripts of children's conversations were read with attention to the nature of the activity in which conversation was embedded, differences in classroom patterns such as those discussed above could be understood.

At the conclusion of Study One it was clear, in a general way, that an open kindergarten classroom provided a context for more sustained, less Regulative and more Interpersonal and Instructional interaction and that in contrast, a traditional classroom enabled less back and forth communication and more truncated speech to occur and that all interactions in this classroom were more likely to be Regulative and Imaginative-innovative-expressive than conversations in the open classroom. However, it did not provide definitive answers to questions such as how both production of conversation components and conversation domain were affected by dimensions of the activity such as focus and aspects of children's social characteristics such as sex and number of children engaged in the activity.

A set of expectations emerged after an observation period of two months in an inner city kindergarten classroom. These initial ideas were shaped with reference to a set of regularly occurring classroom activities that varied both in terms of focus (teacher-centered versus child-centered versus task-centered) and in terms of number and sex of group members. Children in teacher-focused activity were controlled by the teacher and appeared to have reduced opportunities for interaction both because of the teacher's central position in the group and because such activity involved the participation of many children. Children in task-focused work appeared to have the most opportunity for interaction because the activity was always performed by a dyad who did their work in a remote area of the classroom and who had to share resources in order to complete the task. Finally, as an intermediate condition, children in the child-centered activity appeared to involve themselves in interaction less often than in task-focused activity but more often than in teacher-focused reading group work. Child-focused work was either cognitively or aesthetically oriented. Most tasks were accomplished independently, though children could either informally kibbitz with peers or more fomally instruct them. Cognitive work centered upon the child's manipulation of materials in operations, such as puzzle play or more elaborate experiments as the "sink or float" activity in which the buoyancy of soap, a block of wood and other articles, was tested. Aesthetic activity consisted of art projects as kite making or music activity, for example, determining the pitch and tone of musical sounds. A specific set of hypotheses were formulated for the research.

RESEARCH HYPOTHESES

Level I

Children in teacher-centered activity were expected both to initiate and respond to fewer conversation units than in either child-centered or task-centered activities. The same pattern was expected to hold for conversation that did not gain appropriate response (NI). Self guiding or cognitive egocentric speech (NI-CE) (Rubin, 1973) was also expected to increase in task centered and child centered activity and decrease in teacher centered activity.

Level II

Children's speech in the teacher-focused activity was expected to express predominantly an Instructional function while the teacher's speech was expected to express a Regulative purpose. The Imaginative-innovative-expressive domain was expected to be a likely outcome of child-centered activity. Speech displaying an Instructional purpose was most likely to predominate in task-centered work.

SAMPLE

The sample in this study consisted of 28 transcripts of variable length and focus. All transcripts were gathered during a twelve week observation period in a kindergarten classroom. The classroom was located in a public elementary school that drew children from families which were distinctly ethnic (urban Appalachian) and low income. The school has relatively high rates of student absenteeism and mobility, and a relatively low student academic standing in comparison with other schools in the same city. The city itself is an older settlement than the midwestern community in which Study One was conducted and has more of the problems typically associated with major eastern urban industrial centers. As in Study One three boys and three girls alternately served as the focal child for tape recording in the classroom.

CLASSROOM ACTIVITIES

The transcripts made were the audio taped records of three sets of classroom activities: reading group, table work, pegboard math.

Reading group. (teacher-centered activity, N=8) There were two reading groups which met approximately two times a week. Typically, first one group and then the second were summoned by the teacher to sit with her in a circle on the floor for a period of approximately ten minutes. The activity can be characterized as focused upon reading "readiness" exercises such as identifying words and naming letters presented on flash cards or in actual "reading events" which consisted of each child reading aloud in turn from a primer. Each reading group was arranged by the teacher to include half of all the children whose names appeared on the classroom attendance roster. There were 30 children listed "on role." Therefore, each group potentially consisted of approximately 15 children. However, since rates of absenteeism were high, the groups were never observed to include more than eight children (range = 5-8; mean - 7.5). A sort of "random assignment" of children to reading groups had been carried out by the teacher who had structured the reading groups to reflect her informal assessment of the children's verbal skills. The teacher expressly wished to avoid tracking children into either a "slow" or "fast" reading group and had arranged reading groups to reflect her perception of the intellectual heterogeneity of the classroom.

Table work. (child-centered activity, N=12) Table work was a category of classroom activity that included a number of events which typically engaged children while they were seated at one of the six low rectangular tables in the classroom. Activities categorized as table work were alike in several respects. First, all of the recorded activities occurred during a period of the classroom day specifically designated as work time by the teacher. Second, all children engaged in table work were expected to select a project (puzzle, sorting task, matching exercise, etc.), complete it independently, allow the teacher to check the finished project, disassemble the array, and return the materials to the proper storage niche. Table work varied as to the central cognitive or aesthetic purpose of the activity.

Pegboard math. (task-centered activity, N=8) Pegboard math activity was a specific subset of table work activity in that the pegboard math task was available to children during the same period of the daily classroom schedule as an option. Work at the pegboard was structured to include several operations related to mathematical concepts such as set and to the specific mathematical process of addition. Materials included a supply of paper, pencils, pegs and two boards in which 20 holes had been drilled of a size to fit the pegs. The left half of the board was painted white and the right half green to indicate that two sets of pegs were to be utilized by the child in carrying out the work on a given problem. Pegboard math activity varied from other table work activities in several important ways. Though each child did his own set of problems, monitoring the other child's work was encouraged by a set of structural or environmental arrangements. The pegboard table was itself located in a room connected by a wide passageway to the room in which the rectangular tables were located but at a remove of some 50 feet from the tables at which most of the other children were engaged in work during this activity. The two chairs fit tightly together side by side at the table and faced the wall on which was hung a chart printed with the numbers 1-30 in sequence to be used as an aid in writing the problems. These features appeared to encourage children to interact with one another.

DATA COLLECTION

As in Study One, collection of the data was managed in as unobtrusive a manner as possible. A specific focal child was chosen for recording on a given occasion and generally for very practical reasons, e.g., the child had not been recorded engaging in one or another of the three sets of activities and the opportunity to audio tape the activity and the child presented itself. When there were two or more focal children present in the classroom who might serve as targets for the recording of a specific activity, a coin was tossed to determine which of the children would be selected as focal children.

Activities were recorded in their entirety. To insure the collection of complete records the tape recorder was turned on in advance of the initiation of the activity of interest and left on for a period of time after it appeared the activity had been terminated. Judgments about activity boundaries were made by the investigator in consultation with another person who had participated in data collection in the classroom and was familiar with the organization and management of primary grade classrooms. Subsequent analysis focused only upon the interactions bracketed as specific to the activity of interest, i.e., reading group, table work or pegboard math.

RESULTS

Level 1

A set of t-tests were performed in order to compare conversation patterns across the three sets of activities. The three contrasts were (1) Reading Group and Pegboard, (2) Pegboard and Tablework, and (3) Reading Group and Tablework (Tables 4-6). Within each of the first two contrasts two sets of data were compared. One comparison was made for Reading Group and Tablework data (Table 4). In each of these comparisons a set of six transcripts constituted the sample for each activity. Equal numbers of transcripts for boys and girls were used in each comparison. Finally, all transcripts were combined by sex and a comparison made between girls and boys on all recorded activities. No significant differences on any dimension of conversation were found when this latter analysis was made.

The conversation of Teacher, All Children and Focal Child recorded on the set of 28 transcripts used in these analyses varied accroding to the context or activity in progress at the time the audio tape was made. The greatest number of significant differences between conversation behavior in one context and another occurred in Contrast One (Reading Group versus Pegboard Math). These results are presented in Table 4.

TABLE 4 Level I Comparisons - Contrast One

	Comparison 1		Comparison 2	
	(a) Reading Group	(b) Pegboard Math	(a) Reading Group	(b) Pegboard Math
Social Speech	Mean Number	Mean Number	Mean Number	Mean Number
Initiations Responded to (I)				
Teacher	27.6[a]	18.5n.s.[b]	36.8*[a]	16.6[b]
All Children	23.8	38.8n.s.	25.0	40.2n.s.
Focal Child	1.2	16.2***	1.0	15.8***
Initiations Not Responded to (NI)				
Teacher	41.6***	8.6	35.4***	7.8
All Children	46.6	63.0n.s.	54.8	59.3n.s.
Focal Child	2.8	23.2***	3.8	20.8*
Responses (R)				
Teacher	55.2***	32.6	49.6***	31.2
All Children	89.6	102.8n.s.	90.4	108.5n.s.
Focal Child	5.2	42.5***	3.8	42.5***
Non-Social Speech				
Initiations Not Responded to - Cognitive Ego-centric Speech (NI-CE)				
All Children	1.2	19.5***	0.8	17.2***
Focal Child	0.6	9.8**	0.4	7.7n.s.

*p < .05
**p < .02
***p < .01

Of the three groups (Teacher, All Children and Focal Child), focal children, considered as a unit, were most variable in their production of successful and unsuccessful conversation. Specifically, in the dyadic Pegboard Math context, children produced significantly greater amounts of both successful and unsuccessful conversation than in the teacher-focused Reading Group. Indeed, other statistical tests reported in Table 4 suggest that small group work, whether defined as Tablework or Pegboard Math enhances children's production of speech. These results contrast with findings reported in the same table showing decreased production in the context of Reading Group activity in which children are part of a larger group and may have to await a turn to talk.

Finally, at Level I, nonsocial speech which functioned as cognitive-egocentric speech for self was found to emerge in situations in which the child was engaged in a difficult task requiring cognitive self-guiding. Such overt, self-guiding behavior was recorded with greater frequency in the Pegboard Math situation than in Tablework (Table 5) and was more persistent in the latter context than in the Reading Group (Table 6).

TABLE 5 Level I Comparisons - Contrast Two

	Comparison 1		Comparison 2	
	(a) Pegboard	(b) Aesthetic Tablework	(a) Pegboard	(b) Cognitive Tablework
Social Speech	Mean Number	Mean Number	Mean Number	Mean Number
Initiations Responded to (I)				
Teacher	18.5[a]	23.3 n.s.[b]	16.6[a]	15.5 n.s.[b]
All Children	38.8***	25.8	40.2	46.3 n.s.
Focal Child	16.2	12.0 n.s.	15.8	16.5 n.s.
Initiations Not Responded to (NI)				
Teacher	8.6	24.8**	7.8	14.7 n.s.
All Children	63.0	43.0 n.s.	59.3	86.7 n.s.
Focal Child	23.2	18.5 n.s.	20.8	37.2 n.s.
Responses (R)				
Teacher	32.6	37.5 n.s.	31.2	26.2 n.s.
All Children	102.8***	56.0	108.5***	53.0
Focal Child	42.5	29.3 n.s.	42.5	32.8 n.s.
Non-Social Speech				
Initiations Not Responded to - Cognitive Egocentric Speech (NI-CE)				
All Children	19.5***	2.7	17.2*	4.6
Focal Child	9.8	1.3	7.7	3.2 n.s.

*p < .05
**p < .02
***p < .01

TABLE 6 Level I Comparisons - Contrast Three

	Comparison I	
	(a) Reading Group	(b) Aesthetic Tablework
Social Speech	Mean Number	Mean Number
Initiations Responded to (I)		
Teacher	27.6[a]	15.5 n.s.[b]
All Children	23.8	46.3 n.s.
Focal Child	1.2	16.5***
Initiations Not Responded to (NI)		
Teacher	41.6**	14.7
All Children	46.6	86.7 n.s.
Focal Child	2.8	37.2**
Responses (R)		
Teacher	55.2***	26.2
All Children	89.6**	53.0
Focal Child	5.2	32.8***
Non-Social Speech		
Initiations Not Responded to - Cognitive Egocentric Speech (NI-CE)		
All Children	1.2	4.7*
Focal Child	0.6	3.2

*p $<$ .05
**p $<$ .02
***p $<$ .01

Not only did overt, self-guiding non-social speech increase in the context of Pegboard Math, but social speech was also observed to accelerate. Significantly more initiations and responses were recorded for Pegboard Math participants in both sets of comparisons with participants in Tablework. Since Pegboard Math always involved a core dyad in addition to a variable number of ephemeral on-lookers and commentators interaction was more accessible to children engaged in this activity. Children did not have to vie with seven or eight others as in Reading Group or up to five others at the same table as during Tablework for their turn at conversation.

The Pegboard data suggest that children can use self-guiding speech but can also produce extensive social conversation in the same situation. These children were, in fact, observed to be alternately caught up in their problem-solving work and intensely involved with building and maintaining social relations during the twenty-minute interval they were at work at the pegboard.

Level II

As an overall finding, results from this set of comparisons indicate that when the contexts are most dissimilar, speech function diverges most dramatically. Thus, Reading Group activity with its teacher-focused organization and the presence of seven or eight children provided the most dramatic contrast to Pegboard Math in which problem solving work demanded each child's full involvement. Regulative and Interpersonal speech functions varied at high levels of statistical significance while conversation accomplishing Instructional or Imaginative-innovative-expressive work also varied but less dramatically.

Table 7 displays the Reading Group/Pegboard Math contrasts in terms of group means for All Children's data (including focal children's data as a subset) recorded in these activity contexts. Significantly more successful conversation in both the Regulative and the Interpersonal domains was recorded in the Pegboard contexts. However, unsuccessful Regulative bids at conversation occurred significantly more often in the Reading Group context, a circumstance in which children, seated in a circle and involved in a task directed by the teacher, were conversationally inhibited. This latter finding suggests that children may be acquiring an understanding of the situational inappropriateness of Regulative speech in a reading group setting. They may, in fact, be learning to generalize this situational knowledge to other similar contexts. In this regard, a larger number of group participants as in Reading Group or Tablework is associated with an increased production of nonconversational Regulative Units (Table 8).

Though none was statistically significant, there were important trends in these data indicating that Pegboard Math provides the most likely setting for conversation that displays an Instructional intent. In terms of the domain expressed in their conversational exchanges, children appear to be more task-oriented in a context that demands highly focused attention to their work. Moreover, because the task itself is typically performed in the presence of only one other child, conversation is likely to be sustained and uninterrupted by the distraction of others as implied in Level I results showing more successful conversation and less unsuccessful social speech in the Pegboard task (Tables 4, 5, and 6).

The final contrast at Level II matched Reading Group and Cognitive Tablework (Table 9). Children were recorded as engaged in more successful conversation which displayed either a Regulative or Interpersonal function significantly more often in the Tablework context than in their Reading Group work. On the other hand, though results did not attain statistical significance, there is reflected in these data the marked tendency for children to produce more Instructional speech in their Reading Group interactions than in their Cognitive Tablework speech. Child-centered Tablework projects, whether cognitively or aesthetically themed, were selected by the children with little if any strict assignment by the teacher of a child to a particular task. Tablework had less the aura of business than did work in the Reading Group which probably accounts for the greater frequency of Instructional conversation in the latter situation.

DISCUSSION

Children in the classroom observed during Study Two were recorded in three specific activity contexts in order to understand how different classroom task situations would affect their conversation in terms of their growing situational competence. The anticipated finding of more conversation initiated and maintained by children in both the project-focused, dyadic arrangement

TABLE 7 Level II Comparisons - Contrast One

	Comparison 1		Comparison 2	
	(a) Reading Group	(b) Pegboard Math	(a) Reading Group	(b) Pegboard Math
	Mean Number	Mean Number	Mean Number	Mean Number
All Children - Initiations Responded to (I/CU units)				
Regulative	5.2[a]	10.3 n.s.[b]	3.6[a]	11.8*[b]
Imaginative-Innovative-Expressive	0.0	0.0 n.s.	0.0	0.0 n.s.
Interpersonal	1.8	10.2***	1.0	8.7***
Instructional	5.0	12.5 n.s.	8.4	11.2 n.s.
All Children - Initiations Not Responded to (NI units)				
Regulative	20.0*	8.2	16.8	11.2 n.s.
Imaginative-Innovative-Expressive	1.2	1.8 n.s.	1.2	2.3 n.s.
Interpersonal	5.0	6.5 n.s.	4.6	6.7 n.s.
Instructional	10.4	21.0 n.s.	20.4	14.3 n.s.

$*p < .05$
$**p < .02$
$***p < .01$

TABLE 8 Level II Comparisons - Contrast Two

	Comparison 1		Comparison 2	
	(a) Pegboard Math	(b) Aesthetic Tablework	(a) Pegboard Math	(b) Cognitive Tablework
	Mean Number	Mean Number	Mean Number	Mean Number
All Children - Initiations Responded to (I/CU units)				
Regulative	10.3[a]	20.5 n.s.[b]	11.8[a]	20.0 n.s.[b]
Imaginative-Innovative-Expressive	0.0	1.7 n.s.	0.0	1.7 n.s.
Interpersonal	10.2	5.7 n.s.	8.7	7.3 n.s.
Instructional	12.5	6.8 n.s.	11.2	5.0 n.s.
All Children - Initiations Not Responded to (NI units)				
Regulative	8.2	23.7**	11.2	26.3 n.s.
Imaginative-Innovative-Expressive	1.8	12.5 n.s.	2.3	11.2 n.s.
Interpersonal	6.5	10.2 n.s.	6.7	8.8 n.s.
Instructional	21.0	11.3 n.s.	14.3	8.5 n.s.

*p $<$ .05
**p $<$ .02
***p $<$ .01

of Pegboard Math and the child-selected small group situation of Tablework needs little additional comment. It seems clear from the reported results that the context defined by the two parameters of focus and group size explains the reported differences. The findings reported at Level II which describe conversation domain in terms of its variation according to task and group context are of importance because they too denote qualitatively different patterns of interaction which are consistently associated with specific activity spheres. Examination of recorded conversation reveals the specific qualities of these patterns.

TABLE 9 Level II Comparisons - Contrast Three

	Comparison 1	
	(a) Reading	(b) Cognitive
All Children - Initiations Responded to (I/CU units)	Mean Number	Mean Number
Regulative	3.6[a]	20.0*[b]
Imaginative-Innovative-Expressive	0.0	1.7 n.s.
Interpersonal	1.0	7.3**
Instructional	8.4	5.0 n.s.
All Children - Initiations Not Responded to (NI units)		
Regulative	16.8	26.3 n.s.
Imaginative-Innovative-Expressive	1.2	11.2 n.s.
Interpersonal	4.6	8.8 n.s.
Instructional	20.4	8.5 n.s.

*$p < .05$
**$p < .02$
***$p < .01$

As an example, children's Tablework conversation contained significantly more Interpersonal messages than their conversation recorded in Reading Group work. While Pegboard Math was purposefully structured as a dyadic arrangement and displayed even greater amounts of Interpersonal speech than Tablework, Tablework interactions often developed spontaneously and informally into two person exchanges. In addition, conversation in the Tablework situation was a much looser, more fragmented affair. Children were usually not focused upon the same piece of business as in Pegboard Math, but, rather, had different projects in progress. The informal task arrangements of Tablework allowed for the mix at a table of equal numbers of both sexes. The two children in the example that follows are both drawing pictures. Rose is coloring squares on her paper with a green crayon; Joel is drawing a picture of several trees and a house. At this point in the transcript, forty-five seconds have passed since the last recorded utterance.

Rose: What happened to your finger, Joel?
Joel: Cut it.
Rose: Cut it where?
Joel: Out in the yard. My sister//my sister was mad at me 'cause

hit her. ((Her)) (( )) and then I told her (( ))
that time when I said, uh, (( )) and she got mad and
(( )) started chasing me and I almost fell (( )).
(( )) and I jumped over//and I jumped over it and then//
so she had to come up this one (( )) 'cause she can't
jump over water. She got a broken finger. So I broke her
finger and then//and then she pushed me against the slide
and there's these sharp things I cut my fingers on it.
(Pause) See?
(Joel leans over basket with hand in basket to talk to
Roxanne who is looking at him intently.)

Joel: See it right there.
Rose: Ooooh.
Joel: See ((the other one?))
Rose: No, I never seen the other one. (three second pause) Can I
take it off? Ohh. (two second pause) That's terrible.
Joel: I broke her finger for it. She punched me and I broke her
finger for it. (four second pause)
(()): Okay, okay.
(three second pause)
Rose: I//Well, I couldn't go swimming in the pool. I got a cold.
Joel: (( )) swimming, huh?
Rose: I couldn't go in the pool because I have bronchitis and
(( )) all over it.
Joel: My brother's//My cousin's only four years old and he knows
how to swim better than me.
Rose: Oh, my goodness gracious.
Joel: Well, he does. It's true. (two second pause) Four years old
and know//know how to//Do you believe that?
Rose: My sister's only two years and she's gonna go to this school.
Joel: Where is she?
Rose: She's not coming yet...but I'll be starting first grade be-
fore she goes into school. I'll be ((there)). I'm gonna be
there (( )).
Joel: Yeah, I'll be//I'll be//I'll be in first grade before my
cousin is even in school.
Rose: Well, my//my sister (( )).//
Joel: //I just turned six. I just turned six Monday. Is today
Monday?
Rose: Tuesday.
Joel: Tuesday. Good. I just turned six Monday.
Rose: Yesterday?
Joel: (( )). Yesterday was Monday.
Rose: (( )). You know the day after tomorrow?
Joel: Sunday.
Rose: You know the day after//you know last night. You know the
day after that day?
Joel: Yeah.
Rose: Well, you know the day after that day?
Joel: Saturday?
Rose: No//you//you know the day after that day?
Joel: The day after that day I turned six. I'm six now. ((It's
pretty rough being six.))
Rose: How can//how//how did you find out?
(two second pause)
Joel: 'cause it was my birthday. I'm done. (Turns paper over,

picks it up and leaves.)

In this conversation, Rose and Joel have explored a number of interpersonal topics -- Joel's injured finger, his relationship with his sister, Rose's health, Joel's cousin, Rose's sister, Joel's recent birthday and more. Building and maintaining friendly relations appears to be a preeminent purpose in this exchange.

Children in this classroom appeared to use Interpersonal conversation for purposes in addition to the one just described. Indeed, such conversation appeared to accomplish several kinds of work at once. It often accompanied task-related behavior and, unlike the Rose and Joel exchange, tended to be brief and accompanied by limited eye-to-eye contact or other attending gestures. In many cases the interaction occurred midway through the task and appeared to serve as a tension release or breather similar to an adult's mid-morning coffee break. The above example included conversation units numbered 23-35 of the 64 units recorded in the full text of Rose's Tablework transcript.

The tension-release provided by Interpersonal exchanges was particularly apparent in Pegboard Math conversation. After a particularly intense period of concentration and attention to the task at hand, all children were observed to swap observations on topics such as the weather, shared past experiences in the classroom, and gossip about classmates. In the following example, Rose and Carol discussed their classmate Ollie in an interaction that occurred approximately one-third of the way through their recorded Pegboard Math activity and after they had each solved two of the mandatory four sums.

(Rose holds up a pegboard that has a red line drawn in ink through one row of holes.)
Rose: Un, look.
Carol: I know.
Rose: Somebody [scribbled it]
Carol: [Ollie done] that with this. Ollie done that with this pen.
Rose: Why
Carol: Because she's a smart aleck. She wanted to do that. 'Kay, now. Mines all right.
Rose: Yeah mine's all right.
Carol: Okay one, two, three, four, five

Unlike many Interpersonal exchanges recorded during Tablework, Interpersonal conversations taped during Pegboard Math were generally quite brief as in this example. Children's attention would in relatively short order be directed back to their problem solving. However, though task-focused (Instructional) outweighed Interpersonal behavior (see, for example Table 8), the relationship that developed between the two problem solvers was generally a mutually supportive one with one participant expressly offering to write the numerals for the other or both explicitly engaging in parallel work on the same sum.

Dan: Four.
Paul: Three.
Dan: Two plus two.
Paul: Three. Three plus.
Dan: Two. Equals.
Paul: Equals.

Dan: Seven.
Paul: Equals. (Whispering) One, two, three, four, five, six. Six. (two second pause) Hey. How do you make a six again?
Dan: Like this. (one second pause) Like this. Whooeesh. (Traces outline over the table with pen.)
Paul: Oh, yeah. Now I remember. Yeeumm.
Dan: Go like this. Yeeummm.
Paul: (( )).
Dan: Here's a six. (half stands and points to the number six in the sequence of numbers on paper over the table.)
Paul: Ah. Oh, yeah, yeah, yeah. I got 'em (( )). (five second pause)
Paul: Yeah, you got 'em all like this. Oooooooommm. It goes oooooommmmmm. (rising intonation)
Dan: That isn't how it goes.
Paul: uh, huh. (yes) Look. Ooooooh. (rising intonation)
Dan: So, it be like this. Ooooooh. (rising intonation)
Paul: It doesn't go oooooohh. (rising intonation)
Dan: That's how I'm doin' mine.
Paul: You was goin'//you was goin' like this. It goes. You was goin' oooooh. (rising intonation) Doesn't go like that.
Dan: I thought it (( )).
Paul: Six doesn't go like this, does it?
Dan: It can go//
Observer: It's a nine.
Paul: I know. This is a six. I can write you a six out of nine. I can make a six to a nine. I just take the six and just go oooohh. (rising and falling intonation)
Dan: Nuh, uh. (no) Turn it up like this.
Paul: You can't turn it up like this. No way you can.
Dan: Uh, huh. Yes you can. I make a nine out of it, see?
Paul: See what//look. It'd make a different equals. (one second pause)
Dan: I know it.

In the preceding interaction, Dan solves the equation "four plus three" while Paul, working on the problem "three plus three," expressly asks for assistance with the question "How do you make a six again?" Dan outlines the shape of a six in the air with his pen and then later indicates the number on the chart over the table placed there by their teacher for children to use for this purpose. The boys and the irrepressible observer then discuss the similarity in shape of the numerals six and nine and the difficulties this phenomenon poses in working addition problems. The conversation has an overriding Instructional purpose but also appears to accomplish some interpersonal work.

Since there were only ten holes on each of two sides of the board and since each side was used to represent half of the equation, the largest sum that could be constructed was "ten plus ten." Ignoring the restrictions imposed by the pegboard, the same dyad later took on the problem "twelve plus twelve." Attention to problem solving was in this instance short lived. A lengthy conversation, most of it judged to be expressive of the Interpersonal domain followed. The unusual length of this interpersonal exchange may well be related to the difficulty of the task Paul has posed for himself and, therefore, to some extent, for his partner Dan as well. First having successfully computed the sum "two plus two," Paul begain to write another problem on his sheet.

Paul: Four. (two second pause) These are right. Now. How about twelve plus twelve.
Dan: Five.
Paul: ((See)) if you don't know how much twelve plus twelve is. (two second pause)
Dan: Yeah, huh.
Paul: [How many?]
Dan: [Like] simple. Twelve plus twelve equals two.
Paul: No, it doesn't, does it?
Dan: (( )).
Paul: Equals one. Ha, ha, ha, ha, ha, ha.
Dan: I know five plus five equals seven.
Paul: I know nothing' equals nothin'.
Dan: I know equals is nothin' but your eyebrow.
Paul: I know.
Dan: I'll paint your eyebrows. Sch, sch, sch. (Pretends to paint by waving pen in Paul's face.)
Paul: I//I will write you. (two second pause) Danny, I ain't gonna write ya, but I'm gonna write ya.
Dan: Oww. (( ))
Paul: Sch, sch, [sch.] (They pretend to "tattoo" each other with numbers)
Dan: [Sch, sch,] sch, sch.
Paul: ((Stop)).
Dan: I got two of 'em done.
Paul: I do, too, Danny. One more done.
Dan: That's mine.
Paul: Heeey, that's mine. (giggle) (Begins taking out pegs.)
Dan: Hey, take your pegs out.
Paul: Oh, take your bugs out.
Dan: Take 'em out.
Paul: Take your//take you mouth out. Heh, heh, heh, heh.
Dan: Take your big butt out.
Paul: Oooooh. Tellin'.
Dan: I'm puttin'//I'm puttin' a whole bunch in. I'm puttin' a hundred and three hundred.
Paul: Ahh. There's no such//there ain't as much of these pegs as three hundred.
Dan: Yuh, huh. That's a thousand pegs. Paul, you know what? No more stitches. No more//
Paul: //Two hundred and thousand//two hundred thousand.
Dan: Paul, I got my stitches out. (Shows forehead.)
Paul: Where?
Dan: Right there. They're out.
Paul: Oh, great.
Dan: I can run faster, and faster, and faster, and faster. (two second pause) You can outrun yourself.
Paul: They gave you bionics, right?
Dan: Yeah.
Paul: Okay, now let's see you run//outrun everybody in this whole town.
Dan: I can.
Paul: I'll bet you can't.
Dan: I'll bet (screech) I can. Anyways, you can't even whoop a flea. (( )).

Paul: I'm gonna take all these and measure 'em. See how much all is all this. All this plus all this.
Dan: Paul, what's a number. It cost five dollars.
Paul: Know how much this cost?
Dan: Ten dollars.
Paul: Eight, a hundred.
Dan: Eight hundred. Ain't no hun//eight hundred.
(one second pause)
Paul: One, two, three, four, five, six, seven, eight, nine, ten. Ten [plus.]
Dan: [Ten.]

With his last utterance, Paul has returned to the task at hand and is in the process of setting up and solving a feasible problem, one within the scope of the pegboard materials. He is working on the equation "ten plus ten" which he later successfully solves. This example is particularly interesting because it illustrates the sort of interpersonal interplay that characteristically served as a tension release for pegboard math problem solvers who happened to be boys. Though work on the sums was generally characterized by cooperation and mutuality, themes of interpersonal conversation reveal a strong competitive orientation. Thus, boys are developing a specific kind of situational competence, one that emphasizes the importance of characteristics usually associated with masculinity in our society. Boys are learning to assert their masculinity in terms of almost super-human physical and intellectual prowess.

Though girls were less likely to play out competitive themes and more likely to discuss everyday matters such as the weather or their classmates in their Interpersonal conversation, they were as likely as were boys to engage in conversation that similarly enabled building and maintaining friendly relations. In fact, the finding of no significant differences between boys and girls on <u>any</u> conversation measure is perhaps the most interesting finding of this research. Pronounced sex differences in amount of conversation and in domain of conversation was a hallmark of the recorded interaction in Study One's traditional classroom. The classroom observed in Study Two was located in a traditional school and in a neighborhood composed of working class and welfare (ADC) families who might be expected to inculcate traditional sex-role related values in their children (Kohn, 1969). However, Appalachian folkways dominate this neighborhood which for approximately thirty years has been inhabitated by in-migrants from farmlands and coal mining towns of eastern Kentucky. Appalachian values of independence, equality and autonomy are not sex-specific. Rather, both men and women in the culture are often expected to assume important responsibilities in adult life. Though women are often expected to be in charge of family while men are accountable for family dealings outside the home, women's domestic responsibilities often extend beyond meal planning to include managing family financial responsibilities and holding a job outside the home. These cultural characteristics may outweigh social class norms in determining value systems held by members of this community.

IMPLICATIONS OF THE TWO STUDIES

The importance of studying situational competence in the natural setting of the classroom has to do with the outcomes attached by their classroom teachers to children's performance of the range of social skills that constitute this competence. Children are formally evaluated in terms of their performance on tests that measure verbal, number and other skills. Test performance is assumed to be the objective measure of their ability and as such ostensibly determines placement in slow or fast reading groups and later in academic or vocational programs. However, the informal learning of situational competence is indirectly evaluated by teachers who often implicitly use their judgments about children's social skills to help accomplish the task of sorting children. Ray Rist's (1973) ethnography of a St. Louis elementary school documents the practice of teachers in this school of placing children in reading groups on the basis of such features as children's manner of dress and bodily odor. In addition, skills related to social class such as the use of Black English as opposed to Standard English determined the pattern of teacher attention or neglect which became established toward a given child. For example, teachers systematically refused to respond to children who used Black English in the classroom.

Children observed in the two studies reported here were, in the first case, middle class children whose parents were affiliated with the major university situated in the general neighborhood of both schools. The children in the second study were offspring of the urban poor. Yet, my impression of these children formed after many weeks' observation time in each setting is that children were equally sensitive to the demands of most classroom situations in which I observed them and recorded their conversations. There were, of course, individual variations. For example, some children were less likely than others to use Interpersonal breaks in their Pegboard Math activity to advantage. The behavior of these children was fundamentally distracting to themselves and to others working with them. Fortunately for the children in this classroom, their sensitive and alert teacher was able to channel "deviant" behavior effectively. She regarded her arrangement of activities in the classroom as an important determinant of children's behavior and modified curricular arrangements principally according to children's interests and her determination of the intrinsic worth of a particular activity. In this regard, Pegboard Math was established in the classroom only after children were judged by their teacher to have the levels of interest and skill to profit from the inclusion of the activity in the curriculum.

Both studies underscore the importance of the teacher in terms of his or her role as the constructor of the curriculum. If teachers are at pains to arrange activities which provide a clear and compelling focus for children's behavior and if the activity is pursued by a small number of children, preferably a dyad, the development of children's situational competence can be enhanced. These two characteristics, clear and apparent focus, and limited number of participants, are associated with increased production of sustained conversation and situationally appropriate conversational behavior in classroom. Activities in the classroom should be structured in terms of these two characteristics as follows:

A. Clear and apparent focus. The children occupied in the task have in advance determined a specific outcome to their work as in the lego construction of a ship or the objective of their work has been framed and carefully explained to them by their teacher as in the Pegboard Math activity.

B. Limited number of participants. Children work upon the task as a dyad similar to the Pegboard Math arrangement which fostered both the specific qualities of sustained and appropriate conversation and the more general behaviors of mutuality and cooperation as demonstrated by children's concern to share resources while engaged in the performance of the task.

At what point, in terms of the number of participants, the interaction among children will begin to deteriorate and lapse into modes of uncooperative behavior is unclear. A best guess is that four participants constitute an upper limit to group size. Five or six, especially if the group is mixed by sex, would have difficulty maintaining a harmonious interaction.

As much as these studies emphasize the teacher's importance as the constructor of a classroom milieu appropriate to the development of young school children's situational competence, they also point to the importance of the situation itself in determining the manifestation of these skills in actual conversational exchanges. The importance of the speech situation or milieu to children's social behavior including their conversational behavior is beginning to be very apparent to investigators. Edward Mueller and Jeffrey Brenner in a recent (1977) report of Mueller's continuing research in natural (playgroup) settings, describe social interaction not as stemming from social competence the child may have already acquired but as dependent upon the milieu. Specifically, Mueller and Brenner conclude that "object-focused contacts were found to be central to the evolution of social interaction..." Finally, Mueller and Brenner's study of toddler dyadic interaction points up the benefits to peer interaction which are derived from children's involvement in parallel play situations. In other words, focus and number of participants were critical to social skills and social interaction in the latter study in the same way these variables were crucial to situational competence as measured by conversational markers in the current research.

Study One and Study Two view conversation of young school-aged children as dependent upon situational features of the classrooms in which the groups of kindergartners included in these two studies were observed. The perspective, therefore, is an interactionist one. Yet, the structural features of conversational behavior examined in the research are only one set of a full complement of situationally-based oral skills required by classroom task demands. For example, children who speak both a Black English and Standard English variant need to be able to switch language codes appropriately. Likewise, girls and boys both may be penalized for using sex-linked language codes their teacher, perhaps unwittingly, sees as inappropriate. Thus, other skills such as code switching are significant in determining children's classroom performance and therefore teachers' evaluations and are, consequently, important for future study. Finally, the specific ethnic and social class characteristics of classrooms must be controlled if variations in children's behavior are to be understood.

BIBLIOGRAPHY

Bernstein, B. (1971) Class, Codes and Control, 1, 2, London: Routledge and Kegan Paul.

Bruner, J. A. (1975) The ontogenesis of speech arts. Journal of Child Language, 2, 1-19.

Cook-Gumperz, J. (1973) Social Control and Socialization. London: Routledge and Kegan Paul.

Flapan, D. (1968) Children's Understanding of Social Interaction, Columbia University: Teachers College Press.

Flavell,J. H., Botkin, P. T., Fry, C. L., Wright, J. W., and Jarvis, P. E. (1968) The Development of Role-taking and Communication Skills in Children, New York: Wiley.

Florio, S. (1976) Issues in the analysis of the structure of social interaction. Unpublished paper. Harvard University. (Mimeographed)

Garvey, C. (1975) Requests and responses in children's speech. Journal of Child Language, 2, 41-63.

Garvey, C., and Hogan, R. (1973) Social speech and social interaction: egocentrism revisited. Child Development, 44, 462-468.

Gumperz, J. (1971) Language in Social Groups, Palo Alto: Stanford University Press.

Halliday, M. A. K. (1973) Explorations in the Functions of Language, London: E. Arnold.

Hoyt, C. J. (1941) Test reliability estimated by analysis of variance. Psychometrika, 6, 153-160.

Hymes, D. (1972) Models of the interaction of language and social life. In J. Gumperz and D. Hymes (eds.), Directions in Sociolinguistics: The Ethnography of Communication, New York: Holt, Rinehart and Winston.

Kohlbert, L., Yaeger, J., and Hjertholm, E. (1968) Private speech: four studies and a review of theories. Child Development, 39, 255-266.

Kohn, M. (1969) Class and Conformity, The Dorsey Press.

Mueller, E. C. (1971) An Analysis of Children's Communications in Free Play. Unpublished doctoral dissertation, Cornell University.

Piaget, J., and Inhelder, B. (1967) Child's Conception of Space, New York: W. W. Norton.

Rist, R. C. (1973) The Urban School: A Factory for Failure, Cambridge: The MIT Press.

Rosen, C., and Rosen, H. (1973) The Language of Primary School Children, Penguin Education.

Rubin, K. (1973) Egocentrism in childhood: a unitary construct? Child Development, 44, 102-110.

Shapiro, E. (1973) Educational evaluation: restructuring the criteria of competence. School Review, 81, 523-549.

Wells, G. (1973) Handbook for coding the language of young children. Bristol University. (Mimeographed)

Wells, G. (1975) The context of children's early language experiences. Educational Review, 27, 114-125.

Wells, G. (1974) Children and their parents--who starts the talking--why and when? Paper presented at the Conference on Language and the Social Context.

Zimmerman, D. H. and West, C. (1973) Sex roles, interruptions and silences in conversation. Paper presented at the Linguistics Symposium, California State Polytechnic University, Pamona.

A Sociocognitive Approach to Language Development and Its Implications for Education*

LOUISE J. CHERRY
Department of Educational Psychology, University of Wisconsin, Madison

INTRODUCTION

The purpose of this chapter is to explore the relationship between children's language development and their social interactions with others. Language development is conceptualized as the development of communicative competence, which consists of the knowledge of language structure and function, including the rules of phonology, grammar, and semantics, as well as the rules of the appropriate use of language to communicate (Hymes, 1971). The author has argued elsewhere in favor of a unified model of development. This model is defined by the assumption that language, social, and cognitive knowledge are interrelated and interdependent, since all are aspects of the same unified development of the individual (Lewis & Cherry, 1977). The sociocognitive approach to language takes the view that the social interactions in which the child participates directly in the alternating roles of speaker and listener are among the most important expreiences for the child developing communicative competence. These conversational experiences create a demand for the child to use language appropriately and effectively to communicate with another person. In addition, conversational interactions provide the child with opportunities to test language and communicative rules and receive information about the adequacy of those rules.

This chapter begins with a brief overview of approaches to children's language development. Recent research in language development began with a focus on children's acquisition of syntactic structure and underlying semantic relations. Subsequent studies have examined the relationship between language and cognition. More recently, some research has focused on children's use of language for a variety of communicative purposes and examined the relationship between language use and social context. The chapter provides a discussion of a sociocognitive approach to language development and includes examples of the kind of research problems which can be addressed from this perspective. Using the sociolinguistic method of analysis, an examination of two types of adults' requests to children is provided. The chapter concludes with a discussion of the implications of a sociocognitive approach to language development for education.

---

*Support for this work was provided by an NIMH postdoctoral fellowship, (MH #08260). The author is grateful to Linda Berman, Peg Griffin, Freddi Hiebert, Deborah Keller-Cohen, Marilyn Shatz, Catherine Snow, Barbara Stevens, William Ward, and Eve Wilkie for their helpful comments on earlier drafts of this chapter.

OVERVIEW OF APPROACHES TO LANGUAGE DEVELOPMENT

The development of language knowledge, in relationship to social and cognitive knowledge may be viewed in several ways. The following discussion is intended as an overview of recent approaches to language development (for comprehensive reviews of the literature see: Bloom, 1975; Blount, 1975; Brown, 1973; Edmonds, 1976). Lewis & Cherry (1977) have outlined three models which describe the relationship of these three domains of human knowledge: the reductionist, the interactionist, and the unified models. The reductionist model is defined by the assumption that language, social, and cognitive knowledge exist independently of one another. The knowledge which underlies language behavior is restricted to the structure of language. The purpose of scientific inquiry within this model is to satisfactorily explain observable language behavior from underlying language knowledge. Social or cognitive behaviors are regarded as "noise" and are excluded from analysis. The interactionist model is defined by the assumption that language, social, and cognitive knowledge are interrelated in unidirectional ways. For example, language knowledge is derived from cognitive knowledge. Within this model, language, social and cognitive knowledge are discrete domains even though each affects the other. The purpose of scientific inquiry within this model is to define the relationship among language, social, and cognitive domains and formulate a model of their interaction. The unified model is defined by the assumption that language, social, and cognitive knowledge are interrelated and interdependent, since all are aspects of the same unified development of the individual. These domains are not necessarily discrete; for example, one version of this model describes the relationship among language, social, and cognitive knowledge as an interaction; another version describes this relationship as a dynamic flow. These models can be used to characterize each of the major approaches to the study of children's language development within the last 25 years, including the learning, linguistic, and cognitive approaches.

The Learning Approach

The earliest explanations of language development were formulated within learning theory; these explanations fit within a reductionist model. Learning models of language development proposed that language knowledge consists of a set of sentences, which are chains of word associations with conditional probabilities describing the relationships between words and word classes (Skinner, 1957). The learning models proposed that explicit teaching, utilizing the principles of imitation and reinforcement results in the child's acquisition of language (Skinner, 1957). This explanation does not accord with the evidence that children produce utterances which have no plausible adult model (Cazden, 1972; McNeill, 1960). For example, children say "foots" instead of "feet" and "goed" instead of "went", when they are in the process of acquiring the rules for forming noun and verb endings (Cazden, 1968). These words are the result of overgeneralizing the rules for forming endings for many nouns and verbs. In addition, this explanation for language development is rejected because of the evidence that explicit teaching of new syntactic forms before the child has developed them "naturally" is not successful, particularly if the criterion for acquisition includes generalized use of the form in mandatory contexts (Cazden, 1972).

The Linguistic Approach

Chomsky's (1957, 1965) linguistic theory of the syntactic structure of language provided the impetus for a redirection in research on language development. His monograph, Syntactic Structures (1957), described a model of language in which a finite set of language rules could be used to describe an infinite set of sentences. This model of language challenged the most prominent models at the time, the finite-state grammars, which were characterized by the assumption that any word in a sentence determines the word in that sentence. Chomsky (1965) argued that the finite-state grammar is similar to the stimulus-response chain of learning theories, because of the relationships of sequential dependency among language elements.

Chomsky proposed that language knowledge, specifically syntactic structure, is innate and develops through the process of maturation; this view also fits within a reductionist model (Lewis & Cherry, 1977). Chomsky has described language knowledge as a biologically preprogrammed structure, which is "triggered" by the environment at the appropriate time during the life-span of the individual (Chomsky, 1975). An example of this view is the Language Acquisition Device (LAD) first introduced by Chomsky (1965) and later elaborated by McNeill (1966). LAD consists of linguistic universals--a hierarchy of syntactic categories and a set of basic grammatical relations. Chomsky proposed an innate explanation of language development because grammatical structure is complex and is acquired so rapidly; in addition, Chomsky assumed that children have only a brief and fragmentary exposure to grammar in their early conversations with adults.

There are several problems with Chomsky's explanation of language development as the triggering of innate language structure. First of all, this position provides no way of dealing with the significant individual variation in language development (Bloom, Lightbown, and Hood, 1975; Cherry, in press a; Braine, 1976; Dore, 1976; Nelson, 1975). Any theory which attributes individual variation in development to innate and preprogrammed factors is incomplete and inadequate. Very little practical application follows from an innate model. The complementary position is that some individual variation must be explained with reference to environmental factors, but the suggestion that "triggering" (Chomsky, 1975) is the model for these environmental influences does not explicate the processes of development.

A second problem for the innatist position is that some recent research suggests that certain aspects of adults' speech to children guide language development. A number of studies provide evidence that mothers' speech to young children is more grammatically well-formed, syntactically simpler, and more repetitious than is speech to adults (see Snow, 1974, for review). There is also evidence that mothers' speech to young children differs acoustically from speech to adults (Broen, 1972; Ferguson, 1964; Phillips, 1973) and mothers "track" the linguistic production of their children in terms of the length and complexity of speech (Baldwin & Baldwin, 1973; Cross, 1975; Lord, 1975). Mothers adjust their choice of the linguistic form of clarification requests with two year old children according to the children's level of language development; as a result, children at different levels of development are roughly equal in their success at responding appropriately to adults' requests (Cherry, in press c). Neither the origins nor the consequences of what Newport (1976) has called "motherese" has been established. The style may be a consequence of the child's limited knowledge of language. Seitz and Stewart (1975) suggest that mothers adjust their speech as a result of children's responses to speech directed to them.

No evidence presently available fully explicates how the use of "motherese" assists the child's development of language; however, several studies provide suggestions that the modifications are functional for the child's process of development. For example, a study of Nelson, Carskadden, & Bonvillian (1973) provides some evidence that exposure to sentences with new but related syntactic information in response to the child's utterance significantly facilitated the syntactic development (as measured by verb construction, auxiliarities, and sentence imitation) of their children compared with a control group. The control group received no responses of this type, but rather received short and grammatically complete sentences which did not include any of the content words of the child's utterance. A study of Newport, Gleitman, & Gleitman (1977) provides evidence that mothers' deictic utterances are related to children's development of referential speech. A study by Cross (1975) of mother-child pairs provides evidence that there are major differences at the conversational level of speech between mothers of fast and slow language learners. Mothers of fast learners used more utterances that were semantically related to the child's preceding utterance, experienced fewer instances of disrupted speech, and employed a fine degree of grammatical tailoring to the child's level of linguistic development than did mothers of slow language learners.

The focus on the syntactic aspect of language is a third problem with Chomsky's approach to language development. Research in children's language development in the 1960's was characterized by the study of the underlying semantic relations in children's early linguistic productions. This shift within the field of language development mirrored a shift in linguistic theory from the Chomskyian emphasis on syntactic structure to an emphasis on the semantic-syntactic relationships within language. Semantically-based theories of Fillmore (1968) and Schlesinger (1971), and others, provided the impetus for subsequent research in language development.

The Cognitive Approach

The view that language knowledge includes both semantic and syntactic structures fits within the interactionist model, which holds that language knowledge and cognitive knowledge are interrelated. Cromer (1974) formulated one version of the interactionist position as the "cognitive hypotheses": Children develop linguistic structures only after they have developed the prerequisite cognitive structures. The research of Bloom (1973) and Edmonds (1976) among others, provides support for this view. For example, the results of Edmonds' (1976) research suggest that the following sequence for the development of the symbolic function of language:

(1) attain a minimum of sensori-motor intelligence (Stage V);
(2) assimilate words to sensori-motor organizations;
(3) develop and consolidate representational ability;
(4) begin to separate the word from sensori-motor organization;
(5) join words together for a more precise specification of meaning.

One implication of the interactionist model is that language is not acquired suddenly and rapidly at a specific point in development. Language originates within the pre-linguistic period of sensori-motor intelligence, even though linguistic forms emerge at a later period of development. This version of the interactionist model takes the view that language development, specifically, the referential function of language, is derived from prior cognitive development.

THE SOCIOCOGNITIVE APPROACH TO LANGUAGE DEVELOPMENT

The sociocognitive approach to language development is characterized by the study of the development of communicative competence, which consists of the rules of language structure and use. This approach is a life-span approach and fits within the unified model of human development, which is defined by the assumption that language, social, and cognitive knowledge are all aspects of the same unitary development of the individual. The sociocognitive approach emphasizes the importance of conversational experiences, the social context of language development; conversation provides children with both the opportunity and motivation to test and modify their developing system of language rules.

Language Knowledge As Communicative Competence

Language serves many functions in addition to the referential; the exclusive focus upon the referential function of language is one limitation of the cognitive approach to language development. Hymes (1971) has clearly expressed the distinction between a model of language "that restricts the design of language to one face toward referential meaning, one toward sound, and that defines the organization of language as solely consisting of rules for linking the two. Such a model implies naming to be the sole use of speech, as if languages were never organized to lament, rejoice, beseech, admonish, aphorize, inveigh, for the many varied forms of persuasion, direction, expression and symbolic play" (p. 278). Furthermore, Hymes (1971, 1974), has characterized language knowledge as communicative competence, which includes the "knowledge of sentences, not only as grammatical, but also as appropriate. He or she acquires competence as to when to speak, when not, and as to what to talk about with whom, when, where, in what manner. In short, a child becomes able to accomplish a repertoire of speech acts, to take part in speech events and to evaluate their accomplishment by others" (p. 277). Children develop more than linguistic competence; they develop sociolinguistic competence, which enables them to participate in society as a speaking and communicating member.

Communicative competence involves the knowledge of language structure; specifically, the rules of phonology, syntax, semantics. Communicative competence also involves the knowledge of language use; specifically, the rules of the paradigmatic and syntagmatic relationships that hold among language elements and the rules of the sequential organization of discourse including conversation. The principle of the paradigmatic relationships that hold among language elements is that there is a choice among alternative ways of expressing at least approximately the same meaning or accomplishing the same function. The initial choice of a form of expression is effected by the social context, including the age and sex of the speakers, the topic, etc. This principle is also referred to as the rule of alternation (Ervin-Tripp, 1974). The principle of the syntagmatic relationships that hold among language elements is that there is an interdependence within the choice of language elements in expression. The choice of an initial form of expression effects all succeeding choices within the discourse unit. This principle is also referred to as the rule of co-occurrence (Ervin-Tripp, 1974).

An example involving the use of address terms illustrates these two sociolinguistic rules. A recent article in the Wisconsin State Journal described the coronation of Emperor Bokassa I, of the Central African Empire. The following sentence appeared in that article: "Emperor Bokassa I will be crowned at the Bokassa Sports Palace, next to Bokassa University on Bokassa Ave., not far from the Bokassa statue." There are many address terms which refer to the same man, including: "Emperor Bokassa I," "Jean Bedel Bokassa," "the ex-lieutenant," "Jean," "Dad." The set of these terms includes paradigmatic alternates, and only certain terms of address are appropriate within this discourse unit, the newspaper article. The choice of the address term is determined by the relationships among the language elements within the discourse unit, that is, the syntagmatic relationships. In the example given, only the term "Emperor Bokassa I" is an appropriate reference.

Rules of sequencing account for coherence in any sequence of utterances in a conversation. Labov (1972) has argued that coherence involves formulating rules of interpretation, which relate "what is said"--statements, interrogatives, imperatives--to "what is done"--actions such as refusals, assertations, denials. There is no simple match between utterances and actions. The analysis of the linguistic structure of the utterances will not reliably provide the meaning of the utterances, even though they are made possible by and are performed in accordance with the rules of linguistic structure. Two utterances may accomplish different actions even though they have the same grammatical representation, as the following utterances, which are both declaratives: "You are standing on my foot." and "You are driving a new car." The first utterance functions as a request for the listener to remove his/her foot, while the second utterance functions to provide information to the listener. Two utterances may have different grammatical representations but accomplish the same action, as in the following utterances: "You are standing on my foot." and "Get off my foot." Both utterances function as requests for the listener to remove his/her foot. The first utterance is a declarative form, while the second is an imperative form. Rules of interpretation and production relate utterances to actions, and sequencing rules operate between actions performed with utterances themselves.

Unified Model Of Human Development

The sociocognitive approach to language development fits within the unified model of human development, which assumes that language, cognitive, and social knowledge are interrelated and interdependent (Lewis & Cherry, 1977). Language, social, and cognitive aspects of individual development are investigated within the unified model so that these systems can be explicated and observable human behavior can be satisfactorily explained. Thus, the investigation of human behavior is primarily oriented toward uncovering the common basis that makes possible what some observers separate into language, social, and cognitive components. These goals are achieved by formulating a model of individual development which includes language, social, and cognitive rule systems. The unified model implies that all human behavior is to be understood, not just that which is regarded as linguistic. This model also implies that causal chains go from the language, social, or intellectual behavior back through the individual before resurfacing as new language, social, and cognitive behaviors. For example, individuals do not respond passively to the language behavior of others, but actively process this information before producing language and communicative behavior. These behaviors, then, originate within the individual's interrelated rule systems and not within any one, abstract domain of knowledge.

Life-Span Approach

The sociocognitive approach to language development is a life-span approach. Communicative development does not begin with the appearance of language and is not completed at the end of childhood, although the interactional process of language and communicative development is the most dramatic in the first four or five years of life. For example, Halliday (1975) investigated the developing communicative functions in the speech of his son Nigel from 9 to 18 months; this study provides the most comprehensive system for the analysis of the early development of communicative functions. Halliday observed three phases in the development of his child's speech and characterizes the first phase as a "content-expressive" system or protolanguage in which the child used language to satisfy material needs, control behavior, establish and maintain contact with others, express himself, comment on his environment, and construct a fantasy world. The second stage is transitional between the first and the third. The child adds dialogue and grammatical structure to the functional system and so provides a prerequisite for the informative function of language--the use of language to provide information--which emerges in the third phase of language development. At this stage the child's transition to the "adult" system has begun, and from here on the child will abandon his/her own grammatical rules as (s)he creates the rules which govern the speech (s)he hears; (s)he will increase vocabulary, articulate speech more conventionally, and be able to sustain increasingly longer conversational interaction.

Language development begins when a child is born into a social world of other people and interacts with them. In infancy, communication modulates the caretaking process where the caretaker becomes aware of the success and failure of his/her interaction behavior; and the child, in turn, develops rules in the context of these communications. Shutz (1964, p. 324) has characterized such transactional situations, where the joint behavior of both caretaker and child are in sychrony and determine their own course, as an "intersubjective time process, . . . by which the fluxes of inner time, that of speaker and that of listener, become synchronous one with the other and both with an event in outer time." Mead (1934) also recognized the importance of communicative gesture for the regulation of social actions among people by cooperation. That the child uses language as a tool to establish a relationship that was previously accomplished through communicative gesture (which often accompanies speech) illustrates the continuity between preverbal and verbal stages of development (Bruner, 1975; Carter, 1975; Halliday, 1975; Snow, 1975).

Conversation: The Social Context Of Language Development

The sociocognitive approach to language development takes the view that the communicative contexts in which the child participates directly in the alternating roles of speaker and listener are the most important experiences for the child developing communicative competence. These conversational experiences provide the child with opportunities to test language and communicative rules and receive information about the adequacy of those rules from a co-speaker in conversation. The process of conversational interaction between the child and co-speaker creates a demand for the child to use language appropriately to negotiate communication with the co-speaker, thus providing the child with an opportunity to formulate and test language and communicative rules. Communication breakthroughs and breakdowns provide opportunities for the modification of rules. Both the pressures occasioned by communication breakdown and the rewards occasioned by communication breakthrough motivate this learning process. Thus, the child develops communicative competence as an adaptation to the pressures generated by the environment of conversational interactions in which (s)he participates.

Conversation is a social activity, and as such, is structured as much by the rules of social order as by the rules of grammar. Conversational interaction is the cooperative, goal-directed, reciprocal exchange of information by speakers (Grice, 1968). The initiation, maintenance, and termination of actions among participants are involved in conversation. There is a constant effort by participants to maintain conversation through the resolution of ambiguity, and clarification by reformulation, elaboration, and modification. Goffman (1964) sees the study of conversation as the study of turns at talking and things said during those turns. Conversation has a unique structure and its own processes. Labov & Fanshell (1977) see conversation as "a matrix of utterances and actions bound together by a web of understandings and reactions... We have come to understand conversation as a means that people use to deal with one another. In conversation, participants use language to interpret to each other the significance of the actual and potential events that surround them and to draw consequences for their past and future actions" (p. 30). Labov & Fanshell see parallels between the structure of conversation and the structure of language, even though they concur with Goffman that conversation is not exclusively a linguistic form. Both language and conversation are sequentially ordered phenomena; both are characterized by a multi-level structure; and both involve the communication of meaning. The study of conversation is the study of sequential actions accomplished by speakers through their utterances. The paradox of conversation, as the social context of language development, is that while conversation is not exclusively a linguistic form, it is the experience within which children develop language.

In sum, the sociocognitive approach to language development takes the view that the child develops language rule systems, including the rules of language use and structure, through interactions with his/her social world. The child participates in the roles of speaker and listener, and observes these roles in others. The child's interpersonal need to communicate and to be understood, the need to influence people, as well as the pleasurable experience of social interaction, provide powerful motivation for the child to develop the rule systems which enable both the production and comprehension of language. Through communicating with other people, children both accomplish actions in the world and develop the rules of language structure and use.

THE REQUEST FOR CLARIFICATION AND THE REQUEST FOR KNOWN INFORMATION: TWO RESEARCH QUESTIONS

Conversations between adults and children are situations when children can use language appropriately for communication. Participation in conversation involves assuming the alternating roles of speaker and listener. There is a constant effort between speaker and listener to maintain conversation by providing information, clarifying misunderstandings, and resolving ambiguities. An adult's request for information from a child is a situation which encourages the child to respond. Once the adult has made the request, there is social pressure for the child to provide an appropriate response, which can include providing the information requested or a reason why the information cannot be provided. If the child does neither of these, the adult may continue in an attempt to have the child respond to the request. Labov and

Fanshell (1977) have formulated the general rule for requests for information as: If A addresses to B an imperative requesting information, I, or an interrogative focusing on I, and B does not believe that A believes that a. A has I, b. B does not have I, then A is heard as making a valid request for information. The analysis of two types of requests for information will be provided as an example of the kind of research questions which can be addressed from a sociocognitive approach to language development. This analysis includes a definition of each type of request, the various forms of the request, and examples and observations of these forms from mothers' conversations with their two year olds. These observations and examples are based on a reanalysis of conversations between mothers and their two year old children (Cherry & Lewis, 1976). Requests for information were chosen for study for several reasons. The use of this function is common in adults' speech to young children, accounting for approximately a third to a half of all adults' utterances. Ervin-Tripp & Miller (1977) and Lewis (1976) have pointed out that requests for information are the first clearly conversational obligation to which children are sensitive. In addition, adults often use these requests to keep the conversation going; often "the facade of information exchange is used for other purposes" (Ervin-Tripp & Miller, 1977).

The Request For Known Information

The request for known information functions to test the ability and knowledge of the listener to provide information, since the speaker already knows the information. This particular type of request for information violates one of the defining characteristics of requests for information, that the speaker (A) does not have the information (I). In response to a request for known information, the listener may provide the information or a reason why the information cannot be provided; the first speaker then provides an evaluation of the adequacy and appropriateness of the response. This conversational sequence is used frequently in instructional contexts, such as teacher-student interaction in the classroom, and in some instances of mother-child interaction. These sequences involve:

Speaker A: Request for known information
Speaker B: Response
Speaker A: Feedback

The following example is taken from a conversation between a mother and her two year old child:

Example 1: (Mother and child are playing with a toy hammer.)
Mother: What is that? (Pointing to the hammer.)
Child: Hammer.
Mother: Hammer, right.

There are two types of requests for known information according to the kind of information requested: those which request that the listener provide a confirmation or denial of a proposition and those which request that the listener provide a specific product. In mother-child conversations, confirmation requests for known information take the form of either (a) statements with a rising question, interaction, such as "Twelve times thirteen is 155?" or (b) interrogatives with subject-verb inversion, such as "Is twelve times thirteen 155?". Product requests for known information take only the wh-form in the mother-child conversations; for example "What is twelve times thirteen?". Figure 1 illustrates the different types of requests for known information.

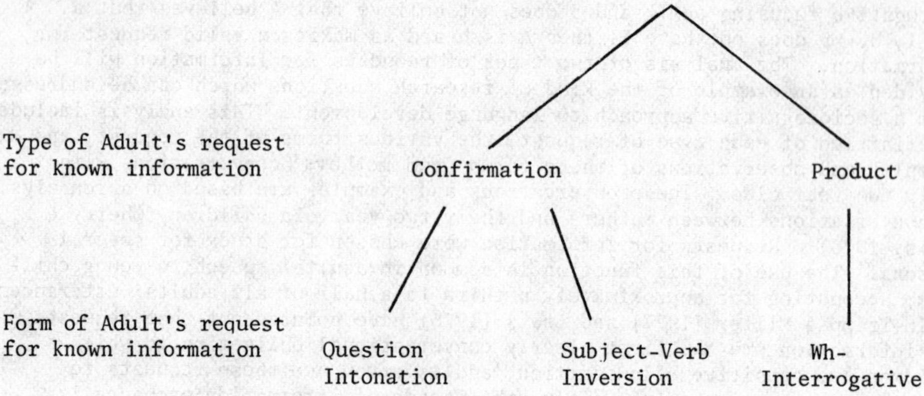

Fig. 1. The types of requests for known information in mother-child conversations

<u>The Confirmation Request For Known Information</u>

The <u>confirmation</u> request for known information is a request by the adult for the child to provide a confirmation or denial of a proposition in the adult's utterance. These requests take the form of either statements with a rising question intonation or an interrogative with subject-verb inversion.

In the first example the mother requests information using a rising question intonation with a statement; in the second example the mother uses the subject-verb inversion form.

Example 2: (Child is playing with mother.)
Mother: That's a cuckoo-clock?
Child: No.
Mother: No.

Example 3: (Mother and child are looking at a book.)
Mother: Is that a little girl? (Points to a picture.)
Child: Yes.
Mother: That's a little girl.

<u>The Product Request For Known Information</u>

The product request for known information is a request by the adult for the child to provide a specific product. Product requests for known information differ along the dimension of explicitness, which refers to the amount of inferencing required by the listener to react appropriately to the request (Cherry, in press b). The proposed wh- requests observed in mother-child conversations are always explicit, since they are interrogative forms which focus upon the kind of information requested as in "What's the name of the first thing?"

The explicit form, "what," is the most frequent type of product request for known information in mother's conversation with their two year olds, as exemplified in the following:

Example 4: (Mother and child are looking at a book.)
Mother: What is that? (Points to a picture.)
Child: A stick.
Mother: A stick.

In the next example the mother uses a variety of "What" questions, and switches to a confirmation request for known information form when the child does not provide an appropriate response.

Example 5: (Mother and child are playing with a "pop" toy.)
Mother: What's that? (Pointing to the toy.)
Child: Uh.
Mother: What is that? What do we call it?
Child: Uh.
Mother: Do we call it a "pop-pop"?
Child: Yeah.
Mother: (nods.)

"Which," "where," and "who" are also used by mothers very infrequently with their two year children as in the following example, but there were no instances of "how," "when," and "why." Ervin-Tripp & Miller (1977) have observed that these forms do not appear in adults' speech to children until the children are speaking in multi-word utterances.

Example 6: (Mother and child are playing with colored balls.)
Mother: Which is the yellow one?
Child: Um.
Mother: Where's the yellow one?
Child: (giggles.)
Mother: Where is the yellow one? Just guess. Which one's the yellow one?
Child: That (points to the red ball.)
Mother: That. No, that's red.

The Request for Clarification

The request for clarification functions to indicate that the listener has not fully heard the speaker's utterance. The speaker is confronted with the fact that his/her utterance has failed to communicate. The speaker may then provide clarification by repeating or reformulating the utterance or else by confirming the listener's reformulation of it. The use of this conversational sequence can thus have the effect of clarifying what was misunderstood so the speakers can resume the conversation. These sequences involve:

Speaker A: Initial utterance
Speaker B: Request for clarification
Speaker A: Response
Speaker B: Acknowledgment

The following example is taken from a conversation between a mother and her two year child:

Example 7: (The child is holding a toy airplane.)
Child: It's broken.
Mother: It's broken?
Child: Yeah.
Mother: That's too bad.

There are two types of requests for clarification according to the kind of information requested: those which request that the speaker repeat the initial utterance, such as "Whad' ja say?" and "Hmm?" and those which request that the speaker confirm or deny the listener's repetition or reformulation of the speaker's initial utterance, such as "You say you have a ticket?" In adult-child conversational interaction, adults used three types of requests for clarification in requesting that the child repeat the original utterance: (a) lexical forms such as "What?" "What did you say?" (b) non-lexical forms such as "Huh?" "Hmm?" or (c) non-verbal forms such as cupping the hand over the ear and bending towards the speaker. Adults used three types of requests for clarification in requesting that the child confirm the formulation of the child's utterance by using a question which is (a) a repetition of the complete initial utterance or some part of it; (b) a repetition of the initial utterance with expansion, expressing in syntactically-complete form the meaning of the first speaker's utterance as the second speaker understands it (after Cazden, 1972); or (c) a repetition of the initial utterance with reformulation due to changes in person. Figure 2 illustrates the different types of requests for clarification.

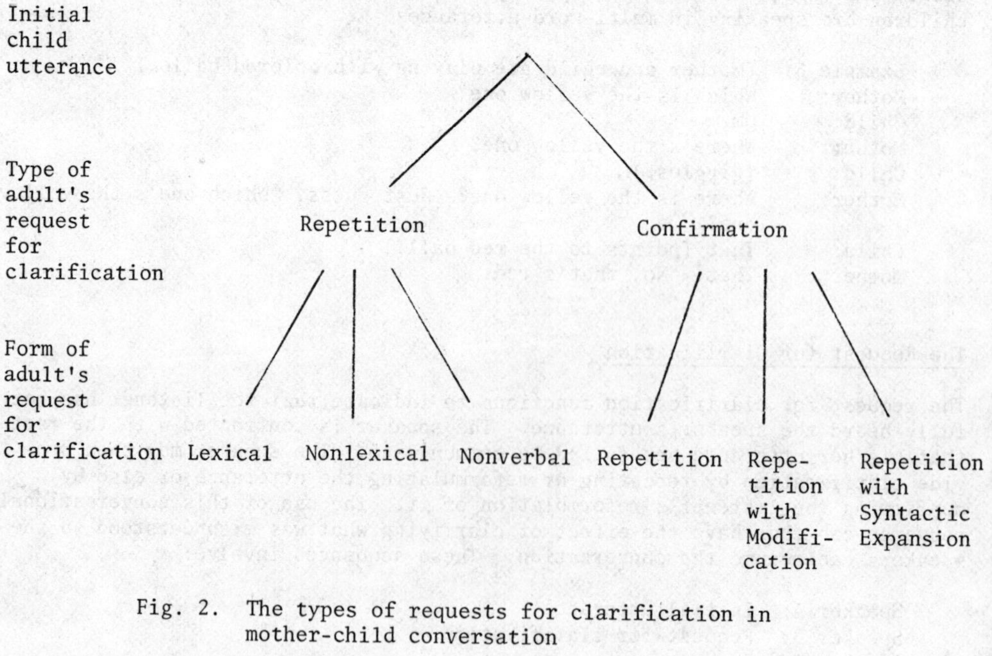

Fig. 2. The types of requests for clarification in mother-child conversation

The Repetition Clarification Request

The repetition clarification request is a request by the adult for a repetition of the child's utterance by using interrogative words and phrases. Both lexical forms such as "what" and nonlexical forms such as "huh" are used and are characterized by rising intonation.

In the following example, the nonlexical "huh" is used to induce the child to repeat her utterance:

Example 8:	(Child is sitting on the floor with her mother.)
Child:	(unclear.)
Mother:	Huh?
Child:	What's this?
Mother:	Raggedy.

The repetition clarification request can also prompt paraphrase and elaboration as in the following example:

Example 9:	(Child is sitting on the floor with her mother playing house.)
Child:	Wanta live there.
Mother:	Huh?
Child:	I wanta live in here.
Mother:	You live in here?
Child:	Yes.

The Confirmation Clarification Request

The confirmation clarification request is a request by the adult for a confirmation or denial from the child of the adult's repetition of the child's preceding utterance. The adult repeats as a question either some part or the entire child utterance with rising intonation. By repeating the child's utterance, the adult requests confirmation on the accuracy of her perception or comprehension of that utterance, as in the following example:

Example 10:	(The mother and child are playing with blocks.)
Child:	More and more.
Mother:	More and more?
Child:	More and more.
Mother:	All right.

Some confirmation clarification requests involve modifications of the child's initial utterance, which are considered to be "speaker-based" adjustments, including changes in pronoun form or verb form due to changes of person. For example, in the following interchange the mother demonstrates the adjustment for first and second-person pronouns:

Example 11:	(Child and mother are playing house.)
Child:	I like this house.
Mother:	You like this house?
Child:	Yes.
Mother:	I'm glad.

Some confirmation clarification requests involve the adult's expansion of the child's preceding utterance by adding missing grammatical elements. This question is produced with a rising intonation. The child's utterance which precipitates the expansion question is incomplete in its syntactic form. As a result, the utterance is occasionally further incomplete in propositional content. The adult then provides a syntactically expanded version of her interpretation of the child's utterance thereby repairing the syntax and simultaneously formulating the proposition which she believes to be intended by the child, as in the following example:

Example 12: (The mother and child are playing with a toy hammer set.)
Child: Stuck.
Mother: Is it stuck?
Child: Yes.

In using the syntactic expansion clarification question, adults may demonstrate speaker-based adjustments as in the repetition questions with modifications, but most saliently, this type of sequence provides syntactically correct form for what the adult believes the child meant in his initial utterance. The expansion clarification request functions as a request for information on the accuracy of the listener's interpretation of the speaker's intended proposition. The very young child is limited in the amount of information he can organize and incorporate into any one utterance. The child is unable to express conventional grammatical relations which are necessary, and it is often left to the linguistically-sophisticated adult to supply the missing elements with which efficient messages are constructed. The <u>confirmation</u> requests are more difficult for the child in comparison to the <u>repetition</u> requests, since the child must make a judgment which often involves complicated grammatical structures in the former, while (s)he must only repeat the original utterance in the latter.

Observations Of Mothers' Requests For Known Information And Clarification With Two Year Old Children

Mothers' requests for known information and requests for clarification were examined in a corpus of data consisting of 38 mother-child dyads in 15 minutes of free play activity. Requests for known information sequences were identified and categorized as <u>confirmation</u> or <u>product</u> requests, and requests for clarification sequences were identified and categorized as: <u>repetition</u> and <u>confirmation</u> requests. Appropriate responses and inappropriate responses were also categorized. Reliabilities were calculated on these categories as percentage agreements between the author and a research assistant who each coded two transcripts, the mean percentage agreement was 86%. Contextual notes made during the data collection were used during coding when this information made more clear a particular category. Conditional probability scores were calculated for each mother-child dyad for each measure. The mothers' requests for known information, and their requests for clarification were each scored as the proportion of all her requests for information that were requests of each of these types. The mother's use of each sub-type of request was scored as the proportion of all requests of that type (known information or clarification) that were of this particular sub-type (confirmation and product for known information requests and repetition and confirmation for clarification requests). The child's responses were scored as the proportion of all the mother's requests that were responded to appropriately by the child. The children's level of language development was calculated according to mean length of utterance (Brown, 1973) and ranged from 1.13 to

3.05 ($\bar{X}$ = 1.87, σ = .47) in this sample. Correlations were computed between the request and response scores and mean length of utterance and two-tailed t-tests were performed to test the significance of these differences.

The analysis showed that 4% of all mothers' requests were requests for known information (128 utterances) and 9% of all their requests were requests for clarification (289 utterances). The wh- product form was the most frequent type of request for known information, accounting for 85% of all known information requests, while 15% were confirmation requests. Mothers' overall use of requests for known information was unrelated to the children's level of language development (r = .11, NS). Mothers' differential use of the two types of requests for known information was also unrelated to the children's level of language development, r = -.22(NS) for confirmation requests and r = -.11(NS) for product requests. In addition, there was no relationship between children's responding appropriately to these requests and their level of language development (r = .08, NS). This analysis reflects the fact that range different types of requests for known information is limited. Mothers used different wh- request forms, including the "what" and "where" forms given in the examples, to play "the naming game" with their children. All children seemed to be able to respond appropriately to these requests. Ervin-Tripp & Miller (1977) have pointed out that the use of these different wh- forms to accomplish the same function is characteristic of this stage of development: "Viewed from the standpoint of syntax or referential semantics, <u>where</u> and <u>what</u> questions seem very difficult, as do identifying and locating. Viewed as a classifying game, <u>what + (pointing) = Name equals Where + Name = (point)</u>, though the latter may <u>be easier</u> (p. 11)." These results suggest that mothers do not differentiate the type of requests for known information during these early stages of children's language development; children at different levels of early language development are equally successful at responding appropriately to these requests.

Confirmation requests were the most frequent types of requests for clarification in mother-child conversations, accounting for 57% of all clarification requests. Repetition requests accounted for 43% of all requests for clarification. Mothers' overall use of request for clarification was unrelated to the children's level of language development, (r = .25, NS) but use of different types of clarification requests was related to the level of language development. Mothers used fewer repetition clarification requests with children of higher mean length of utterance ($r = -.66$, $p < .05$) but used more confirmation questions with them ($r = .63$, $p < .05$). There was no relationship between children's responding appropriately to requests for clarification and their level of language development for all types of requests for clarification or for any particular type. These results suggest that mothers request clarification from children in a way that is appropriate to their level of language development, children at different levels of language development are equally successful at responding to these requests.

These cross-sectional observations of mothers' conversations with their two year olds provide evidence that mothers adjust certain kinds of requests to the children's level of language development. One result of this maternal behavior is that children at different levels of language development are roughly equally successful in responding appropriately to these requests. The question arises regarding the effect of such sequences upon language development of children. Adults' use of the request for clarification provides the child with the information that his/her utterance has failed to communicate effectively, and thereby encourages the child to reformulate the utterance or confirm the adults' (re)formulation of it. Adults' use of the request for known information provide the child with an opportunity to test his/her developing lexical rule system by playing "the naming game". The direct information about language use is available to the child in request sequences as well as the immediate opportunity to produce language may be important experiences for the process of language development. Longitudinal studies, which allow the examination of the effect of such sequences upon children's language development, are critical in investigating individual differences in both the rate and course of language development.

CONCLUSION: IMPLICATIONS OF THE SOCIOCOGNITIVE APPROACH FOR EDUCATION

The overall implication of the sociocognitive approach to language development is that attention be directed to the child's development of communication skills involving language functions. There is a wide range of functions for which language is used including informing, requesting, expressing, among others. All aspects of language use are included within the sociocognitive approach, including nonverbal communication and social actions which accompany language use. In some communicative contexts, some of these functions may be emphasized while others may be used very little or ignored, so that the child may not have experience with the complete range of language functions. There may be an optimal amount of conversational interaction with adults which fosters and facilitates language development, and noninheritable individual differences in development would then be a consequence of these different patterns of social interaction. Several investigators have suggested that children may prefer or specialize in one set of language functions and express other functions nonverbally or not at all (Halliday, 1975; Nelson, 1973). Caretakers need to be aware of this pattern and be responsive to the differing needs of children as they develop.

One of the implications of the sociocognitive model for bilingual education is that contexts which motivate communicative intent and provide a responsive environment may be the most effective for learning a second language as well as a first. Snow (1977) in a study of children's second language acquisition of Dutch, found that communication pressures of various types operated in a classroom situation. All kindergarteners participated in activities even though they could not understand Dutch, which was not their native language. These children who did not require that language for communication and participation hardly ever learned the second language. In contrast, adolescents had to deal with fairly complex abstract material; these children managed to acquire enough of the language to do so very quickly, or else they dropped out of the school. Communicative pressure seemed to motivate learning Dutch for these children.

Cazden has characterized language development as paradoxical. One paradox is that children rapidly and successfully learn the grammar of their native language, even though either the caretaker(s) nor the child is overtly concerned with this aspect of development; mothers seldom consciously teach grammar and children seldom consciously learn it. A second paradox is that deliberate attempts at language education are very rarely successful, particularly if the long term effects are examined. She concludes that: "Because everything we know about language development suggests that it develops best--in function as well as structure--when motivated by powerful communicative intent, and because we want to stimulate development and not just mimic it, it is important to try to make natural, less didactic, group environments more effective (p. 218)."

In conclusion, the sociocognitive approach implies that educators need to maximize communicative opportunities for students in as many possible contexts and involving as broad a range of uses of language as possible. This approach can serve to guide future research on how children develop language as a communicative and cognitive system.

BIBLIOGRAPHY

Baldwin, A. & C. Baldwin, (1973) The study of mother-child interaction. American Scientist, 61.

Bloom, L. (1970) Language Development: Form and Function in Emerging Grammars. Cambridge, MA: MIT Press.

Bloom, L. (1973) One Word at a Time: The Use of Single Word Utterances Before Syntax. Cambridge, Mass.: MIT Press.

Bloom, L., Lightbown, P. and Hood, L. (1975) Structure and Variation in Child Language. Chicago: University of Chicago: Monographs of the Society for Research in Child Development, Serial no. 160, 40(2).

Blount, B. (1975) Studies in child language: An anthropological view. American Anthropologist, 77, 580-600.

Braine, M. (1976) Children's First Word Combinations, Chicago: University of Chicago Press: Monographs of the Society for Research in Child Development, Serial no. 164, 41(1).

Broen, P. (1972) The verbal environment of the language learning child. ASHA Monographs, #17.

Brown, R. (1973) A First Language: The Early Stages. Cambridge, Harvard University Press.

Bruner, J. (1975) From communication to language: A psychological perspective. Cognition, 3, 225-87.

Carter, A. (1975) The transformation of morphemes into words. Journal of Child Language, 2, 233-50.

Cazden, C. (1968) The acquisition of noun and verb inflections, Child Development, 39, 433-48.

Cazden, C. (1972) Child Language and Education. New York: Holt, Rinehart and Winston.

Cazden, C. (1974) Two paradoxes in the acquisition of language structure and functions. In K. Connolly, & J. Bruner (Eds.), The Growth of Competence. London: Academic Press.

Cherry, L. J. and Lewis, M. (1976) Mothers and two-year-olds: a study of sex differentiated aspects of verbal interaction. Development Psychology, 12(4), 228-282.

Cherry, L. J. (in press, a) Individual differences in language development: a sociocognitive approach. In L. Waterhouse (ed.) Sources of Individual Variation in Language Development, New York: Holt, Rinehart and Winston.

Cherry, L. J. (in press, b) Teacher-student interaction and teachers' expectations of students' communicative competence. In M. Griffin and R. Shuy (eds.) The Study of Children's Functional Language Development and Education in the Early Years, Final report to the Carnegie Corporation of New York.

Cherry, L. J. (in press, c) The role of adult's requests for clarification in the language development of children. In R. Freedle (ed.) Discourse Processing: A Multi-disciplinary Approach, II, N.J.: Ablex Publishing Company.

Chomsky, N. (1957) Syntactic Structures, The Hague: Mouton.

Chomsky, N. (1965) Aspects of the Theory of Syntax, Cambridge: MIT Press.

Chomsky, N. (1975) Reflections on Language, New York: Pantheon Books.

Cromer, R. (1969) The development of language and cognition: the cognition hypothesis. In B. Foss (ed.) Determinants of Infant Behavior, London: Methuem.

Cross, T. (1975) Motherese: its association with rate of syntactic acquisition in children. Paper presented at the Third International Child Language Symposium, London.

Dore, J. (1977) Children's illocutionary acts. In R. Freedle (ed.) Discourse Relations: Comprehension and Production, New York: L. Earlbaum Associates.

Edmonds, M. (1976) New directions in theories of language acquisition. Harvard Educational Review, 46, 2, 175-198.

Ervin-Tripp, S., and Miller, W. (1977) Early discourse, some questions about questions. In M. Lewis and L. Rosenblum (eds.) Interaction, Conversation, and the Development of Language: The Origins of Behavior, New York: Wiley.

Ferguson, C. (1964) Baby talk in six languages. American Anthropologist, 66, 103-114.

Fillmore, C. (1968) The case for case. In E. Bach and R. Harms (eds.) Universals in Linguistic Theory, New York: Holt, Rinehart and Winston.

Goffman, E. (1964) The neglected situation. American Anthropologist, 6,2, 133-6.

Grice, P. (1968) Logic and Conversation. Unpublished manuscript.

Halliday, M. (1975) Learning to Mean, London: Edward Arnold.

Hymes, D. (1971) On communicative competence. In J. Pride, and J. Holmes (eds.) Sociolinguistics, Baltimore: Penguin Books.

Hymes, D. (1974) Foundations in Sociolinguistics, Philadelphia: University of Pennsylvania Press.

Labov, W. (1972) Sociolinguistic Patterns. Philadelphia: University of Pennsylvania Press.

Labov, W. & D. Fanshell (1977) Therapeutic discourse: Psychotherapy as conversation. New York: Academic Press.

Lewis, M. (1976) A theory of conversation. The Quarterly Newsletter of the Institute for Comparative Human Development, 1(1), 5-7.

Lewis, M., & Cherry, L. (1977) Social behavior and language acquisition. In M. Lewis, & L. Rosenblum (eds.), Interaction, Conversation, and the Development of Language: The Origins of Behavior, New York: Wiley.

Lord, C. (1975) Is talking to babies more than baby talk? Paper presented at the Society for Research in Child Development, Denver, Colorado.

McNeill, D. (1966) Developmental psycholinguistics. In F. Smith, & G. Miller (eds.), The Genesis of Language. Cambridge: MIT Press.

Mead, G. H. (1934) Mind, Self, and Society. Chicago: University of Chicago Press.

Nelson, K. (1973) Structure and strategy in learning to talk. Monographs of the Society for Research in Child Development, 38 (1-2, Serial no. 149).

Nelson, K., Carskaddon, G., & Bonvillian, J. (1973) Syntax acquisition: Impact of experimental variation in adult verbal interaction with the child. Child Development, 44, 497-504.

Newport, E. (1976) Motherese: The speech of mothers to young children. In N. Castellan, D. Pisoni, and D. Potts (eds.), Cognitive Theory: Volume III, Hillsdale: L. Earlbaum Associates.

Newport, E., Gleitman, H., & Gleitman, L. (1977) Mother, I'd rather do it myself: Some effects and non-effects of maternal speech style. In C. Ferguson & C. Snow (eds.) Talking to Children, Cambridge: Cambridge University Press.

Phillips, J. (1973) Syntax & vocabulary of mothers' speech to young children: Age and sex comparisons. Child Development, 44, 182-85.

Schlesinger, I. (1971) Production of utterances and language acquisition. In D. Slobin, The Ontogenesis of Grammar. New York: Academic Press.

Shutz, A. (1964) Collected Papers. (A. Broderson, ed.) The Hague: Martinus Nijhoff.

Seitz, S. & C. Stewart (1975) Imitations and expansions: Some developmental aspects of mother-child communication: Developmental Psychology, 11, 763-69.

Skinner, B. (1957) Verbal Behavior. New York: Appleton-Century-Crofts.

Snow, C. (1975) The development of conversation between mothers and babies. Unpublished Manuscript, Unit for Research in Medical Application of Psychology, University of Cambridge, Cambridge, England.

Snow, C. (1977a) Mothers' speech: An overview. In C. Snow & C. Ferguson (eds.) Talking to Children, Cambridge: Cambridge University Press.

Snow, C. (1977b) The biological and social factors in the development of communication. Paper presented at the Minnesota Symposium on Child Development, Minneapolis, Minnesota.

The Boys have the Muscles and the Girls have the Sexy Legs: Adult - Child Speech and the Use of Generic Person Labels

OLGA K. GARNICA
The Ohio State University

INTRODUCTION

The current revival of interest in the role of environmental factors in the intellectual development of the young child has brought about an increasing number of studies on interactions between the adult (usually the mother) and the child (Clarke-Stewart, 1973). Of these studies, a large portion emphasize the role of adult language as an important--perhaps the most important--mechanism in intellectual and social development. This is certainly reflected in the view that the language directed to the young provides a major contribution to the child's learning of language forms and usage rules (Snow and Ferguson, 1977). The majority of investigations of speech directed to young children by adults and older children have dealt solely with the form of the speaker's utterances. Examinations of the syntactic form (Snow, 1972; Cross, 1977; Shatz and Gelman, 1973), prosodic and paralinguistic features (Garnica, 1977a), phonological forms and vocabulary words (Ferguson, 1964) have been conducted. Many of the earlier studies on the form of utterances directed to children are conveniently classified in Snow (1977). Subsequent studies investigating form appear in most papers contained in Snow and Ferguson (1977). The nature of gestures accompanying such adult utterances have also received some attention (Garnica, 1977b).

Although by far the primary focus of attention has been on the forms of utterances directed to the young child, the content of such utterances has also received some attention. As researchers began to notice that the forms in which adults conveyed information to the child were different, they also observed that the information the adult was conveying to the child in this special format was special as well. Specifically, adults talk to young children about those objects and activities that are present in the child's immediate environment and that are of direct concern to the child--food, toys, animals, etc. (Ferguson, 1964). It is not surprising then that children talk about these things as well when they first begin to produce single-word utterances. Nelson (1973), for example, found that there was considerable uniformity in what children first talk about. Specifically, she found that the categories animals, food and toys were referred to most frequently in the first ten words of the eighteen children studied. By the time these children had acquired vocabularies of about fifty words, most had words for foods, body parts, clothing, household items, vehicles, and people. The categories of items talked about were quite similar even though the exact words used varied, with the naming of movers (persons, animals), moveables (food, toys), and recipients (people) being most common. So too with the content of adult speech directed to children. The category of objects referred to is quite stable across adults and the same words are used repeatedly, as is reflected in the type-token ratio.

Although it is useful to know what general topics are used by adults in speaking to children and the focus of the adult's conversational contribution (the here-and-now), this provides little or no information on how the adult structures utterances to provide the child with information as to (a) the physical nature of persons and objects in the child's surroundings, (b) how these persons and objects are viewed--socially and otherwise--by the adult, and (c) how the child is expected to view and behave toward these entities. Investigation of these latter questions involves detailed analyses of the actual conversational sequences that transpire during adult-child conversation, information which is lost in the summerization process which goes on when a list of topics discussed represents the level of specificity which is reported in a study. Speech directed to children does not simply provide the child with a data base from which she/he may learn the language form and their usage patterns in the language spoken to her/him. It also provides the child with a view of the social world which surrounds her/his existence--a world view that is firmly entrenched in language and inseperable from its use. Even the strongest critics of theories like the Sapir-Whorf hypothesis cannot deny that some sort of relationship holds between social and cognitive categories on the one hand, and language categories on the other. The conclusion that there are such connections is inescapable and suggests that a closer examination of the content of adult-child utterances is important. Specifically, such an examination could establish what sort of connections are being made and transmitted to the child.

In this paper I examine in detail some conversational sequences produced by adults in dyadic interaction with young children. The particular set of utterances that is analyzed consists of several terms selected from the greater set of words available in the English language used to designate persons. The great variety of vocabulary of this type available in English (as well as other languages) points to the personal and social importance of this sphere to speakers. Words used to designate persons include proper names, personal pronouns, kin terms, and certain generic person words. Some examples from this latter category having reliable perceptual foundations are man, woman, boy, girl, baby, etc. Investigations on the structure and use of such labels by children and adults have been most extensive on kin terms (Romney and D'Andrade, 1964; Elkind, 1962; Haviland and Clark, 1974) and personal pronouns (Brown and Gilman, 1960; Maratsos, 1976). The other labels used to designate persons, e.g., generic labels, have been little studied--even in the adult population.

The present study focuses on the use of a subset of these generic person words in adult speech directed to young children. The study is somewhat limited in scope because this is an initial investigation in this area and because of certain restrictions on the amount of material that was collected and analyzed. Nonetheless, it represents a first step toward a new approach to the analysis of the content of adult speech to young children, one which I believe adds new importance to conducting more detailed examinations of what adults say to children and examining the consequences of what is said or (sometimes more importantly) not said to the child.

METHOD

Subjects

Six children participated in the study. The children were all female and attending a daycare center on a fulltime basis. They ranged in age from 0;11 to 2;0. The age and MLU level for each child is listed in Table 1 below.

TABLE 1 Age and MLU Level of Children Participating in Study

	Age	MLU
TE	0;11	1.2
UU	1;0	1.3
EG	1;3	1.5
YJ	1;6	1.7
EB	1;9	1.7
MC	2;0	3.1

All children came from a middle class home environment where English was the only language spoken in the home. Each child's behavior was observed on two separate occasions by a developmental psychologist. These observations lasted for approximately 20 minutes each. The observer kept a running log of the activities of the child during the normal, everyday activities of the daycare center--feeding, free-play, cleaning up, etc. The adult caretakers were also questioned informally about the everyday behaviors of the child. On the basis of these observations each child was judged to be functioning at a level that was average to above average (for the child's age) in social and intellectual development.

Data Collection

Each child was brought by a caretaker well known to and very much liked by that child to a playroom in the daycare center. The playroom was equipped with a 5' x 7' rug and a large variety of play materials. The toys in the playroom included (a) a large doll house equipped with furniture and a family of dolls (mother, father, boy, girl, baby), (b) a two seater car complete with boys and girls from the Brady Bunch® toy collection, (c) an assortment of picture books containing photographs of animals and children of all ages (with and without adults present in the photos), and (d) a small suitcase containing assorted extra clothes for the doll family (dresses, shirts, shoes, etc.).

A Sony Video Porta-Pak recorder was set up in one corner of the room. A Sony TC 55 audio tape recorder was placed on the floor facing the center of the rug and at one corner of it. The tape recorder was partially concealed by a table leg to protect the recorder from damage that might ensue as the result of being bumped or handled by the child.

The adult accompanying the child was a staff member at the daycare center and had been in daily contact with the child from three months or more. The adult was told that the study was concerned with how adults and children play with toys together and that they were to respond to the child in whatever way seemed most natural and appropriate given in this playroom environment. The spontaneous behaviors of adult and child were audio and video taped for a 20-25 minute period. For all but one child, the same adult interacted with a particular child on both occasions. However, since the children were taken from different classroom groups in the daycare center, five different adults participated in the sessions. The adults were all female and ranged in age from early 20s to late 30s. They were all monolingual speakers of Standard Midwest American English.

In each session the adult and child were engaged in what Goffman has called "focused interaction" which is "instances of two or more participants in a situation joining each other openly in maintaining a single focus of cognitive and visual attention--what is sensed as a single mutual activity" (1963, p. 89). Their activities included playing with the toys available in the play-room as well as other activities such as playing "pattycake" and singing songs.

Data Analysis

The speech material from these sessions was transcribed along with a running word commentary of concurrent nonverbal contextual information. All speech sequences in which the child and/or the adult used one of a subclass of generic person words, i.e., mother (including variants such as mommy, etc.), father (including daddy, etc.), woman (including lady, etc.), man, boy, girl and baby, were extracted for further analysis. In this paper only the sequences containing the terms boy, girl and baby are discussed. The focus is on the adult usage patterns in sequences containing these three terms.

In the analysis, the following questions were considered to be of central interest. Do adults use same-sex (in relation to the child) and cross-sex generic terms referring to persons equally often in their spontaneous speech directed to young children? Are there any differences in the presentation of same-sex versus cross-sex terms? What are the ways in which adults present information to the child about the meanings of the pair of sex specific (boy, girl) terms? What information is supplied to the child about the semantic and social specification of these terms? Is there variation in the manner in which this information is presented? The data presented in the following section serve as a basis for beginning to answer some of these questions.

RESULTS

Use of Same-sex Versus Cross-sex Person Words

A tabulation of the frequency of use of same-sex and cross-sex generic person words appears in Table 2.

TABLE 2 Frequency of Use for Selected Generic Person Terms with All Sessions Combined

Type of Sequence	Baby	Girl	Boy
	Generic Person Term		
Elaborated	28	11	1
Unelaborated	26	14	26
Total	74	25	27

The term used most often is the sex neutral term--baby. It is used approximately three times more often than either of the sex marked generic terms--boy, girl. Furthermore, in the overall results these female caretakers used the same-sex person word, i.e., girl, as often as the cross-sex person word, i.e., boy. However, the types of sequences in which the words boy and girl appear are different. The two kinds of sequences noted are termed "elaborated sequence" and "unelaborated sequence."

A sequence is called an "elaborated sequence" when one of the terms (boy, girl, baby) is simply designated in one or more utterances of the adult's conversational turn, without reference to attributes or associated activities. In such instances, the term simply appears in the utterance(s) as for example in (a), as an identifier used to indicate to a person that is being referred to in the course of the conversation. In unelaborated sequences no attempt is made by the adult to associate the term with any possible attributes, behaviors, potential or routine actions with the type of person designated by the term. The following two excerpts from the transcripts are examples of unelaborated sequences. Example (a) contains the person term girl; example (b) contains the person term baby.

> (a) Context: Adult and child looking at successive pages of a book.
> Adult: There is a house (Adult turns page). There's a girl (Adult turns page). What's this? (Adult points to picture). That's a kitty. Nice. Fuzzy. Kitty.
>
> (b) Context: Child looking around at toys in playroom.
> Adult: What do you want to see? Do you want to see this baby? (Adult picks up baby doll). Do you want to see this one? (Child shakes head and turns head away) No? Okay. (Adult puts baby doll on rug).

In example (a), the term girl appears but it is simply produced and the conversation moves on to a discussion of another picture, of a kitten. In example (b), the term baby appears in the text of the adult's conversation turn but it is again there solely for the purpose of referencing an individual pictured in the book of photographs.

Example (a) is of further interest to us here because this conversational turn consists of a sequence of utterances in which the term kitty is elaborated. The term kitty is, of course, not a generic person label and therefore not of direct interest to us here except as an illustration of what is meant by "elaborated sequence." In (a), the turn is made up of several sequential utterances containing the word kitty, i.e., "That's a kitty. Nice. Fuzzy. Kitty." The term kitty is not only repeated in these sequential utterances but additional attributive words appear in the sequence that are juxtaposed to it, i.e., "nice" and "fuzzy." These latter words are related to kitty and provide information on particular features of the object (the kitten) that is being referred to by the term in the sequence of utterances. In other words, the term, i.e., kitty, is expounded on or elaborated through a concatination with other words which are commonly associated with it or which the speaker wants to associate with the term.

The following is an example of an elaborated sequence containing the generic person term girl.

(c) Context: Adult and child examining contents of doll house. Adult: Look at this pretty little girl over here (Adult points to girl doll) See the hair? (Adult picks up doll and touches doll's hair) She has lo::ng lo::ng hair, doesn't she? Wanna touch it? (Adult moves doll within reach range of child. Child reaches toward doll) Touch her hair (Child strokes doll's head repeatedly) Feel how so::ft it is.
(Note: The colon after the vowels in certain words indicates that the vowel was prolonged for an extended duration of time.)

This elaborated sequence also contains a variety of words indicating features and attributes of the person being referred to by the generic person label. In (c) above, the word "pretty" appears and there is reference to the girl doll's hair, specifically to its length (long) and texture (soft). The use of these terms in concatination with the term girl elaborate on the meaning of the term. An example of the term baby appearing in an elaborated sequence can be found in (d) below.

(d) Context: Adult and child examining baby doll in doll house. Adult: Look at the ba:by. See the little baby in the back there in the crib? Hm? She's so cute.

In this example the term (baby) is used in combination with other words that "elaborate" on the evaluative and attributive aspects (little, cute) of the person being referred to by the term.

In the speech samples collected, the terms girl and baby appeared in all but one of the elaborated sequences while the term boy appeared primarily in unelaborated sequences such as (e) below.

(e) Context: Adult and child examining doll houses. Adult: What's that? (Adult points to boy doll) Is that a boy? (Child looking at boy doll) Is that a boy? Yes it is.

There was only one elaborated sequence containing the term boy and this sequence also contained the term girl. The adult's turn containing the sequence was as listed in (f).

(f) Context: Adult and child examining several boy and girl dolls sitting in a toy car. Adult: Hey look. There a car. And a girl and a boy. The girl (Adult points to girl doll) has a dress on and the boy (Adult points to boy doll) has pants on. They look different, don't they? They are different.

There are several interesting aspects of the language used in this example. First, the order in which the persons referred to are mentioned (same-sex person mentioned first) violates the normal conventions in everyday conversation which is to mention the male member of a mixed sex group first, as in expressions such as "boys and girls" or "the man and woman." In (f) the speaker says "a girl and a boy" rather than the expected "a boy and a girl." Furthermore, the elaboration is of a contrastive nature which also includes an elaboration of the term girl. There were no examples in the transcripts of an elaborated sequence with the term boy all by itself, although there were numerous examples of unelaborated sequences containing the term boy.

The Nature of Elaborated Sequences Containing Same-sex Person Words

The next step of the analysis was to examine the elaborated sequences in an attempt to classify these sequences into types according to the way the additional information was provided in the sequence. There were two basic types of elaborated sequences for the person terms being studied: (1) contrastive, and (b) substitutive. The latter type contained several subtypes. The contrastive elaborated sequence has already been illustrated in (f) above. In these elaborated sequences an attribute or an action of the person referred to by the term is compared to another attribute or action. Example (f) is the only instance of the terms boy and girl appearing in such an elaborated sequence. However, there were four examples in which the terms girl and baby appear, as in (g), below.

> (g) Context: Adult and child examining several dolls.
> Adult: Oh look. A baby. And a girl. The baby has a diaper on. The girl. The girl has a dress on, doesn't she?

In (g) both the terms baby and girl are used and the attire of each person referred to by these terms is given in the account. Thus the terms are juxtaposed in one conversational term and in addition there is a juxtaposition of a salient attribute of the juxtaposed persons. It is stated in (g) that a significant contrast between persons referred to as babies and those referred to as girls has something to do with the type of attire that one commonly associates with each type of person. Although female infants can be seen wearing dresses, they also inevitably are wearing diapers, whereas non-infant females, i.e., girls, stereotypically wear dresses (presumably without diapers). It seems from their example that stereotypic attributes, e.g., type of attire, are assigned to each person associated with the terms used (baby, girl) and that the message is that these attributes separate the persons referred to by the terms mentioned in unequivocal ways. In other words, diapers and dresses separate the babies from the girls in a manner like dresses and pants separate the girls from the boys. The rule which the adult seems to convey is: If you see a diaper on a young person, you can refer to the term baby, if you see a dress on a young person, use the term girl. I elaborate this point in the discussion section below.

I have termed the second basic type of elaborated sequence substitution. Illustrations of these types of sequences appear in several of the examples already listed above. In substitutive elaborated sequences of the attributive type, an action appears in the same utterances as the term or in an adjacent utterance. In such sequences, the attribute or the action "stands for" the term. An example of a substitutive sequence of the attributive subtype is in (c) above. In this example the attribute being singled out is the doll's long, soft hair. It is not the hair itself that serves to elaborate on the meaning of girl, but its texture and length. Both boys and girls (and some babies) have hair, but usually only girls (as opposed to boys) have long hair, and furthermore, it is usually expected to be well kept (hence soft). The use of paralinguistic cues, as indicated partially in the transcript by the colon and double colon, i.e., "long, lo:ng hair" and "Feel how so:ft it is," serve to highlight these portions of the utterances. Note that there is no such marking of the word hair in the entire conversational turn of the adult. Another example dealing with an attribute linked to the term girl appears in the following example.

> (h) Context: Adult and child playing with dolls and other toys. Adult: Oh my goodness! What is this? A little girl. With pigtails. She's got hair the color of yours. She's got a buggy. (Adult picks up toy automobile and tries to put doll in) Oh! She doesn't fit. She's too long. Here. (Adult holds doll toward child) Got a basket. She's going shopping. Here. You wanna hold her? (Adult touches doll to child's hand)

In (h) another reference to hair is made. In this case it refers to the style of hair--pigtails. Wearing hair in pigtails is a way that only girls wear their hair.

The conversational turn cited in (h) above also includes an example of a substitutive elaborated sequence of the second subtype. In the second subtype of substitutive elaborated sequences, it is an action rather than an attribute that is being conveyed. Here the action of going shopping is associated with the term girl. An examination of the substitutive elaborative sequences shows the following actions (activities) to be associated with girl and baby.

Baby	Girl
cry	go shopping
sleep	hug an animal (dog, kitten)
shake rattle	hug a person (another doll)
smile	sit on a chair

The list of actions (activities) related to the term baby is just about exhaustive for a young infant (except for wetting, which was not mentioned by the adults). On the other hand, the list of actions (activities) related to the term girl no where near represents the full range of actions, that normally active female children pursue. It does, however, include activities which would fall exclusively under the stereotypes of the feminine person--a passive, nurturing homemaker/caretaker. It is always possible, of course, that a larger sample of elaborated sequences of this type will reveal a different picture, but that remains to be demonstrated.

DISCUSSION

In considering the theoretical implications of these findings I will focus my remarks on what is being achieved by the adult through the use of the linguistic terms that were examined--boy, girl, baby--especially within the particular usage patterns that were observed. I suggest that what is transmitted to the young child (such as the ones in this study) are two separate, but intimately related, types of information. First, the adult's behavior as discussed above, with regard to the use of certain nouns, i.e., boy, etc. and verbs (action) i.e., cry, hug, etc., serve as markers of social categories and associated attributes and activities. The adult's use of these linguistic forms is one source (perhaps the primary source) of learning for these categories with these associated attributes and activities. Thus, such verbal activities on the part of the adult assist in the explication and delineation of social categories and the semantic fields associated with these categories. Second, partially because the first point is the case, the adult verbalizations that were observed in the study of these terms (boy, girl, baby) contribute to the child's knowledge of the coherence of texts both in terms of the production and recognition of particular juxtapositions of words and sentences as possible or potentially valid instances of a piece of discourse. This particular dual function of the adult utterance is most easily and immediately evident if discussed in the terminology of the conventional analyst Harvey Sacks (1972a, 1972b). This is not to imply that the frameworks suggested by others who have dealt with similar issues, e.g., for coherence of texts consider (Halliday, 1973; 1975; etc.) could not be adequately used to achieve an explanation to a greater or lesser degree, but simply reflects my preferences as to which framework is most useful in this respect. Thus, the ensuing discussion will first focus on that portion of the theoretical apparatus developed by Sacks which is relevant to the results of the study presented above. Next follows a discussion of the results in relation to those formulations. Finally, there appears a few preliminary remarks on possible sex differences in the development process which are partially reflected in the data already presented.

Linguistic Categories and Social Categories

One of the most important general theoretical statements from the Sacksian perspective, supported by others who preceded him (Goffman, 1967; Garfinkel, 1967; Cicourel, 1968; and others), is that linguistic material can be used and is to be used to analyze social categories and activities. It is maintained, furthermore, that the formal language system performs an important social function in that it incorporates the objectification of experience gained in the varied contexts of life. Thus, language plays a primary role in the mediation of a socially constructed reality. This stance dictates an analysis of verbal material which goes beyond the investigation of the overt content of what is said in a piece of discourse to discover what is achieved by the use of a particular utterance in a social/interactional sense. Intentions are of great consequence in this type of analysis. The interpretation of intentions must take into account the social categories used by the speaker of an utterance and the cultural associations they convey to him, since intentions are expressed by assigning others to these categories and, moreover, ascribing to these categories certain category-related activities.

The young child is ignorant of many aspects of the social categories which are deemed important by the adult social community in which she/he lives and the activities commonly associated with these social categories. Yet, the child must learn this information in order to function in the speech community with a satisfactory degree of competence. Otherwise the child will not be able to decode other speakers' intent properly or to encode intent that will be decipherable by others. Two concepts proposed by Sacks which are useful in the further conceptualization of the significance of adult utterances directed to the young child are: (a) membership categorization device, and (b) category bound activity. A membership categorization device is a collection of member categories plus rules of application. The rules of application are not of particular relevance to us here so I will not devote any further attention to them. They are discussed in detail in Sacks (1972b). The notion of device, however, is worthy of further discussion. An example of a device is "family" usually consisting of the following member categories: father, mother, baby, and nonnuclear family categories such as aunt, uncle, grandfather, etc. Another device discussed by Sacks is the "stage of life" device--baby, child (boy, girl), adolescent, adult, etc. As is evident, the categories in a collection go together in the sense that they are internally grouped and related to one another in specific ways.

Category-bound activities are activities, usually actions, to be done by some particular category (or categories) of members. For example, a category-bound activity for the category baby is "cry." Category-bound activities are then behaviors routinely associated with a certain member category and, in fact, normally expected to be produced by members of that category. The same activity bound to different member categories are evaluated differently. Sacks cites the activity "cry" as an example. The activity "cry" produced by an adult is usually evaluated negatively, i.e., degraded. Cessation of this activity by an adult is construed as a return to a normal state. On the other hand, the activity "cry" produced by a baby is considered normal and the cessation of this activity usually brings great praise. Therefore, it turns out that the category-bound activities associated with member categories provide a norm which is a set of a set of category-bound activities with a membership category. This existence of such a set of activities allows members of a speech community to attribute a second or third activity to a member of a category given that the occurrence of a first activity which is known to be category-bound to that member category is exhibited. Thus, there is a tendency to group together actions (as well as objects and events) that one observes and to give them an interpretation that makes the most sense given what expectations dictate.

Sacks points out two viewer's maxims which provide for the recognizability of the correctness of observations. To say that observations are recognizable is to say that the observations are not questioned by the viewer. They are:

> Viewer's maxim #1: (for processing observed activities): If a member sees a category-bound activity being done, and if one can see it being done by a member of a category to which the activity is bound, then: see it that way.
>
> Viewer's maxim #2: If one sees a pair of actions which can be related via the operation of a norm that provides for the second given the first, where the doers can be seen as members of the categories that the norm provides as proper for the pair of actions, then: (a) see that the doers are such members and (b) see the second as done in conformity with the norm.

The connection here with coherence in texts is that strings of sentences that have been produced by a speaker who utilized viewer's maxims will be heard as a "recognizably correct possible description," i.e., a correctly formed piece of discourse. This occurs, of course, provided that the hearer utilizes what Sacks calls hearer's maxims. Hearer's maxims do not concern us here so they will not be discussed.

Learning about Membership Categorization Devices and Category-bound Activities

Learning about the salient membership categories, the category-bound activities associated with these categories and how these activities are to be evaluated takes place as a result of the child's interaction with the environment. No doubt there are several mechanisms through which the child learns such information which are prerequisite for the production and interpretation of utterances occurring in the course of conversational interaction. In my opinion, the types of sequences which were discussed in the results portion of this paper constitute one such mechanism by which the child learns about social categories. It is through conversational interactions with the adult (and older children) that the child learns to participate in conversational exchanges. This point has been discussed elsewhere (for example, see Halliday, references above) with primary regard given to the proper formation of the structural aspects of conversation, i.e., conversational turns, opening (primary greetings), closings, etc. But, in fact, this analysis can be extended to the content (at least some of it) as well. An overwhelming amount of emphasis has been placed on the child's learning of the formal (structural) aspects of conversation--the positioning of turns in a sequence, etc.--with little consideration for how the child learns what the relevant categories are and what there is to say about these categories.

The adult utterances seem to call attention to those persons, objects, actions, and events that are most salient socially in the environment. There are a multitude of things in the visual world of the child. The child no doubt notices some because of their inherent properties, e.g., their movements or bright color; others are specifically brought to the child's attention through the adult's verbal and nonverbal references to them. There were many more references to persons during the adult-child interactions than there were to objects. The ratio was approximately 3 to 1. Nonperson animate items, e.g., animals, were in between. The generic person labels are the terms which appear in the two devices that would serve to be most important to a child in the second year of life--"family" and "stage of life." The latter is especially salient since at this point the child is moving out of being a baby into being a child, i.e., a boy or a girl.

More interesting, however, is the juxtaposition of the member category with category-bound activities. Once the child knows what term can best serve as an interesting and attention-holding topic of conversation, the child must know what to say about the item. The elaborated sequences produced by the adult, as illustrated in the results section above, contain the information that the child needs to build the same system of rules for relating activities to their appropriate categories as possessed by the adult. The results of analyzing the adult-child sequences suggest that, in fact, it is the norms of "stereotypic" activities that appear repeatedly in the adult productions. It is noteworthy that the theoretical apparatus developed by Sacks (1972b) was based on a story told by a child two years and nine months old. The story was: "The baby cried. The mommy picked it up. She went to sleep." The story contains one instance of the terms studied, i.e., baby and two instances of activities often associated with this term--crying and sleeping. Also, although this study did not investigate the adult usage patterns for mommy or daddy, it should be noted that nurturant activities (i.e., hugging) were noted in the caretakers conversational turns as activities bound to the term girl, a person who, like mommy, is female. The fact that this young child was able to produce a three sentence story such as that quoted above illustrates what Sacks calls "the fine power of a culture" which "does not, so to speak, fill brains in roughly the same way, it [culture] fills them so that they are alike in fine detail" (1972b, p. 332, the underlining is mine). A major point of this paper is that people's minds are filled alike in fine detail very early in life and a major mechanism through which this is achieved is by presentation of material in the utterances of adults as they interact conversationally with the child.

Learning about Coherence in Discourse

It should be clear by now that if one accepts the theoretical framework proposed by Sacks and the proposition that adult speech directed to the child plays a significant role in the learning of social categories and category-bound activities, then it follows that learning to identify "possible descriptions," i.e., well-formed discourse, has its source at least partly in the types of elaborated sequences observed in this study. The viewer's maxims suggested by Sacks are operative in the story told by the child (cited above) and it is these viewer's maxims that reinforce and combine with the content of the adult utterances in adult-child conversations to provide the child knowledge about orderliness necessary to interpret and produce discourse that is coherent.

Sex Differences and Adult Usage

One interesting aspect of the data which warrants some further discussion is the marked absence of elaborated sequences for the term boy in adult-child discourses where the child involved is female. Admittedly, the sample is relatively small and thus this result may be biased by the particular utterances that happened to arise in these materials. However, if upheld by further investigations this point is of some interest. The data would suggest that (at least for female children) terms which can be applied to the child being spoken to, in this case girl, is in fact applied in elaborated sequences. The rule seems to be: first learn what you are and what activities are appropriate to what you are. This contrasts with another possible rule which could apply, e.g., learn what you are not. If the latter rule were the case, we would expect the elaborated sequences to be associated with the cross-sex term, i.e., boy, and, also perhaps a large number of contrastive elaborated sequences containing both terms--boy and girl. Furthermore, it seems as though it is the characteristics that form the core of the sex role stereotype that appear in such elaborated sequences. This suggests that the rule be modified to read: learn what society expects you to be and what activities others expect of someone to whom the term refers. More evidence can confirm or disconfirm this proposal. However, popular folk sayings passed on from one generation to another, such as the chant known by practically every three year old nursery school child (at least in the Midwest) "The teachers have the brains, the boys have the muscles and the girls have the sexy legs" reinforce this point.

The question arises as to whether a study of adult-child conversational interactions which involve male children will show a similar pattern, i.e., will the same-sex term (boy) appear most frequently in elaborated sequences? The answer to this question is not immediately obvious. Studies by Meredith

(1975) indicate that boys take on female behavior patterns initially and only later (at 4 or 5 years of age) reject these patterns for the male patterns. This suggests that perhaps a different pattern of adult language input would be operative for male children at different ages. Further, the study of speech produced by male adults may reveal an even more complicated pattern. In any event, only further investigations along these lines can provide the answers.

BIBLIOGRAPHY

Brown, R. and A. Gilman. (1960) The pronouns of power and solidarity. In T. A. Sebeak (ed.), Style in Language, New York: M.I.T. Press

Cicourel, A. (1968) The Social Organization of Juvenile Justice, New York: Wiley.

Clarke-Stewart, K. A. (1973) Interactions between mothers and their young children: Characteristics and consequences. Monographs of the Society for Research in Child Development, 38(6-7), Serial no. 53.

Cross, T. (1977) Mother's speech adjustment: The contribution of selected child listener variables. In C. Snow and C. Ferguson (eds.), Talking to Children, Cambridge: Cambridge University Press.

Elkind, D. (1962) Children's conceptions of brother and sister: Piaget replication study V. Journal of Genetic Psychology, 100, 129-136.

Ferguson, C. (1964) Baby talk in six languages. American Anthropologist, 17, 1-14.

Garfinkel, H. (1967) Studies in Ethnomethodology, New York: Prentice-Hall.

Garnica, O. K. (1977a) Some prosodic and paralinguistic features of speech directed to young children. In C. Snow and C. Ferguson (eds.), Talking to Children, Cambridge: Cambridge University Press.

Garnica, O. K. (1977b) Nonverbal concomitants to language input to children. In C. Snow and N. Waterson (eds.), Development of Communication: Social and Pragmatic Factors in Language Acquisition, New York: Wiley and Sons.

Goffman, E. (1963) Behavior in Public Places, New York: Free Press.

Goffman, E. (1967) Interaction Ritual: Essays in Face-to-Face Behavior, New York: Doubleday Anchor.

Halliday, M. A. K. (1973) Explorations in the Function of Language, London: Arnold.

Halliday, M. A. K. (1975) Learning how to mean. In E. H. Lenneberg and E. Lenneberg (eds.), Foundations of Language Development, New York: Academic Press.

Haviland, S. and H. Clark. (1974) What's new? Acquiring new information as a process in comprehension. Journal of Verbal Learning and Verbal Behavior, 13, 512-521.

Maratsos, M. (1976) The Use of Definite and Indefinite References in Young Children, Cambridge: Cambridge University Press.

Meredith, A. (1975) The development of sex-specific speech patterns in young children. Anthropological Linguistics, 17(9), 421-433.

Nelson, K. (1973) Structure and strategy in learning to talk. Monographs of the Society for Research in Child Development, 38, Serial no. 149.

Romney, A. and R. D'Andrade. (1964) Cognitive aspects of English kin terms. American Anthropologist, 66, No. 3, part 2.

Sacks, H. (1972a) An initial investigation of the usability of conversational material for doing sociology. In D. Sudnow (ed.), Studies in Social Interaction, New York: Free Press.

Sacks, H. (1972b) On the analysability of stories by children. In J. Gumperz and D. Hymes (eds.), Directions in Sociolinguistics, New York: Holt, Rinehart and Winston.

Shatz, M. and R. Gelman. (1973) The development of communication skills: Modifications in the speech of young children as a function of listeners. Monographs of the Society of Research in Child Development, 38, Serial no. 152.

Snow, C. (1972) Mothers' speech to children learning language. Child Development, 43, 549-565.

Snow, C. (1977) Mothers' speech research: From input to interaction. In C. Snow and C. Ferguson (eds.), Talking to Children, Cambridge: Cambridge University Press.

Snow, C. and C. Ferguson (eds.). Talking to Children, Cambridge: Cambridge University Press.

*Sex Differences in the Language of Children and Parents**

JEAN BERKO GLEASON
Boston University

If sex differences exist in language, whether in the distribution of abilities or in different kinds of linguistic performance, it is clear that they stem at least in part from environmental or social factors. No one would argue, for instance, that men use more direct imperative constructions than women because of innate differences between the sexes; many sex differences arise out of differing sex role expectations. Children growing up must learn not only to act like girls and boys, women and men, but to talk like them as well. Some sex differences are thus sociolinguistic in nature. It is also possible that there are some innate differences between the sexes in respect to both temperament and to the neuroanatomical structures associated with language. These inborn differences could affect language development directly, or they could affect the way in which the infant interacts with the adults in her or his environment and thus help to shape the social factors that in turn reflect back upon the infant. An analogy can be drawn from a different area of infant development, atypicality, or more specifically, infantile autism, a serious condition that is sometimes blamed on mothers. Some mothers of autistic children have been observed to be less warm and loving with their offspring than the mothers of normal children. Yet it now appears unlikely that it is lack of warmth itself that causes autism; in fact, the autism may cause the lack of warmth. Some babies are born with atypical responses, presumably rooted in neurological irregularities: they avoid making eye contact with adults and, from the earliest days, hold themselves stiff when they are picked up, rather than molding to the body of the adult, as most ordinary, lovable, "cuddly" babies do. Since such infants are singularly unrewarding to pick up, and may dislike being held, a circular pattern can be set in motion: the child is unresponsive, and so the parent pays less attention to it than to an infant that is able to reward and sustain adult caregiving behaviors. The infant-caretaker interaction degenerates, and eventually the child is diagnosed as disturbed, but it is not possible to pinpoint the cause of the disturbance, since there are both constitutional and environmental factors involved, each affecting and fused with the others.

A similar situation may arise with language disturbance or delay. We now know that the quality of the linguistic input a child receives is an important factor in language acquisition; parental language has many of the features of a teaching language which at all levels, phonological, morphological and syntactic, helps the child to arrive at the rules. It must also be added that parental language changes over time in response to both parents' expectations and to feedback from the child. At some point, a parent decides it

*This research was supported in part by Grant No. BNS 75-21909 A01 from the National Science Foundation.

is no longer appropriate, for instance, to refer to himself as Daddy, and assumes that it is time to say I. In the case of language delay, as in Downs' Syndrome, something goes awry with this process. The cues from the child are inadequate to elicit a typically rich linguistic corpus from the parent. Downs' syndrome children have an inherent disability that contributes to their delay in language acquisition, and, at the same time, receive less input from their parents than normal children, and are thus doubly disadvantaged. The interactive nature of language development, with children affecting parents and parents affecting children, becomes increasingly apparent.

The early evidence for sex differences in language development rests on both performance and neurological data. There have been a number of reviews of the literature on sex differences in language development, notably those of McCarthy (1954), Terman and Tyler (1966), Maccoby and Jacklin (1974), and Thorne and Henley (1975). In their exhaustive review of thousands of psychological studies in which sex of the subject was a variable, Maccoby and Jacklin concluded that there are only four areas in which sex differences have consistently been found: males appear to be more aggressive than females, to excel in visual-spatial ability, and to excel in mathematics; females excel in verbal ability. The general findings of many studies indicate that girls begin to talk earlier than boys, that they begin to use sentences earlier, and that they are also advanced in terms of various other measures of articulation and fluency. Maccoby and Jacklin suggest that the clear advantage in favor of girls tends to dissipate after the early school years, while others have contended that females continue to have greater facility than males in such things as spelling, essay writing, and the learning of foreign languages; at the same time, speech disturbances like stuttering and dyslexia are more common among males of all ages (Garai and Scheinfeld, 1968).

While there might be slightly different patterns of development for males and females in language development as well as in mathematical and visual-spatial ability, it must be emphasized that the performance curves for both sexes are very similar, and either sex has many individuals who display the whole range of human potential. This is not so clearly the case when we consider aggression; not only is there strong cross-cultural evidence for substantial differences between the sexes in the amount of physical aggression displayed at all ages, but it is also easier to point to possible biological or hormonal factors that might account at least in part for such sexually dimorphic behavior. Money and Erhardt (1972) point out, for instance, that males and females probably have somewhat different brain structures because they have a different prenatal hormonal environment: ". . . the prenatal hormonal environment does exercise, during a few critical days of brain development, a determining influence on neutral pathways that will subsequently mediate sexually dimorphic behavior." (p. 9) A number of studies cited by Maccoby and Jacklin (1974) have shown a link between hormones and aggression, both in humans and in subhuman primates. Whether the prenatal hormonal environment might also exert an influence on parts of the brain associated with intellectual activity is a fascinating question that remains unanswered. No such postulation is needed to account for sex differences in language, since there are observable environmental variables that can be evoked to explain the differences, but the possibility that male and female brains are organized differently remains.

A number of observations on sex differences in language development were made in the 1930's and 1940's by McCarthy (1954) and her colleagues. McCarthy had studied the speech of nursery school children between the ages of 1:6 and

4:6 and had concluded that girls produced speech that was generally easie[r] to understand, more complex and more grammatical than the speech of boys. It is interesting to note that whether or not sex differences are found dep[ends] very much upon the epoch in which the studies are conducted: in the 1930's and 1940's, when the dominant mode of study was through enumeration (number of words per sentence, number of grammatical errors, mispronunciations, etc.) girls were frequently found to excel. In the 1950's and 1960's, where the search was for evidence of the internalization of generative language systems, sex differences typically were not found. Now, in the 1970's, when conversational, interactional, and stylistic variables are topics of study, sex differences once again emerge.

McCarthy's evidence indicates that boys perform less well on language tasks than girls, but it does not show why this might be so. In discussing her findings, McCarthy herself (1953) felt that environmental differences rather than genetic ones were responsible. She claimed that girls had an easier task because they could match their voices to their mothers' more easily than boys could match their voices to their fathers', that boys were more likely to be rejected as infants than girls, and to develop language problems because of this rejection, and that because of sex role expectations boys get less time to learn language, since their parents are more likely to send them outside to play and to give them toys that are not easy to talk about.

Some of this argument appears a bit thin. McCarthy assumed that girls were less likely to be rejected because there was more demand to adopt them, but it would be difficult to show that girls are actually the preferred children in our own, or any other, society. The other arguments are equally weak. But we do know that boys and girls are treated differently, and it is easy to assume that the language differences we see are the result of the different treatment. One could, however, make an argument that is just the opposite: that there are innate differences between the sexes in respect to language development, and that the reason there are *so few* observable differences between the abilities of boys and girls by the time they get out of school is because of different treatment. The bias that we see in school books, with a heavy emphasis on males and their importance, along with the general trivializing of females, probably has a negative effect on girls' motivation and self confidence and a positive effect on boys. One could argue further that school programs, like "reading readiness," or the special reading classes that exist in most schools, are designed primarily to close the gap between girls and boys, who are the primary beneficiaries of such programs. What we may have, in effect, is a kind of compensatory education that has been remarkably successful. Sex role expectations for both boys and girls call for basic skills in literacy and self expression, and if some individuals have difficulty in attaining this proficiency the educational world is geared toward providing special help which, in the end, minimizes what might otherwise be a more observable manifestation of inherent sex differences.

Unfortunately, there are no comparable mathematics readiness classes or programs to enhance the acquisition of spatial visualization that might help girls catch up with boys. And, in fact, sex role expectations for girls are that they will not perform well in these areas. While the image of a male who moves his lips when he reads or cannot write a simple letter is not acceptable, the image of a female who cannot add up her checkbook or follow a map is rather stereotypic. With mathematical and spatial abilities, the sex role expectation that girls will not do well enhances what might be inherent sex differences to begin with, and the gap between males and females becomes demonstrably wider with age.

The evidence for inborn differences is somewhat equivocal, but worth considering. One possibility is that constitutional factors contribute to different patterns of parent-child interaction in early infancy. Male infants, on the whole, according to some observers (Moss, 1967) are more irritable than female infants, and this might explain at least in part another consistently observed sex difference, namely that throughout the first two years of life, girl infants are looked at and spoken to by their mothers more frequently than are boy infants (Lewis, 1972). It is easier to talk to an attentive child than to one who is fussing and crying. Girls may therefore receive more and higher quality linguistic input at an earlier age than boys, and this extra input may lead to earlier and more highly motivated language development on the part of girls; while mothers tend to interact more physically with their infant sons, they tend to speak more to their infant daughters, and this interpersonal style may have far reaching effects on the development of girls' language and their ways of dealing with others in their world. Thus, innate constitutional factors, not originally related to language, could exert some influence on language development.

Another frequently offered explanation for differences is that girls mature at a rapider rate than boys. There appears to be some physiological evidence for this general finding, but it is not clear how it applies to cognitive functioning, or to what extent it is a sufficient explanation for what is observed. If maturational differences explain girls' linguistic superiority, perhaps they should also be called upon to explain boys' mathematical superiority. If male and female brains mature at different rates and in different ways, then they are very different indeed. The maturational argument also leads to some conclusions that simply do not follow. Earlier maturation would be a good explanation for why girls begin to speak earlier, but if girls' verbal superiority were based purely on maturational factors, we would expect them to lose their advantage once they had matured. In fact, since language acquisition is so much easier for children who have not yet reached puberty than for adolescents, and since girls on the whole reach puberty before boys, we might expect that around the age of 12 boys would become much better second language learners. This simply does not happen; girls continue to do well as foreign language students even at a time when their earlier maturation might be expected to work to their disadvantage.

Two other kinds of evidence suggest the possibility of genetic differences between males and females: the differential incidence of language disabilities, and neuroanatomical evidence obtained by dissecting the brains of males and females at post mortem and examining and comparing homologous structures.

First, all language-related disabilities, like stuttering, dyslexia, and developmental aphasia, are much more frequently found in the male than the female population. (Even strephosymbolia, the inability to learn foreign languages, a disability that excuses Harvard students from the foreign language requirement, has proven quite uncontagious--the female students at Radcliffe rarely catch it.) For some of these language disabilities the ratio of male: female is as high as 8:1. It is difficult to postulate a consistent environmental cause of these sex differences in language disability, but, of course, this has been done, particularly in the case of stuttering, where environmentalist theories abound; it is claimed, for instance, that males stutter because there is greater pressure on them to speak well, or because they have a poor relationship with their mothers. Some of the disabilities, however, are accompanied by soft neurological signs. Since males are more vulnerable to neurological insult of all types than females are, it is likely that many of the disabilities syndromes can be subsumed under more general categories of neurological impairment. There is also the possibility that language is more broadly represented in the female than in the male brain, and is hence more resistant to disturbance. Recent findings from aphasiological studies indicate that it requires a good deal more brain damage to produce aphasia in females than in males (McGlone, 1975). There are also many more male aphasics than female aphasics, but there are also many more male stroke victims. If, however, language is more resistant to dissolution in even damaged female brains, there exists the possibility that males may be more strongly lateralized for language, while females may have some language areas in both hemispheres. (Perhaps where their multiplication tables should be.)

It might be noted parenthetically that sex differences in the onset of lateralization for speech have been found. Kimura (1967), using a dichotic listening task, found that young girls show a right ear advantage for speech sounds earlier than boys. This indicates earlier left hemisphere specialization for language in girls. Earlier lateralization of language functions may, of course, be a result, rather than a cause of the differences; learning to speak earlier, for whatever reason (for instance, because one is spoken to more frequently) may lead to lateralization of speech functions, but, at any rate, a measurable difference between boys and girls has been demonstrated.

Finally, more recent brain studies may have shown actual morphological differences in the brains of male and female neonates. A number of neurologists have pointed out that the human brain is visibly asymmetrical; not only is the interhemispheric fissure angled from the left to the right as one looks down on the brain, there is also an area in the left temporal lobe that is larger than the homologous structure in the right temporal lobe. This area is called the planum temporale; this extra left hemisphere "bump" is believed to be an area that mediated incoming language, and the difference between the left and right sides of the adult brain had been shown in 1968 (Geschwind and Levitsky). Then, in 1973, Witelson and Pallie published a study in Brain called "Left hemisphere specialization for language in the newborn: neuroanatomical evidence of asymmetry." These authors found in measuring the plana of a group of very young infants who had died for various non-language-related reasons that the females had significantly larger left hemisphere structures than right, while the males of comparable age (1-19 days) had no significant difference between left and right hemispheres. In other words, newborn infants, whose brains have not had the opportunity to be affected by language experience, already have asymmetrical brains, with extra tissue in what will be the language area. This extra tissue is observable in females but not in males during the first three weeks after birth. The brains of male infants who were older than about a month also showed a larger left-sided planum.

The sample size in this study was very small--the sex difference data were obtained by comparing the brains of only 10 infants, 5 males and 5 females who were matched for age, but the possibility that male and female infants are born in different states of readiness to process language has been raised by this work.

All of these neurological data are very tantalizing, and should be entered into the complex set of variables that eventually will be called upon to explain the phenomena of language acquisition. While there may be actual differences in the neurological endowment of males and females, there are also environmental forces that have a powerful effect on the course of a child's development. One of the most pervasive of these forces is the set of sex role expectations parents and society at large bring to any interaction with boys and girls. In a recent study, for instance, researchers have shown that from the first day of a child's life parents have different attitudes toward girls and boys (Rubin, Provenzano and Luria, 1974). These researchers interviewed and presented a rating scale to parents of 30 neonates in a hospital setting, where the parents had not yet had an opportunity to interact with their babies. Although the 15 boy infants and 15 girl infants did not differ in their mean birthweight, their size, or their Apgar scores, parents, especially fathers, had quite different beliefs about the female and male infants; daughters, for instance, were more likely to be rated _little_, _pretty_, and _cute_. And fathers saw their sons as hardier, stronger and better coordinated and their daughters as weaker and more delicate, while mothers did not make such strong distinctions. Since parents have different expectations about their children from the day they are born, and probably earlier, it is easy to postulate that those different expectations will manifest themselves in differential language treatment.

Parents probably have beliefs about the language capabilities of their children as well. It is not known, for instance, if they believe that female infants understand them earlier or are more eager to talk than males. An ideal study might look for families with male and female twins and investigate the parents' beliefs and their ways of talking to each infant. Even in the absence of such data, it is clear that the sex of the child is an important determining factor in how it is regarded and treated, and it is inconceivable that this important distinction would not be underlined in the way the child is treated verbally. The mere knowledge of what sex the baby is, is enough to start parents off with particular sets of expectations and behaviors. What is not clear is to what extent parents readjust their expectations on the basis of their experience with their own child and to what extent they persist even in the face of contrary evidence--some parents might, for instance, continue to give sex-typed toys like dolls to their daughters who prefer other toys, while other parents might be more sensitive to the individual child rather than to stereotyped notions of what children should be like. Parents expect that their children will speak in ways that are appropriate to their sex role, and undoubtedly provide differential reinforcement to the children. At the same time, parents' speech is sex-typed as well, and children will eventually take on the speech characteristics of the same sexed parent through imitation or social learning.

There have been very few studies that have looked specifically at these kinds of processes. Our own studies have thus far shown some sex differences in speech directed at preschool children. The kinds of differences we have seen have been related both to the sex of the child and to the sex of the parent. Observations were made in a naturalistic setting in the subjects' homes and in a laboratory study. In general, speech addressed to both sexes by either parent had typical input features; that is, speech to the children was simplified and contained many short sentences and repetitions, was delivered at a slow rate, and was seriously limited in topic and scope. In some families, there were stylistic differences in the ways that boys were addressed. Even at the age of two or three, boys were more likely to be called by a variety of jocular names, like _Tiger_, _Buster_, _Monster_, or _Dingaling_. They were also more likely to be threatened; in one middle class family we observed, the father offered to "knock the block off" his 3 year old son. The differences in treatment of the sexes were much more pronounced when we looked at the fathers' speech. This is what one might have predicted after reading the Rubin, Provenzano and Luria (1974) study first: that it is fathers who are the primary agents for maintaining and enforcing sex role distinctions.

Another, more subtle kind of difference, lies in the relationship between the child's language and the parent's. In general, as children's language becomes more complex with increasing competence, parental speech to children also becomes more complex. This is a remarkable phenomenon, and one that has not yet been adequately explained: on what basis does the parent decide, at whatever level, to talk more quickly or in longer utterances? Presumably, on the basis of some sort of signals from the child, even though we may not be able to specify what those signals are. In an earlier study (Gleason, 1975), we found that mothers' utterances were more closely attuned to the children's than fathers' were. For instance, mothers' mean length of utterance more closely resembled the children's than fathers' did, and in a number of other ways mothers appeared to be more attuned to the child's linguistic state of development than fathers. Fathers also tended to be less likely to notice when their children did not understand them. This led to the speculation that another kind of sex difference in parents' language may be in sensitivity to other speakers and the ability to adjust one's speech to the needs of other speakers.

Since our present interest is in finding out the answers to some of these questions, particularly what it is that causes the parental input language to change over time, we decided that one way of going about this is to test parents directly for their knowledge about their own children. We wanted to know what parents know about their children's linguistic and cognitive state of development, as well as how familiar they were with their child's preferences for such things as particular foods or colors. Our initial hypothesis was that there may be differences between fathers and mothers in the kinds of knowledge they have about their children. These differences could arise out of basic differences in the language abilities of adult men and women, or they could result from the fact that women tend to spend more time with children and have greater opportunities to interact with them.

What has become clear from recent research is that language acquisition is infinitely more complex than we ever thought; and the question of sex differences in language is fraught with complexities as well. There may be inborn differences between the sexes in their biological endowment for acquiring language; and even if there are not, there are clear differences in environmental forces. The acquisition process involves an elaborate interaction between children and older speakers. Language development is optimized if parents speak at a level that is appropriate to the child's state of development, and this requires a kind of judgment on the part of parents; this ability to judge also appears to be sex related. While it is possible to find some sex differences by recording speech to children (in the use of particular lexical items, for instance) we may learn more about the relationship between language input and language acquisition by studying patterns of parental sensitivity to children. Finally, parents have different expectations for their children, which may lead them to shape the speech of the children, and they themselves speak in sex-typed ways that children may come to imitate.

When we find sex differences in the language of children and parents, it is important to acknowledge that they result not solely from environmental forces, like the pressures of sex role socialization, or from inborn differences, like different patterns of neuroanatomical development; rather, sex differences arise out of a complex interaction between children with particular endowments, and parents, with all of their expectations, special ways of speaking, and patterns of sensitivity.

BIBLIOGRAPHY

Garai, J. E. and Scheinfeld, A. (1968) Sex differences in mental and behavioral traits. Genetic Psychology Monographs, 77, 169-299.

Geschwind, N. and Levitsky, W. (1968) Human brain left-right asymmetries in temporal speech region. Science, 161, 186-187.

Gleason, J. B. (1975) Fathers and other strangers: Men's speech to young children. D. P. Dato (ed.) In Georgetown University Roundtable on Languages and Linguistics. Georgetown University Press, Washington, D.C., 289-297.

Gleason, J. B., Greif, E. B., Weintraub, S., and Fardella, J. (1977) Father doesn't know best: Parents awareness of their children's linguistic, cognitive, and affective development. Paper presented at the biennial meeting of the Society for Research in Child Development. New Orleans, La.

Kimura, D. (1967) Functional asymmetry of the brain in dichotic listening. Cortex, 3, 163-178.

Lewis, M. (1972) Parents and children: Sex-role development. School Review, 80, 229-240.

McCarthy, D. (1930) Language Development of the Preschool Child. Minneapolis: University of Minnesota Press.

McCarthy, D. (1953) Some possible explanations of sex differences in language development and disorders. Journal of Psychology, 35, 155-160.

McCarthy, D. (1954) Language development in children. In L. Carmichael (ed.), A Manual of Child Psychology, New York: Wiley.

McGlone, J. (1975) Sex differences in functional brain asymmetry. Paper presented at the 13th annual meeting of the Academy of Aphasia, Victoria, B.C.

Moss, H. (1969) Sex, age, and state as determinants of mother-infant interaction. Merrill-Palmer Quarterly, 13, 19-35.

Rubin, J. Z., Provensano, F. J. and Luria, Z. (1974) The eye of the beholder: parents' views on sex of newborns. American Journal of Orthopsychiatry, 44(4), 512-519.

Terman, L. and Tyler, L. (1966) Psychological sex differences. In L. Carmichael (ed.), A Manual of Child Psychology, New York: Wiley.

Thorne, B. and Henley, N. (eds). (1975) _Language and Sex: Differences and Dominance_, Rowley, Mass.: Newbury House.

What is an Instructional Context? An Exploratory Analysis of Conversational Shifts Across Time

JUDITH GREEN and CYNTHIA WALLAT
Kent State University

The study of teaching is ultimately the study of the development of social contexts of the classroom. Since teaching is primarily a communicative process, knowledge about the social contexts can be obtained through analysis of how people communicate, that is how people interact with and act upon the messages of others to achieve the social and instructional goals of the classroom. The identification of context is essential to understanding the rules for communication, and the nature of the communicative competence required for both teacher and students in the classroom.

Recent work on the nature of contexts (Erickson & Shultz, 1976; Cook-Gumperz and Gumperz, 1976) indicates that contexts are not predetermined entities but rather are created by and are a part of the unfolding conversations. Therefore, in order to understand the classroom as a social system, an understanding of the types of contexts that are created in classrooms and the demands communicatively within and across the contexts is necessary.

This paper presents an exploratory analysis of what is an instructional context and what are the rules for functioning communicatively within and across each context. To answer these questions, a linguistic ethnographic analysis of thirteen minutes of a videotape recording of a kindergarten classroom on the third day of school was undertaken. The discussion is divided into two parts. The first part presents a theoretical framework underlying the definition of context as developed and applied in this paper. The second presents a method of linguistic ethnography for capturing the evolving conversation as it evolves in time, for identifying the various contexts created as a part of these conversations, and for defining the social rules within and across these contexts.

THEORETICAL FRAMEWORKS FOR DEFINING CONTEXT

Context as a Theoretical Construct

Work to date concerning the concepts of context and tieing has received attention in the literature. Taken as a whole, past work in these areas has been invaluable for building a framework for answering the question What Is An Instructional Context?

In 1971 James Britton suggested that those concerned with analysis of the functions of an extended dialogue had received "salvation" in the notion of context (p. 245). Citing John Lyons' (1963) interpretation of context as an overall language function that dominates in a hierarchy of functions, Britton spoke of context as man's view of the world. Through this view of the world an individual creates "his true theatre of operations since all he does is done in the light of it; his hopes for the future depend upon its efficacy; and above all his sense of who he is and what it is worth for him to be alive in the world derive from it" (p. 246).

While Britton was concerned with the individual's established view of the world, Etzioni (1968) was more concerned with describing strategies that an individual uses in order to enact his view of the world. Etzioni defined the strategies of social action according to two major segments. The first segment is composed of symbolic processes such as the processing and synthesis of information, while the second segment results in the process of implementing a particular action. Etzioni referred to these two segments under the umbrella term contextuating orientation. Although like Britton, Etzioni was concerned with the individual's established view of the world he employed the term context less esoterically and in its active form contextuating. Following Britton, Etzioni also used the phrase hierarchial when referring to the cognitive aspect of context.

> It is fruitful to view societal knowledge as having a hierarchial structure which provides a contextuating orientation for bits (or items) of knowledge. The bits are more concrete, specific and cognitive than the context. A fact is a bit; a theory is a context. An attitude is a bit; a world view is a context. (p. 157)

The utility of Etzioni's theory of contextuating orientation to the question, What is an instructional context? becomes clearer when we put all of the features he used to define context together. First, contextuating is active i.e., the hierarchial relationship between the bits is open to change (p. 158). Second, contextuating or the individual's enactment of his view of the world "is neither metaphysical nor psychological but structural" (p. 14). This developmental view of context is useful for researchers concerned with processes and structures children may attend to in developing competence in the ability to communicate and enact a participant role in classroom groups. Before a child can make decisions concerning what is appropriate verbal and nonverbal behavior in a group he has to be able to read and interpret structural cues. Since the cues or bits are active and open to change, the child's task is to focus not only on words and phrases in social situations but also "focus upon how context is realized as part of the interaction" (Cook-Gumperz and Gumperz, 1976, p. 11).

Although the analysis of what is taken to be context is still an open question in the analysis of social interaction (Cook-Gumperz and Corsaro, 1976), child language studies have contributed a great deal in identifying specific features of what Etzioni referred to as concrete or specific cognitive and structural bits. The following list of features of context is representative of the cues identified to date that are useful in identifying instructional contexts.

kinesic shifts	-	body movement (cf. Kendon, 1970)
proxemic shifts	-	changes in interpersonal distance between speakers (cf. Erickson and Schultz, 1977)
postural shifts	-	changes in gaze direction and facial expression (cf. Scheflen, 1972)

prosodic shifts -	changes in voice tone and pitch (cf. Cook-Gumperz, 1977)
sequential shifts -	changes in relationship among different behavior from first, second, third (cf. Sacks, Jefferson, Schegloff, 1974; Argyle, 1975)
modality shifts -	shift is full battery of communicative signals that adults use to mark, for example, arrival and leave taking, e.g., movement, kinesic gesture, semantic routine (cf. Cook-Gumperz and Gumperz, 1976)
situational shifts -	within lessons shifts from less formal and instrumental activity to more formal and instrumental and back again (cf. Erickson and Schultz, 1977)
participant structure shifts -	within lessons differing rules of appropriateness for paying attention, getting the floor, maintaining topical relevance (cf. Erickson and Schultz, 1977; Phillips, 1972)
audience shifts -	class as a whole or one individual at a time (cf. Hymes, 1974)
temporal shifts -	referents to events in the past, present, or future (cf. Cook-Gumperz and Corsaro, 1976)
stylistic shifts -	message spoken with raised pitch and loud voice or a call to attention shifts to message still in a loud voice but slow rhythm and measured pace with dropped pitch or an announcement (cf. Cook-Gumperz and Gumperz, 1976)
register shifts -	shift from formal and careful Language Instruction Register such as baseless, e.g., We'll have to locate a container for that insect, to less formal Ugh, look at that bug - get rid of it. (cf. DeStefano, 1975)

The identification and interpretation of specific cognitive and structural cues such as the above as they may occur in social interaction is not the whole story in the child's task of identifying context and enacting the correct social rule.

> The interpretation of any utterance depends upon the negotiated understandings that have developed during the interaction, and on the situated character of that utterance such as its prosodic shape in relation to previous utterances and any semantic ties to previous utterances, to previous events, or to any factors of the environmental setting. (Cook-Gumperz and Corsaro, 1976, p. 7)

Cook-Gumperz and Gumperz give recognition to previous work identifying contextual features but their definition takes the researcher one step further in their suggestion that "a notion of context can be developed which can be shown to be more than a source of background" (p. 4). That notion should address two premises:

(a) context as socially dynamic
"What we are stressing is that people including children talk to achieve certain social goals or projects . . . and that these goals constitute an interpretive input to the semantic field" (p. 5).
(b) context as part of the total message
"Therefore in order to study how context enters into speakers and listeners judgment and performances in social situations we have to focus upon how context is realized as part of the interaction" (p. 11).

Researchers have demonstrated that the concept of context and tieing can be approached from different points of view. While Etzioni was concerned with macro contextuating orientation of our society, such as American attitudes towards military aggressive nations in the 40's and 50's, his explanation of how bits are related to the maintenance of an overall context in a social group is useful for understanding the answer to What Is An Instructional Context? Etzioni argues that under "most circumstances the relationship between the bits of knowledge and the context will be loose; that is bits can be changed at relatively low cost as long as the new ones fit the existing context" (p. 158). In the case of establishing a context for classroom group discussion, for example, once the contextuating orientation has been established in that children have internalized the bits over time and now know that this is a group then some bits such as reminders to talk one at a time may not have to be concretely referred to all of the time. Etzioni's argument is that once a context orientation has been established individuals will use different examples from their experience to reinforce that context. Even if no new bits of information are supplied "the orientation may still be maintained on normative grounds alone" (p. 158). Although Etzioni does not describe exactly how many or what type of specific concrete bits must be structured to maintain a normative rule in a social group, he does suggest that without reinforcement the contextuating orientation would be strained and "potentially open to rapid . . . transformation" (p. 158). The maintenance of social rules is therefore not merely an arithmetic sum, "but are in part the result of processes the social unit brings to bear on its members" (p. 52).

Erickson and Schultz (1977) have described a theoretical and procedural approach to capture what Etzioni described as the result of processes a social unit brings to bear on its members. In answering the question When is a context? Erickson and Schultz have outlined the need for a multi-dimension description of social interaction. In their definition of context as interactionally constituted environments that can change from moment to moment, the authors suggest that contexts are constituted by what people are doing and where and when they are doing it. Citing McDermott's (1976) phrase that people in interaction become environments for each other, Erickson and Schultz suggest that a researcher interested in capturing the instructional context will have to have a way of recapturing the entire lesson. The need for going back again and again to the video tapes of a lesson is apparent in the following.

> Despite the redundancy of cues it usually is not possible to determine . . . an exact moment when the definition of situation has changed. It is only after the cues for a change in context have occurred that it is possible to determine that something has indeed changed. Thus, it would seem that it is by retrospective evaluation that (researchers can) determine that the context has changed. (p. 6)

In this section we presented the broad theoretical framework for the definition and identification of context. The following sections of the paper focus on context applied to instruction, the methodology used to capture and define what is an instructional context, and an exploratory analysis of the social rules within and across the context identified.

Context as a Theoretical Construct Applied to Instruction

The need for retrospective evaluation of teacher/child interaction in educational settings has been recognized by researchers concerned with the study of teaching and teacher effectiveness. Whereas researchers such as Britton and Etzioni have been concerned with the concept of context in relation to processes in the wider society, Cook-Gumperz and Gumperz (1976) have drawn our attention to this process in the classroom. The selection of the classroom as a research focus for sociolinguistic analysis is a source of both potentialities and problems: potentialities because ultimately the classroom dialogue is the educational process (Stubbs, 1976); problems because we cannot generalize findings from free conversation to instructional conversation (Green, 1977) nor can we generalize from classroom conversations to rules for free conversations (Kendon, 1976).

The approach taken in this paper is that recent work on concepts of sociolinguistics provides a sound basis for exploratory analysis of instructional contexts if one keeps in mind the pedagogical constraints on language in the classroom. In other words, sociolinguistic theory can be related to actual data on classroom language. Furthermore, the usefulness of the concepts and methodology can be related to the wider issues of social skill development and the study of teacher style in the natural setting of the classroom.

The following premises from the marriage of sociolinguistic and pedagogical concepts form the basis for the systematic description of instructional conversation:

(1) Conversations are created by people acting on and working with the messages from others;
(2) the roles for teacher and student are specified;
(3) the instructional conversation is goal directed;
(4) the teacher determines the structure and direction of the conversation;
(5) the structure of the conversation may be tied to the students' interactions, the teacher's messages or the materials or topic central to the lesson;
(6) the structure of the conversation includes nonverbal and coverbal aspects of the instructional chain;
(7) a description of the instructional conversation must be obtained on a message by message basis;
(8) messages are context bound, therefore, interpretation of any part of the instructional conversation requires the consideration of the immediate context in which the aspect under consideration occurred;
(9) the cues to message realization, message boundary, and message ties (kinesics, proxemic, postural, prosodic, sequential, modality, situational, participant structure, audience, temporal, stylistic, register) used by participants are available to an observer;

(10) pedagogical actions on the part of student and teacher overlap conversational strategies, i.e., strategies such as focusing, confirming, and clarifying are at the same time pedagogical and conversational in nature;
(11) relationships or ties exist between some messages in an instructional conversation but not between all messages;
(12) consideration of thematic cohesion on a variety of levels provides the basis for the identification of tied message units of varying length and type;
(13) the instructional conversation is composed of phases. A lesson has different parts each of which is tied on a broad level to previous phases.

The premises of the system outlined above permits analysis of instructional patterns as well as demonstrate that a context cannot be created a priori in the classroom. Context is created in the process of teaching and must be defined in retrospect as Cook-Gumperz and Gumperz have demonstrated.

The remainder of this paper will present a two-step analysis procedure used to identify instructional context. The first step involves a systematic means of describing on a message by message basis the evolution of the instructional conversation. Step two is the identification of context within and across instructional conversation based on the message by message description obtained in step one.

A Sociolinguistic Description of Instructional Conversations

Definition of features used in coding. The methodology used to describe the units and structure of the instructional conversation is based on a retrospective analysis of each message as it unfolds. Each message is described structurally in terms of its source; its form, the strategy or strategies present; the level of comprehension required; the person or activity to which it is tied; and how it is resolved conversationally. The boundary of a message is defined post hoc by consideration of the messages that follow the given message and the contextualization and semantic cues that co-occur with the form of the message. The features identified are: message units, source of message unit, form of message, strategy (purpose of message unit), level of message unit, ties, interaction units, and instructional sequence unit. These are defined as follow.

Message units. A message unit (MU) is the minimum unit coded in this system. An MU is a minimal unit of conversational meaning on the part of the speaker. Each MU is defined in terms of its source, form, purpose, level of comprehension, and its tie. A message unit is comparable to a free morpheme in structural linguistic terms. The boundary of an MU is linguistically marked by contextualization cues.

The source. The source identifies the speaker -- the teacher or the student. The person to whom the message is directed is also recorded whenever possible. In the MDIAS the source of a message unit is coded by recording the appropriate number code -- 2 for teacher and 3 for student -- in the appropriate column of the coding form for the MU under consideration.

The form. Two general forms are identified--the question and the response. Each is linguistically marked. The manner of describing message units is based on the assumption that all messages in an instructional conversation which are not questions are responses to either the question, another participant, or the internal purpose of the speaker. However, not all responses are of the same type; therefore, three categories of response types have been identified:

Type A Response +: This category encompasses all responses that could be expected and/or are predictable given the previous contiguous behavior. An expected or predictable response refers to those responses that meet the social, cultural, psychological, and semantic aspects of the situation. For example, if a teacher asks the question, "How much is one plus three?" a predictable or expected response would be a number. In contrast, an unpredictable response to this question would be "boys," or "bananas."

Type B Response 0: This category encompasses nonpredicted responses. Three types of unpredicted responses have been identified:

(1) a spontaneous message by a student
(2) a response by a student other than the one designated in the previous contiguous behavior
(3) an incorrect response by a student.

Type C Response -: This category encompasses student nonresponses and comments such as "I don't know," and "um."

The strategies. This feature refers to the purpose of the message unit. The categories that compose this aspect of message structure were designed to be identified from linguistic cues rather than from inference.

Focusing: A message is defined as focusing if used to initiate the discussion or an aspect of the discussion. Focusing is marked by a shift in content of what is being discussed. It can be a question or response strategy. Although focusing behavior could also be coded as confirming, raising, etc., it is coded as focusing because of the overriding function it performs, the shift of focus.

Ignoring: This strategy is solely a response strategy. If a participant asks a question or makes a response that requires another response and does not receive one, ignoring is occurring. This message type is marked nonverbally.

Confirming +: This feature refers to verbal and nonverbal acceptance of a preceding response. It is also used to code the answer to a yes-no question. Confirming + may take the form of a question or a response.

Confirming -: This strategy refers to nonacceptance of the previous contiguous response or to an unpredicted no in response to a request for confirmation. Confirming - may take the form of a question or a response.

Continuance: A nonverbal or verbal message which can provide a cue to the speaker that the listener is following the speaker's message and the listener may continue his turn.

Extending: This strategy refers to messages aimed at providing additional information about a topic. This information can be spontaneously added, or it may be elicited, therefore extending may take the form of a question or a response.

Raising: This strategy refers to a message that is aimed at raising the level of the discussion. This message is required to be tied to the preceding one. This message cannot be an initiatory one. This strategy takes the form of a question.

Clarifying: This strategy refers to messages meant to bring about explanations or redefinitions of a preceding behavior. This strategy may take the form of a question to a response.

Editing: This strategy encompasses shifts or changes in content, form, or strategy after the original message began. This strategy also encompasses false starts.

Controlling: This strategy refers to messages concerning the control of the interaction and/or the behavior of the participants. This strategy takes both a question and a response form.

Refocusing: This strategy encompasses refocusing on a previous question or response.

Restating: This strategy refers to repeating all or part of the previous message of the original speaker either by the original speaker or by another individual in the group.

The levels. An interaction or message unit can be classified according to the level of understanding required of the listener.

Factual: Factual level comprehension is the lowest level of comprehension. It refers to information that was stated in the story or the discussion. Factual comprehension requires recall of facts from memory.

Interpretive: Interpretive level comprehension requires that information be inferred. This level requires that the participant provide information not specifically stated in the lesson.

Applicative: Applicative level comprehension requires that the information obtained during the lesson be used in new ways or in new situations. This is the highest level of comprehension.

The ties. This feature of message unit structure refers to the fact that a message which occurs in a lesson is related to or builds on other behaviors. For the lesson under analysis in this study, three sources of ties have been identified: the teacher, the student, and the story.

Teacher: A message is said to be tied to a teacher if the purpose of the message is a teaching focus. If a message is not built on a student or the teaching aide directly, it is said to be built on the teacher's own purpose, internal or external.

Student: A behavior is said to be tied to a student if its purpose is to provide feedback to the student or to extend the student's response, or use the response as the basis of the next response.

Story (Material): A message is said to be tied to the text or material if it is observed to be the direct trigger for a message unit.

Interaction units.

Resolved Interaction Units: Multiple Units. A resolved interaction unit is defined as a series of messages that are related by topic and by intent. A conversational action on the part of a participant achieves its general purpose.

Resolved Interaction Unit: Single Unit. An interaction unit may be composed of a single message unit if the message unit is a completed message that requires no response.

Unresolved Interaction Units. Four types of unresolved interaction units can occur in an instructional conversation:

Type I Non-completed or interrupted units. If a behavior is begun and is not completed, it is coded as a message and the structure of the unit is coded for as many features as possible. For example, the teacher begins to ask, "WHO CAN . . ." and a student interrupts with a question. This unit has been interrupted, but the source and the form can be coded. The identification of the other features is not possible from this fragment; therefore the message unit and the interaction unit are unresolved. If all features of a message unit cannot be determined, then the message unit is said to be unresolved.

Type II No response is given. If a participant initiates a message that requires a response but receives none, the interaction unit is unresolved or open. For example, a teacher asks, "WHO IS THIS?" and receives silence. The teacher then asks the question in another way: "WHAT ANIMAL DO YOU THINK THIS IS?" The interaction unit begun by the first question is unresolved since the teacher does not receive the expected response and asks another question or shifts direction.

Type III Expected response not achieved. The student in this type of unresolved interaction unit asks a question which is postponed. The teacher overtly ignores this question. For example, a student asks, "Why did the tiger do that?" and the teacher responds with, "WE'LL COME BACK TO THAT LATER." The expected response was not given, and the student, from a pedagogical point, does not receive closure.

Type IV Overt ignoring. An unresolved unit can occur if the teacher or student who is to respond to an initiation overtly, as indicated by a direct nonverbal gesture, indicates lack of cooperation. For example, if the teacher asks a question of student B and student B turns away from the teacher, this unit is said to be unresolved from a pedagogical point of view.

Instructional sequence unit. An instructional sequence unit is composed of a series of tied interaction units (IU). The instructional sequence unit is the equivalent of an instructional episode. An instructional episode is defined in terms of content. All interaction units which focus on the same aspect of the total conversation belong to a single instructional unit. The ties for the instructional sequence unit are ties that exist across units semantically. The end of an episode is marked by a shift in the general content within the lesson. Contextualization cues do not play a central role in the identification of instructional sequence units. The instructional sequence unit corresponds to a step the teacher takes in building the structure of the lesson. An instructional sequence unit (ISU) is composed of smaller units, the interaction units, which focus on a single sub-content of the lesson. Like message units and interaction units, the instructional sequence unit is determined only in retrospect. It is not possible to determine in advance whether or not an interaction unit will be part of the preceding instructional unit or will form a new unit.

The Analysis of Classroom Instructional Sequence Units

To illustrate how these features can be used to identify the various contexts created as part of the conversations that occur in classrooms and to show how this leads to the definition of the social rules within and across these contexts, we chose for analysis 13 minutes of classroom interaction videotaped in a kindergarten on the third day of school during the fall at the Kent State University Laboratory Elementary School. A complete transcript of this videotape appears in Appendix A.

First, we illustrate the system of description outlined in the previous section by considering in detail lines 001 through 009 from the transcript. The coding of this first instructional sequence (and the second instructional sequence, i.e., transcript lines 011 through 015) is illustrated in Appendix B.

Transcript line 001, i.e.,

001 Teacher: WELCOME, WELCOME, WELCOME HERE TODAY (sung)

is described as a focusing response on the part of the teacher at a factual level tied to the lesson, the song of welcome, that is not conversationally or pedagogically complete. The basis for the determination of this message as not conversationally complete resulted from the consideration of the phrasing of the line of the song. There is a pull or tie between this message and the next line

002 Teacher: WELCOME, WELCOME MEANS HELLO PLEASE STAY.

This message unit is described on Transcript line 002 in Figure 1 as a second focusing response by the teacher at a factual level tied to the lesson, the song.

However, conversations are composed of more than simple strings of unrelated messages. Conversational units greater than the individual message can be reliably described through observation of the ties or relationships between and across the message units (Green, 1977). Simultaneous consideration of the semantic, pedagogical and contextual ties between and across units permits identification of four types of hierarchical units in instructional conversations which we will discuss in turn: (1) sequences of tied message units called Interaction Units, (2) sequences of thematically tied Interaction Units called Instructional Sequence Units, (3) sequences of thematically tied Instructional Sequence Units to form Phase Units, (4) sequences of tied Phase Units to form a lesson. As with message unit determination, the determination of the boundary of each of these hierarchical units is possible only through retrospective analysis of observable cues, e.g., prosodic shape, semantic intent, proxemic shift, etc. The key to the descriptive analysis is the observation of the actions and messages of the participants as they act upon and work with the utterances of others (Gumperz, 1976).

To continue with the analysis, we consider two of the four types of hierarchical units: Interaction Units and Instructional Sequence Units. Transcript lines 001 and 002, presented previously, are examples of a non-resolved or interrupted Interaction Unit. These two lines, the lines of a song, are thematically and structurally tied but are conversationally incomplete. Lines 003 and 004 form a completed Interaction Unit:

003 Rogan: (enters for first time)
004 Teacher: ROGAN, WELCOME

This unit although complete by itself acts as a potentially divergent unit for previous unit, the song. The teacher uses this break to welcome a new child who entered late and to absorb him into the group and lesson. The focus returns to the group in line 005:

005 Teacher: WELCOME, WELCOME EVERYONE

The Interaction Unit formed by lines 003 and 004 is tied thematically to the previous one and to the second unresolved unit on line 005. The instructional sequence is still not complete, the end of verse one of the song has not been reached. The sequence continues with a potentially divergent unit, lines 006 to 008:

006 James: (inaudible sounds plus nonverbal actions)
007 Teacher: WE'RE SINGING NOW. (Teacher points to James)
008 James: (stops vying for teacher attention and refocuses)

Relationships exist thematically between each message in this unit. This Interaction Unit, while a part of the instructional sequence of the lesson, is not directly tied to the lesson, the song. It forms a potentially divergent behavior unit within the lesson. However, a semantic analysis shows that the teacher uses this unit to provide a refocusing response to the student and that the student complies.

The instructional sequence ends on line 009, with the end of the verse:

009 Teacher: WE WILL SHARE AND LEARN AND HAVE SOME FUN.

The number 50 in the Unit Resolution column for Instructional Sequence indicates the end of this larger unit.

Once the systematic description of the instructional conversation is obtained, the second step, the identification and definition of instructional contexts by the researcher is possible. As discussed previously, people "know" when contexts occur since the creation of context is part of the evolution of the conversation. The exact moment in which a context shift occurs, however, can be identified for research purposes if the contextualization cues are considered. Context in this definition is an outcome of the process of interaction within the instructional conversation.

The creation of maps based on observation of the strategies used by participants in a conversation as they enact their view of the situation permits systematic identification of contexts. In other words, map descriptions of individuals interacting with and acting upon the messages of others to reach an instructional goal provides the basis for context identification.

For the purpose of this paper, maps of the descriptive analysis of a continuous seven minute segment of a rug area or circle area class meeting in a kindergarten will be discussed with regard to context specification. The conversational segment is composed of a welcome or greeting lesson and a "News and Views" lesson that occurred on the third day of school. The sample is part of a larger corpus of classroom conversations being systematically collected to permit exploration of the evolution of social rules in this kindergarten class. The current analysis is exploratory in nature and was undertaken as a first step in the analysis of how social rules evolve over the school year within and across the various contexts of the classroom. Space does not permit presentation of each map. Sample maps of the first two phases of the welcome or greeting lesson will be presented and the definition of context for each phase discussed.

The maps obtained from the descriptive analysis depict the existence of and relationship between the various elements of the instructional conversation. The maps in Appendix C and Appendix D provide graphic representations of two separate contexts. Appendix C contains a map of the first phase of the welcome or greeting. Appendix D contains a map of the second phase of the welcome or greeting lesson. These maps are illustrative of the method and will provide the basis for the discussion of the question -- What is an instructional context?

Each unit identified in the descriptive analysis is represented on the maps. Each figure on the maps represents the source, form, strategy or strategies, the tie and the resolution of a message. For example, the teacher is represented by the large square and capital letters while the student is represented by the small squares and lower case letters. A circle is used to identify those messages that are spontaneous or self-initiated by students. Numbers on the figures refer to the strategy and the tie of the message. Related messages are indicated by a single line between these messages. Relationships across interaction units are indicated by arrows. The end of an Instructional sequence is indicated by two solid double lines, while interruptions are represented by a combination of a solid line with a broken line.

The map in Appendix C can be glossed in terms of conversational actions as follows: the teacher's first message is a focusing response tied to the lesson. This message is followed by a second response message tied to the lesson and thematically tied to the previous message. This sequence is diverted by a student, entering the lesson for the first time. The teacher welcomes and brings him into the group by making his entry and welcome a part of the song. The direction of the conversation then returns to focus on the entire group and the lesson.

The sequence of the lesson is now interrupted by the teacher's message to indicate what she expects of an individual in the group for this phase of the lesson. The student responds appropriately by refocusing and the teacher then moves on to complete the Instructional Sequence and to end the verse.

At this point a natural break in the conversation occurs, the end of a verse is reached, and the teacher interrupts the instructional chain by asking Stephanie to move back. The communication to Stephanie requires two requests. Stephanie does not act on the first message accurately and simply sits back on her heels rather than moving back. This action requires the teacher to ask her to move to a specific space in the circle. This is indicated by both the verbal message and the nonverbal kinesics by the teacher. The unit ends with a thank you by the teacher to Stephanie for moving and completing the requested behavior. The thank you segment is said simultaneously with the beginning of the next Instructional Sequence.

The lesson sequence continues unbroken until the last verse of the song is completed. In this sequence the children spontaneously sing with the teacher as indicated in lines 018 and 019 as well as 023 and 024. The teacher in the manner of presentation, indicates that response is appropriate; that is, that the children are invited to join in.

The Instructional Sequence in the next phase of the lesson has a different structure. In Appendix D, the map of the second phase of the welcome or greeting lesson is presented. The theme of this as derived from the transcript is the greeting of each individual student in the group. The first

Interaction Unit, lines 025 to 029 of Appendix D, shows that the teacher moves her focus from speaking to the total group to speaking to the individual. The teacher accomplishes this shift in focus by using a series of three messages each tied to her own actions before giving the new lesson theme:

026 Teacher: I'M GOING TO GREET ALL OF YOU THIS MORNING BECAUSE (said almost in a whisper)
027 Teacher: I'D LIKE TO SAY (said louder)
028 Teacher: HELLO, JAMES

The voice level of the teacher and the prosodic shape of each message provide the basis for this gloss of the first Interaction Unit.

Each Interaction Unit that follows the first has the same structure:

Teacher: HELLO
Student: Hi, hello

The exception is the Interaction Unit found on lines 052 and 053:

052 James: Hello, Peter (side comment-not part of main conversation)
053 Teacher: (Teacher and Peter ignore James)

This unit is a side unit, a unit from one student to another. The timing of the teacher's messages before and after this unit and the reaction of the teacher/students indicate that this unit is not part of the main structure of the lesson sequence. However, it is tied to actions by James on line 052:

052 James: Hello, Peter

The Instructional Sequence ends on line 055 with the response of Nicholaous, the last child in the circle:

054 Teacher: AND HELLO, NICHOLAOUS
055 Nicholaous: Hi

Closure of the instructional sequence is indicated in the shift in content of the next Interaction Unit, Line 056 and 057, and by the prosodic shape of the teacher's message to Nicholaous. This message is said slowly and with a drop in voice and the inclusion of the word "and."

The new unit is interrupted by a message by James who suggests the teacher missed Peter. The teacher completes this unit by stating she had not missed Peter. The Interaction Unit by James reopened the Instructional Sequence. Peter then introduces a new message, a hello to the teacher, which the teacher accepts. These two messages by Peter and James, indicate that these students read the expectation of the sequence; everyone in the group gets a turn to be greeted individually. Peter's comments indicate that the teacher is part of the group.

The descriptive analysis discussed in the preceding sections produced descriptions of the structure of various phases of the instructional conversation. Once the maps are obtained the last step in the definition of context is possible. The definition of context is obtained by a retrospective analysis of the structures identified on the maps. For the present study context shifts were observed to coincide with the Phase boundaries of the lessons in the 13 minute segment. Comparison of Phase I (Appendix C) and Phase II (Appendix D), of the greeting lesson will illustrate this finding. In Phase I, the song, the group is the appropriate unit of message focus. The teacher's messages are directed to the group as a whole with two exceptions: first Rogan entered and was welcomed into the group as part of the song; and second, James began a message to the teacher to which the teacher responded with a statement that "we're (the group) singing now." The teacher's statement had the effect of refocusing James on the singing. The "we're singing" meaning the group is singing is reflected in the fact, thus spontaneous instances of group singing are accepted. Context, then, for this Phase is group singing.

In contrast, in Phase II the individual is the recipient of the teacher's messages and the appropriate responder. Each person receives attention from the teacher in turn as she moves in a clockwise fashion around the circle. Each individual within the group forms a context for the teacher's interaction. Based on this observation of conversational structure, Phase II is a new context. Context defined this way has thematic coherence and a basic unit of interaction, the group or the individual. In the present study the question, "What is an instructional context?", can be extended to, "When is a group?"

Consideration of the question, "When is a group?", led to the identification of three additional contexts that occurred in the remainder of 13 minute segments explored in this study. To summarize what we have already established, Context 1, i.e., Phase I of the welcome lesson which consisted of singing the welcome song, had a group focus. Context 2, i.e., Phase II of the welcome lesson which consisted of "hello" greetings, had an individual focus. As with the identification of Contexts 1 and 2, the new contexts are described in terms of thematic cohesion and the unit of focus, the group, or the individual. Context 3, i.e., Phase III of the welcome lesson, is an extension of the song. In this phase and context the teacher introduces the Spanish word for hello, ola, and repeats the song. Singing and saying the Spanish word is observed, appropriate behavior. The unit of focus is primarily the group. However, an individual as a member of the group, may respond to questions. The questions, though, were open to or directed to the group as a whole.

Context 4 coincides with the beginning of a lesson entitled News and Views. The structure and spatial distribution of students within the rug circle setting, remains the same. Phase I of News and Views is concerned with the rules for speaking and participation during News and Views. The group is the primary focus for teacher's messages; however, as in Context 3, an individual may respond to a given message. The final context, Context 5, is thematically concerned with providing sharing time for each of the individual children. The individual child is, in interaction with the teacher, the context for the sharing. In each instance in which an individual was the immediate context, the interaction of teacher and child was conducted in a manner that while personal made it open to the group. This observation suggests that even though the general focus for the entire segment was the group, the immediate context within the broad context shifted.

The findings of this exploratory study indicate that the definition of context cannot be equated with the physical structure of lesson except on a gross level. Context is created by the participants in the creation of the instructional conversation. Context, then, is a dynamic entity that can be described in sociolinguistic terms. Researchers interested in the study of teaching as a communicative process need to concern themselves with the definition of the various contexts for learning created in the process of teaching. Answers to questions about the evolution of social rules, miscommunication in the classroom, and teacher style are dependent on the identification of the appropriate context for analysis.

BEYOND THE IDENTIFICATION OF CONTEXT: THE EXPLORATORY ANALYSIS OF THE EVOLUTION OF SOCIAL RULES

The identification of context through sociolinguistic analysis opens a wide range of possibilities for exploration of process outcomes of the instructional conversation. One such possibility for exploration of process-process outcome is the overtime description of the evolution of the social rules and the development of sociolinguistic competence of children in the classroom. This area of research is the focus of the extended study from which the 13 minute segment used for this study was taken. To permit exploration of social rule evolution a systematic sample of the first hour of school is being collected, beginning with the first day of school in September and progressing through the entire year.

An initial exploratory analysis of the teacher's conversational shifts across and within contexts in the 13 minute segment led to the identification of three rules for social interaction.

Rule 1: Being a member of a group involves cooperative effort. This rule can be seen in the responses of the students, e.g., spontaneous singing with the teacher by the students, and in the lack of interruption while another student was sharing during news and views.

Rule 2: Becoming a member of the group involves clear avenues of access. The right of access may depend upon a child's position in the circle (e.g., clockwise) or on contribution of additional information on the theme of the subject or contributions of group rules. For example: children state the rule in the transcripts that we talk "one at a time."

Rule 3: Being a member of a group includes rights and responsibilities. Although each individual has the right to speak, this right is dependent upon the concept of turn taking. For example, if a person has been designated as the one who is to share, it is not appropriate to then interrupt to share a different idea. Eleven interruptions of this type across all contexts resulted in refocusing statements, e.g., "We're listening to ________ now."

These rules indicate that the children are beginning to develop a contextuating orientation for answering the questions when is a group and what should my actions be in a group. How these rules evolve over time is one of the directions that will be addressed in the longitudinal study.

BIBLIOGRAPHY

Britton, J. (1972) What's the use? A schematic account of language functions. In A. Cashdan and E. Grugeon (eds.) Language in Education: A Source Book, Boston: Routledge and Kegan.

Cook-Gumperz, J., and Corsaro, W. A. (1976) Social-ecological constraints on children's communicative strategies. In J. Cook-Gumperz and J. J. Gumperz, Papers on Language and Context, University of California, Berkeley: Language Behavior Research Lab.

Cook-Gumperz, J., & Gumperz, J. J. (1976) Context in children's speech. In J. Cook-Gumperz & J. J. Gumperz, Papers on Language and Context, University of California, Berkeley: Language Behavior Research Lab.

DeStafano, J. D., & Rentel, V. M. (1975) Language variation: Perspectives for teachers. Theory into Practice, 14, p. 328.

Erickson, F., & Schultz, J. (1977) When is a context? Some issues and methods in the analysis of social competence. Institute for Comparative Human Development Newsletter, 1(2), 5.

Etzioni, A. (1968) The Active Society, New York: Free Press.

Green, J. L. (1977) Pedagogical Style Differences as Related to Comprehension Performance: Grade One Through Three, University of California, Berkeley: PhD Dissertation.

Gumperz, J. (1976) Teaching as a Linguistic Process. Unpublished paper for National Institute of Education Conference on Language in the Classroom.

Kendon, A. (1975) Introduction. In A. Kendon, R. M. Harris, & M. R. Key (eds.), Organization of Behavior in Face-to-Face Interaction, Chicago: Aldine.

Kendon, A. (1970) Movement coordination in social interaction. Psychologica, 32, pp. 100-124.

McDermott, R. (1976) Kids Made Sense: An Ethnographic Account of the Interactional Management of Success and Failure in One First Grade Classroom. Stanford University: PhD Dissertation.

Phillips, S. U. (1972) Acquisition of rules for appropriate speech usage. In C. B. Cazden, V. P. John, & D. Hymes (eds.), Functions of Language in the Classroom, New York: Teachers College Press.

Sacks, H., Jefferson, G., & Schegloff, E. (1974) A simplest systematics for the organization of turn taking. Language, 50, pp. 696-735.

Scheflen, A. E. (1972) Communicational Structure, Bloomington, Indiana: Indiana University Press.

Stubbs, M. (1976) Language, Schools, and Classrooms, London: Methusen.

APPENDIX A: TRANSCRIPT OF 13 MINUTE SEGMENT FROM THE THIRD DAY OF SCHOOL IN A KINDERGARTEN CLASSROOM

Key - Teacher's message units: CAPITAL LETTERS
Student's message units: Lower case letters

---

001 WELCOME, WELCOME, WELCOME HERE TODAY
002 WELCOME, WELCOME MEANS HELLO PLEASE STAY.
003 Rogan: (Rogan enters circle for first time)
004 ROGAN, WELCOME
005 WELCOME, WELCOME EVERYONE
006 James: (Inaudible + nonverbal action)
007 WE'RE SINGING NOW. (T points to James)
008 James: (Stops vying for T attention and refocuses)
009 WE WILL SHARE AND LEARN AND HAVE SOME FUN
010 STEPHANIE, IF YOU'LL SIT BACK HERE SO I CAN SEE NYLA, PLEASE
011 Stephanie: (She was kneeling and sits back)
012 SIT BACK HERE (points to space in circle)
013 Stephanie: (Sits back)
014 HELLO
015 THANK YOU (To Stephanie simultaneously with new unit to complete previous unit on lines 012-013)
016 HELLO, AND HOW ARE YOU TODAY?
017 HELLO (points to left side of circle)
018 HELLO (points to right side of group)
019 All: hello (sung simultaneously with T)
020 I'M FEELING FINE TODAY.
021 COME OUT, COME OUT (waves hand toward self)
022 COME OUT WITH ME AND PLAY (waves hand toward self)
023 ALL RIGHT, ALL RIGHT, I'LL BE THERE RIGHT AWAY
024 All: I'll be there right away (sung simultaneously with T while T sings in quieter tones)
025 MY VOICE IS GOING TO GET VERY SMALL AND
026 I'M GOING TO GREET ALL OF YOU THIS MORNING BECAUSE (said almost in a whisper)
027 I'D LIKE TO SAY (said louder)
028 HELLO JAMES
029 James: Hi
030 HELLO STEPHANIE
031 Stephanie: Hi
032 HELLO NYLA
033 Nyla: Hi
034 HELLO SHAUNA
035 Shauna: Hi
036 HELLO JOY
037 Joy: Hello
038 HELLO ERIN
039 Erin: Hi
040 HELLO PETER
041 Peter: Hi
042 HELLO MISS BRIENIK (turns to student T who brings in materials for T)
043 Miss Brienik: Good morning Mrs. Marx
044 HELLO ROGAN
045 Rogan: Hi

046 HELLO BRIAN
047 Brian: Hello
048 HELLO THAD
049 Thad: Hello
050 HELLO ERIC
051 Eric: Hello
052 James: Hello Peter (side comment - not part of main conversation)
053 (Teacher and Peter ignore James)
054 AND HELLO NICHOLAOUS (Rhythm changes - said stressed and slower)
055 Nicholaous: Hi
056 ALL TOGETHER
057 AND CAN WE S --
058 James: Peter, You didn't said Peter
058 I DID SAY PETER.
059 Peter: And hello yourself
060 WELL THANK YOU. HA! HA! HA! HA!
061 St. X: Well, well, well
062 St. X: Well hello yourself
063 YOU KNOW
064 DO YOU KNOW HOW YOU SAY HELLO IN SPANISH?
065 WE COULD CHANGE THE SONG TO SAY HELLO IN SPANISH AND LEARN THE SPANISH WORDS
066 OLA, OLA, AND HOW ARE YOU TODAY?
067 All: Ola, and how are you today? (sung simultaneously with T)
068 LET'S TRY IT
069 OLA, OLA, I'M FEELING FINE TODAY
070 All: Ola, ola, I'm feeling fine today (sung simultaneously with T)
071 COME OUT, COME OUT, COME OUT WITH ME AND PLAY (T volume decreases with third come out)
072 All: Come out, come out, come out with me and play (sung with T)
073 ALL RIGHT, ALL RIGHT, I'LL BE THERE RIGHT AWAY (volume increases to normal)
074 All: All right, all right, I'll be there right away (sung with T)
075 THE WORD FOR HELLO IN SPANISH IS?
076 James: Ahla
077 OLA
078 James: Ola
079 OLA
080 OR BUENOS DIAZ. THAT'S ANOTHER WAY OF SAYING GOOD DAY
081 BUENOS DIAZ (looks at James and Stephanie)
082 Stephanie: You know what? I want to be --
083 (Teacher looks at Stephanie and waits for comment)
084 Stephanie: (no additional response)
085 WE'RE GOING TO HAVE --
086 REMEMBER YESTERDAY WE TALKED ABOUT
087 (off camera Shauna triggers something)
088 SHAUNA
089 NEWS AND VIEWS
090 AND IF EACH OF YOU WOULD LIKE TO HAVE A CHANCE TO SAY SOMETHING
091 AND WE TALKED ABOUT THE PROBLEM --
092 James: You know what I'd like to --
093 JAMES, EXCUSE ME
094 James: (ceases actions)
095 WE TALKED ABOUT THE PROBLEM WE HAVE IF FIVE PEOPLE TALK AT A TIME
096 IS THERE A PROBLEM WITH LISTENING IF THAT?
097 St. X: Uh huh

098 WHAT HAPPENS IF ALL OF US TALK AT ONCE?
099 All: I don't know. Can't hear.
100 WELL, IF ALL OF YOU TALK AT ONCE AND YOU CAN'T HEAR, IS THERE A WAY WE COULD DO IT SO WE CAN HEAR EACH PERSON?
101 All: Yea
102 Peter: One at a time (said loudly)
103 WHAT DID YOU SAY PETER?
104 Peter: One at a time (said loudly)
105 LET'S TRY YOUR IDEA
106 MAY WE TRY YOUR IDEA?
107 Peter: (shakes head yes)
108 OK WE'LL START WITH JAMES
109 JAMES, DO YOU HAVE SOMETHING TO SHARE WITH US?
110 James: Yea, um
111 James: Tomorrow I think I'll, I'll play with Rogan and make --
112 Rogan: What?
113 James: In the, in the, in
114 James: Tomorrow I think, I'll find some rocks outside, and then --
115 James: The day after tomorrow, I'm gonna bring it here and give it to Rogan
116 THAT'S AN INTERESTING IDEA
117 STEPHANIE, GOOD MORNING
118 YOU HAVE SOMETHING TO SHARE WITH US THIS MORNING?
119 Stephanie: Uh
120 Peter: I got something to --
121 WE'RE LISTENING TO STEPHANIE NOW
122 Peter: (stops talking)
123 Stephanie: I got, I got it. I got a baby puppy.
124 OH, THAT'S RIGHT
125 HOW IS THE PUPPY DOING?
126 Stephanie: (no response)
127 Stephanie: And my cat died Charlie
128 CHARLIE DIED?
129 Stephanie: Um huh
130 WHEN DID CHARLIE DIE?
131 Stephanie: Um a month ago
132 HOW DID YOU FEEL ABOUT THAT?
133 Stephanie: Sad
134 DID YOU?
135 Stephanie: (no response)
136 Stephanie: I said, "Mamma why does he have to go there every time?"
137 Stephanie: Because and I go and she goes, "because he's sick."
138 Stephanie: Then we took her to the doctor, you know
139 UH HUH
140 Stephanie: With a, um, box, a baby box
141 I SEE (said with extended tones)
142 Stephanie: A kitten
143 IT'S SAD SOMETIMES WHEN YOU LOSE A CAT, I KNOW
144 Erin: Uh, I lost a pet
145 DID YOU LOSE A PET ERIN?
146 Erin: (shakes head yes)
147 WHAT KIND OF A PET DID YOU HAVE?
148 Shauna: I lost a cat
149 I'M LISTENING TO ERIN RIGHT NOW (first two words accented and stressed)
150 Shauna: Excuse me
151 ERIN

152 James: (James starts an action as indicated by Stephanie's response)
153 I'M LISTENING, I'M LISTENING TO ERIN RIGHT NOW JAMES
154 James: (ceases actions and attends)
155 Erin: Do you know our dog Emma?
156 I DIDN'T KNOW EMMA
157 WHAT WAS EMMA LIKE?
158 Erin: U, she was white and she had black spots. She got hit.
159 I'M SORRY TO HEAR THAT
160 Erin: By a car
161 I'M SORRY TO HEAR THAT
162 James: (fingers walk up T's leg) You know what?
163 (Teacher shifts body position away from James)
164 NYLA, DO YOU HAVE SOME NEWS FOR US?
165 James: (fingers walk up T's leg again)
166 WE'RE LISTENING TO NYLA (whispered to James as teacher shifts total body position)
167 James: (ceases actions and refocuses)
168 Nyla: Um huh um
169 Nyla: Did you know I had two cats?
170 I DIDN'T KNOW
171 Nyla: And my, and my friend named Carl gots this rabbit because he, he put it out and it ran away
172 I SEE
173 Nyla: But he wasn't sad
174 Joy: Uh! uh! uh! uh! (said by Joy who is not next speaker in sequence)
175 SHAUNA (Joy ignored)
176 SHAUNA, DO YOU HAVE SOME NEWS FOR US?
177 James: (again puts hand on T's knee)
178 WE'RE LISTENING TO SHAUNA NOW, JAMES
179 James: (ceases actions and refocuses)
180 Shauna: Guess what? um
181 Shauna: A long time ago or a month ago, or um ...
182 Shauna: A cat died, one of them
183 WHAT WAS THE NAME OF THE CAT THAT DIED?
184 Shauna: Maria
185 MARIA, OHHH WHAT A PRETTY NAME, MARIA.
186 Joy: but, but
187 Joy: You know what?
188 JOY
189 Joy: But you know, you know Shauna had a gerbil
190 I SAW, I WENT VISITING
191 I WAS VISITING WITH SHAUNA THIS SUMMER AND I WAS ABLE TO MEET THE GERBIL
192 AND HE HAS A LONG CAGE DOESN'T HE?
193 Shauna and Joy: Yea
194 AND IT'S REALLY HIGH AND THERE'S ALL KINDS OF SPACES FOR HIM TO TRAVEL
195 Stephanie: (Takes two pieces of wood Nicholaous brought in from shelf)
196 THANK YOU STEPH, THANK YOU STEPHANIE FOR FINDING THIS FOR ME. I APPRECIATE THAT.
197 Nyla: Um, um, um, um
198 OH, I'M LISTENING TO SHAUNA NOW
199 Shauna: I'm going to get my gerbil a new wife
200 YOU'RE GERBIL'S GOING TO GET A NEW WIFE?
201 Shauna: (shakes head yes)
202 GREAT

203 WHERE ARE YOU GOING TO FIND THE WIFE?
204 Shauna: Pet shop where I got my gerbil
205 UH, OK
206 HI ERIN
207 DO YOU HAVE SOMETHING
208 DO YOU HAVE SOME NEWS?
209 Joy: I got something
210 Joy: What, um, what, um, what
211 Peter and Rogan: (talking together)
212 PETER
213 PETER, WE'RE LISTENING TO SH-- TO JOY NOW
214 Peter: (ceases talking and refocuses)
215 Joy: My gerbil got a shute to go through and a top to jump out then they, them they crawl back in the shute and go out the other way
216 AHH
217 ERIN, DO YOU HAVE ANY OTHER NEWS FOR US?
218 Erin: (shakes head no)
219 MISS BRIENIK, DO YOU HAVE ANY NEWS FOR US?
220 Miss Brienik: I have good news
221 THAD
222 Miss B: I got a surprise present yesterday, baby guppies
223 Miss B: Does anyone know what baby guppies are?
224 Rogan: Yeah fish
225 Miss B: They're fish, that's right Rogan
226 Rogan: I have some too
227 Miss B: Do you?
228 Miss B: Do you have a lot of them?
229 Rogan: I have only one
230 Miss B: Only one
231 Rogan: Because one of them died
232 Miss B: Well my little sister has one guppie and got another guppie
233 Miss B: They had babies
234 Miss B: Now we have some baby guppies
235 Miss B: They're fun to watch
236 Miss B: They're very tiny and we have them in a little bowl
237 Peter: And they're going to grow bigger and then you'll have to put them in a bigger bowl
238 Miss B: That would be a good idea if they grow
239 James: If they grow like a shark, you have put them in, in, in the ocean (said loudly with stress on first part of sentence)
240 Miss B: Do you think they grow that big?
241 James: (shakes head yes)
242 All: Nooooo
243 SOME FISH ARE THAT BIG, AREN'T THEY?
244 Erin: Yea the sharks are --
245 Nicholaous: Some fishes are --
246 Erin: Whales are bigger than sharks
247 St. X: confusion (all simultaneous)
248 James: Remember, one at a time (said in loud tones with high stress on each word)
249 JAMES, I APPRECIATE YOUR REMINDING US OF THAT
250 AND PETER
251 PETER DO YOU HAVE SOME NEWS FOR US?
252 Peter: I got a hat

253 WOULD YOU LIKE TO SHOW US?
254 Peter (shakes head yes and goes to get hat)
255 WHILE PETER'S GETTING HIS HAT, ROGAN WAS VERY BUSY DURING ARRIVAL
256 ROGAN, WOULD YOU LIKE TO SHOW US THE STRUCTURE THAT YOU CREATED?
257 Rogan: (nonverbal yes and gets structure)
258 DO YOU WANT TO COME IN THE MIDDLE AND LET US SEE IT AND TELL US ABOUT IT? (T points to center)
259 Rogan: (indicates yes by moving)
260 Shauna: (trigger off camera)
261 SHAUNA, WE'RE LISTENING TO THE STRUCTURE NOW
262 LISTENING ABOUT THE STRUCTURE
263 TELL US ABOUT THIS ...
264 Rogan: I built it by myself
265 AND IS THERE ANYTHING MORE YOU'D LIKE TO TELL US ABOUT IT?
266 Rogan: It can't stand up on its own
267 AHH
268 Rogan: Cause it'll fall down and break
269 DID IT TAKE YOU A LONG TIME TO BUILD IT?
270 Rogan: (shakes head yes)
271 DID YOU HAVE A SPECIAL IDEA WHEN YOU STARTED OR DID YOU JUST START THINKING ABOUT IT AS YOU WERE BUILDING?
272 Rogan: (nonverbal yes)
273 Peter: (enters with hat and sits in own space)
274 LOOK AT HOW TALL IT IS IF HE STANDS IT UP (to group)
275 IF YOU STAND UP, I WONDER HOW TALL IT WOULD BE NEXT TO YOU?
276 COULD YOU STAND UP AND WE'LL SEE HOW TALL IT IS NEXT TO YOUR BODY?
277 Rogan: (stands up with structure)
278 Nyla: (stands up almost simultaneously with Rogan)
279 WE'RE LOOKING AT ROGAN'S BODY
280 LOOK HOW TALL
281 I WONDER WHO'S TALLER, THE STRUCTURE OR ROGAN?
282 Rogan: (puts hand on head and on structure)
283 Rogan: Me
284 ROGAN SAW IT
285 James: Well, I'm taller though (said loudly simultaneously with teacher's next message)
286 (no response by teacher)
287 IS THE STRUCTURE SHORTER?
288 Rogan: (nonverbal yes)
289 WHERE WOULD YOU LIKE TO PUT THIS NOW?
290 James: I, I
291 James: You know what?
292 (teacher ignores James)
293 Rogan: On the shelf
294 ON THE SHELF?
295 Rogan: (indicates yes)
296 OK
297 THANK YOU ROGAN
298 James: (touches Teacher)
299 AND JAMES (touches James), I WONDER WHAT BRIAN HAS TO TELL US?
300 BRIAN
301 Brian: (no response)
302 BRIAN, GOOD MORNING
303 Brian: Hi
304 THAD, HI
305 Thad: Hi

306 HOW ARE YOU?
307 DO YOU HAVE ANYTHING TO TELL US?
308 Thad: (nonverbal no)
309 Nicholaous: I have something to tell you (simultaneous with teacher)
310 JUST A MINUTE, AND I'LL BE HAPPY TO HEAR ABOUT IT, TOO (to Nicholaous)
311 HI ERIC
312 HOW'S THAT DOG OF YOURS DOING?
313 Eric: Fine
314 DOES SHE STILL BARK WHEN THAT STRANGE BLACK DOG COMES AROUND?
315 Eric: Yea
316 HE DOES?
317 Eric: Once my dog was outside you know and the other dog came and licked each other
318 REALLY?
319 Eric: Yea
320 DID THEY LICK?
321 DID HE GO?
322 WAS YOUR DOG ABLE TO GET OUTSIDE OR DID THE OTHER DOG COME UP TO THE WINDOW OF YOUR HOME?
323 Eric: My dog was outside on a chain
324 OH
325 Eric: And ____________ (inaudible)
326 WHAT WOULD HAPPEN IF HE GOT OFF OF THE CHAIN?
327 Eric: He'd run away
328 DO YOU THINK HE MIGHT?
329 Eric: Um huh
330 Peter: I've got something to tell you
331 Peter: When we were going to the dog, um, doctor
332 UM HUH
333 Peter: We had B.J., our dog, B.J. on a tr___, on a chain him
334 Peter: and you know what?
335 Peter: He got unloose and ran all the way down and under somebody's car lay ahead of her all the way down gettin 'im
336 WERE YOU ABLE TO GET HIM BACK?
337 Peter: Yea we got 'im back
338 James: Mrs. Marx?
339 YES JAMES?
340 James: You know...
341 James: You know what?
342 James: What day is today?
343 TODAY
344 WE'RE GOING TO TALK ABOUT THAT
345 TODAY IS THURSDAY, SEPTEMBER 15
346 WE'RE GOING TO PICK OUR LEADER IN A MINUTE
347 Stephanie: (inaudible)
348 AND STEPHANIE, AS SOON AS WE'RE FINISHED TALKING TO NICHOLAOUS HERE, WE'RE GOING TO DO SOMETHING ELSE SPECIAL
349 NICHOLAOUS, DO YOU HAVE SOME NEWS FOR US?
350 James: You know what? (said simultaneously with previous teacher message)
351 AND JAMES, JAMES, I'M LISTENING TO NICHOLAOUS, WE'LL TALK ABOUT THAT IN A MINUTE
352 James: OK
353 YES, NICHOLAOUS?
354 Nichalaous: And in the ocean they sometimes go in the big shark
355 IN THE OCEAN? YES

356 HAVE YOU SEEN PICTURES OF SHARKS IN THE OCEAN?
357 Nicholaous: (shakes head no)
358 Stephanie: I have
359 James: I have
360 All: I have, too (general comments by all students)
361 IF YOU'RE HAPPY (teacher begins singing, then stops)
362 OH, I HAVE SOME NEWS
363 Student X: I have some news
364 (teacher ignores)
365 DO YOU KNOW WHAT HAPPENED TO ME TODAY?
366 I OVERSLEPT
367 All: (laugh)
368 HAVE YOU EVER
369 All: (start comments...)
370 HAVE YOU EVER, HAVE YOU EVER OVERSLEPT AND THEN WOKE UP AND HAD A PROBLEM GETTING READY?
371 St. X: Me
372 St. X: I did
373 WELL THAT WAS MY PROBLEM, IT WAS VERY FRUSTRATING TO ME TODAY
374
375 All: (general comments -- all at once)
376 IF YOU'RE HAPPY AND YOU KNOW IT COME AND SIT BY ME (teacher begins singing)
377 NOW FIND A COMFORTABLE SPOT

APPENDIX B SAMPLE DESCRIPTIVE ANALYSIS OF INSTRUCTIONAL CONVERSATIONS

	SOURCE		FORM				STRATEGIES												LEVEL			TIE				UNIT RESOLUTION			
Transcript Line	Teacher	Student	Question	Response +	Response 0	Response -	Focusing	Ignoring	Confirming +	Confirming -	Continuance	Extending	Raising	Clarifying	Editing	Controlling	Refocusing	Restating	Factual	Interpret	Applicative	Teacher	Student	Lesson (Welcome Song)		Resolved Interaction	Unresolved Interaction	Instruction Sequence	Phase
1	2	3	4	5	6	7	8	9	10	11	12	13	14	15	16	17	18	19	20	21	22	23	24	25	26	30	31	50	60
001	2			5			8									17			20					25		0			
002	2			5			8									17			20					25			31		
														SKIP															
NV 003		3R			6		0	----------						(off camera)				----------	0	------			24			0			
004	2R			5			8		10							17			0				24			30			
														SKIP															
005	2			5			8									17			20					25			31		
														SKIP															
006		3J			6		8									17							24			0			
007	2J			5												17								25					
NV 008		3J		5												17			0	------		23				30			
														SKIP															
009	2			5			8																	25		30		50	
														SKIP															
010	2S+			5												17			0	------			24			0			
NV 011		3St		5												17			0	------		23				30			
														SKIP															
012	2St			5												17			0	------			24			0			
NV 013		3St		5												17			0	------		23				0			
015	2St			5					10										20				24			30		50	
														SKIP															

APPENDIX C: MAP OF AN INSTRUCTIONAL CONVERSATION: PHASE I OF WELCOME LESSON

Lines	Text
001	WELCOME, WELCOME, WELCOME HERE TODAY
002	WELCOME, WELCOME MEANS HELLO PLEASE STAY
NV 003	Rogan: [Rogan enters circle for first time]
004	ROGAN, WELCOME
005	WELCOME, WELCOME EVERYONE
006	James: [Inaudible + nonverbal action]
007	WE'RE SINGING NOW [Teacher points to James]
008	James: [Stops vying for Teacher's attention and refocuses]
009	WE WILL SHARE AND LEARN AND HAVE SOME FUN.

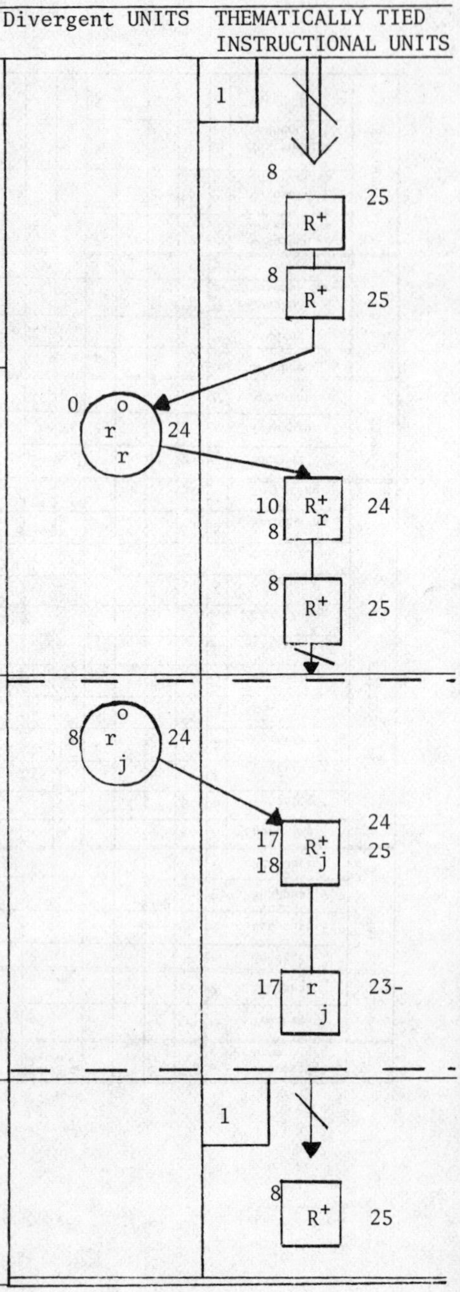

APPENDIX C (cont'd)

010	STEPHANIE, IF YOU'LL SIT BACK HERE SO I CAN SEE NYLA, PLEASE
011	Stephanie: [She was kneeling and sits back]
012	SIT BACK HERE. [Points to space in circle]
013	Stephanie: [Sits back]
014	HELLO
015	THANK YOU [To Stephanie simultaneous with new unit to complete previous unit on lines 012-013]
016	HELLO, AND HOW ARE YOU TODAY?
017	HELLO [points to left side of circle]
018	HELLO [points to right side of group]
019	All: hello [sung simultaneously with Teacher]
020	I'M FEELING FINE TODAY.
021	COME OUT, COME OUT, [waves hand toward self]
022	COME OUT WITH ME AND PLAY [waves hand toward self]
023	ALL RIGHT, ALL RIGHT, I'LL BE THERE RIGHT AWAY
024	All: I'll be there right away [sung simultaneously with T while T sings in quieter tones]

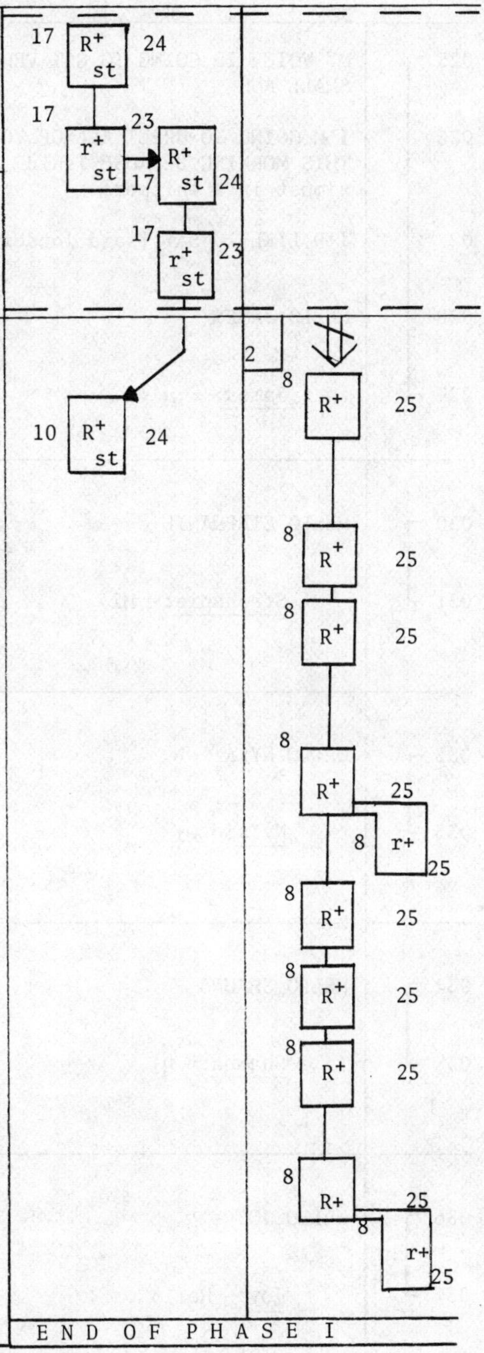

APPENDIX D: MAP OF AN INSTRUCTIONAL CONVERSATION: PHASE II OF WELCOME LESSON

Line	Message		Level	Unit	Code
025	MY VOICE IS GOING TO GET VERY SMALL AND		3 8	R^+	23
026	I'M GOING TO GREET ALL OF YOU THIS MORNING BECAUSE [said almost in a whisper]		8	R^+	23
027	I'D LIKE TO SAY [said louder]		8	R^+	23
028	HELLO JAMES		15 8	R^+_j	25
029	<u>James</u>: Hi		8	r^+_j	25
030	HELLO STEPHANIE		3 8	R^+_{st}	25
031	<u>Stephanie</u>: Hi		8	r^+_{st}	25
032	HELLO NYLA		3 8	R^+_{ny}	25
033	<u>Nyla</u>: Hi		8	r^+_{ny}	25
034	HELLO SHAUNA		3 8	R^+_{sh}	25
035	<u>Shauna</u>: Hi		8	r^+_{sh}	25
036	HELLO JOY		3 8	R^+_{jo}	25
037	<u>Joy</u>: Hello		8	r^+_{jo}	25

APPENDIX D (cont'd)

038	HELLO ERIN		3 8	R^+_{er}	25
039	Erin: Hi		8	r^+_{er}	25
040	HELLO PETER		3 8	R^+_{p}	25
041	Peter: Hi		8	r^+_{p}	25
042	HELLO MISS BRIENIK [turns to student teacher who brings in materials for the teacher]		3 8	R^+_{nb}	25
043	Miss Brienik: Good morning Mrs. Marx		8	r^+_{nb}	25
044	HELLO ROGAN		3 8	R^+_{r}	25
045	Rogan: Hi		8	r^+_{r}	25
046	HELLO BRIAN		3 8	R^+_{b}	25
047	Brian: Hello		8	r^+_{b}	25
048	HELLO THAD		3 8	R^+_{th}	25
049	Thad: Hello		8	r^+_{th}	25

APPENDIX D (cont'd)

050	HELLO ERIC
051	Eric: Hello
052	James: Hello Peter [side comment - not part of main conversation]
053 NV	[TEACHER AND PETER IGNORE JAMES]
054	AND HELLO NICHOLAOUS [rhythm changes-said stressed and slower]
055	Nicholaous: Hi
056	ALL TOGETHER
057	AND CAN WE S ___
058	James: Peter, You didn't said Peter
058	I DID SAY PETER.
059	Peter: And hello your-self
060	WELL THANK YOU. HA! HA! HA! HA!
061	St. X: Well, well, well
062	St. X: Well hello your-self.

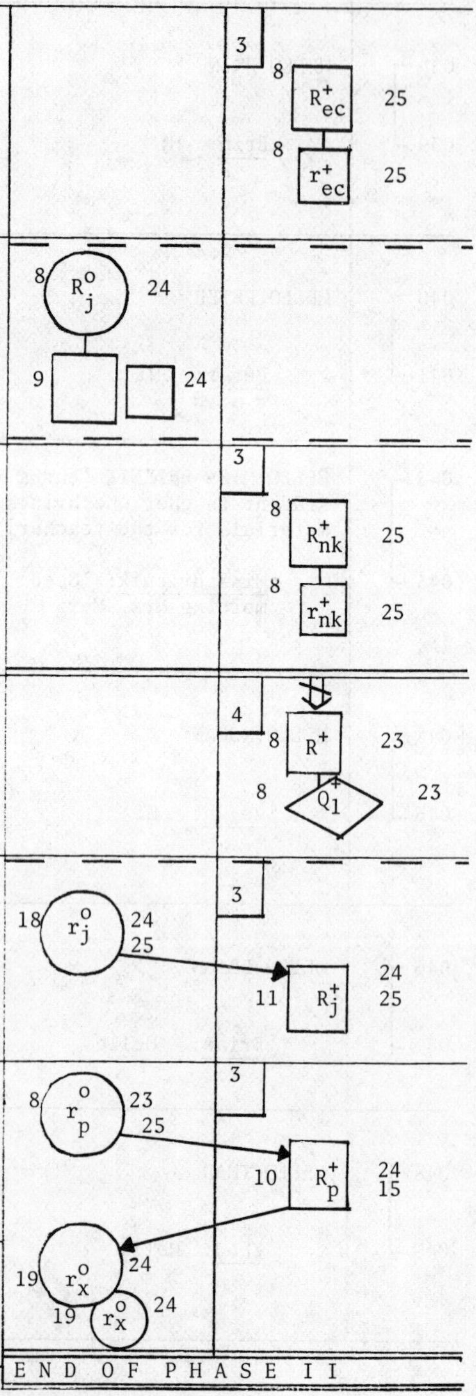

*A Cross-cultural Investigation of Children's Imagery**

VERA JOHN - STEINER, PATRICIA IRVINE, and
HELGI OSTERREICH
University of New Mexico

INTRODUCTION

Humans of all ages are hard at work creating order, frequently of a temporary kind, out of their complex, and often contradictory, environments. Children's activities are particularly noteworthy in this respect as they are more overt and thus open to observation than those of adults.

The inward flow of sensations and experiences are organized by the brain in a variety of ways; some sense impressions are stored in long-term memory requiring re-coding. The transformation of what is heard, seen or touched is dependent upon the skill of the human mind in presenting anew, or representing events as images, as inner language, and as other forms of symbolic representation. It is difficult to ascertain the nature of inner cognitive processes. We are dependent to a large extent upon subjective reports as our source of information. Individuals do specify visual, verbal, kinesthetic and more elusive elements as components of their memory skills and thoughts. There are variations in introspective report among individuals in the same culture and between individuals from differing cultures in their reliance upon one or another aspect of these inner processes.

We know more about the role verbal representation plays in thinking and learning than we do about the role of visual or other modes of representations. In this paper we are only examining imagery and verbal processes at the exclusion of other modes. Language is more accessible to study. It is a more socially conditioned and a more socially supported process of communication and representation than imaging. The visual representation of experience is less easily understood, as it is bound to the internal, subjective life of the mind to a greater extent than are verbal processes.

Nevertheless, psychological theorists have stressed the importance of the iconic, particularly in the course of development, as an essential stage in the growth of thinking. The two questions which provide the focus of this paper are: (a) To what extent are children's and adult's images the same or different? and (b) Do children rely on images more than adults?

Developmental psychologists approach the issue of varying modes of representation from the point of view of stages. In one theory at least (Bruner, 1966), verbal processes are placed in the context of an age-linked progression: "At first the child's world is known to him principally by the habitual

*The research reported here was supported by the National Institute of Education, HEW: NE-G-00-0074.

actions he uses for coping with it." (p. 1). This enactive stage is followed by iconic representation in his schema, and the third stage is that of the verbal-symbolic mode. Around the age of seven or eight a shift to language takes place, or as Bruner states it, "gradually, there is added a new and powerful method of translating action and image into language, providing still a third system of representation." (p. 1).

Piaget's (1968) views differ as to the role of language as a representational process. He does not conceive of it as the central process of thought, which, once internalized by the child, dwarfs other representational processes. Piaget argues that abstract thinking includes both imaginal and verbal processes. Paivio (1971) has summarized a large body of empirical work in his book Imagery and Verbal Processes, and his approach to representational processes is closer to Piaget than to Bruner. Paivio defines these processes as follows:

> Images and verbal processes are viewed as alternative coding systems, which are developmentally linked to experiences with concrete objects and events as well as with language . . . In addition, it is assumed that chains of symbolic transformations can occur involving either words or images, or both, and that these can serve a mediational function in perception, verbal learning, memory, and language. (p. 8).

In our view, words and images are primarily complementary methods of representation, but individuals can also succeed in fusing them in particularly productive ways. The way in which differing representational systems are combined into functional systems is dependent upon many individual, historical and cultural variables.

Although Piaget and other developmental theorists emphasize the importance of both verbal and visual processes and their interaction in the course of cognitive growth, contemporary educational practice tends to stress the development of verbal skills at the expense of visual ones. The question we raised earlier concerning the reliance of individuals of varying ages upon images, becomes more complicated at this point. If we find that children's images differ from adults', is it because of a necessary developmental trend across all cultures, or can a preference for one mode or the other be shaped by social and cultural experiences?

The impact of specific cultural variables emerged as significant while we were involved in a study of learning styles among Pueblo Indian children. It was clear from the beginning while working in these communities that these children approached learning in ways that were different from those we were familiar with from studying urban children. These Indian children live in a well-integrated village community where a great amount of adult time is spent on activities which are available for their inspection. Relatives are engaged in farming, crafts (production and selling), and other kinds of work of traditional value in their communities. Adult activities and preoccupations are not separated from the sphere of the children's lives. Unlike Western urban children who experience discontinuity in learning because they have had limited chances to observe significant adults at work, these Indian children have the opportunity to be present, to monitor and observe adult behavior.

Previous research underscores the possibility that Indian children excel in spatial and visual skills if they are raised in tribal communities (Bland, 1970, 1974; Dennis, 1942). All these children may function well in the visual mode of learning and representation as a consequence of a distinctive artistic tradition which is part of their daily lives. The scope of this paper does not allow for detailed discussion of the many ramifications of differences in learning styles among children from different cultural backgrounds. In the particular exploration of imagery which we discuss here, we are concerned with the question of whether the reported images of urban children and those of children raised in traditional village communities reflect cultural differences.

THE STUDY

Method

We tested sixty-two children, ranging in age from 5 to 14 years, using word association and imagery tasks. The children were approached in classrooms in these locations: the South Valley of Albuquerque, New Mexico; a Tanoan Pueblo located in northern New Mexico; and in Chinle, Arizona, which is part of the Navajo Nation. We also collected information on imagery tasks from thirty adults, ranging in age from 22 to 42 years. There were ten Navajo, ten Crow and ten non-Indian women in the adult sample at The University of New Mexico. Both groups of Indian adults were involved in bilingual bicultural teacher-training programs.

Adults were tested in groups. In the imagery task the children were interviewed individually. They were asked to play a "game" by listening to a word given by the field worker, then closing their eyes and looking for the first "picture" to appear "inside their heads." We then asked them to say out loud what they saw. The eight words chosen for this task were sadness, sky, house, schoolbus, mountain, office, man, and teacher. The heavy reliance on words dealing with the physical environment was dictated by our experience in working with children who had difficulty associating to more abstract words. The field worker began by giving some examples, and sometimes prompted with questions. Failure to understand these instructions occurred in only one case out of sixty-three, and this child's responses were not used in the analysis.

Results

We analyzed the imagery responses by assigning each to one of four categories which had been previously developed for studying the images of adults. Response categories used to group children's and adults' images were:

1. visual: details of the image were described in purely visual terms, e.g., house, masonry house, beige-colored walls, post fence surrounding it, in the mountains . . ."

2. verbal: no visual component, e.g., house, "A house is a shelter full of love."

3. composite: both visual and verbal elements are present, e.g., house, "House with a roof and a yard -- both full of whatever it takes to make up a life."

4. constructed: an integrated image, constructed from several levels into a whole; symbolic, visual, e.g., house, "I am in a Victorian mansion, the walls are high and dark, there is a sea crashing outside; it is secure but makes me uneasy."

The percentage of children's images to the words teacher, house and man which were assigned to each of the response categories is shown in Table 1.

TABLE 1 Percentages of Imagery Responses of Navajo, Pueblo and Non-Indian Children in Each of Four Categories

Response Category	Navajo Responses N = 34*	Pueblo Responses N = 48	Non-Indian Responses N = 89	All Children N = 171
Visual	62	81	78	76
Verbal	6	8	4	6
Composite	32	10	16	18
Constructed	0	0	2	1

In looking at the content of the images more closely, we found that children tended to enumerate, i.e., to list a series of things in no apparent order. One young child's response to schoolbus illustrates this: "yellow, seats, kids, driver, window." A pre-teen's image to schoolbus shows a developmental trend from a straightforward listing of random detail to a more narrative, integrated style: "When I sit at the bus stop, I look up and see lots of kids looking out, some of them spitting at people, some of them throwing rocks and some of them asking for cigarettes with their hands." This type of image, wherein details are integrated around a theme, occurred among both children and adults. The most striking difference, however, is to be found in the larger number of purely verbal responses given by adults, and conversely, the primarily visual images reported by children.

The percentages of adult responses to the same words given to the children are shown in Table 2.

TABLE 2 Percentages of Imagery Responses of Navajo, Crow and Anglo Adults in Each of Four Categories

Response Category	Navajo Responses N = 68**	Crow Responses N = 53	Anglo Responses N = 70	All Adult Responses N = 191
Visual	50	70	33	49
Verbal	40	21	31	31
Composite	9	8	30	16
Constructed	1	2	6	3

*N is the number of responses. The responses of 12 Navajo, 16 Pueblo and 34 non-Indian children were analyzed.

**N is the number of responses. These results include the responses of ten Navajo, ten Crow and ten non-Indian adults.

A content analysis suggests a qualitative difference between the images of children and those of adults. Children tend to view spaces from the inside, showing a personal involvement lacking in adult images. To the stimulus word house, more than half of the children responded with images like, "a bed, a dresser, a mirror"; "a room in a house and a living room, and a TV and a kitchen"; "my family talking and eating"; or "my dad is laying in bed and my mom is washing dishes." Adult responses are both more highly integrated than children's and, in contrast to children's images, view a house from the outside: "my parents' front yard, rosebushes, a couple of trees, a white screen door, a blue painted porch" (female, age 20); or "a white clapboard farmhouse, two-story, mid-western, 50 years old or so, with a high pitched roof and large long old-fashioned windows" (male, age 36).

Children's responses to other words similarly revealed an actual involvement in the setting. To the stimulus word mountain, for example, they rendered a close-up view. They mention, in various combinations, weeds, snakes, flowers, ants, worms, bushes, wind, rock, sand, ground and piñon trees. These are all things a child can experience directly. Adults, on the other hand, often reported images of mountains from a distance: "large, jagged sky -- snow-capped mountain -- horizon is at a great distance" (male, age 25); "large peaks which meet with the sky" (female, age 22); "a distant mountain rising out of the flat lands with ragged ridges and sharp shadows and a bluish haze" (male, age 36).

Of additional interest was the presence of cultural themes in the content of images. The imagery of both children and adults contained culturally specific references. In response to mountain a nine year old Navajo girl reported seeing "a girl standing on top . . . she is looking for sheep," which is a common activity for children on the reservation. A Pueblo kindergarten child responded also to mountain: "Indians." (Probe: What are they doing?) "Shooting arrows and a girl is cooking." Another Navajo child reported the following image to the word man: "jewelry on . . . a necklace . . . he's weak . . . (Probe: How do you know?) . . . he has those wrinkles . . . a bun on his hair." She was clearly describing an old, traditionally-dressed Navajo man. The stimulus word house elicited two direct references to "hogan," the traditional Navajo-style house, from other Navajo children. An adult from the same community reported this image: "Man and woman sitting in a hogan eating."

Some Anglo adults responded to the word fantasy with references to Walt Disney's animated cartoon characters or to characters in J. R. R. Tolkein stories: "Children at a movie theater watching a movie with comic strip characters, maybe Snow White and the Seven Dwarfs" (female, age 25). "A Walt Disney film Fantasia. Mickey Mouse was under the spell of the sorcerer and he's getting water at a well" (male, age 26). "I see Tinkerbell flying around the castle at night at Disneyland" (female, age 35). "Pictures from Tolkein's Hobbit (Smaug, Bilbo, etc.)" (female, age 20). "Feeling of freedom -- childlike-- books like The Hobbit" (female, age 46). This sample of such references indicate these adults' participation in popular Anglo-American culture.

Among children, visual responses were predominant, regardless of ethnic background. The adult groups, on the other hand, showed variation. Indian groups responded on the whole with more visual components than the non-Indian group. These differences among adults are congruent with ethnographic observations which stress the high visual literacy prevalent among Native Americans. In one such study, Collier (1967) attributes an astuteness of perception to people who, by "living close to nature, have to be specialists in natural phenomena to survive."

Diverse Uses of Imagery

These findings further support our view that imaging is a universal aspect of the life of the mind: images are condensed units of meaning which have referential, connotative and symbolic properties. But the extent of reliance upon this function varies among individuals from different cultures, and among individuals of varied ages from the same culture. Children rely on iconic representations of their experience more than adults. Although their images are vivid and easy to elicit, they are not sufficiently powerful or integrated for use in the diverse intellectual tasks they will encounter in later life.

The cultural and educational emphases upon language in contemporary Western societies precludes the full development of imagery for cognitive purposes. Those individuals who are able to maintain a continuity in iconic representation, in spite of such emphasis upon language, succeed in developing more mature forms of images than children. These iconic symbols can then be used, along with verbal representation, for complex cognitive tasks.

One of the most powerful statements on the role of imagery in creative thought is Einstein's description (Einstein, 1955) of his own cognitive process in a letter to Jacques Hadamard, a fellow scientist:

> The words or the language, as they are written or spoken, do not seem to play any role in my mechanism of thought. The psychical entities which seem to serve as elements in thought are certain signs and more or less clear images which can be 'voluntarily' reproduced and combined . . .
>
> The above mentioned elements are, in my case, of visual and some of muscular type. Conventional words or other signs have to be sought for laboriously only in a secondary stage, when the mentioned associative play is sufficiently established and can be reproduced at will.

Thus, imagery is viewed by Einstein as an active process, the functions of which go beyond a mere visual storage of experience to its elaboration and transformation.

More recent studies report the extensive use of imagery by scientists (Krueger, 1976) not only in physics and mathematics but also in biology and in the human sciences. In an important case-study, Howard Gruber (1977) discovered that Charles Darwin relied upon the characteristic visual representation of a tree structure to help him pull together different concepts of evolution. In studying the notebooks and writings of other major thinkers such as Jean Piaget and Mary Wollstonecraft, Gruber and his co-workers found these "wide-ranging images" to be a significant cognitive process for these creative people.

Another approach to the study of image use in thinking and creating is found in DeGroot's (1965) study of chess-players. He compared the approaches used by masters, experienced players and novices; Chase and Simon interpret his findings as follows:

> In order to perceive chess relations a player must be able to visualize a path of a piece in order to see what lies ahead. This capacity to construct an image combining perceptual structures from internal memory with sensory features from external memory is probably one of the very basic cognitive processes. The most important processes underlying chess mastery are immediate visual perceptual processes, rather than subsequent logical deductive thinking processes.

Both the representational and the symbolic uses of imagery are emphasized by these various studies of men and women engaged in intellectual labor. Imagery processes are perhaps most apparent in the work of visual artists and poets, whose artistry is a result of their ability to transform intense visual memories into metaphorical and symbolic meaning.

The varied and important functions of imagery in mental life are but briefly sketched in this paper. However, once it is recognized that imaging is a crucial process in the work of many creative adults, the critical role of imagery in complex thinking will no longer be neglected by educators, but encouraged. At present, most adults, particularly those who experienced early pressure to excel in verbal tasks, find their facility for imaging masked by the flood of language. Most of the "images" reported by college students are verbal associations or redefinations, lacking visual or other sensory information. The early shift in education to a focus on language seems to happen at the expense of the development of diverse uses for imagery. We suggest that the educational experience would be enhanced by a more conscious effort to balance the emphasis on verbal ability with encouragement of our imaginal facilities.

BIBLIOGRAPHY

Bland, L. L. (1970) Perception and Visual Memory of School-Age Eskimos and Athabascan Indians in Alaskan Villages. Monograph I, Human Environmental Resource Systems, Anchorage, Alaska.

Bland, L. L. (1974) Visual Perception and Recall of School-age Navajo, Hopi, Jicarilla Apache and Caucasian Children of the Southwest. Unpublished Ph.D. dissertation, University of New Mexico, Albuquerque, New Mexico.

Bruner, J. S. (1966) On Cognitive Growth. In J. S. Bruner, R. R. Olver and P. M. Greenfield (eds.), Studies in Cognitive Growth. New York: John Wiley & Sons.

Chase, G. and H. A. Simon (1973) The Mind's Eye in Chess. In G. Chase (ed.), Visual Information Processing. New York: Academic Press.

DeGroot, A. D. (1965) Thought and Choice in Chess. The Hague: Mouton.

Dennis, W. (1942) The Performance of Hopi Children on the Good-enough Draw-A-Man Test. Journal of Comparative Psychology., 34, no. 3.

Einstein, A. (1955) Letter to Jacques Hadamard. In B. Ghiselin (ed.), The Creative Process: A Symposium. New York: The New American Library (Mentor Books).

Gruber, H. E. (1977) Darwin's Tree of Nature and Other Images of Wide Scope. In J. Wechsler (ed.), On Arsthetics in Science, MIT Press.

Krueger, T. H. (1976) Visual Imagery in Problem Solving and Scientific Creativity. Derby, Connecticut: Seal Press.

Paivio, A. (1971) Imagery and Verbal Processes. New York: Holt, Rinehart, and Winston.

Piaget, J. (1968) Six Psychological Studies. New York: Vintage Books.

*Learning to Say No: Functional Negation in Discourse**

DEBORAH KELLER-COHEN and CHERYL A. GRACEY
University of Michigan

INTRODUCTION

In acquiring a language, a child learns to manipulate not only rules governing the syntactic and semantic structure of utterances, but also rules of discourse which coordinate utterances between speakers. The distinction between relations within a child's utterances and between the child's utterances and those of other speakers is a natural outgrowth of recent attention to the ontogenesis of conversation.

It has been observed that propositions within children's speech may at first develop out of propositions that the child creates jointly with other speakers (Scollon, 1974; Keenan, Schieffelin, and Platt, 1976). Our recent research on children's acquisition of English as a second language has been aimed at examining the development of this phenomenon in the non-native child. This chapter examines one communicative function that is expressed when the child builds on a previous proposition (or its associated presuppositions) by another speaker. In particular, we examined functional negation (discourse negation), a sequential unit of conversation occurring when the child's utterance or set of utterances is negatively related to that of a prior speaker. Internal negation (negation within an utterance) was examined only if the utterance was a negation of a proposition (or its presupposition) produced by another speaker.

THE FORM OF FUNCTIONAL NEGATION

Linguistic descriptions of the adult model of negation have primarily considered the formal features of negatives, examining how they combine with modals and auxiliaries and describing such processes as negative incorporation and do-support (Klima, 1964; Quirk, Greenbaum, Leech and Svartvik, 1972). These analyses have generally overlooked the fact that negation can be expressed functionally without the presence of a negative morpheme. In this vein, investigators of children's language have observed that children sometimes communicate negation without explicitly using a negative morpheme. Lord (1974) and Weeks (in Lord) report children's expression of negation through the use of contrastive intonation. For example, Lord's daughter

*This research was supported by Faculty Research Grants 387105 and 387188 from the Graduate School, the University of Michigan. The authors wish to thank Karen Chalmer and Janice Bogen for helpful discussion.

used elevated intonation rather than a segmental morpheme to express negation. Bloom (1970) found utterances with clear negative intent "as evidenced, for example, by the child shaking his head, pushing an object away, or refusing to follow a direction although a negative element was not expressed" (p. 171). [emphasis ours] Such observations led us to a broader characterization of negation detailed in the section below.

The Adult Model

The adult has at his disposal a number of mechanisms for expressing functional negation including rejection, contradiction, denial and rebuttal. These are illustrated below. In examples (1) - (3) the negation contains a negative marker that may (1, 2, 3a) or may not (3b) be incorporated into the aux.

(1) X: Are you guilty?
Y: No (I'm not).

(2) X: (Why don't you) give me that.
Y: No (I won't).

(3) X: That's a truck isn't it?
a) Y: No, it doesn't have wheels.
b) Y: No, it flies.

The expression of discourse negation does not require a segmental negative as is demonstrated by examples (4), (5), and (6a). In (4) speaker Y disagrees with X's utterance. Since X's assertion is in the negative, Y's disagreement (a functional negation) is in the affirmative.

(4) X: This isn't a tree.
Y: Yes it is.

(5) X: That's a picture of Marilyn Monroe.
Y: It's Jayne Mansfield.

In (6) Y does not negate an overt proposition in X's utterance, but rather a negation of one of its presuppositions.

(6) X: When is your mother leaving?
a) Y: My mother's in Florida.
b) Y: My mother's not here.

Finally, the presence of a negative element may in fact signal agreement and is therefore not a negation of the propositional content of the other speaker's utterance (7).

(7) X: You don't have enough food?
Y: No (I don't).

There are of course other devices available for negating the propositions or presuppositions of another speaker's utterance including polite hedges (Are you sure?, But I thought that . . . , Maybe, but . . .) and put-downs (8).

(8) X: John is so smart.
Y: I think he has the brain of a pencil.

Some additional observations will further clarify the relationship between the treatment of negation presented here and that found elsewhere in the literature. With little exception, in prior child language research on negation all utterances containing negative morphemes were examined and characterized. In contrast, we included utterances with negatives only when the utterance expressed a negation of a prior utterance or its presuppositions. In addition, we required that the negation be in opposition to an utterance by a prior speaker. Hence, the child's negation of a prior utterance of his own was not examined. These two criteria meant that we excluded some instances of negation described in previous research. However, we included utterances without a negative morpheme if they negated the propositional content of prior other-speaker utterances. In this sense, we included data excluded in prior analyses. Our definitional criteria arose naturally from the examination of a particular phenomenon in children's speech that is apparent only when propositions created jointly by the child and another speaker are considered. Figure 1 characterizes the focus of our investigation.

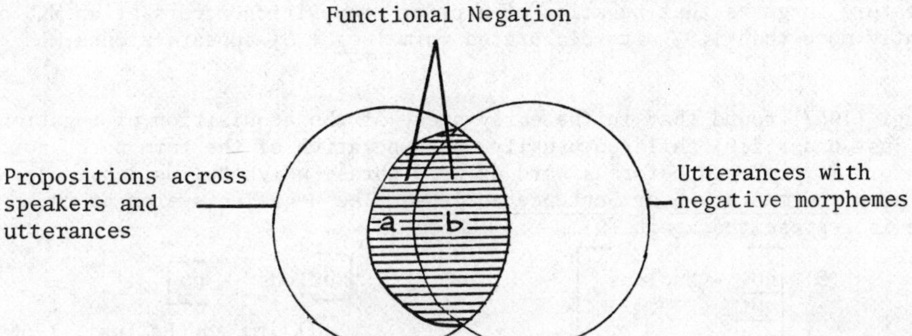

Fig. 1.

As one can see from this figure, functional negation contains both utterances across speakers that do not contain a morpheme (a) and utterances across speakers that do contain an explicit negation (b).

PRIOR RESEARCH*

The acquisition of negation both within a child's utterances and between a child's speech and that of another's has been a recent focus of investigation (Bellugi, 1967; Bloom, 1970; Bowerman, 1973, 1975; McNeill and McNeill, 1973; Lord, 1974). In each of these studies, negation was examined in children's spontaneous conversations with adults although the nature of the adult-child interaction was not the focus of investigation. The attention of these authors was toward describing the form (Bellugi) and form-function

*Formal negation has been investigated in several studies of children learning English as a second language. However, the adjacent child and adult utterances were not reported; hence, it was not possible to examine them for evidence of discourse negation.

covariance (Bloom, McNeill and McNeill, Lord) of negation in children's speech. Adult input was treated in three ways: First, as an aid in identifying the function of the negation or in determining the presence of negative intent where an overt negative was not present (all authors). Second, negation in adult speech was considered in order to describe the model toward which the child was working (Bellugi). Third, the frequency of different negative forms in the mother's speech was examined in order to predict order of acquisition in the children's speech (Bellugi).

Overlap for some of the age periods investigated in prior research makes it possible to compare the data reported in Bellugi, Bloom, Lord, and the McNeills with that presented here. The period of development considered by these authors covers language acquisition from an MLU of 2;0 - 3;0 as do the data reported in this chapter. However, because adjacent adult speech is not consistently reported in these studies, it was not possible to determine when the child's utterance was a negation of another speaker's utterance. In addition, negation of propositions without negative morphemes was generally not reported. Nevertheless, the picture of negation that emerges from the literature suggests that negation of a prior proposition occurs at an MLU of slightly more than 1;0. Its elaborated form [*neg* + S] appears around MLU 2;0.

Bellugi (1967) found that in the early stage of the acquisition of negation (MLU just under 2;0) children usually use a negative of the form *no* or *not*. This form is produced before a word or word phrase which Bellugi characterized as a *rudimentary S* or *Sentence nucleus*. The negative system at this stage is represented as in (9):

(9) [{*no*, *not*} - Nucleus] or [Nucleus - *no*]

(Klima and Bellugi, 1966)

Bellugi reports the following kinds of utterances for this stage:

(10) No heavy
No Mom sharpen it
No the sun shining
No a flag

Her claim that the negative occurs outside the sentence nucleus arises from two sources: the non-anaphoric use of the negative, and the placement of the negative before Indef + N or NP. The use of the negative was thought to be non-anaphoric because there was no clear evidence that it referred back to a prior utterance and because there was no pause between the negative and the S. Bellugi also argued that this early rule of negation was dropped in favor of later rules rather than serving as a primitive form for future rules. Of greatest consequence for our discussion of discourse negation is Bellugi's claim that the negation was non-anaphoric during the earliest stage of acquisition. This means that the child during this period (MLU $<$ 2;0) is not yet able to negate a proposition in a prior adult utterance.

Like Bellugi, Bloom (1970) also found that the negative was a prepositional operator occurring before nominals and predicate forms in the child's earliest utterances (188). Hence, she observed utterances like the following:

(11) No pocket
No turn
No morning

However, in contrast to Bellugi, Bloom and Bowerman took the position that the negative was located before nouns or verb forms and *not* before a nucleus S. Support for her view was drawn from two sources: 1) To posit Neg + nucleus S is to claim that there is no constraint on utterance complexity, when in fact negative utterances were found to be less complex than non-negative utterances; 2) *neg* + $\left\{\begin{matrix}N\\V\end{matrix}\right\}$ was occasionally anaphoric. That is, the negation applied to a prior adult utterance and not to the co-occurring elements.

Bloom observed that the *neg* + X utterances expressed three semantic types of negation: non-existence, rejection and denial (or in the terms used by McNeill and McNeill for Japanese children, "existence-truth, internal-external, and entailment-non-entailment". Both sets of investigators found that the syntactic expression of negation was acquired first for non-existence and later for rejection and denial, the latter developing last. Other investigators, however, (Bowerman, 1973; Lord, 1974) have not found the distinct stages reported by Bloom. For example, one of Bowerman's Finnish subjects expressed denial much more often than non-existence. Each child expressed the different functions of negation (non-existence, rejection and denial) before different syntactic forms were acquired to express each function. In Kathryn's case, for example, *no* was used to signal all three functions at first. Only in the later phase of negation did she acquire more fully developed syntactic means for expressing the categories differentially. So the function, in a sense, preceded the form. In addition, there were differences between the children in Bloom's study in the form of the negative used to express these functions.

Bloom's finding that denial developed last can be explained in part by the fact that the cognitive demands on the child are greater for denial than for non-existence and rejection: In denial the child negates a symbolic referent, i.e., what is denied is not present. Also, the negation is of a proposition in a prior utterance. In contrast, non-existence and rejection are simpler: non-existence does not require negation of a prior utterance while denial does; in rejection, the negated referent is present or imminent whereas in denial it is absent. (Rejection can include rejecting a proposition in a prior adult utterance, although Bloom does not discuss this aspect of rejection.)

The acquisition of negation reported in Lord (1974) differs from that of Bellugi and Bloom. Lord observed that her daughter used elevated intonation to express negation in the earliest stage. In addition, she used *no*, *not* + NP and *can't*, *don't* + VP to express negation. Apparently the semantic expression of negation as non-existence, rejection and denial did not follow the distinct stages reported in Bloom. There were however, many examples of negations of prior adult utterances in Lord's data even at the beginnings of negation.

Although concensus is not great, there is agreement that negation is at first pre-positioned to the rest of the utterance and only subsequently positioned internal to the utterance. In addition, it appears that anaphoric negation of the form [*neg* + S] comes into use at an MLU of 2;0, although it comprises a minority of the negative utterances.

If one argues as Lewis and Cherry have (in press) that learning to communicate through language is the result of the interaction of linguistic, social and cognitive factors, then it is highly appropriate to examine a phenomenon like functional negation that displays this interaction. In terms of the child's social cognition, negating another's speech requires some understanding of "the thoughts, emotions, intentions, and viewpoints of others" (Shantz, 1975). The ability to create functional negation also places heavy cognitive demands on the child since it requires the simultaneous retention of three propositions: keeping in mind what the other person has said, what you think is wrong, and what claim(s) you would instead make. That the simultaneous retention of different kinds of information is not an easy task is demonstrated by Bowerman's investigation of the acquisition of causative verbs. She found that causatives are not used early in language development because the child must retain in mind both "an act upon a patient and the change of state or location which the patient undergoes" (p. 72). This retention of dual action in the case of causative verbs or three propositions in the case of functional negation, is a significant achievement in the child's language development. The cognitive requirements for denial, coupled with the expression of alternatives, present particular problems for the child and must therefore represent a significant accomplishment.

In sum, functional negation places the following demands on the child. It requires:

1) some semantic and syntactic interpretation of another speaker's prior utterance;
2) simultaneous retention of two or three propositions;
3) being able both to recognize that you and others have points of view and being able to evaluate possible discrepancies in viewpoints;
4) that the child must be able to understand and express causation, reasons, and alternatives, depending on the type of functional negation.

METHODS

The data presented here were drawn from a larger longitudinal study of four children's acquisition of English as a second language. For the analysis of functional negation, we examined the speech productions of Maija, a native Finnish speaker. Maija was 4;3 at the outset of our investigation, and had been in this country for three months. While both her parents spoke English to varying degrees, English was not spoken in her home nor did Maija have any real contact with native English speakers prior to coming to this country.

Like the other children in our study, Maija was videotaped approximately every week for one-half hour in a structured play setting interacting with a native English speaking investigator. The same graduate student investigator interacted with Maija each session.

The nature of the interaction between the child and the adult in our study can be characterized by what Goffman has called "focused interaction." In Goffman's words, focused interaction is "the kind of interaction that occurs when persons gather close together and openly cooperate to sustain a single focus or attention, typically by taking turns in talking" (p. 24). Focused interaction is typical of adult-child discourse in a physical setting like that in our study. Two speakers were the only ones present; they occupied a relatively confined area of space and were engaged in cooperative play activity. The adult paid close attention both to what the child said and did.

FUNCTIONAL NEGATION: THE CHILD'S CONTRIBUTION

As suggested in the introduction, we were interested in the ways in which children learn to construct discourse by implicitly or explicitly building on a previous proposition from another speaker. We addressed this concern by isolating and describing the sequence of interactions characterized by the notion "functional negation". In particular, we were interested in characterizing in very general terms the child's expression of functional negation and the nature of the adult's subsequent response. (For more discussion of functional negation see also Keller-Cohen, Chalmer, and Remler, in press.) The characterization of functional negation presented here is constructed so as to articulate the direction of future investigation. We hope that the description presented here will clearly indicate further areas of research on this topic.

In general, the mode of expressing negation in discourse changed from nonverbal to verbal. In the early stage Maija relied on a head shake to express functional negation (13); this was followed by a transition to nonverbal + verbal expression (14) and finally to verbal expression primarily (15).

(13) (Playing with clay)
Myra: ...Shall I make a dog?
(Maija shakes head)
Myra: No? OK. I think I'll make a tree. How's that?
(Maija nods head)

(14) (Maija is trying to separate pieces of a grocery game)
Myra: Can you get it apart?
(Shaking head) Maija: no/
Myra: Want me to do it?
(Nodding head) Maija: yeah/

(15) Myra: Uh huh. I wonder. Do you know what that elephant's name is?
Maija: n/ no/
Myra: His name is Babar. Yeah.

Flowchart notation was employed to characterize the organization of the conversational unit "functional negation". The steps in a functional negation can be many since each speaker has alternatives at different points in the sequence. This is presented in Appendix A.

The initial point in a child's functional negation is an utterance or set of utterances by another speaker, in this case an adult. Once the child selects to respond to the adult's contribution in a functionally negative manner, he is confronted with the task of selecting from his present linguistic inventory a means of conveying the negation.

One simple way of signaling functional negation is to shake your head. In the first two months of our study, Maija's most frequent means of signaling negation in discourse was the headshake. (16) is an example of this:

(16) (Maija puts a hat on the doll's head)
Myra: There we go. It fits doesn't it? And she has a purse, and her hat on. She's going someplace, huh?
Is she going to school maybe?
(Maija shakes her head)
Myra: No.
(Maija picking up baby doll) Maija: baby/

An expression of functional negation that developmentally appeared somewhat later was a combined verbal-nonverbal response, i.e., a headshake in combination with no. This can be seen in (17).

(17) (Myra and Maija are playing store)
Myra: Oh, that's too much. Do you have a smaller bunch?
That's too much. I don't have that much money.
(Maija shaking head) Maija: aah/ no/
Myra: No? OK. I'll take an apple then, instead.

Still a third means of communicating discourse negation is no plus nonverbal behavior. We distinguish here between nonverbal behavior and nonverbal response. A nonverbal response is headshaking which can function as a complete response. Nonverbal behavior is any behavior other than a headshake. Such behavior serves to reinforce the child's verbal negation but can occur by itself. Some instances of nonverbal behavior cannot be interpreted unambiguously and such examples were therefore excluded from the description reported here.

The way in which nonverbal behavior reinforces a verbal negation can be seen in (18) where Maija's no is accompanied by placing her hand on the tablet page to prevent the proposed activity from taking place.

(18) (Myra and Maija are drawing)
Myra: Let's see if we can draw one, ok?
(Maija puts hand on page when Myra tries to turn to a clean sheet of paper)
Maija: no/

Although nonverbal behavior and nonverbal responses were prominent throughout the duration of the study, the most frequent means of expressing functional negation was no. This is illustrated in (19).

(19) (Maija dresses a doll)
Myra: She's gonna disappear in there, isn't she? That's not so good. Can we get some clothes that fit her?
Maija: no/
Myra: Why? (unbuttons doll's coat) Want that off?

This form of functional negation occurred consistently over the eight months of the investigation.

A shared feature of examples (16) - (19) is the absence of elaboration accompanying the negation (as seen in 20a and 20b). Although such examples appeared throughout the data, they were uncharacteristic of the early stages of development. Apparently, Maija had learned an unambiguous signal for negation in discourse but had not yet learned when or how to elaborate on a functional negation. These negations therefore tended to be syntactically less complex than non-negative utterances produced during the same time period. The significance of this fact is discussed later.

Since functional negations typically exhibited reduced complexity initially, it was expected that the course of Maija's linguistic development would display functional negations with greater semantic and syntactic complexity. This is borne out beginning with the third month of the study when Maija began to spontaneously elaborate on her discourse negation.

Elaborated functional negations tended to be expressed by syntactically and semantically less complex means in the early months of the study. The elaborations were expressed by utterances that were shorter than non-negative utterances produced by Maija during the same period. It appears that the semantic load that negation carries is sufficiently great such that the child is constrained by some limitation on storage or processing space (Bloom, 1970).

The constraints of the semantic weight carried by negation can also be seen in the absence of internal negation in functional negations with no. Whereas Maija used the negative no and not within an utterance, when the anaphoric no was present no other negatives occurred. This indicates the presence of an operating constraint that allows for the expression of only one negative element per utterance, hence blocking the production of utterances of the form No, it's not X, it's Y. To argue that the absence of more than one negative element is simply the reflection of a more general constraint on production would overlook this important cooccurrence restriction.

Support for the relationship between semantic weight and utterance complexity can also be found in utterances that did not contain functional negation. In (21) Maija explains why Babar the elephant uses his trunk to hold a carving knife. Her single word explanation is substantially less complex than utterances produced at the same time period.

(21) (Myra and Maija are examining a picture of Babar carving a turkey, holding the knife with his trunk)
Myra: Look at how he's cutting. Why do you suppose he's doing that?
Maija: hands/
Myra: Doesn't he have any hands?
Maija: no/

One way in which a functional negation can be expanded is to provide a reason or explanation for the negation. In (20a) for example, Maija explains why the postman can't go through the light; in (20b) she justifies turning down an invitation.

(20a) (Myra and Maija are playing with the Fisher-Price Village)
Myra: Postman. (Puts mailman in car) OK. Here comes the postman, Maija. Vroom. Delivering the mail. Can he go through (the stoplight)?
Maija: no/ red/
Myra: It's red.
Maija: yeah/

(20b) (Myra and Maija playing with dolls)
Myra: So would you like to go shopping with me today?
Maija: no I am . looking baby now/ I am babysitting/

Myra: You're a babysitter? Ah.

We have already seen that a negation can be expanded by the child providing reasons for the negation. Another means of elaboration is the presentation of alternatives. In supplying alternatives, the child in effect says X is not the case, Y is. This can be seen in (22a) and (22b).

(22a) (Myra and Maija are discussing Maija's father's back injury)
Myra: He sleeps, huh, stays in bed.
Maija: no/ floor/
Myra: Huh?
Maija: floor her sleep/[4]

(22b) (Examining Babar book)
Myra: Where do you suppose they're going? They're in a boat.
Do you think they're going back to the zoo?
Maija: no/ go home!/

Functional negation has thus far been characterized as: 1) the unelaborated negation of a prior proposition by the use of no (not) or 2) an elaborated negation of no + reasons or alternatives. Functional negation need not negate a prior proposition however; it can negate the presuppositions or background information of a particular proposition. In light of the demands placed on the child, it is not surprising that such examples seldom occurred. The infrequency of negated presuppositions can be explained as follows. Like any functional negation, the child negates another speaker's proposition: As with elaborated functional negations the child provides an alternative. But unlike other functional negations, the negation is of covert material, information not explicitly expressed in the other speaker's proposition. An example of negated presuppositions appears in (23a). Here Maija and Myra have been discussing seasonal temperature changes in Finland. They have also been dressing dolls in different clothes appropriate to different changes in temperature. Myra has been unable to determine whether Maija's claims are with regard to the dolls at hand or with regard to real life events. Maija's functional negation clarifies the confusion.

(23a) (Myra and Maija are dressing dolls)
Myra: So hot he d- that he doesn't need to be dressed up warm then, does he, 'cause it's summer.
Maija: no/ I playing it's cold day/

A similar example appears in (23b). Myra and Maija have been playing with the Fisher-Price Village. Myra has misinterpreted how Maija has set up the play scene, confusing the barbershop and the dentist's office.

(23b) Myra: What will you be doing after your haircut?
(Maija indicating barbershop on opposite end of village; her doll is in the dentist's office)
Maija: no/ here's haircut/
Myra: Oh.
Maija: is go to here teeth/

One alternative to elaborated functional negation is topic change. If the child does not wish or is unable to pursue the proposition introduced in the other speaker's utterance beyond negating it, she may simply change the topic. This can be seen in (24a) and (24b).

(24a) (Myra and Maija playing store)
Myra: This is an awful lot of money, you know. I don't want to pay that much for bananas.
(Maija gives Myra some coins)
I have another coin. Do I have to give that to you now?
Maija: no/ what more you want/

(24b) (Myra and Maija playing with dolls)
Myra: What about the hippopotamus? Can he go to Florida with Mama?
Maija: no/ oh mama you take your boots off/ clothes off mama take/ daddy everything sunglasses on/ mommy's sleeping/

In the preceding section we have characterized the shape of the child's functional negation. The reader may have observed that in many sequences, the adult probed the child's functional negation. The regularity with which the adult queried the child's negation suggested that the adult might be providing a post hoc model for elaborated functional negation. That is, in the event that the child produces an unelaborated functional negation, the adult's subsequent response may serve to illustrate what more the child could say. The form and function of the subsequent adult response are considered in the following section.

THE ADULT RESPONSE

The preceding discussion of functional negation represents only a portion of the picture. When a child produces an utterance that negates another speaker's proposition, the co-present speaker asks herself "Is this response sufficient? Has it given me the information I am interested in?" In the case of unelaborated functional negation, the adult frequently decides that the child's negation is insufficient because an unelaborated functional negation halts the progress of the conversation. It rejects or denies a prior proposition, claiming Not X, but does not add Instead Y. The absence of new information interrupts the flow of speech between the two speakers. That this new information is essential is demonstrated by the regularity with which the adult probes the child until Y is supplied. This is illustrated in (25).

(25) (Myra and Maija are playing with toy schoolhouse)
Myra: It looks like the animals decided to come to school today.
Maija: no!/
Myra: Why not?
Maija: they are not going school/
Myra: Why not. Lookit. Here's a camel and he's sitting in the desk.
(Maija grabbing camel and tossing it aside)
Maija: no:!/ no/
Myra: And there's the kangaroo sitting in the desk. Why can't he go to school?

Maija: no:/ I don't want/ teacher don't want/

One of the most significant features of the sequences in discourse negation is the adult's response to the child's negation. The adult's response assumes one of three forms: a) in the case of a nonverbal response (headshake) the adult often provides the verbal equivalent (no?) and optionally provides an alternative. In the event of a verbal functional negation the adult: b) queries the child's reasons or probes the alternatives or, c) acknowledges receipt of the functional negation (no?) and provides a possible reason or alternative, i.e., the adult elaborates the child's negation. We suggest that the function of the adult response is to provide a model for a more complete expression of the functional negation. The subsequent adult response seems to offer the child a potential paradigm for communicating elaborated negation in discourse.

For example, in (13) the adult's response to the negation is an example of Type A above since it both signals the child that the message has been received and indicates what the child could have said. (26) is a Type B response; it requests an elaboration, indicating that a reason would be appropriate.

(26) (Holds binoculars up to doll)
Myra: Binoculars. Think she can see anything out of 'em?
Maija: no/
Myra: Why?
Maija: this dolly/

In (27), also Type B, the adult's subsequent query suggests that the expression of an alternative would appropriately expand the initial functional negation.

(27) Myra: What are we going to do with the blocks?
Maija: no/
Myra: Shall we build something with those?
Maija: first we play with these/

The adult need not always provide the frame for the elaboration by indicating that reasons or alternatives are appropriate. Instead, the adult may optionally confirm receipt of the negation and supply a specific reason or alternative as in (28). This is a Type C response.

(28) (Picking up the turtle)
Myra: What about the turtle? He's-
(Maija grabbing turtle and putting it back in place)
Maija: no/
Myra: No? Oh, he can't move.

The regularity with which the adult facilitated conversational flow until the child provided elaboration was both consistent over time and across a wide range of discourse topics. The adult's probes apparently provide the child with a pattern that he eventually comes to master. By either suggesting the direction of the elaboration (reasons or alternatives) or providing a sample elaboration (as in (28)) the adult is able to indicate how the functional negation can be expanded. This is not to say that a child could not learn to expand negations in discourse without the adult probe. Yet it suggests that sequential units in discourse are available to the child as data for the structure of conversational units, in this case functional negations.

The data above suggest the following organizational features of discourse negation. First, functional negation occurs most often after yes-no questions. The frequency of negations following adult declaratives was more limited. This suggests that responding no to yes-no questions is easier because it explicitly requests affirmation or negation. Negating an assertion by someone else appears to be a later acquired type of discourse negation. Second, the most common means of signaling functional negation is the headshake or no. The co-present speaker may, however, interpret these responses as insufficient because they do not add new information. Unelaborated functional negations therefore appear to halt the forward flow of conversation. Third, more complex and conversationally more facilitative means of functional negation include offering reasons and alternatives. When the child does not offer an elaborated functional negation, she may still move the dialogue along by changing the topic. Fourth, the frequency of elaborations in negation increased over time. The acquisition of the paradigm for functional negation may be facilitated by the adult probing or offering a sample elaboration of the child's functional negation. Fifth, a happy discourse negation can therefore be characterized as one which both negates and introduces new information. This information can be supplied by either speaker.

IMPLICATIONS FOR UNDERSTANDING CHILDREN'S DISCOURSE

In this paper we have described the sequential organization of a conversational unit, functional negation. This unit is an example of a class of conversational sequences that are created across speakers and utterances. It is a significant development in terms of the child's conversational competence because it requires the retention and expression of two propositions. The negated proposition is expressed by the anaphoric no while the alternatively proposed proposition is expressed syntactically. It is likely that the first proposition is elliptical because of limits on the child's storage and processing space (see Keller-Cohen, in preparation). Expression of the anaphoric no eliminates the need to express No, it's not X and instead permits the reduced form, No, Y.* This suggests that children may first develop discourse skills that permit expression of complex ideas in structurally simple forms. Economy must be a compelling operating principle in the early stages of discourse development, be it in first or second language acquisition.

Examination of the structure of functional negation revealed that unelaborated functional negations in effect stop the forward movement of the conversation because they do not add sufficient new information. The regularity with which the adult probed unelaborated functional negations is evidence for this. Further research ought to be directed toward examining the relation between information structure (the juxtaposition of old and new information) and the structure of conversational units like functional negation.

---

*This argument is only meaningful if the child produces utterances of the form it's not X. Expressions of this form were frequently found in utterances that were not functional negations. Hence, the claim that there is a restriction on the simultaneous expression of two negative propositions is supported.

The structure of functional negation was also found to have import for our understanding of the role of input in the child's development of discourse skills. The adult's response following the child's functional negation was found to consist of the conversational frame or sample expansion for an unelaborated functional negation. This conversational framing offers a new interpretation of the frequent observation that adult's speech to children contains many questions. Further examination of the placement of adult questions in adult-child discourse may reveal that questions serve to indicate directions in which the child can expand discourse structure in general and specific conversational units in particular.

Scollon (1974) and Keenan (1974), among others, have argued for the importance of examining the development of child language in terms of the development of discourse skills. The examination of functional negation reported here is consistent with such a view. Continued examination of the developing interactional patterns between the child and the adult will certainly cause us to re-examine existing conceptions of the nature of language development.

BIBLIOGRAPHY

Bellugi, U. (1967) The Acquisition of Negation. Unpublished doctoral dissertation, Graduate School of Education, Harvard University.

Bloom, L. (1970) Language Development: Form and Function in Emerging Grammars, Cambridge, MIT Press.

Bowerman, M. (1973) Early Syntactic Development, Cambridge: Cambridge University Press.

Bowerman, M. (1974) Learning the structure of causative verbs. Papers and Reports in Child Language Development, 8, pp. 142-178.

Bowerman, M. (1975) Cross-linguistic similarities at two stages of syntactic development. In E. Lenneberg and E. Lenneberg (eds.) Foundations of Language Development, 1, New York: Academic Press.

Goffman, E. (1963) Behavior in Public Places, New York: Free Press.

Keenan, E. O. (1974) Conversational competence in children. Journal of Child Language, 1(2), pp. 163-183.

Keenen, E., Schieffelin, B. and M. Platt. (1976) Propositions Across Speakers and Utterances. Paper presented at the Child Language Research Form, Stanford.

Keller-Cohen, D., Chalmer, K. and J. Remler (in press) The development of discourse negation in the non-native child. In E. Keenan (ed.) Studies in Developmental Pragmatics, New York: Academic Press.

Keller-Cohen, D. (in preparation) Memory in the bilingual child.

Klima, E. (1964) Negation in English. In J. Fodor and J. Katz (eds.) The Structure of Language, New Jersey: Prentice-Hall, pp. 246-323.

Lewis, M. and Cherry, L. (1977) Social behavior and language acquisition.

In M. Lewis and L. Rosenblum (eds.) Interaction, Conversation and the Development of Language, New York: Wiley.

Lord, C. (1974) Variations in the acquisition of negation. Papers and Reports in Child Language Development, 8 pp. 78-86.

McNeill, D. and N. McNeill. (1973) What does a child mean when he says "No"? In C. Ferguson and D. Slobin. Studies of Child Language Development, New York: Holt, Rinehart and Winston, pp. 619-627.

Quirk, R., Greenbaum, S., Leech, G. and J. Svartvik. (1972) A Grammar of Contemporary English, New York: Seminar Press.

Scollon, R. (1974) One Child's Language from One to Two: The Origins of Construction, University of Hawaii dissertation, May 1974. [Also in Working Papers in Linguistics, University of Hawaii, 6(5).

Shantz, C. (1975) The development of social cognition. In E. Hetherington (ed.) Review of Child Development Research, 5, Chicago: University of Chicago Press.

APPENDIX A STEPS IN FUNCTIONAL NEGATION

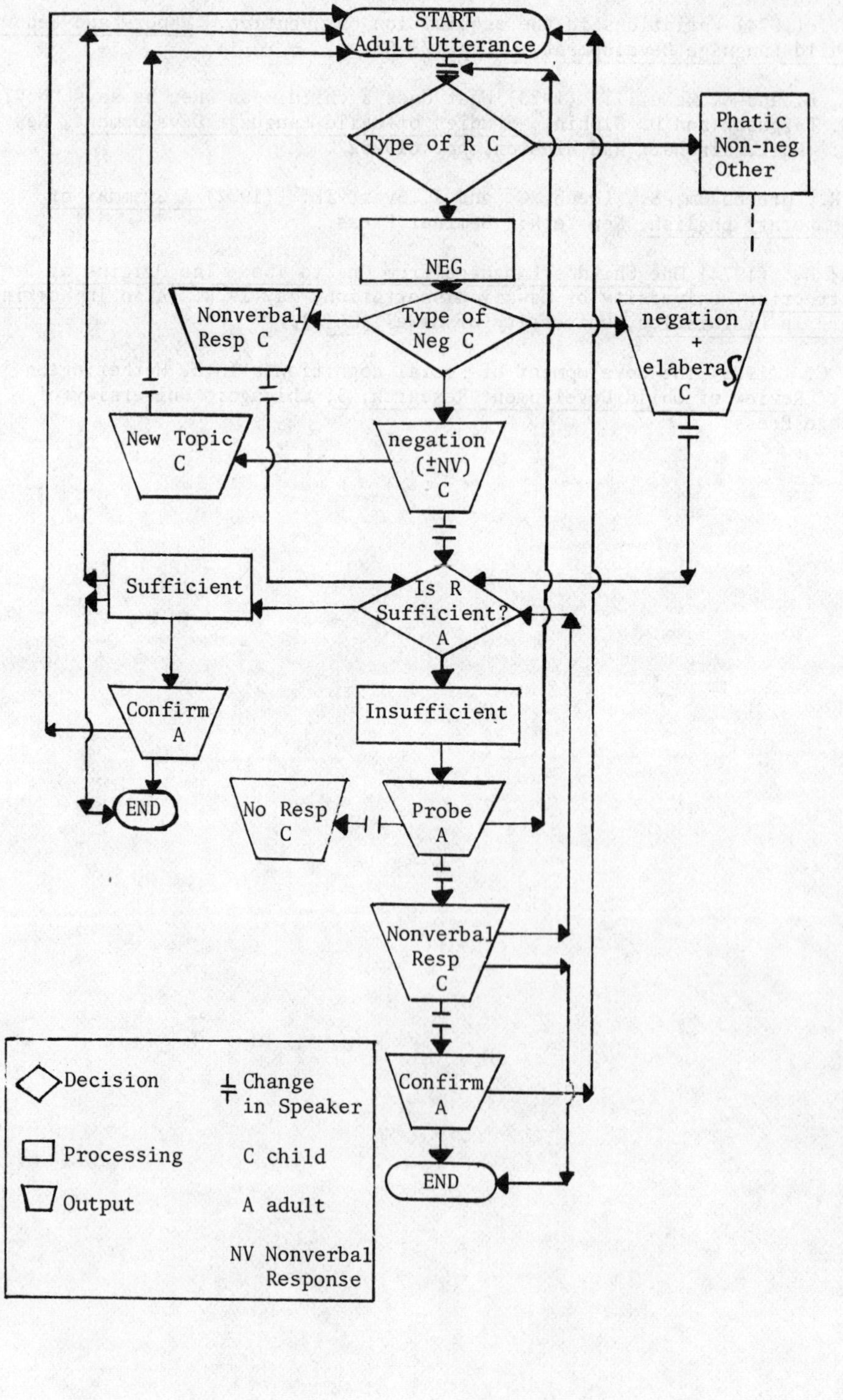

Development of Paralinguistic and Kinesic Expression of Roles

MARY RITCHIE KEY
University of California at Irvine

An infant's first communicative and cognitive experiences are expressed nonverbally (see Key, 1975; 1977). Infant vocalizations and infant motor activity are precursors of language. Some vocalizations eventually result in language sounds; some result in paralinguistic phenomena. Motor activity results in kinesic expression, among other things.

The development of suprasegmentals (intonational features) appears to start at birth, if not before -- if we consider rhythm. For example, the cry can be described in terms of pitch range, intensity, timing, intervals and rhythm, all elements of adult intonation patterns in every language. Vocalizations and motor activity are intimately integrated, and in correlation with each other, though only recently they have been studied from the point of view that they are inseparable.

The development of nonverbal behavior (paralanguage and kinesics) is crucial in the acquisition of language; there is evidence that disruptions of nonverbal behaviors may result in disruptions of acquisition of language. Many scholars have noted the close relationship of body language to the development of speech. Bullowa's (1970) studies corroborate this relationship.

Rhythm is a basic element of life and behavior, and with the advent of technology scholars are now able to record and film the rhythmic interactions of human beings. Studies that speak to this interactional synchrony are accruing, providing abundant proof that interactive behaviors and responses have their effect on learning and maturing.

Rhythms may be biologically based, or they may be culturally learned. Knowledge of the circadian rhythms or the biologic clock is a commonplace these days. Lieberman's work (1968) on intonation in infant vocalizations is based on the hypothesis that there is an innate physiologic basis in the properties of intonation, and that the "linguistic use of intonation reflects an innately determined and highly organized system..." (p. 38). Abercrombie (1967) believes that rhythm in language is one of the most fundamental properties, and cites a study of a type of aphasis "in which brain damage has caused every feature of the production of speech to be lost except the pulse systems of the pulmonic air-stream mechanism, as if these were the most resistant to damage to the speech-centres of the brain." (p. 36, italics added).

It is thought that learned rhythms begin in utero. Brazelton, et al., (1975) suggest that "pathways may be set up in intrauterine life, ready to be entrained, especially by the mother, immediately after birth." (p. 148) They go on to hypothesize that the "messages which are communicated to the infant via the mother's face and movement seem to be at the root of their communication." Condon and his colleagues (1974) have been writing on interactional synchrony for over a decade. Their microanalysis of sound films reveal "a complex interaction system in which the organization of the neonate's motor behavior is entrained by and synchronized with the organized speech behavior of adults in his environment." (p. 101) This sociobiological entrainment is basic to communicating. Brazelton, et al., speak of the mother-infant interaction as a regulated homeostatic system. This system involves the achievement of affective synchrony, the substitutability of behaviors within a phase, and the cyclic rhythms. In their observations, they notated vocalizations of both mother and infant, direction of gaze, head position, body position, facial expression, blinks, amount of movement, and specific handling of the infant. These nonverbal behaviors indicated phases in the dyad which moved through: initiation, mutual orientation, greeting, play-dialogue, and disengagement. They found the interactants regulating their behavior in response to each other in a defineable homeostatic system. Rosenfeld has also studied mother-infant interaction. His studies are concerned with a time-series analysis, or the temporal association between infant and mother behaviors. He recorded cooing and fussing, and four variables of the mother: neutral voice, soothing voice, animated voice, and unusual voice (such as whistling and clicking). He has diagrammed the correlations of these interacting behaviors.

The relationship of physiology to communication is immediately evident when one observes extra-linguistic aspects of communication. A surprising number of physiological acts function as communicative devices, or at least contribute to communication. Though linguists do not record such acts as coughing, clearing the throat, or yawning in syntactic analysis, no one could doubt that these physiological acts often occur in human interactions. More subtle relationships having to do with perception of movement, the use of the body in space, the affect of intense sounds, the diurnal fluctuation of the voice, and many others, are more difficult to recognize in correlation with linguistic patterns. I feel strongly that future studies will reveal their importance in human communication.

Dominating all other functions and organs in physiology is the brain which guides human behavior as well as physiology. Attention has been given recently to the relationships of language and the brain. I suggest that attention also be given to the relationship between the brain and nonverbal expressions of human behavior. It is recognized nowadays that nonverbal behavior/communication gives the overriding meaning to the language of the interaction between human beings. Both kinds of behavior are governed by the brain, where thoughts are processed and where many physiological functions are guided.

Gross anatomy of the brain shows two hemispheres -- the right and the left. Recent studies indicate that there are small but consistent anatomical differences between these hemispheres, especially locations near Wernicke's area (Geschwind, 1970). The right and left hemispheres are asymmetrical, at least in that speech-attributed area. Though this fact is widely accepted, it is by no means clear what the distribution of "duties" is for the right and left hemispheres, nor whether it is mutually exclusive. Over a century ago Broca popularized among neurologists the relationship of the left hemisphere and language. This premise has been widely accepted and has led to further declarations that the left hemisphere is the logical, intelligent, and analytic side of the brain which controls rational thinking. The left side is often referred to as the dominant or the major hemisphere. The right hemisphere is said to be minor and "primitive" -- the one from which originate the emotional, intuitive and artistic responses in the human being. This labeling has even been taken to extremes by some who have called the dominant left side "male" and the emotional right side the "female."

It might be seen that the nominal dichotomy of the functioning of the brain is the origin of the apparent dichotomy of verbal and nonverbal behavior. Could it be that the left hemisphere guides language (verbal) and the right hemisphere guides nonverbal acts? A review of the literature on language and the brain gives many examples that lead to this idea. If the extent and importance of nonverbal behavior is recognized, it might subsequently be shown that the "dominant" side is not the left side.

The duties of the left hemisphere are said to specialize in the following: cognitive and propositional language; sounds made by the speech apparatus (Kimura, 1973); some types of movement of the hand (Kimura, 1973); speech played backwards, foreign languages, and nonsense syllables (Kimura, 1973); consonants (Shankweiler, 1971); verbs (Gazzaniga, 1970). Kimura makes other observations about gestures and their relationship to speech. She notes that the manual activity during nonspeech events is different in kind.

The duties of the right hemisphere seem more numerous and varied and are difficult to delimit. The right hemisphere, Kimura says, plays a dominant role in the human being's perception of the environment. This side processes melodies, timbre and tonal properties, "emotional tone" of sentences (see Gazzaniga, 1971; Kimura, 1973; Van Lancker and Fromkin, 1973). The right side also is said to describe colors and objects. It processes visual tasks, such as spatial relationships and depth perception; emotional behavior, such as humor, displeasure, profanity; environmental sounds and sonar signals; nonlanguage vocalizations; coughing, laughing, crying; tactual behavior; olfactory stimuli; abstract notions, ideation, mental concentration, and high-order mental capacities. The right side qualifies statements which are made by the left, by such modifiers as "if, and, but, however" (Gazzaniga, 1970; Geschwind, 1970). The right side recognizes faces and tells the face to frown, or to shake the head (Gazzaniga, 1970). It also deals with the negative/affirmative concept (Gazzaniga, 1970; Gazzaniga and Hillyard, 1971). This should be of interest to linguists who have recently analyzed these concepts in a "pre-sentence" construct. With regard to acquisition of language and the negative/affirmative concept, is there a relationship between the brain development and children who go through the "No" stage? The right side specializes in concrete nouns. As far as gestures are concerned, Charlotte Wolff (1945) noted a preference for the left hand in expressive movement. She felt that the left hand, under the control of the right hemisphere, has a closer link with emotional than voluntary impulses. (See this reference for other comments on the right-left distinction.)

Linguistic studies have been done at UCLA recently on Genie, the deprived and isolated girl whose case came to light when she was thirteen years old. Because of her deprivation she resembles split-brain patients as well as left hemispherectomies. Since she has passed the critical stages of maturation, here language is not normal. Nevertheless, Genie performs surprisingly well on abilities normally localized in the right hemisphere (Curtiss, et al., 1975). For the most part she performs well on "appositional" tests. They note that her performance on some of these tests is "simply sensational."

On the Mooney Faces Test, which involves gestalt facial recognition, she scored far above the responses of a normal child. As far as they could discover, it was the greatest performance reported on this test for child or adult subjects. They conclude that Genie is proficient in at least some duties of the right hemisphere that have to do with spatial, configuration, appositional, and nonverbal abilities.

The relationship between the right and left hemispheres is not clearly understood yet, in spite of all the impressive research and publications. There are difficulties in testing and some of the experiments seem even more ingenious than the brain itself. For instance, the brain manages to compensate, and the behavioral strategies, cross-cueing, interlocking, and cooperation between the right and the left can only remind one that the human brain belongs to an "endlessly clever primate" (Gazzaniga, 1970; p. 126). In reviewing the studies, one also becomes aware that the term "nonverbal" is sometimes used in different ways than I am using it here, and we are not always talking about the same behaviors. At times the experiments are inadequate because they record only the verbal responses of the subject, though we know that other interactions take place -- as eye movement, facial expression, body movement -- which add to the meaning of the response.

Nevertheless, there is enough anecdotal information to hypothesize that the verbal and nonverbal systems have different origins in the brain. For one thing, the consciousness of control of these systems is different. Language is voluntary and conscious while nonverbal behavior is usually out-of-awareness (except, of course, when it is brought into awareness). For another thing, people do not react the same to sounds which are in the sound system of language as to sounds which they use in the paralinguistic system. A teacher in Germany once told me of the difficulty experienced by his students (from another dialect area) in pronouncing a "z" even though they used the sound freely to accompany a certain gesture. English speakers use at least two"click" sounds in their paralinguistic systems, but find it difficult to use these sounds in a language such as Zulu, where they occur in the language system. Also, there is a "perceptual" difference between singing and talking. While some people cannot carry a tune, they have no problem with pitch in intonation. There are differences between the singing and speaking behavior of aphasic patients and people who stutter (Geschwind, 1970). For classifications of right and left behavior, we should again consider linguistic structures that show classes of words which reflect nonverbal categories, such as sensory verbs, and verbs which indicate paralinguistic activity, such as shout, holler, scream, yell, bellow, whisper, shriek, wail, growl, grunt, mumble, moan, howl, mutter (Zwicky, 1971; Ross, 1970). Compare Gazzaniga's discussion of "smile, laugh, nod, frown."

There are other curiosities which must be brought to light in discussions of specialities of the two sides of the brain. For example, male and female responses. Kimura notes that males tend to have a greater left-visual-field superiority for dot location and dot enumeration than do females, and that females tend to have more verbal fluency than males (Kimura, 1973). Someone has conjectured that females do somewhat better than males in music performance. In prelinguistic behavior one notes that infants coordinate seeing and reaching. Gazzaniga notes that there is a clear link between eye and hand, and I am reminded of the remark by Juana Ines de la Cruz: "I hold in my hands two eyes, and see only what I touch." The matter of tactile interaction between humans is of concern in that some scholars have suggested that the act of touching and being touched is essential to the development of the brain, as well as to other physiological maturation.

The cognitive, social and emotional development of an infant begins much earlier than speech development. These features are expressed in vocalizations and kinesic behavior. The infant relates to categories and concepts in nonverbal ways. The kinds of things which later are articulated in language to give meaning are being developed before speech begins. For example, infants begin to distinguish between human and nonhuman (animate and inanimate categories in morphological or syntactical structures). Brazelton, et al., observe the responses of infants to objects and humans, and indicate that the infant is able to differentiate inanimate and animate events as young as two or three weeks of age. Infants gain control over: affirmation/negation; deictic processes; demand/request/command; alternatives (if, and, or); cause-effect (pushing, dropping, hitting). The infant relates to imaginative and pretend concepts by pretending to pick things out of the air, or dressing up in Mommy's purse and shoes (legendary and fable linguistic categories). The infant is defining categories by inserting or removing certain objects from the toy box, a purse, clothes hamper, wastepaper basket, diswasher, and drawers. Infants understand rejection and denial, as well as various question types: Who? Where? What?

Infants make up vocabulary items to cover categories which are meaningful to them. One infant I observed said [šiši] every time she heard a lawn mower, vacuum cleaner, automobile, or any motor that sounded similar. Infants also use syntactic structures of more than one element before speech develops. One infant I know used a three-constituent construction at one year of age. It was composed of recognizable syllables and a three-element intonation pattern, which could be recorded something like the following:

[da-da-da iiiii da-da-da]

It occurred while the family was out riding and a vehicle with a siren shrieking crossed their path suddenly. Complete with uplifted facial expression and pointing gesture toward the sound, it could be translated something like, "Mommy, a siren went by" or "Listen! The siren made a noise!" Infants are often heard to make two-constituent constructions, such as [da-da-da Ummmmmm], which might be translated "These (are) good" -- an equational construction. Halliday (1975) has some further discussion on early utterances of this type.

Infants use conversational styles, "talk" in whole paragraphs, and "tell" stories before they develop speech. These are expressed with nonsense (to the adult) syllables, using intonation patterns with breath groups and rising-falling pitches as are heard in dialogue and paragraph structure. Appropriate gestures and movement complete the "conversation", which may take place with a toy phone, with dolls, or with other small children. One infant I observed folded her arms at the end of the "conversation" just as her daddy did.

It seems that it would be profitable to investigate infant communication in much the same way that linguists record an unwritten language in a monolingual approach -- when there is no common language between the native language and the linguist. One would discover that before speech the infant uses communicative devices in a systematic and meaningful way.

In summary, it can be seen that paralinguistic and kinesic expression begin at birth and are essential to the development of language. The relationship of physiology to communication is evident in the observations of extralinguistic aspects of communication. It is possible that the origin of nonverbal behavior is in the right hemisphere of the brain, even as the origin of language apparently is in the left hemisphere of the brain. Attention to these findings should lead to a new approach to the study of the acquisition of language.

BIBLIOGRAPHY

Abercrombie, D. (1967) Elements of General Phonetics, Chicago: Aldine.

Brazelton, T. B., Tronick, E., Adamson, L., Als, H., and S. Wise. (1975) Early mother-infant reciprocity. In Parent-Infant Interaction, Ciba Foundation Symposium 33, Amsterdam: North Holland, pp. 137-154.

Brazelton, T. B., Young G. C., and M. Bullowa (MS). Inception and resolution of early developmental pathology.

Bullowa, M. (1970) The start of the language process, Actes du Xe Congres International des Linguistes Bucarest, 1967. Editions de l'Academie de la Republique Socialiste de Roumanie, pp. 191-200.

Bullowa, M. (1974) Non-verbal communication in infancy. Paper presented at the First Congress of the International Association for Semiotic Studies, Milan.

Bullowa, M., Fiedelholtz, J. L., and A. R. Kessler. (1973) Infant vocalization: communication before speech. Paper at the 9th International Congress of Anthropological and Ethnological Sciences.

Bullowa, M. and E. Putney. (1973) A method for analyzing communicative behavior between infant and adult from film. Paper presented at the International Society for the Study of Behavioral Development, Ann Arbor, Michigan.

Condon, W. S., and L. W. Sander. (1974) Neonate movement is synchronized with adult speech: interactional participation and language acquisition. Science, 183, pp. 99-101.

Condon, W. S. and L. W. Sander. (1974) Synchrony demonstrated between movements of the neonate and adult speech. Child Development, 45, pp. 456-462.

Curtiss, S., Fromkin, V., Harshman, R., and S. Krashen. (1975) Language development in the mature (minor) right hemisphere. Paper presented at the Linguistic Society of America, San Francisco, Calif.

Engel, W. (1964) Il prelinguaggio infantile. Brescia: Paideia Editrice.

Gazzinіga, M. S. (1970) The Bisected Brain, New York: Appleton-Century-Crofts.

Gazziniga, M. S., and S. A. Hillyard. (1971) Language and speech capacity of the right hemisphere. Neuropsychologia, 9, pp. 273-280.

Geschwind, N. (1970) The organization of language and the brain. Science, 170, pp. 940-944.

Geschwind, N. (1972) Language and the brain. Scientific American, 226, pp. 76-83.

Halliday, M. A. K. (1975) Learning How to Mean, London: Arnold.

Key, M. R. (1975) Paralanguage and Kinesics (Nonverbal Communication): With a Bibliography, Metuchen, New Jersey: Scarecrow Press.

Key, M. R. (1975) Male/Female Language, Metuchen, New Jersey: Scarecrow Press.

Key, M. R. (1977) Nonverbal Communication: A Research Guide and Bibliography, Metuchen, New Jersey: Scarecrow Press.

Kimura, D. (1973) The asymmetry of the human brain. Scientific American, 228, pp. 70-78.

Kirk, L. (1973) An analysis of speech imitation by Gã children. Anthropological Linguistics, 15 (6), pp. 267-275.

Kirk, L., and M. Burton. (in press) Maternal kinesic behavior and cognitive development in the child. Annals of the New York Academy of Sciences.

Krashen, S. (1972) Language and the left hemisphere. UCLA Working Papers in Phonetics, 24.

Lieberman, P. (1968) Intonation, Perception and Language, Cambridge: MIT Press.

Middlemore, M. P. (1941) The Nursing Couple, London: Cassell.

Rosenfeld, H. M. (1973) Time series analysis of mother-infant interaction. University of Kansas Symposium on the Analysis of Mother-Infant Interaction Sequences, Philadelphia.

Ross, J. R. (1970) On declarative sentences. In R. A. Jacobs, and P. S. Rosenbaum (eds.) Readings in English Transformational Grammar, Waltham, Mass.: Ginn and Company, pp. 222-272.

Shankweiler, D. (1971) An analysis of laterality effects in speech perception. In D. L. Horton and J. J. Jenkins, Perception of Language, Columbus, Ohio: Charles E. Merrill, pp. 185-200.

Stern, D. N. (1971) A micro-analysis of mother-infant interaction: behavior regulating social contact between a mother and her 3 1/3 month-old twins. Journal of the American Academy of Child Psychiatry, 10, pp. 501-517.

Tonkova-Yampol'skaya, R. V. (1973) Development of speech intonation in infants during the first two years of life. In C. A. Ferguson and D. I. Slobin (eds.) Studies of Child Language Development, New York: Holt, Rinehart and Winston, pp. 128-138.

Van Lancker, D., and V. A. Fromkin. (1973) Hemispheric specialization for pitch and 'tone': evidence from Thai. Journal of Phonetics, 1, pp. 101-109.

Wolff, C. (1945) A Psychology of Gesture, London: Methuen. [Reprinted by Arno Press, New York, 1972.]

Zwicky, A. M. (1971) In a manner of speaking. Linguistic Inquiry, 2 (2), pp. 223-233.

*"Wou' You Trade Cookies with the Popcorn?" The Talk of Trades Among Six Year Olds**

ELLIOT G. MISHLER
Harvard Medical School and Massachusetts Mental Health Center

The task of the present paper is to analyze how children do trading, a social activity which results in an exchange of objects through a process of bargaining. This process is organized, regulated and guided by norms, conventions, and values with regard to property rights, relative worth of objects, preference scales, considerations of equity and fairness, and a variety of other principles and rules. Of most importance for our purposes, the work of trading is usually done through talk.

Let us consider a series of exchanges, presented in Appendix A and B, which begin with "Wou' you trade cookies with the popcorn?" and "I gotta-I gotta Su:zy Q." These have a structure and coherence that is intuitively apparent. The first, a request to trade, is recycled and transformed in the face of the other party's reluctant response, is followed by some hard bargaining and some difficulties in reaching a mutually acceptable agreement, and finally terminates with a resigned "oh well." The second begins with an announcement that the speaker has a desirable object, meets with a series of failures to work out a trade, achieves success, and is terminated by an explicit politeness exchange.

In both instances, the process appears to have a degree of orderliness and an integrity. That is, their internal development and organization are guided by rules, apparently understood by both speakers, and the sequences are set off by linguistic boundary markers at either end from the ongoing flow of conversation and social action within which they occur. The problem for analysis is to develop a set of methods and concepts that are adequate for describing how the speaker-participants "do the work" of trading through their talk. The ultimate aim is to understand how social structure emerges through and is constructed by language. (See Bauman and Scherzer's discussion of speech events, 1975, pp. 108-112.)

In that trading is "accomplished" through the talk, that a trade is a joint achievement of the participants, the problems which are posed for analysis

---

*This is the fifth in a series of papers entitled, "Studies in Dialogue and Discourse" that focus on conversations in first grade classrooms. The study was supported in part by a research grant from the National Science Foundation (GS-30001). The work on trading talk, reported here, benefited from discussions with Anita Pomerantz and George Psathas. This revision also reflects Bruce Fraser's helpful comments on an earlier draft.

offer several advantages for the purpose of developing sociolinguistic models and theories. Foremost among these is the fact that since the trade is constructed through the process of trading, that is, we and the participants recognize that a situation of trade exists because trading is being done, our analysis must be consistent with the "analysis" being done by the participants themselves. In other words, the participants have the same problems as the observer-analyst of determining when they are in a "state of trade" and when it begins and ends. If we can describe how they solve these problems, we will at the same time have provided an analysis of the event. It should be evident that this approach relies upon the perspective of ethnomethodology as developed in the work of Garfinkel and Sacks, and their co-workers and students.

A related problem/advantage of the types of speech events that occur during the ongoing flow of conversation in a natural social setting is that the language itself is the primary source of information and data. Sociolinguistic analyses of speech events, particularly those of ethnolinguists and anthropologists, often refer to rituals and ceremonies where linguistic forms and sequences are provided by general cultural norms, which also specify the meaning and significance of the talk (see for example, Frake, 1972). This allows the analyst to use his/her general understanding of the culture to understand what is being said, and how it is accomplished. The language itself, however, is frequently treated "merely" as illustrative of the more general cultural analysis. In the instances under examination here, we will not have the advantage of a formal and prescribed ritual to rely upon. We are thrown into the sea of talk and will have to find its structure from the inside.

Although the work of ethnomethodologists and conversational analysts informs the approach followed here, my emphasis is somewhat different. Rather than being interested primarily in how speakers solve certain general (and perhaps universal) conversational problems, such as turn-taking (Sacks, Schegloff, and Jefferson, 1974) or "openings" and "closings" (Schegloff and Sacks, 1973), I am interested in how problems of social process are expressed in and solved through language. My focus, then, is on the "realization" of the social process in talk and on the ways in which linguistic resources of speakers are used to solve the problems of speakers as social actors rather than the problems of speakers as conversationalists.

Nonetheless, the work of the conversational analysts provides some of the principle resources for this effort in much the same way that models of grammar developed by theoretical linguists provide resources for the work of psycholinguists and sociolinguists. I shall, therefore, be concerned with specific ways in which turns are taken, and conversations opened and closed, but always with attention focused on how the particular forms used serve the functions of "trading".

Trading: Some Preliminary Concepts

I am proposing that trading is one type of framed activity, to use the Bateson-Goffman term (Goffman, 1974). This suggests that it has certain features that set it off not only from "just talk" but from other framed events, particularly those that may also involve verbal "exchange" between speakers, such as games, insult rituals and verbal dueling (Dundes, Leach, and Özkök, 1972; Labov, 1972; Mitchell-Kernan, 1972), or the exchange of gifts or compliments.

The essential conditions for trading are, simply put, two or more parties with tradeable objects and trading motives. The problem for participants is to express the trading relevance of their own objects and motives, to assess the presence of similar relevances in others, and to elicit their expression from them. There is a further and special feature of trading which generates the specific features of the bargaining process through which the trade is accomplished. This feature is that, in order to be tradeable, objects must differ from each other; we do not trade identical objects. Note the following exchange, which begins like some trading sequences but does not become one:

S1 Wanna sit with me?
S2 Ha Ya got any snacks?
S1 Yup. Gotta snack pack.
S2 I do too.

Since the objects are not identical, they must be assessed relative to each other on some standard of judgment. This is likely to be a mix of external reference scales of value and the preference scales of the parties involved. Trading requires the ongoing specification of these standards of value, the mutual assessment of the relative value of the objects, and the determination of the general preferences and situational motives of the two parties. This is done through such negotiating exchanges as the following (from Trading Sequence I, Appendix A), which form the core of the trading sequences.

S1 Want some popcorn?
S2 Those are smaller. So if I give you one, you'd hafta give me like fiv:ve.
S1 You give me two and I'll give you 'bout this much.

The centrality of bargaining, and its uniqueness as a characteristic of trading, has another important consequence for the participants and for the analysis of their talk. The problem faced by the participants is that a successful trade, excluding such instances as coercion or deception, requires that the exchange be viewed as an equitable one by both parties; but this result must be achieved from a situation which begins with nonidentical, and hence unequal, objects. If an objective standard existed on which the relative value of the objects could be calculated with some degree of exactness, then bargaining would simply involve rational calculation. Obviously, bargaining is always more than this and its qualities are captured more clearly by social cliches like "hard bargaining" or "bargaining from strength."

Each party has an interest in "bargaining from strength." It is through the bargaining process itself that their respective strengths (relative to each other) will be demonstrated, given the limited utility for this purpose of any external reference scale. Except perhaps for defining a range within which certain classes of objects may be viewed as tradeable within particular circumstances, the relative bargaining power of parties will depend in part on their expressed need or wish for the other's object. That is, if I want what you have more than you want what I have then I am likely to find myself in a weaker bargaining position. As we shall see, in the detailed analysis of the next section, efforts to elicit the expression of such wishes, from the other party, and to restrict the expression of one's own wishes, are a critical feature of the bargaining process.

My analysis will focus primarily on how the essential conditions for trading are displayed in the talk. This includes making visible to each other the existence of tradeable objects and motives as well as their respective strengths as bargainers. These are not considered to be 'preconditions' for trading which, when set in place allow for some separate process of 'trading' to get underway. Rather, the talk itself is the realization of these conditions. To be doing the talk of trading is to be in a state of trade, and this definition of the situation for the two parties is being constructed and affirmed continuously through the announcements, assessments, offers and counter-offers of the speakers acting/speaking as traders. Thus, the opening utterance, "Wou' you trade cookies with the popcorn?" both expresses the speaker's readiness to trade and, at the same time, probes for the presence of a tradeable motive in the other. It already makes explicit that, from the speaker's point of view, the other has a tradeable object. In addition, the utterance is also part of the bargaining process, and its function in this respect has the consequences, as we shall see, for the way the trading sequence develops.

While the position adopted here is consistent with the general orientating idea that "social structures" emerge through speech events (Bauman and Sherzer, 1975), the emphasis is different in ways that may be important for sociolinguistic analysis and theory. To say that a structure "emerges" from a process suggests two discrete phenomena, one of which is the product of the other. This is not what is intended here. I am suggesting instead that the social structure of a state of trade exists in and through the "talk" of trading, and consists in the structure of this talk as it develops and is recognized by the speakers as trading. I take this to be one of the central meanings of Garfinkel's concept of reflexivity (Garfinkel, 1967).

A further implication of this approach is that each utterance is viewed as both affirming and assessing the sense of the conversation as "trading" (or, reaffirming/reassessing the continuing existence of the state of trade.) At the same time, I am asserting that the sequence of utterances that constitutes the trading talk has a particular structure and is not simply a stretch of talk with each speaker at each point having an equal option to make or not to make a statement that is relevant to the trade. That is, once the trading process is initiated, or an effort is made to initiate it, there are constraints on what may be said in the sense of what it would be appropriate to say. Such constraints on the appropriateness of next utterances are familiar from analyses of various types of exchanges, such as adjacency pairs with first and second pair parts (Schegloff and Sacks, 1975), greetings (Ervin-Tripp, 1972) and questions and answers (Mishler, 1975a, 1975b, 1976). This is an essential feature of the claim that the trading process is a structure, i.e., the component elements have some form of dependence on each other.

A further implication of this meaning of structure as constraining, is that there are certain points where we would expect evidence of the constraints. These are likely to be at points of transition from non-trading to trading, or the reverse, and would be marked by changes in the fluency of speech, attention markers, or perhaps be repairs of the inappropriate act. Another way to state this is that shifting in or out of the structure of a trade, or any other structured social activity, requires "work" and it should be possible to find evidence of this work in the text.

Analysis of Trading Talk

In introducing the problem of trading, we noted that the "popcorn" (Appendix A) and "Suzy Q" sequences (Appendix B) have a structure and coherence that is intuitively apparent. From our remarks in the previous section, it should also be apparent that we, as readers, may have arrived at this sense of these passages in ways and on grounds that are not parallel to or in accord with the ways in which participants both create and simultaneously recognize that they create a state of trade.

We, as observer-analysts, made our judgment on the basis of the full text. By seeing how it came out, we "know" that a trade was "really" in process. But, where did it begin? And, how was it brought into being through the sequential exchanges of utterances? The "popcorn" example seems to pose no problem for locating a beginning since it starts with a trading request. But, where does the "Suzy Q" sequence begin as a structured trading sequence? Does it begin, as I seem to have assumed, with the announcement that "I gotta-I gotta Su:zy Q"? Or, does it "really" begin with the explicit trading request "...What will ya give me fer a Suzy Q?" I shall argue that the first announcement is the proper place to begin, and that there is internal evidence for treating this as an "opener" for trade. But, this first attempt fails. It does not generate the essential conditions of mutually recognized tradeable objects and motives. So, the effort is repeated, in this example, in systematically different forms until a state of trade is achieved.

Whereas the Suzy Q exchange begins with an announcement of what turns out to be a tradeable object, the cookies-for-popcorn opener is in itself a request for a trade which specifies the tradeable objects held by each party. Of the four requisites for trading that we proposed earlier, three are provided in first utterance -- the tradeable objects that each possesses and the motive to trade on the part of the first speaker. In contrast, the Suzy Q announcement is less complete and less definite; neither a trade-relevant object nor motive are explicitly expressed by the first speaker. Nor does he indicate a trade-relevant object or motive on the part of the other. The announcement is a much more general search procedure; the speaker is a potential seller looking for buyers who might have something equally "interestin" to offer.

A third example of a trading sequence includes a different type of search procedure. "Alan, whadda you got?" does not, on its surface, indicate that the speaker himself has either a trade-relevant object or motive. This sequence is presented in Appendix C.

Despite their differences, there is one common feature to the trading exchanges which follow these different openers. In each instance, the first speaker is forced into a weaker trading position. That is, second speaker(s) respond in such a way that when the actual trading process or negotiation "begins" the first speaker has become more of a pleader asking for something that the second speaker has. Thus, the announcement "I gotta-I gotta Suzy Q" is an effort to gain another's attention by the claim, expressed through the slightly teasing intonation and the emphasis of the stretched vowel in 'Su:zy', that the speaker has a valuable and prized object. This is a strong statement that gives nothing away to the other, in that neither a wish to offer the object nor a wish for something the other has is expressed. The response denies the presence of the prized object. Note that the value of such an object is not questioned, but rather the speaker's possession of the object as claimed. The exchange which follows centers on the justification of the claim that indeed what the first speaker has is a real Suzy Q. The evidence offered turns out to be unarguable not only did "My mamma" say it was a Suzy Q, but "She bought them." The first speaker wins the argument, since no further rebuttals are forthcoming, but the cycle terminates without leading into a trade.

The first speaker tries again with another announcement. There is a change, however, and the combination of a repetition of the announcement with a change offer some evidence that more is being done than simply announcing. The change is further specification of the value of the object: "I got somethin interestin Suzy Q's." The specification within the reannouncement must be read within the context of the failure of the previous exchange to engage another's attention for further business. In this sense, although the utterance is more explicit, it reflects a weakening of the first speaker's position; he has been forced to specify the value of the object rather than being able to leave it implicit, and thereby loses some bargaining power.

The first reannouncement produces no results. There is a long (45 second) break and then he starts again, but this time with a specific trading request. The full statement includes a repeat of the original announcement prefaced by the name of another child specifically selected for a possible trade (thus, further ensuring the other's attention) and ends with a specification of the other's tradeable object "An apple?". The elements for a trade that are now present are equivalent to those in the opening utterance of the "popcorn" example--tradeable objects and a motive to trade on the part of the speaker.

At the same time, this second reannouncement with its explicit request for a trade represents a further weakening of the speaker's bargaining position. The first announcement represented an attempt to elicit a request from the other, an expressed wish for the Suzy Q. If that had been forthcoming, the first speaker could have bargained from strength since he had not expressed any wish of his own for the other's object. The trading request represents instead an effort to elicit an offer from the other party. This shift marks the change in relative bargaining strength.

The next cycle has a peculiar feature. Although the first speaker specifies the tradeable object "An apple?", he then refuses the offer when it is made. A direct refusal of an offer, particularly in response to one's request, is unusual and appears to require justification. This is provided in the excuse about the lost tooth. A direct offer of the Suzy Q is then made, although presumably with the reservation that something else will have to be given in exchange. This also produces no results. Finally, someone else makes a direct offer which is accepted with alacrity and emphasis (as if "some of these" had been wanted all along in exchange for the Suzy Q). The counter-offer is made to complete the transaction and the trade terminated with a politeness exchange.

We proposed earlier that a trade is achieved through the talk of the trader-participants, that the trading process has a structure which is not predetermined but is nonetheless systematic and emerges through the interchange, and that our analysis must follow the analysis being made by the speakers as they construct, recognize, and enter into the trading process. The conversation that begins with "I gotta-I gotta Su:zy Q" and ends with the same speaker's "you're welcome" has a coherence, a structure, and an integrity as a bounded social unit. Our analysis of the shift in the bargaining power of the initial speaker reveals a systematic weakening of his position through a series of utterances, each a step-down from the previous one resulting from a failure to make a trade come off. This systematic shift is one of the principle structures of the trading process.

A similar progressive step-down in bargaining power is evident in the "popcorn" example (Trading Sequence I in Appendix A). Here an initial request to trade becomes a more pleading offer, "Want some popcorn?" Although the form of the second speaker's response to the initial trading request differs from the denial and silences that followed the Suzy Q announcements, the functions of the "What?" and "Umm umm" are the same and they produce the same results. The first speaker is attempting to initiate a trade; the responses are signs of trouble. He is being informed that the proposed trade will not simply run off. Nonetheless, he tests to see whether there is an alternative explanation, namely, that the second speaker has not heard him, by repeating the trading request. The lack of a direct response the second time around seems to convince him that it is trouble and not a lack of comprehension that is being expressed. He then moves to the form of a direct offer.

The second speaker's response indicates clearly that he has understood that a trading request was being made. Through his negotiating comment, he brings the full state of trade into existence since all the required elements are now present. His first remark is deprecatory, "Those are smaller" which also marks his relative strength in the bargaining process now that he has forced the other into an offer.

The depreciation of the offered object provides some further evidence that the offer is recognized as part of a trading process rather than as a direct offer, as of a gift. One would not respond to a present by belittling what is being given. Similarly, the denial of the Suzy Q-ness of the object in the other example indicates that the second speaker is aware that more may be involved in the announcement than the display of a prized possession. In both instances, the response to the opening statement is directed to diminishing the strength of the first speaker's position before the explicit bargaining begins. Although, in the Suzy Q example, the second speaker loses the round of the argument (and does not enter into the trade, perhaps as a result of not being able to reduce the other's bargaining position), the result is a weakening of the first speaker's power for successive rounds, as we have seen above.

The "popcorn" sequence involves a more complicated bargaining process since amounts are involved rather than single objects, and the amounts of popcorn can only be vaguely specified, "bout this much" or "a whole hanful." This makes for some difficulty, after the first cycle, in determining whether the trade has been completed to each party's satisfaction. These difficulties continue through at least two more cycles, further complicated by a quality assessment, "I don't wanna broken one" and, at the end, the entry of a third party. Nonetheless, the sequence seems to come to an end, if not with politeness at least with resigned acceptance, "mm mm uh oh well."

The third illustrative sequence (Appendix C) begins in yet a different way with what seems to be a simple request for information -- "Alan, whadda you got?" The second speaker's silence forces two successive repetitions, each with increasing emphasis. The final utterance in the first speaker's turn might appear to have become stronger with each word now given emphasis and the form changed to an imperative from the original question from "Alan, whadda you got?" to "Alan, tell me what you got." Nonetheless, within the context of the two earlier requests and their lack of success in generating a response, I would argue that it represents a weakening of the bargaining position of the first speaker. He has been forced into the role of a pleader; the increased intensity of the statement reflects his stronger need to know rather than his power to command a response.

The second speaker counters with the same question -- "What do you got?" -- and immediately proposes a trade. It is important to note that he does not answer the question and that his proposal to trade is in a strong form, "I'll trade ya'", rather than the weaker "Would you trade..." statement in the "popcorn" example. The first speaker is forced to ask again, and again, for information about what is being offered by the other. The second speaker's second utterance -- "you have Johnnie" -- still does not provide this information but specifies the first speaker's object which the first speaker then further specifies. The "yummie yummie" utterance presumably makes the second speaker's object visible, but it has not been stated. Rather, he indicates how good and valuable it is. The first speaker is forced, finally, into a specific trading request. By this point, as in the "popcorn" and "Suzy Q" sequences, the first speaker has become a pleader and the second is in full command of the situation, able to delay the consummation of the deal by further questioning and reflection -- "I think I -".

The Structure of Trading

Through the delicate and subtle process of trading that has been described, one strategic rule appears to guide the participants: don't be the first to make a specific trading offer. Those who do so find themselves forced into a weakened bargaining position where the other speaker is able to set the terms of the trade to his/her advantage.

This poses a problem for the person who wishes to set a trade in motion, either because the other has a preferred or desirable object or because he/she has a nonpreferred object. The task is to get the other to take the first step. This may be accomplished in alternative ways. Among our speakers, these include: announcements in which attention is called to the possession of a desirable object, presumably with the intent of eliciting a trading request; a request to know what the other has (in another sequence, "Will you give me one?"); and finally, a generalized trading request which doesn't specify the exact terms of trade.

The second speaker's problem is similar -- to avoid making the first explicit offer in the trading process and to force the first speaker to do this. In our materials, second speakers do this through a variety of utterances that are not directly responsive to the trading possibilities that may be implicit or explicit in the first speaker(s) statement. Either they do not "hear" what was said, or they counter the claim made -- "That's not a Suzy Q." -- or counter-question the questioner -- "What do you got?" These responses force the first speaker to take the first step, although this may take several exchanges and perhaps involve some failures to accomplish a trade, as in the Suzy Q excerpt.

These initial exchanges are both bargaining in and of themselves, and at the same time set the stage for the explicit trading exchanges which follow. If neither of the parties is willing to take the first step, and thus risk entering the trade at a disadvantage, then the cycle may be aborted as in the first series of Suzy Q exchanges.

I have been arguing that trading involves a jockeying for advantage, that first offers to trade place that speaker at a disadvantage, and that the structure of these exchanges displays the ways in which speakers try to maintain their relative advantage by forcing the other person to make the first step. This is an organized and structured process and by engaging in it these children bring the social structure of a trade into being through their talk.

This joint accomplishment, the production of a trade through participants' talk, represents one half of the argument that underlies the analysis presented of trading sequences. The other half is that recognition by participants that they are engaged in trading, and not 'merely' talking or doing something else like telling a joke or exchanging greetings, has consequences for what they say and how they hear what the other says. Sacks asserts this principle in his analysis of the course of a 'joke's telling' in conversation, "...the fact that this is a joke that is being told figures in the course of its telling and that it is a dirty joke also figures." (Sacks, 1974, p. 347).

Without this condition, it would not be possible to understand the central features of these sequences as discourse, that is, as organized stretches of talk which have cohesion, internal structure, and boundary markers that set them off from the ongoing flow of conversation in which they occur. I am referring to the structured downgrading of successive trading requests that represents a weakening in bargaining power and to the systematic efforts to elicit trade-initiation statements from the other speaker.

It may be useful to contrast this approach with an alternative which has gained some prominence in recent work, namely, the analysis of speech acts. Garvey notes that the speech act has become an attractive construct since it "promises to relate the functional and the formal aspects of language. The construct links the motive force (the communication of social intentions) with the development of systematic means (the linguistic code) for the expression of meaning." (Garvey, 1976)

Her analyses of requests and contingent queries (Garvey, 1975) represents one way in which speech act theory may be applied. A brief comparison of her work with the approach developed here may be instructive with regard to the different implications of the two approaches for theory, analysis and research in sociolinguistics. Following Austin, Garvey argues that "it may be useful to consider the notion that a discourse is composed of illocutionary acts or speech acts." (1976, p. 3) This leads her to specify certain exchanges as structural units of discourse, such as the "Domain of a request" which refers to "the scope of discourse within which the attention of the speaker and addressee is directed to the accomplishment of the request." (1975, p. 49)

By Garvey's definition, many of the utterances in the trading sequences could be classified as direct requests. These would include: "Gimme a whole hanful. C'mon..a whole hanful." (I); "Get your hans outta here. Get your hans outta here." (I); "Alan, whadda you got?...Alan, tell me what you got." (III). Others appear to be indirect requests: "What about some of these?" (II) However, there are problem cases. For example, the initial announcement in the Suzy Q episode, "I gotta - I gotta Su:zy Q" turns out, on analysis of the full sequence which follows, to be an indirect request but this cannot be determined on the basis of the immediate exchange which follows. It is only when we can see that this was one cycle, a failure to trade, within the full trading sequence that we can specify it as an indirect request.

A similar problem of interpretation presents itself for other exchanges within the overall structure of the trade. For example, take the politeness exchange that concludes the Suzy Q sequence:

S5 What about some of these?
S1 I <u>do</u> want this fer a Suzy Q. Do you wanna Suzy Q?
...
S5 Thank you Steven.
S1 You're welcome.

If this exchange were treated in isolation, it would appear that the first speaker's (S5) statement had the illocutionary force of an offer. In such a case, we would expect that the recipient of the offer would produce the first part of the politeness exchange which follows an offer, that is, "Thank you." Instead, he restates the terms of the trade and makes the counter-offer. By accepting the trade, the first speaker (S5) has now been relocated so that it is now appropriate for him to begin the closing exchange and for the initial 'trader' to terminate the sequence with "You're welcome."

Similar questions may be raised with regard to the meaning and function of contingent queries. In the "popcorn" trading sequence, the first two responses by the second speaker, "What?" and "Umm umm" would meet Garvey's criteria for unsolicited contingent queries. The first is a nonspecific request for repetition; the second might be a request either for confirmation or specification of the information in the prior utterance. However, from an analysis of this sequence, I have argued that these responses serve a critical function in the bargaining process in that they help to establish the relative strengths of the two parties.

It is easy to understand why the study of speech acts has proved attractive to developmental psycholinguists and other investigators of language in use. It offers a way out of the constraints set by formal models of linguistic structure and reaffirms the social communicative functions of speech. Nonetheless, the notion of an illocutionary act brings its own constraints to the study of these problems and these are particularly evident when it is applied to the analysis of discourse.

Garvey takes note of one particular form of the problem: "... it may not be possible to extricate the conditions essential to defining or discriminating among speech acts until the way in which discourse context contributes to the operation of these conditions is taken into account." (1976, p. 40) The difficulties I've described in applying this model to the analysis of utterances and exchanges within the overall context of a 'trade' illustrate this problem. However, a more serious issue is involved. The model of illocutionary acts works outwards from the features of language to social meaning. This results both in the formal proposal that discourse is constituted by illocutionary acts and to the substantive definition of social behavior in terms of linguistic features.

Put another way, the social functions/meanings are "read off," often in an ad hoc way, from linguistic features and implicit conditions for presumed illocutionary intents and effects. Thus, Garvey proposes that the "intent" of contingent queries is to elicit information via forms that press "selectively" for responses that are repetitions, clarifications, or specifications. However, she then concludes with a comment on the interpersonal functions of unsolicited and solicited queries, with the former being the "maintenance of mutual understanding" and the latter, the promotion of "mutual attention or rapport."

Rather than concluding an analysis of conversation and discourse with a casual and unsystematic reference to some presumed interpersonal functions, which are not located within any larger framework of social theory, I would propose that this is the place to begin. A model of social relationships, processes, and functions should be an essential part of the analysis of speech as communicative action. The development of such models merits the same degree of serious attention that is given to the features of speech. To begin, we must recognize speakers as social actors and not simply as language users.

BIBLIOGRAPHY

Bauman, R. and Sherzer, J. (1975) The Ethnography of Speaking. In B. J. Siegel, A. R. Beals, and S. A. Tyler (eds.) Annual Review of Anthropology, Vol. 4., Palo Alto, Calif.: Annual Reviews.

Dundes, A., Leach, J. W., and Ozkok, B. (1972) The Strategy of Turkish boys' dueling rhymes. In J. J. Gumperz and D. Hymes (eds.) Directions in Sociolinguistics, New York: Holt, Rinehart and Winston.

Ervin-Tripp, S. (1972) On Sociolinguistic rules: Alternation and Co-occurence. In J. J. Gumperz and D. Hymes (eds.) Directions in Sociolinguistics, New York: Holt, Rinehart and Winston.

Frake, C. O. (1972) Struck by Speech: The Yakan concept of litigation. In J. J. Gumperz and D. Hymes (eds.) Directions in Sociolinguistics, New York: Holt, Rinehart and Winston.

Garfinkel, H. (1967) Studies in Ethnomethodology, Englewood Cliffs, N. J.: Prentice-Hall.

Garvey, C. (1975) Requests and responses in children's Speech. Journal of Child Language, 2, 41-63.

Garvey, C. (1976) The contingent query: A dependent act in conversation. In M. Lewis and L. Rosenblum (eds.) The Origins of Behavior: Communication and Language, New York: Wiley.

Goffman, E. (1974) Frame Analysis, New York: Harper and Row.

Labov, W. (1972) Rules for ritual insults. In D. Sudnow (ed.) Studies in Social Interaction, New York: Free Press.

Mishler, E. G. (1975a) Studies in dialogue and discourse I: An exponential law of successive questioning. Language in Society, 4, 31-52.

Mishler, E. G. (1975b) Studies in dialogue and discourse II: Types of discourse initiated and sustained through questioning. Journal of Psycholinguistic Research, 4, 99-121.

Mishler, E. G. (1977) Studies in dialogue and discourse III: Utterance structure and utterance function in interrogative sequences. Journal of Psycholinguistic Research, in press.

Mitchell-Kernan, C. (1972) Signifying and marking: Two Afro-American speech acts. In J. J. Gumperz and D. Hymes (eds.) Directions in Sociolinguistics,

New York: Holt, Rinehart and Winston.

Sacks, H. (1974) An analysis of the course of a joke's telling in conversation. In R. Bauman and J. Sherzer (eds.) Explorations in the Ethnography of Speaking, London, England: Cambridge University Press.

Sacks, H., Schegloff, E. A., and Jefferson, G. (1974) A simplest systematics for the organization of turn-taking for conversation. Language, 696-735.

Schegloff, E. A., and Sacks, H. (1973) Opening up closings. Semiotica, 8, 289-327.

APPENDIX A

Trading Sequence I: First Grade Classroom

S1 Wou' you (trade) cookies with the popcorn?
S2 What?
S1 Would you change cookies with the popcorn?
S2 Umm ummm
S1 Want some popcorn?
S2 Those are smaller. So if I give you one, you'd hafta give me like fi:ve.
S1 You give me two and I'll give you 'bout this much.
(7" Background noise and conversation)
S2 Yeah, I have a drink.
Here, one. Now gimme some.
S1 But you didn' gimme my second one.
[
S2 Ah- Gimme a whole hanful. C'mon
...
a whole hanful.
S1 (Giggle) Ya ready?
(60" Background noise and conversation)
S1 W' you gimme another one.
....
S2 Wel:l
......
S1 All I did was (...)
Hey mister.
[
S2 If I give you one o' these, you give me a whole hanful-cuz If I give ya just that (giggle) (...)
S1 Look I don't wanna broken one (...)
[[
S2 Here. Yer supposta gimme a whole hanful. (Giggle)
S1 Gimme another cookie and I'll give ya (...) Gimme another hanful an I'll=
[
S2 Thanks.
S1 =give ya all this.
....
No, not that one.
..
S2 Take it.
[
S1 (...) Andrea.
S2 Take it or nothin.
S3 Get your hans outta here. Get your hans outta here.
[
S1 Nope. It's my popcorn. My popcorn.
S2 No:o. Take this if you haven't eaten. Errr.

Appendix A (cont'd)

S1 Jus that one. (Giggle)
Jus- mm mm uh oh well

Note to the Appendices: Within the limits of the page, an effort is made in the typescripts to represent the temporal relationship of utterances by locating the beginning of an utterance after the completion of the prior utterance, rather than bringing it back to the left-hand margin as if it were a written text. Pauses of 2" or more, within and between utterances, are marked by "...." with each "." representing 1"; stretching of a word is indicated by ":" and emphasis by underlying. Points of overlap or interruption are marked by a single bracket connecting the utterances ([).

APPENDIX B

Trading Sequence II: First Grade Classroom

S1 I gotta- I gotta Su:zy Q.
S2 That's not a Suzy Q.
S1 Yes it is.
S2 Who said?
S1 My mamma.
..
She bought them.
......
I got somethin interestin Suzy Q's.
(45" Background noise and conversation)
S1 Jimm:ie, I gotta- I gotta Suzy Q. What will ya give me fer a Suzy Q. An apple?
S3 Yeh.
S1 I don't wan an apple. I got the- I lost a tooth an it's hurting.
....
You like a Suzy Q Beth?
(8" Background noise and conversation)
S4 Nobody'll listen ta you binglebang.
S5 What about some of these?
S1 I do want this fer a Suzy Q. Do you wanna Suzy Q?
....
S5 Thank you Steven.
S1 You're welcome.

APPENDIX C

Trading Sequence III: First Grade Classroom

S1 Alan, whadda you got?
....
Whadda you got?
....
Alan, tell me what you got.
S2 What do you got? I'll trade ya. I'll trade ya the bag for my bag.
S1 What do you have Ala:n?
(Background C whispers: Talk in here)
S1 So whadda you have?
S2 You have Johnnie.
S1 Puddin. I mean (...)
[
S2 Ahh yummie yummie yummie yum yum yum yummie yuma. I love it.
S1 Hey I'll trade ya - I'll trade ya this.
S2 For this?
S1 Yea, for that.
...
S2 I think I -
(Giggle)
(6" Background noise)
S2 You'll trade me that.
(15" Background noise, crunch eating noise)
S1 Jus when I talk.
S2 Want dis?
S1 No.
S2 Crumbs.

A Study of Story Retelling Among Young Bilingual Indian Children

HELGA OSTERREICH* and VERA JOHN - STEINER**

**Albuquerque Indian School, Albuquerque, N.M.*

***Department of Educational Foundations and Department of Linguistics, University of New Mexico, Albuquerque, N.M.*

The exploration of children's stories, both those they make up themselves and those they fashion based on stories told or read to them, is of increasing interest to psychologists and linguists. At first, it was the content of children's narratives which intrigued the developmental scholar. Pritcher and Prelinger in Children Tell Stories (1963) examined the themes of their making. They analyzed the stories according to Erikson's psycho-social framework. They found that young children gave expression to their fears, wishes, rivalries, and imaginative facilities in these accounts. Though their interest was not focused upon the cognitive and structural features of these narratives, they found certain related developmental trends, as, for instance, in the expansion of the spatial setting in which children's invented stories were situated.

In recent years it is the formal or structural features of children's narratives which are being studied. Botvin and Sutton-Smith (1977), in their study of spontaneously told stories, conclude that the complexity of structural organization increases with age. Stein and Glenn (1975) studied retold stories of first and third graders. They found that children's recall of narratives is highly organized and that the amount of information recalled increases with age. Informational elaboration, e.g. causal connections not explicit in the original text, is common and also increasing with age. Zimeles and Kuhns (1976) were interested in "what the child chooses to remember of material to which his attention is directed without, at the same time, being instructed to remember," and how different aspects of memory that are involved in the recall of narratives change as a function of age. In examining the patterns of forgetting in retold stories, Zimeles and Kuhns found that children retained the skeletal plot of a story, even over a two-month interval between the hearing of a story and its retelling. They also found that variation in age is reflected in the older children's better recall of the set of circumstances which put a story into play and which affect the hero's state of mind.

While psychologists and linguists have been interested in developmental trends in children's narratives, educational researchers have focused their interest on the possibility of using narratives for the assessment of language proficiency, both in monolingual and bilingual children. Lambert and Macnamara (1969) and John, Horner and Berney (1970) have used stories for this purpose. Stemmler (1967) designed a test of spontaneous language and methods of thinking, called the Language Cognition Test. Cohen (1975), in his Redwood City study, devised the Storytelling Task, through which children can be rated on general fluency, grammar, pronunciation, rhythm and intonation, and language alternation. Most of these types of language measures attempt to capture multiple aspects of language production, such as the aspects listed for Cohen's Storytelling Task. In addition, many require linguistically trained raters to interpret the results (Cohen, 1975; Natalicio and Williams, 1972).

The technique described here was originally developed by John during the early days of Head Start as a method of working with children whose languages and cultures differed from the mainstream. The first studies using the story retelling method were conducted in the mid-sixties with young children drawn from differing ethnic communities (John and Berney, 1967 and 1968). The method is an attempt to capture both linguistic and cognitive patterning in children's performance. In this specific study, we have attempted to use the method for the purpose of assessing comprehension and production of language in bilingual children. Since we believe that there are many other tests which adequately measure such discrete features of verbal performance as vocabulary, pronunciation and the specifics of grammar, our focus is on another important aspect of general communicative ability - the ability to comprehend and reproduce a simple narrative.

All children are exposed to the thematic discourses of their elders. In tribal communities, traditional tales are an integral part of community life and the socialization of children. In urban communities, the exposure to sequential language is manifold and includes the mass media as well as face-to-face experiences. All children have ways of selecting, transforming and storing these streams of words. It seems reasonable to assume that a general cognitive process that consists of a simplification of sequential language is shared by all children, but that children differ in the extent to which they rely upon key words and/or images in storing a theme or story sequence. During recall or retelling, a simplified internal version is reexpressed in communicative language. The style in which the child retells the story, and the themes which now appear salient in the child's retold version, may reveal the particulars of cultural emphasis.

The findings of the studies conducted in the sixties showed that in their retold stories children differed greatly. Ethnic membership emerged as a crucial variable correlating highly with length, style and thematic content (John and Berney, 1968). The data showed similarities to the work of Stodolsky and Lesser (1967), who have found ethnic differences among children in terms of their salient approaches to cognitive tasks. Such differences among children can interfere with the attempt to measure communicative ability, especially if length, style and 'Standard English' grammar are an integral part of the measure. In the task to be described, we will not be concerned with these grammatical aspects, but rather simply with the extent to which children understand the story and can get across their ideas of it to others.

POPULATION

The children we worked with came from a wide variety of environments. Each of the settings are here described briefly.

An Albuquerque Kindergarten

This classroom is a Title I kindergarten in a predominantly Chicano neighborhood of Albuquerque. There is one teacher and one aide, with a morning session of sixteen children and an afternoon session of eighteen children. The language spoken by students and adults is English, although on occasion the aide addresses children in Spanish, and most children understand her. Children among themselves speak only English.

An Albuquerque First Grade

This first grade class has a stable population of Anglo-American children. The community the children come from is a new housing area of upper middle class status. The class size is around twenty-five students.

A New Mexico Commune School

Another site was a school in a commune located east of Albuquerque in the mountains. All but two of the children, however, were children from the surrounding area. Some of them were children of counter-culture parents; some members of rural families of a more traditional kind. Although some of these children's parents came from upper middle class and middle class families, none are now engaged in professional occupations. Approximately 40 elementary age children attend the school.

A Keresan Pueblo Day School

This school is located within a southwestern Indian Pueblo which is very much continuing its ancient traditions, while participating in the majority culture at the same time. Extended family and kinship relationships, religious ceremonies, and language are among the important traditions being maintained. The B.I.A. Day School has about 300 children in kindergarten through fourth grade. We worked with children in one of the kindergartens and one of the first grades. Most of the children had entered school speaking little or no English, and so the dominant language for these children was Keres.

A Tanoan Kindergarten

The Tanoan Pueblo served by this school is not as "traditional" as the Keresan Pueblo. However, native religion, the extended family, and traditional crafts are still important, while knowledge and use of the native language is declining. The B.I.A. Day School is located within the Pueblo and has about 120 children in kindergarten through sixth grade. We worked in the kindergarten class at this school. All instruction was carried out in English. Only one of the fifteen children was dominant in the native language. However, all the children took part in the bilingual program, which consisted of half hour lessons in the native language per day.

METHODOLOGY

We used two modified versions (Navajo and Pueblo) of the original story retelling book (John and Berney, 1967: see Appendix A for the text). The pictures were slightly different. In most of the story retelling the following procedure was used. The field worker read the story to the child, making certain that he/she had a good view of the story pictures. Next the tape recorder was turned on, and the child was asked to tell the story to the field worker while being shown each of the pictures in sequence. No prompting, aside from encouragement, was done after the first picture. When the child completed retelling the story, he/she was given a 12 x 18 sheet of white construction paper and a set of crayons, and asked to draw a picture of something he/she particularly liked in the story. (For analysis of drawings and a comparison between drawings and language analysis, see John-Steiner and Osterreich, 1975.)

The kindergarten aide in the Keresan Pueblo classroom administered the task in the native language. She proceeded as described above, except that she did not tape the children's stories. Instead, she transcribed them by hand, translating the story into Keres orally and taping several versions of it until she felt it was adequate. However, she told the story herself when doing the task, rather than using the tape.

For the first graders we recruited an aide who had worked with many groups in the school. She played the tape prepared by the first aide to four children at the same time, while turning the pages of the book. She then had the children retell the story individually, out of earshot of the others, while she transcribed directly into English.

In the Tanoan Pueblo, the kindergarten teacher herself collected the stories from the children. In this school, as we have indicated, the majority of the children are native English speakers, but a bilingual program is in operation. Consequently, about four months after the original story retelling was done, a former teacher in the bilingual program administered the Story Retelling task to the same children in the Tanoan language. The procedure she followed was exactly the same as for all English versions. Only one of the children, however, retold the story in the native language; the others retold it in English, despite the fact that all instructions and encouragements were given in the Tanoan language.

We transcribed the taped stories as soon as possible after the activity and as completely as possible, including all pauses, redundancies and prompts by the field worker.

Our analysis was done in terms of the following categories.

Phrase — A unit usually marked by a pause, and usually containing a subject and verb. The main criterion, however, was that it be a thought unit or meaning unit that could stand by itself and still convey information to the listener.

Types of phrases:

Pictorial (P) — The phrase refers to something present in both picture and text; wording need not be close to the actual text.

Textual (T) — The phrase refers to something present in the text only; it cannot be in any way derived by looking only at the picture, never having heard the text. Some of these phrases can be very different from the actual text, but have the same meaning. Others are almost an echo of the text, or even a verbatim repetition.

Elaboration (E) — This category contains two different types of phrases. One is a phrase that refers to something which is in the picture but not in the text (pictorial elaboration). The other type is a phrase which represents something the child has added to the text of the story which makes sense in the context - something that arises out of the child's involvement in the story and his/her creativity (textual elaboration). Although on the analysis sheet we differentiated these two types, in most cases there were not enough total instances to warrant this separate analysis.

<u>Elsewhere in Story</u> (W) The phrase refers to something in the story, but is not related to the particular picture being viewed nor the text that goes with it.

<u>Other</u> Comment unrelated to story or picture content.

<u>Fragment</u> An incomplete phrase, usually arising when a child changes his/her mind after starting a phrase and instead stops and begins another. (Fragments were not counted into Total Phrases in our analysis.)

In the analysis, the retold phrases for the first picture are not counted, since it is here that the task administrator ensures understanding of the task with prompts and questions. Similarly, if prompts or questions occurred in later pictures, the children's productions after such prompts were not counted. For the original text we counted fourteen (14) P phrases and eighty (80) T phrases for a total of ninety-four (94) possible phrases.

RESULTS

Table 1 presents the Story Retelling scores from the English-dominant classrooms where the procedure was used.

TABLE 1 Story Retelling Scores for English-speaking Children

	New Mexico Commune Kindergarten	Albuquerque Kindergarten	New Mexico Commune First Grade	Albuquerque First Grade
N=	6.0	8.0	6.0	22.0
Pictorial	5.5	5.7	8.0	5.4
Textual	9.8	8.7	18.7	16.9
Elaboration	0.7	1.5	1.3	2.4
Elsewhere	0	0	0.7	1.4
Other	1.5	2.8	2.5	1.6
Total	17.5	18.5	31.2	27.7

No statistical tests were done on these or any other results because of the low N's, and because our discussions are intended to indicate trends only. It is evident that the profiles of the classes differ. The kindergarten children told a fairly "basic" story, with little deviation from the text and an average of two phrases per picture (nine pictures, average of 17.5 and 18.5 total phrases for the two kindergartens respectively). On the other hand, the first grade children told fairly long stories (average 3.0 and 3.5 phrases per picture), and their T average was higher than that of the kindergarten group.

In Table 2, the results of story retelling for the Keresan children are presented.

TABLE 2 Story Retelling Scores for Keresan Pueblo Children in English and in Their Native Language

	Keresan Pueblo Kindergarten (English)	Keresan Pueblo Kindergarten (Native Lang.)	Keresan Pueblo First Grade (English)	Keresan Pueblo First Grade (Native Lang.)
N =	7.0	3.0	21.0	4.0
Pictorial	3.6	5.7	4.6	2.8
Textual	6.6	10.7	5.3	15.5
Elaboration	1.3	1.4	1.8	5.3
Elsewhere	0.8	0.7	0.2	1.0
Other	0.9	0	0.3	2.3
Total	13.0	18.4	12.2	26.8

When the two languages are compared, it is evident that the children's stories in Keres were much fuller than those in English. (For example of one child's story in both languages, see Appendix B.) The English versions were what might be called "basic" stories, i.e., the bare essentials of the pictures and text, with very little elaboration. In Keres, the results are comparable to the results obtained at equivalent grade levels in the English-speaking classrooms. That is, the kindergarten children show an average of two total phrases per picture, and the first graders an average of three phrases per picture. Moreover, the ratio of T to P phrases is about two to one for kindergarten, but higher than that for first grade, again a result comparable to the English-speaking classrooms.

The results for the Tanoan Pueblo children are presented in Table 3.

TABLE 3 Story Retelling Scores for Tanoan Pueblo Children in English and in Tanoan

	Tanoan Pueblo Kindergarten (English)	Tanoan Pueblo Kindergarten (Presented in Tanoan, Retold in English)
N =	13.0	12.0
Pictorial	5.0	5.0

TABLE 3 (cont)

	Tanoan Pueblo Kindergarten (English)	Tanoan Pueblo Kindergarten (Presented in Tanoan, Retold in English)
Textual	7.3	3.3
Elaboration	1.6	2.1
Elsewhere	0.8	0.6
Other	0.5	0.2
Total	15.2	11.2

These results were very different. In the Tanoan Pueblo kindergarten, as we have mentioned before, the children's first language is English, except in the case of one child. Thus, the stories they told were fuller in English than in the native language version. It should also be remembered that the children, with one exception, retold the story in English, even when it was told to them in the native language. The likelihood that they did not comprehend much of the story on this occasion is shown by their reliance on the pictures rather than the text - the production of P rather than T phrases. This was the only group of children in our sample whose P average was higher than the T average. Moreover, their elaboration average is somewhat higher than is the case in the other kindergarten groups. An average of 1.2 phrases of the 2.1 elaboration phrases is what we have termed pictorial elaboration, i.e., a reference to something which is in the picture but not in the text. It seems, then, that the children relied minimally on the native language text in retelling the story. In fact, they most probably did not understand much of it, since they failed to reproduce the text even in translation.

To summarize, it is evident that there are both language and age differences in the retelling of the story, and that different groups exhibit different profiles. If one considers the same age group, and if the child hears and tells the story in his/her dominant language, the quantitative aspects of the results are very similar. Thus, all kindergarten groups display similar profiles in total phrases, and in the proportions of Textual to Pictorial phrases. The first grade groups show a higher number of total phrases, and a higher ratio of Textual to Pictorial phrases than do the kindergarten groups. When telling the story in their second language, the children tend to display scores more like those of younger children. Their ratio of Textual to Pictorial phrases is low, and the total phrases are even lower than those of kindergarten groups in their dominant languages. Also, the group which had difficulty in comprehending the second language showed a higher Pictorial score than Textual score, the lowest total phrase score of any of the groups, and did not even attempt the production in the second language. Furthermore, regardless of age, a story told in the child's dominant language has a higher average number of Textual phrases and total phrases than a story in the weaker language. If the child has any productive competence in the language being evaluated, he/she will produce more Textual phrases than Pictorial phrases, and these will be mostly complete sentences. The higher the proportion of Pictorial phrases, the less competence in producing complete sentences the child has, e.g., Keresan Pueblo children. If the child has no productive competence in the tested language, he/she will most likely tell the story in the other language.

If the child is weak in comprehension as well, Pictorial phrases will predominate over Textual phrases, e.g., Tanoan Pueblo children.

CONCLUSIONS

These preliminary results suggest that the Story Retelling procedure is a promising language evaluation method with bilingual children, especially when some measure of sequential speech is desired. The method allows the comparison of the same story in two languages, in order to identify the dominant language and the degree of knowledge of the weaker language. In view of the concern about communicative ability, or ability to use the two languages in varied social contexts, this method of handling comprehension and production of sequential text can prove useful.

In addition, this study reveals that during the early school years children develop rapidly in their skills of processing and recalling narrative material. This finding is in accord with that of other investigators who share our interest in linguistic and cognitive functioning as revealed in children's retold stories.

BIBLIOGRAPHY

Botvin, G. J. and Sutton-Smith, B. (1977) The development of structural complexity in children's fantasy narratives, Developmental Psychology, 13, 377-388.

Cohen, A. (1975) A Sociolinguistic Approach to Bilingual Education, Rowley, Mass.: Newbury.

John, V. and Berney, T. D. (1967) Analysis of Story Retelling as a Measure of Ethnic Content in Stories, Final Report, Office of Economic Opportunity, Project Number 577.

John, V. P., Horner, V. M. and Berney, T. D. (1970) Story retelling: A study of sequential speech in young children. In H. Levin and J. P. Williams (eds.), Basic Studies in Reading, New York, Basic Books, 246-262.

John-Steiner, V. P. and Osterreich, H. (1975) Learning Styles Among Pueblo Children, Final Report, National Institute of Education, Dept. of Health, Education and Welfare.

Lambert, W. E. and Macnamara, J. (1969) Some cognitive consequences of following a first-grade curriculum in a second language. Journal of Educational Psychology, 60, 86-89.

Natalicio, D. S. and Williams, F. (1972) What characteristics can 'experts' reliably evaluate in the speech of Black and Mexican-American children? TESOL Quarterly, 6, 121-127.

Pritcher, E. G. and Prelinger, E. (1963) Children Tell Stories, New York: International University Press.

Stein, N. and Glenn, C. G. (1975) A developmental study of children's recall of story material. Paper presented at SRCD Conference, Denver, Colorado.

Stemmler, A. O. (1967) The LCT, language cognition test research edition--a test for educationally disadvantaged school beginners, TESOL Quarterly, 1, 35-43.

Stodolsky, S. B. and Lesser, G. (1967) Learning patterns in the disadvantaged. Harvard Educational Review, 37, 546-593.

Zimeles, H. and Kuhns, J. (1976) A Developmental Study of the Retention of Narrative Material. Final Report, National Institute of Education. NE-G-00-3-00271.

APPENDIX A One of These Days

Page 1: "What's it like on the moon, Daddy?" James asked.

"Why it's cool and clean as a country rain on the moon. And there's lots and lots of tall grass. Every child has a room of his own to sleep in."

Page 2: When a boy gets to be six years old, his daddy buys him a pony with a shaggy black mane. He rides it every day. And on Sundays he gallops the pony all over the moonlight.

Page 3: That night James lay on his rug and looked up at the moon.

"I'm the only one awake," thought James. "Me and my doll." He hugged the doll and whispered in his ear. "One of these days, doll, one of these days we'll go to the moon."

A small cry floated across the room. Uh-oh. His baby sister was awake too. Mother went to the crib, and said, "Hush baby, hush baby."

Page 4: James fell asleep to his mother's voice. Soon he was dreaming. He dreamed that he and his doll were on the moon. It was raining. James and the doll walked around in the rain.

The rain stopped.

Page 5: Now silver and turquoise began to fall from the sky. It landed in the tall grass without a sound.

"Hooray," shouted the doll, and he and James ran from place to place, stuffing their pockets.

Page 6: "Oh dear, oh dear, oh dear," said the rag doll. "Where will we put it all?"

"In me," said a voice. "Fill me up."

They turned around and saw an enormous medicine bag. James and the doll climbed the tree beside it and emptied their pockets into the bag. Clickety, clickety, clink.

"More, more, more," grunted the bag. "Fill me up."

Page 7: Finally there was only one piece left. The doll clutched it in his hand.

"More," grunted the bag.

The doll began to cry. "I'd like to keep just this one," he said in a very small voice.

"Don't cry," James said. "You may keep it."

Page 8: Now in his dream it was Sunday, the day of his sixth birthday. The little pony which his father had bought him was waiting quietly for him by a big tree. James climbed on the pony and put the doll in back of him.

Soon he and the doll were galloping through the moonlight.

"Faster!" cried the doll, and suddenly he burst into tears.

"What's the matter?" shouted James. "I thought you wanted to go fast?"

The doll cried louder and louder.

Page 9: But when James turned around, it wasn't his doll on the seat behind him. It was his baby sister.

"Hush now," said James. "Don't cry. Please don't cry." And then James woke up.

Even in his dream he had heard his baby sister. She was still crying. Mother had moved the baby outside and had gone back to sleep.

James tiptoed outside and picked up the baby. "Hush baby, hush baby," he said. "If you stop crying, I'll take you for a pony ride on the moon, one of these days, I promise."

His sister stopped crying. James saw that she was asleep. He went back to his rug.

Page 10: James peered up at the cool round face of the moon. "I promised her that one of these days, one of these days . . ."

But he didn't finish what he was saying because he was asleep.

APPENDIX B Two Versions of the Story by a Keresan Pueblo Child.

English	Keres*
1. I: Tell me what's going on in this picture. C: Um . . . the boy woke up.	1. C: Father looking and boy said, "What do you see?"
2. C: The boy, he ride on a pony.	2. C: The boy was six years old. They bought a pony for the little boy and he was riding on the circle . . . was light and dark around. When night, stars were below.
3. C: The boy lay down she look at the moon.	3. C: Little boy looking up at moon and everybody asleep. The doll was also awake and looking up.
4. C: The boy go outside, it's raining.	4. C: Was walking on the moon and grass was long and when walking the rain stopped.
5. C: The jewelry is all getting fallen down.	5. C: Suddenly, the jewelry fell and baby doll screamed . . . they picked them up, and put it in their pockets.
6. C: The bag is all full.	6. C: They took . . . he took them up and put in bag and put the jewelry and the bag said, "Fill me up." That's all.
7. C: The baby doll has another one.	7. C: The boy gave the doll one jewelry to take and the boy got sad.
8. C: The little boy and the doll sit on the pony, they jump over the moon.	8. C: The boy and pony went up and baby in the back was crying.
9. C: The boy is carrying the baby.	9. C: Baby was crying in bed and boy got up and tiptoed and took baby outside and said to baby, "hush, baby, hush.
10. C: The boy is sleeping . . . and she's baby.	10. C: Was dreaming in the moon . . . was dreaming in the moon and was dreaming while on the rug.

*This is the translation of the Keres, exactly as the task administrator set it down. It was assumed that this version conveys the Keres exactly if not grammatically. Grammatical errors are irrelevant for this analysis.

Dialogue, Monologue and Egocentric Speech by Children in Nursery Schools

MAUREEN M. SHIELDS
University of London, Institute of Education

This paper is a personal meditation or spring cleaning exercise aimed at clearing up some of the traditional views and assumptions about child language which are still current in this rapidly advancing field and which at one time or another have formed part of my own mental furniture. It is particularly concerned with examining in the light of recent studies what is meant by 'egocentric language', 'language for self', 'monologue', 'collective monologue', and 'dialogue'. Categories such as these have survived from very early studies, such as those by Piaget (1926, 1959) and Vigotsky (1934, 1962) which were written and discussed in the twenties and thirties and for long formed the staple of language studies for teachers and even for psychologists. The richness of this work is undeniable, and its accessability to the student beginner (in contrast to much of the later work of Piaget) has given the basic ideas contained in these studies an exceptional longevity.

When compared to much of the recent work on language, the half-century old work of Piaget and Vigtosky seems short on data, but, on the other hand, rich in ideas in interesting theoretical formulations. Perhaps this is another reason for its longevity. Collections of data are easily superseded by new data. Theories, ideas and interpretations, however, can survive, grow, intertwine and change in the continuous exchange of intellectual discourse.

This early work is full of contrasts and paradoxes. Piaget held that young children are intrinsically egocentric and subjective in their thinking and that objectivity and ability to take into the account the viewpoint of others develops slowly in reciprocal interaction with others. He held that the world cannot really be shared until it is objectivized and that the encounter with other minds is a powerful influence towards this objectivization. Adult thought, for Piaget, is essentially internalised dialogue:

> The adult, even in his most personal and private occupation, even when he is engaged on an inquiry which is incomprehensible to his fellow human beings, thinks socially, has continuously in his mind's eye his collaborators or opponents, actual or eventual, at any rate, members of his own profession to whom sooner or later he will announce the result of his labours. This mental picture pursues him throughout his task. The task itself is henceforth socialised at almost every stage of its development. Invention eludes the process but the need for checking and demonstrating calls into being an inner speech addressed throughout to a hypothetical opponent, whom the imagination often pictures as one of flesh and blood. (Piaget, 1959, p. 39)

Children, on the other hand, often do not take into account the viewpoint of others, do not adapt their meanings for their audience, and indeed often speak as though they are alone even when in company. Piaget did acknowledge that there are social elements in children's language from the start, but he viewed the language of children from his definition of the mature skill. He therefore categorized as non-social everything which did not match up to his highly intellectualized definition of social. He counted as social any speech whether reciprocated or not which is directed at the behavior of another (criticism), any speech which indicates that the speaker expects some behavior by the addressee (commands, requests), any speech which is in response to another speaker (answers) and any speech which contains what he called 'adapted information', that is, information about anything other than the child's own views and activities which are only counted as information when they enter into a collaborative play sequence in which there may be need for reciprocal definition of activity. However, Piaget counted as conversation or dialogue any remark which evokes a remark from another speaker which is adapted to the theme or intention of the first speaker. Here Piaget stumbled into one of the main problems of looking at language interchange in contrast to monologue, that is, the difficulty of defining the activity of one speaker except in terms of his or her inferred expectations or intentions about others, or in terms of the actual behavior of others to the speaker. By Piaget's criterion, a piece of information about the speaker's own intentions which does not evoke a response is placed in the category of monologue, while a similar remark which does produce a response is placed in the category of socialised speech. Conversely a piece of information about the shared objective world is always classed as socialized whether it elicits a response or not. Piaget's view on intellectual development, which came to be based almost exclusively on the development of intellectual schemes, derived from operations on objects in space and time, did however at this stage allow that the communication of behavioral rules is 'adapted information', but it excluded from information and hence from dialogue any definition or commentary on the speaker's own feelings, perceptions, actions or intentions. When Piaget set out the stages of development of dialogue he put collaboration in abstract thought and genuine argument as the highest stage...a definition which would undoubtedly exclude the major part of adult interactional speech.

Vigotsky, on the other hand, defined speech as originally totally social, but as developing through monologue into speech for self:

> The inner speech of the adult represents his 'thinking for himself' rather than social adaptation; i.e., it has the same function that egocentric speech has in the child. It also has the same structural characteristics: out of context it would be incomprehensible to others because it omits to 'mention' what is obvious to the 'speaker'. (Vigotsky, 1962, p. 18)

Vigotsky, therefore, used as criteria for the transition of socialized speech into thought characteristics such as lack of referential specificity through use of pronouns, which Piaget classified as an index of egocentricity. Some students of child language (Hawkins, 1968; Tough, 1977) have categorised these very same features as indicators of restricted code and communicative incompetence!

Vigotsky's collaborator, Luria, developed a line of study on the relation between language and thinking which tended to concentrate on the effect of language as such, i.e., non-social language as a means of internal behavioral control (Luria, 1961). We thus have the paradox that Vigotsky who believed in the social origin of language, is the originator of much research which concentrates on the within-person or a-social effects of language, while Piaget, who believed that children's language, though partially socialized is in the main egocentrically characterized, developed the idea of language and thinking as internalized social dialogue.

What light do modern studies on children's language throw on the concepts used by Piaget or Vigotsky, concepts such as speech for self, egocentric speech, synpractic or imaginative monologue, collective monologue, and so on?--in some ways a great deal, in others not very much. In one respect Vigotsky has been proved abundantly right. The recent plethora of studies of mother-child interaction have left no doubt that the young baby is socially oriented and that the reciprocal actions and mutual adaptations of mother and baby set up the system of behavioral exchange which is the foundation of human communication (Brazelton, et.al., 1974; Bullowa, 1973; Trevarthen, 1974). There are also an increasingly numerous set of studies which examine social interchange between mothers and toddlers (Bates, 1975, 1976; Edwards, 1978; Howe, 1976), and between very young children and their peers (Lee, 1975; Garvey, 1976, 1977). These studies are focused on the social competencies of children and therefore tend to search out the social implications of interactions. Just as Piaget's intellectual bias led him to exaggerate the egocentric dimension in children's language, it may be that our concentration on the social and interpersonal may lead us to set aside those language activities where the speaker is not in dialogue with another as unimportant. Or we may regard them more as a reflex or epiphenomenon of dialogue without looking at the function that such activities may have for the individual or the part that they may play in his or her language development.

WHAT IS DIALOGUE LANGUAGE LIKE?

If the young child acquires his language within an interactional setting does the language he acquires have intrinsic features which reflect its interactional nature? If it has, would these features disappear or diminish when the child uses language when alone, or when not in an interactional exchange with his audience? Vigotsky held that speech for self was structually different from socialized speech because the operation of reference was unnecessary in monologue, and therefore, language for self would be predicative only. Deictic or nonspecific reference is, however, a universal characteristic of human speech and is itself an index of how much of the intersubjective field is assumed to be shared in normal interaction, i.e., nonspecific language is typically highly social (Aarts, 1971; Lyons, 1975).

In looking at this question most studies in linguistics are of little help, because the structures of language have traditionally been based on monologue texts, often on single monologue utterances. Studies of discourse are in the vast majority of cases based on single source non-interactive texts, and therefore, do not define the functions within dialogue of the structure they describe. Even the important work on Cohesion in English by Halliday and Hasan (1976) is mainly based on literary texts, the only examples of real alternation by speakers being in the dialogue of a play by J. B. Priestley. It is true that many of the cohesive markers that they describe also serve to bind together the utterances of different speakers in dialogue, but some of the main elements of cohesive dialogue are not included.

A few pioneering studies of language in dialogue have been undertaken mainly by those who are primarily interested in sociolinguistic categories rather than in linguistic structure, though there are now a number of important studies on turn taking (Sacks, et.al., 1974; Duncan, 1974; Poyatos, 1977). Harvey Sacks also did foundation work on the dependencies between utterances and the 'ties' which indicate them (Sacks, 1967, pub. 1976). Other studies have concentrated on short individual segments which form part of a sequence of exchanges such as Schegloff's (1972) study of conversational openings or Jefferson's work (1973) on tag positional address terms in closing sequences.

One of the most interesting and ambitious attempts to tackle in linguistic terms what is involved in dialogue exchanges in the language of young children is that currently being undertaken by John Dore and his colleagues at Rockefeller (Dore, et.al., 1977). This takes the speech act as its core functional category, following Dore's previous work (1977) but now also includes presuppositional frames, turns and some interactive processes. However, by adopting a classification of speech acts which sticks very closely to the canonical grammatical form and conventional illocutionary force (such as requests, statements, descriptions, answers, performatives) their system, on their own admission, does not capture social degrees of acts such as the difference between orders and pleas as a social dimension of action requests. This means that the adjustment of a speaker's utterance to the relationship in which he stands to his interlocutor is missed out. The system also misses out reference to particular contents which means loss of the feature of thematic continuity, which is another marker of discourse cohesion. Dore's dialogue descriptions are also closely based on classroom texts and therefore resemble in this respect the work of Sinclair and Coulthard (1975) on class lessons or Bruton, Leather and Candlin (1977) on doctor-patient interviews, in both of which the interpersonal exchanges are governed by a powerful frame of conventions which closely define the respective roles of those communicating.

The snag about all these studies is that the examination of particular features of dialogue, or the examination of dialogue in highly structured contexts may obscure the underlying universal features of dialogue as such.

Beneath all the variations of human verbal communication there must surely be some structural requirements which any act of communication must have if it is to serve as a means for the negotiation of meaning between two quite distinct centers of awareness and experience, each with similar human characteristics. Perhaps such universals are so skeletal and basic that their nature is assumed to be uninteresting and taken for granted. It is not always unprofitable, however, to examine the obvious, and if any contrast is to be made between dialogue and monologue speech it is probably in the more stable and obvious features that the contrast (if any) should lie.

If one examines dialogue skill in the light of what is logically presupposed by its exercise, even in the immature forms used by young children, there appear to be three sets of things to consider. In the first place there are the actual utterances and their surface structure. Underlying these there are presumably certain competencies, because the use of the surface features of language appears to be cued and organised in a way that fits the context and the relationship of the speakers. Beneath the competencies and supporting them there must be a system of representation or knowledge and belief about the perceptual field of other persons, their concepts, their memories, their independent action potential, their experience and the rule systems which they share with the speaker. All this is in addition to the speakers own direct knowledge of the world and his own intentions and abilities (Shields, 1978).

In developing communication skills the child must acquire at least five basic competencies: (a) he must be able to attract the attention of another person, and he must be able to maintain this attention by his own contribution and by turn taking; (b) he must be able to organise and define the interpersonal field to make salient to the mind of another the matter which is central to his purpose and activity; (c) he must be able to initiate verbal and nonverbal acts in the expectation of reciprocity, and must himself act with reciprocity in response to the initiative of others; (d) he must tailor his utterances to avoid unnecessary redundancy by taking account of what has been already done and said and fitting his utterance to it; (e) and lastly, he must be able to evoke or activate in another mind elements from a shared frame of experience about the world, and about human behavior in the world which are presupposed in the current context of activity.

These five competencies would minimally underlie the discourse constitutive universals which are variously manifested on the surface of any language (Habermas, 1970). Without the first three (a), (b), (c), and the last (e), communication would be impossible, and (d) the smoothing out of redundancy is the manifestation in language of a universal feature of any practiced skill. It is not possible to elaborate this analysis here. A more detailed account has been given elsewhere (Shields, 1976, 1977). The five elements of skill are set out together with their underlying cognitive and belief system and some of the surface exponents in Table 1. The fact that some of the surface exponents expound more than one function is not unfamiliar in language where it is usual for a small set of elements to map onto a large and variable set of linguistic products.

Having set out some of the basic constituent features of dialogue, it remains to ask which, if any, are missing from monologue. Address and turn taking would presumably be missing. It might be unnecessary, as Vigotsky suggested, to define the field of attention, the language would not need to be modulated to the status and independence of another, there might be no reciprocity of speech acts. As regards the latent frame which roughly corresponds to Vigotsky's definition of 'sense' because it contains the intentions, context and associative network, that presumably would remain because it would supply the stock of meaning which would underlie the verbalisations.

Now let us look at two extracts from the speech corpus of one little girl aged 4 years and 2 months. This and the other excerpts are from recordings of language collected in London Nursuries and playgrounds in 1971, 1972 and 1973. Recording was by tape and simultaneous manual recording. The direction of address was noted and only 12% of the 6,700 utterances were not classifiable as addressed either by verbal address or gaze and other kinetic cues.

In the first extract Rebecca is playing with friends in the home corner, temporarily transformed into a hospital. There are 49 exchanges in the whole episode, but only 20 are cited here to give the flavor of Rebecca's competence in dialogue.

TABLE 1 Primary Discourse Elements

Level of Representation of Cognition	Level of Communication Skill	Level of Linguistic System
a. Setting up and maintaining an interpersonal field		
Beliefs about (i) the autonomy (ii) the approachability (iii) The social competence (iv) the relative status of others (age, sex, power control of resources etc.)	Grasp of linguistic means for attracting attention, maintaining a communicational field and adjusting language to the autonomy and status of others.	Summons, address, turn taking, personal deixis, acknowlegement such as <u>yes</u> and <u>no</u>, tagging, modulation, politeness formulae.
b. Organizing an interpersonal field of attention		
Beliefs about the perceptions, experiences and cognitions of others. Beliefs about their memory and attentional fields.	Grasp of linguistic means of referring to things and events and locating them in time and space so that they can signal the speaker's frame of reference to the listener.	Specific and pronominal reference field deixis, temporal deixis, definiteness modality, transitivity.
c. Organizing cohesion of verbal and nonverbal acts		
Representations of the intentions, and activities of both self and other persons within a context. Expectations concerning the effects of verbalizations and actions upon others.	Grasp of linguistic rules for the construction of speech acts, their reciprocal cohesion, and their modulation to take account of the autonomy and status of others.	Questions, answers, affirmations, denials, commands, requests, consents, suggestions, refusals, contradictions, etc. Modulation and modality.
d. Maintaining cohesion of expressed linguistic context		
Representation of the utterances and meanings of previous speakers.	Grasp of means to maintain continuity, to foreground topics in the intersubjective field and to avoid redundancy.	Thematisation definiteness, ellipses, conjunctions, substitutions.
e. Evocation and negotiation of both shared and individual latent context		
Beliefs about what is the case in the material and social world and the rules governing action in particular contexts.	Grasp of pragmatic rules about presuppositions governing appropriate utterances in given contexts.	Marking for generality, relevance, sincerity, truth, pretending, degree of seriousness.

Example 1.

Context of activity: Ann (4.7), Kim (4.11) and Reb (4.2) are in the home corner which has two beds at one side and in the other a stove, sink, kitchen dresser, table and tablecloth. The two beds are placed in an L shape with a table between on which there is a toy doctor's bag. Kim and Reb are dressed as nurses and Ann in sitting up in bed. The interaction has been proceeding for about five minutes before the recording begins.

Context	Episode	No.	Speakers	Utterance
	1	1.	Ann-Reb	I WANT AN INJECTION
		2.	Reb-Ann	NO, I HAVE TO COVER YOU UP... DO MY JOB.....LIE DOWN!
Reb begins to tuck Ann in, Ann tries to remain sitting up, but then lies down, screws up her eyes and feigns sleep.		3.	Ann-Reb	I'M GOING FAST ASLEEP AND THEN YOU WON'T BE ABLE TO KILL ME.
Kim is sitting on the other bed looking in the bag.		4.	Reb-Ann	DON'T BE SILLY ANN...ELSE I REALLY WON'T PLAY WITH YOU.
Reb continues tucking in, brief pause.				
Ann turns head from Reb to Kim.	2	5.	Ann-R&K	DID YOU SEE PEYTON PLACE YESTERDAY?
Kim leaves bag and looks at other two.		6.	Reb-Ann	YES.
Reb almost certainly is fibbing, unless the au pair allows what parents wouldn't.		7.	Ann-Reb	DID YOU SEE THE BIT WHERE THE MAN SAID THE BABY WAS DYING?
		8.	Reb-Ann	YES.
Ann widens eye dramatically.		9.	Ann-Reb	AND SHE MADE A FUNNY FACE.
		10.	Kim-Ann	EVERYTIME SOMEONE COMES SHE MAKES A FUNNY FACE. THAT WAS A GOOD PART WASN'T IT? ....
Reb leans over to window in home corner screen which is beside Ann's bed.	3	11.	Reb-Ann	THE WINDOW'S OPEN AND I'LL HAVE TO CLOSE IT.
Ann yanks curtains open.		12.	Ann-Reb	BUT I WANT TO LOOK OUT.
Reb yanks curtains closed and makes locking movements with right hand.		13.	Reb-Ann	LOCK, LOCK, LOCK,--I'VE LOCKED THAT WINDOW.
		14.	Ann-Reb	BUT WE'VE GOT THE KEY.
Reb flounces away in a huff throwing her remark over her shoulder, takes off nurses cap.		15.	Reb-Ann	I'M NOT PLAYING WITH YOU. I'M THE COOK AND I'M GOING TO COOK THE DINNER.

	Episode	Remark	Speech
Ann looks at Kim then Reb.	3	16. Ann-Reb	THE NICE NURSE SAID I COULD OPEN THE WINDOW.
Reb returns with two plates of dinner emptied out of pot on stoves.		17. Reb-Ann	YOU CAN'T....ELSE YOU'LL GET A WORSER COLD....'COS IT'S WINDY TODAY.
			....
Reb hands plates to Kim, but Kim does not take them.	4	18. Reb-Kim	TWO PLATES.
Reb goes up to Ann who lies back in the bed.		19. Reb-Ann	SHE SAID, MY LITTLE GIRL IS DYING.
Kim goes towards stove, brushing past Reb, who drops the plates.		20. Kim-Ann	NURSES DO GO INTO THE COOKING DON'T THEY?

All the remarks are addressed except possibly 19., where Rebecca gazes at Ann but may be soliloquizing. Rebecca also uses formal address by name as a distancer in remarks 4. She uses a self referent I to distinguish her intentions and activities in 2, 3, 11, 13, 15, and during the dispute in episodes 3, both Ann and Rebecca contrast their views in this way. In each of the four episodes, the remarks cohere by field of attention but it is quite clear that the latent frame about nurse/patient behavior differs as between Rebecca and her two playmates. Rebecca's frame is domestic and authoritarian, concerned with tucking up, feeding and managing the environment on the nurses part, and lying down and submitting on the part of the patient. The latent frame of Kim and Ann contains more sinister material, and Rebecca in remark 4, signals what she considers a breach of frame in Ann's mention of her killing her patient by Don't by silly Ann, or I really won't play with you. She uses this standard nursery formula again in 15 in response to the defiance of the patient who has signalled that she is ganging up with the other 'nurse' by using we in We've got the key. Ann, however, does not accept this and uses the nice nurse both to refer to Kim and to imply a criticism of Rebecca's bossiness. Rebecca is drawn back into the interaction justifying her behavior by giving reasons for stopping her patient opening the window. It is impossible within the compass of this paper to go into full intricacy of this interaction, but elements of all the main dialogue constitutive categories set out in Table 1 are exhibited. The interpersonal field is set up and maintained by turn taking, the field of attention is organised both by specific reference and deixis, speech acts cohere even when intentions differ, e.g., the use of but by Ann in 12 and 14. There are powerful latent frames of meaning underlying the exchanges.

The next extract contains a lengthy complete monologue by Rebecca. There is an audience in the shape of Christopher who merits three remarks but the rest of the speech sequence is constructed entirely under the organising power of Rebecca's ideas. The segmentation is by pauses which, however, are filled by the completion of the indicated action.

Example 2.

Context: Christopher (4.1) and Rebecca (4.2) are on the floor with two boxes, and wooden shapes of people and animals.

	A. Reb-Chr	1.	THERE'S ONE OF THEIR TOYS THAT THEY STAND ON...
She looks briefly at the observer with the tape recorder, but after that looks only at the toys. She says names as she picks up and places them in a line formation.	B.	2.	A BUTCHER...
		3.	THE PIG...
		4.	THE LITTLE ONE...
		5.	AND THERE'S A GIRL...
		6.	NOBODY ELSE
		7.	THE DADDY...
		8.	A MUMMY
Starts to put them in 1st wooden box, under a thin beam across one side. Bangs each time with the wooden figure on the beam.		9.	THE DADDY GOES IN FIRST
		10.	UNDER AND IN...
		11.	THE LITTLE GIRL GOES NEXT...
		12.	KNOCK, KNOCK...
		13.	OPENS IT...
		14.	DADDY I NEXT...
		15.	KNOCK, KNOCK...
Chr is just kneeling a few feet away handling one figure.		16.	COME IN...
		17.	GOES IN THE LITTLE BOX...
		18.	NEXT THE PIG...
		19.	KNOCK, KNOCK...
		20.	YOU'RE NOT COMING IN...
Puts him back.		21.	ALL RIGHT I'LL GO BACK IN MY ROOM...
		22.	NEXT THE OLD MAN...
		23.	KNOCK, KNOCK...
		24.	OPEN...
		25.	NEXT THE MAMMY...
		26.	KNOCK, KNOCK...
Handling policemen, Gruff voice. She is putting them all side by side round the edge of the box.		27.	IS ANY ROBBERS HERE?
		28.	NO...
		29.	WHAT'S DOWN THERE...ANY ROBBERS?
		30.	THEN THE BOY...
		31.	KNOCK, KNOCK...
		32.	COME IN THE BOY...
		33.	HE STAYS THERE...
She picks up the butcher.		34.	NEXT THE BUTCHER...
		35.	KNOCK, KNOCK...
		36.	COME IN THE BUTCHER...
		37.	THEN THE LOLLIPOP MAN...
		38.	STAY HERE...
		39.	THE LOLLIPOP MAN STAYS THERE...
Chr chimes in out of the blue though he has been watching a few seconds.	C. Chr-Reb	40.	WHAT NEXT?
	D. Reb-Chr	41.	NOBODY...
She answers indifferently.		42.	NEXT THE HORSE...
She picks up the cow.		43.	MOO-MOO...STRAIGHT INTO MY ENTRANCE...
Then she picks up the horse.		44.	NEXT...
		45.	KNOCK, KNOCK...

Gallops and jumps him over beam this time.		46.	COME IN...
		47.	NEIGH-NEIGH...
		48.	COME IN...
Picks up the dog and puts him in.		49.	WOOF-WOOF...
Turns to Chr.	E. Reb-Chr	50.	WE NEED THE BIG COW...
		51.	WHAT WE HAVE DONE THE BIG COW?
Jumps big cow in and a couple of figures rock.		52.	WHAT A BIG JUMP...
		53.	NEARLY KNOCKED THE POSTMEN OVER...
		54.	NEARLY KNOCKED THE GIRL OVER...
		55.	NEARLY POPPING THE BOY...
		56.	ALL SAFE TOGETHER--EVERYONE...
Sits backs a little looking pleased. All the figures are inside box then she starts to lay them flat, the policemen at the very end.		57.	THEN THEY LAY DOWN IN THEIR BEDS...
		58.	THE POLICE LAYS THERE TO SEE IF ANY ROBBERS COME...
		59.	THE MOTHER WENT TO SLEEP...
Stands policeman up,		60.	THE POLICEMAN STAYED UP AND HE HAD TO HAVE SOME ROOM...
places another figure laying down.		61.	AND ONE FOR THERE...
		62.	THE GIRL WAS LAST BUT SHE DIDN'T MIND...
		63.	THEN THE POLICEMAN HE STAYED THERE...
		64.	THEY ALL WENT TO SLEEP.

The first impression given by the monologue is of fragmentation, especially in the first 50 segments, and of the brevity of each fragment. If, however, one compares the length of main clauses in which there is a verb of some kind, counting subordinated and coordinated clauses separately, Rebecca's basic building block in the monologue is exactly the same length as in the dialogue, 5.0 words. The clauses containing verbs in the monologue are, however, imbedded in a sea of synpractic utterances designed to organise and give meaning to her play with the little toys. These utterances nominate the doll she is handling, and define the activity of placing them in the box as an entry into a dwelling by the rhythmic Knock, Knock and its responses open or come in. What is particularly interesting is that this monologue is in fact set up as a role playing dialogue in which each claimant for entry is formally allowed in by Rebecca's alter ego, in this case possibly speaking for the daddy, who is the first to be put in.

> NEXT THE PIG--Synpractic utterance.
> KNOCK, KNOCK--Role play entrance claim.
> YOU'RE NOT COMING IN--Role play respondence.
> ALL RIGHT...I'LL GO BACK IN MY ROOM--Role play concession by pig.

This monologue exhibits the verbal features of both address, turn taking and speech act cohesion which are characteristic of dialogue. Rebecca also uses distanced commentary like an onlooker,

> WHAT A BIG JUMP
> NEARLY KNOCKED THE POSTMAN OVER...

and she ends with a story-like finale, section E, with everyone going to sleep and the policeman looking after them all.

Contrary to Vigotsky's theory, this synpractic monologue contains a higher count of specific referents or nouns than the dialogue--14% as compared with 12%. Conversely, pronominal reference is higher in the dialogue episode where 16% of the words are pronominals as opposed to only 7% in the monologue. The referential material is more specific rather than less. This is, of course, an established feature of written texts (Ure, 1971).

The sequence is at first sight very similar in many ways to the pre-sleep monologues of her 2½ year old son, Anthony, analyzed by Ruth Weir (1972), except that in Rebecca's monologue there is much more overall cohesion. Her monologue is imaginatively oriented and does not slip gear into pure word play in the way that Anthony's monologues did. That may be because the task in which she is engaged gives a certain thematic continuity, it might also be because she is older, and more able to construct consecutive material. Most likely, it is a combination of the two.

Two further examples of monologue sequences are given below. In the first, Alpana is the organizing spirit of a play hospital. Various illnesses and injuries have been dealt with, and now, in a flight of imagination, Alpana creates a maternity case.

Example 3.

Context: Sheena (4.8), James (3.11), Richard (3.10), Alpana (4.10, East Indian), Carol (4.6) have been playing doctors and nurses for 26 minutes.

Sheena comes along and puts a doll wrapped in a towel on the bed.	Alp.	1.	SHE'S GOT A BABY...
		2.	SHE WAN'S A BABY...
		3.	SHE'S LONELY...
		4.	SHE NEEDS A BABY...
		5.	GIVE HER A BABY...
		6.	GIVE THAT LADY A BABY...
Alpana hands doll to Carol.		7.	SHE NEEDS THIS ONE...
	Alp-Car	8.	HERE'S YOUR BABY BORN...
Alpana pushes up pram with box unit.	Alp.	9.	MOVE OUT OF WAY...
		10.	MACHINE'S COMING TO TAKE PHOTOGRAPH...
Ric who has been a doctor is assigned a new role. Ric looks vaguely at Carol.	Alp-Ric	11.	PRETEND YOU COME TO SEE YOUR BABY, RIGHT?

Although Alpana intermingles her statements with imperatives, these are not, apart from 11, addressed to anyone and they are accompanied by her own actions only. The small patient who is being transformed into an obstetrical case is addressed once but Alpana barely looks at her. Not until she feels she wants to involve another in her play does she request Richard to take the role of a visiting father, tagging her imperative with a right, designed to elicit alright. Some features of her utterances such as the intermittant omission of articles, and the lack of verb inflection, indicate that English is Alpana's second language. The short sentences of her monologue are like brush strokes creating the play scene. Her normal interpersonal communication shows an average main clause of 6.9 words, but here her utterances in her monologues, of which this is a sample, average only 4.5. The whole sequence is geared less to motor activity than Rebecca's, and the actual material props play a far smaller role in the elaboration of the play.

Finally, here is one of several play monologues by Michael (4.10) in which he is moving a toy car over an elaborate layout with roads, rivers and a harbor.

Example 4.

Context: Michael (4.10) is playing with a layout containing roads, a harbor, boats, lorries, cars, houses and trees. An observer (O) is nearby recording. Mark (3.11) is watching.

This refers to an earlier monologue in which the roads were gravelled against ice.	Mic-O	1.	NOW THIS LORRY'S BEEN OUT SO LONG ON THE BOAT THAT IT ISN'T SLIPPERY ANY MORE...
One of the model people falls into the harbor. Mic goes on moving the lorry.	Mic	2.	STRAIGHT INTO THE WATER HE SLIPPED..
		3.	THEY'RE GOING ON HOLIDAY...
		4.	SO HE PARKED HIS LORRY UP HERE AND IS GOING ON HOLIDAY...
		5.	THEN HE DROVE OFF AND SAW THE BUS STOP AND THOUGHT SOMEONE MIGHT WANT TO GET UP HERE...
Mic has put gravel in the lorry.		6.	...BUT I'VE GOT GRAVEL ON THE BACK...
Mic picks up a tree, and puts it on the back of the lorry, and then takes it off and puts it near a house.		7.	...SO HE WENT TO THE GRAVEL SHOP...
		8.	...AND ON THE WAY BACK HE SAW THE LITTLE TREE AND HE PUT IT ON HIS LORRY AND WENT AND PLANTED IT IN HIS GARDEN...
He drives off and stops at the lights.		9.	...AND THEN HE WENT TO THE TRAFFIC LIGHTS...
		10.	...AND THE TRAFFIC LIGHTS SAID...
		11.	YOU SHOULDN'T TAKE THINGS FROM OTHER PEOPLE'S GARDENS...
		12.	SO HE SAID ALRIGHT...
		13.	AND HE WENT AND BOUGHT ONE FROM A SHOP...
	Mic-O	14.	YOU SHOULD MAKE THIS GARDEN BIGGER BECAUSE IT IS ALL GETTING KNOCKED DOWN.

Here, too, the actual props, though providing some referential structure, play a role subordinate to other current experience and to his creative imagination. He is not without an audience as there is another child present and also the observer, who is addressed in the last remark and a tape recorder, so perhaps Michael is creating for an audience as well as for himself. The length and elaboration of his verbal constructions are no different from those he uses normally for interpersonal communication. He is also beginning to use conjunctions and full narrative form. Apart from the moral injunction uttered by the traffic lights and the lorry driver's acceptance of it, there is no manifestation of speech act cohesion, because only one role is elaborated. Address and turn taking are also only shown in this one exchange.

If we consider these three monologues together, the degree to which they differ from each other may indicate one line of development of children's monologue, towards consecutive narrative and imaginative story telling. There is an element of this at the end of Rebecca's monologue. All three are essentially imaginative and creative. They are not directed to problem solving as Vigotsky implied in his description of the transformation of socialized language to language for self and then into inner thought. Nearly all the exchanges of fundamantal information or arguments about rules in this language sample come either in interactional play when the play situations or roles are being elaborated, when there is a clash of intention or viewpoint, or in exploratory play or in argument with an adult. That is the problem solving, information getting role of language apparent mainly in dialogue with others, and not when the child is playing alone.

For example, in the following sequence, there is an impressive exchange based on a clash between the latent rule frame of another Michael (3.11), whom we will call Mick, and the leader of his playgroup. It is clear that Mick has powerful rules about babyish behavior, sucking dummies, and putting dirty things in the mouth. He also has a great respect for rules. The playgroup leader's forthright exposition of her rule frame--that people should not be unjustly deprived of what they like, that little boys should look after little girls under the superordinate rule that the big and strong should look after the little and the weak, obviously causes a deep impression on Mick's thinking and behavior and he attempts to bring his own rule system and that of the playgroup leader into some accord.

Example 5.

Context: Mick (3.11), Susy (2.5), Steven (2.7) and Playgroup Leader. Mick and Susy are using the dough in the home corner. Mick is making cakes. Susy is watching him and is sucking her dummy, she always has this in her mouth whatever she is doing.

Mick leans over and snatches Susy's dummy, Susy cries immediately. Playgroup leader comes up.	1. Mic-Pl SHE'S A LITTLE BABY TO HAVE... TO HAVE A DUMMY...SHE'S LITTLE CRY BABY. Mick justifies with rule, only babies have dummies.
	2. Pl-Mic DON'T TAKE SUSY'S DUMMY MICHAEL... SHE LIKES IT. Playgroup Leader counters with rule, things people like should not be removed.
As he says this Mick wipes the dummy over the table to make it dirty.	3. Mic-Sus YOU DON'T WANT YOUR DIRTY OLD DUMMY...IT'S DIRTY. Direct address to Susy, indirect counter to (2) by new rule--no dirty things in mouths.
	4. PL GIVE ME THE DUMMY, MICHAEL... THERE YOU ARE SUSY.

		Playgroup Leader overrides, formal address by name.
Mick goes back to his pastry.	5. Mic	I'LL MAKE A PICTURE. Mick terminates by new initiative ...pause.
Playgroup Leader watches Susy and Mick for half a minute. Mick has taken all the dough.	6. Mic-PL	SHE HAD ALL THIS BEFORE, DIDN'T SHE? D'YOU THINK SHE WANTS A BIT? Mick's use of she distances Susy link with (2).
	7. PL-Mic	I THINK SHE WOULD MICHAEL, YOU GIVE SUSY HALF...YOU LOOK AFTER HER...BOYS HAVE TO LOOK AFTER LITTLE GIRLS... Playgroup Leader confirms, directs and gives rule.
	8. Mic	WHY?
	9. PL-Mic	BECAUSE THEY ARE BIGGER AND STRONGER. Development by superordinate rule.
Mick looks doubtful. Playgroup Leader leaves them.	10. PL-Sus	MICHAEL'S GOING TO LOOK AFTER YOU SUSY. Directs Mick, informs Susy.
Susy looks sulkily at Mick and does not answer his question.	11. Mic-Sus	WANNA PLAY?
He pushes the cake tray towards her, she takes it and throws it away.	12. Sus	Nonverbal rejection.
	13. Mic-PL	KNOW WHAT...I GIVE...I GIVE HER THAT THING...AN' SHE THREW IT. Mick protests to authority over breach of rule that offers should not be rudely rejected.
Playgroup Leader does not hear Mic--he was perturbed at Susy's reaction. He gives her a piece of dough. Susy pushes it away. Mick leaves to tell the Playgroup Leader.	14. Mic-Sus	THERE YOU ARE.
	15. Sus	NO!
Steven enters and looks at Susy.		
Steven looks blankly. Mick goes off. He collects a chair for Steven.	16. Mic-Ste	SHE'S GOT A BABY'S DUMMY. Susy is distanced.
They sit and play together. There is no conversation.	17. Mic-Ste	THERE YOU ARE STEVEN, EVERYTIME YOU KNOW...I'LL SIT NEAR YOU... AND I'LL PLAY WITH YOU. Elaborate overture with direct address cohesion marked by I/you with you know, long term intentionality by everytime.

Above all this dialogue illustrates how intimately thinking is linked to social exchange. Mick not only takes in and applies to his own behavior the rule frame propounded by the playgroup leader, he does so even when she is no longer hovering over him. His ability to take in and transform the argument for his own purposes is illustrated in the final overture to Steven. This behavior seems to be the externalized precursor of that socialized form of internalized dialogue which Piaget described as mature thinking.

Where do the examples cited leave the argument about language for self and language for and with others? Of the types of language included by Piaget under monologue, i.e., (a) echoic repetition, (b) language accompanying action, and (c) creating reality by words and magical language, (c) is the one which most nearly fits the monologue examples given. But is this really language-for-self? Perhaps it begins as such as a child left on its own summons up experiences both social and nonsocial, playing with and reorganising them in a way uncoupled from the demands of the real. This process may interiorise as fantasy, or later exteriorise in the socially acceptable form of creative writing.

Children who attend nursery schools inevitably have experience of narrative monologue in stories and many other children also have this experience from an early age at home. Both Rebecca's and Michael's monologues appear to show the influence of the story form, which may be the reflex of exposure to stories read or told by adults. The inconsequentiality and lack of sequence in Michael's monologue show the dominance of play-fantasy, but a fantasy which is equally rooted in the world of reality. Two questions arise; the first is that of audience. Do these play monologues elaborate so much when there is no audience? This question is difficult to solve. The work of Gordon Wells based on microtransmitter recordings taken in the home may throw some light on this and one of his collaborators, Peter French, is working on the problem. The available transcripts from Wells' work do not record children older than 39 months, so the scrappiness of the solitary fantasy play episodes may be a function of immaturity. Piaget, however, said about these fantasy monologues:

> the longest and purest monologues show themselves in the language of child to adult, the child uninterruptedly following the thread of his imagination (Piaget <u>loc cit</u> p. 242).

It may be, therefore, that the presence of an audience is a necessary feature for the elaboration of monologue, and that when the child is left to his own company, the linguistic or expressed structure fragments and becomes more interiorized and less explicit. Further evidence is needed.

The second question is: do the monologues have characteristic structural features? There is no evidence in any of the examples cited, or indeed in any of the monologues in the nursery sample from which they are taken, that the language necessarily assumes the inexplicit reference postulated by Vigotsky. In principle, as the function of this kind of monologue appears to be the creating of a world, anything within that world, objects, actions, social interactions, can be reflected in it. The content of the monologue, the age and personal style of the speaker and the context will all be a source of variation. Specific linguistic features might be differently distributed under the influence of any of these variables. Again, further evidence is needed.

What of collective monologue, that uncertain category which helped to swell the quantity of children's language classified as egocentric by Piaget.

Modern English nurseries and playgrounds appear to be more socially oriented than the Montessori type kindergarten in which Piaget's data were collected. But even there the typical group was the dyad, and 78% of the groups in which children only were participating were dyads, and only 11% had more than three members (Shields, 1976). In adult organised activity, groups of three constituted 51% of the episodes. It is within these groups that the kinds of utterance described by Piaget as collective monologue were mainly represented. In most of these recordings the children were engaged in a common activity, often collage or drawing. Each made their own thing and fairly often they describe what they are doing as in the following example.

<u>Example 6.</u>

<u>Context</u>: Ann (4.7), Anna (4.10), Kim (4.11) and Paul (3.10), and Sylvana (4.10) are cutting up old magazines, making collage pictures and crayoning. An observer (O) is present.

Anna picks up a cut out	9. Anna	THIS IS TOO BIG I'M NOT DOING ANYTHING.
	10. Pau	I'M MAKING ANYTHING (something)
Kim cuts a door in some yellow paper	11. Kim	I'M GOING TO MAKE A HOUSE
	12. Pau	I'LL MAKE ANYTHING
Anna looks at Kim's work	13. Anna-Kim	YELLOW IS FOR CRAYONING
Paul holds up collage, the others look without interest	14. Pau-All	LOOK, I MAKE ANYTHING...THERE Y'ARE.
Anna is using yellow crayon, Kim hints	15. Kim-Anna	I NEED..(inaudable) YELLOW ONE IN A MINUTE
Anna responds negatively, but tactfully.	16. Anna-Kim	I WON'T FINISH FOR A VERY LONG TIME
Shows O his collage	17. Pau-O	I MAKE ANYTHING
Sylvana has trouble with stapler	18. Ann-Sylv	PUT ONE THERE...PUT A STAPLE THERE, PUT THAT THERE
Kim wants yellow crayon	19. Kim-Anna	C'M ON, ANNA...
Anna won't part with it	20. Anna-Kim	NO
	21. Ann-Kim	WHAT ARE YOU MAKING...A HOUSE? I'M GOING TO MAKE A HOUSE WITH A LADY AND A PUSSY CAT.

At first sight a number of unaddressed remarks made about the children's own activities might seem to be candidates for classification as egocentric, but it seems more likely that we are looking at children coping with a new social problem, how to function interactively in a group. There are 52 utterances in all in the episode of which 43 are addressed. Numbers 9-21 are given because these contain the highest number of remarks which are not specifically addressed. Three of them are by Paul who is literally odd man out in this group of girls consisting of two pairs of friends. (Ann and Kim figure in the dialogue with Rebecca.) Are his rather immature utterances egocentric or is he attempting an entry into the interactional network?

This is a complex manoeuvre, and Paul is unsuccessful, making a final bid in (14) and then turning to the Observer for attention in (17). The induction and maintenance of an interpersonal field is an interactional skill which children have partially learned within the family, most often in dyadic exchanges with their caregiver. On entering the nursery group the child may be faced for the first time with entry into a group interaction in which turn taking must pass round to several people who stand in no fixed relation, unlike members of a family. There may be several ways of making an entry but all would involve establishing some joint intent. If the setting is one where all children are making their own artifact in a common center of activity, the non-specifically addressed remarks may be a means of defining self role in a joint interaction thus setting the field for possible exchanges. What Piaget termed collective monologue, may in fact be the child's first attempt at collective dialogue or interaction in a non-family group. Some nursery teachers are adept in helping the children to take conversational turns in larger groupings, a skill which is very necessary in educational institutions and probably an important part of what children learn in nurseries.

Creative monologue, and collective monologue have been briefly discussed. What of the kind of synpractic monologue that Vigotsky identified as a precursor of thinking? Unfortunately the nursery recordings cited here hold little that could be described in this way. When children were recorded in play situations without a companion, vocalisation was at a fragmentary level, consisting mainly of accompanying sounds like drurr-drurr-drurr for an imaginary motorbike, or ca-ca-ca-ca-ca marking the march of an animal into the Noah's ark. If another child approached there was usually an increase of verbalization, as though the child had to define his or her activity within the field of attention of another. This usually ended in dialogue. Sometimes, however, the solitary child shut up and retired to silent social surveillance of the newcomer. There were no instances in these recordings of a child using language to tackle a problem when on his own, though there was plenty of problem solving by language in play sequences and in some interaction with adults.

What now is left to egocentric speech since even echoic repetition has been reclassified as social play (Keenan, 1974; Garvey, 1976), and collective monologue redefined as a form of collective dialogue in which the child is attempting a more complex form of interaction. Perhaps it would be best to follow the suggestion of Bates and classify as egocentric only those utterances where communication is intended but fails because the child does not take into account the needs of the speaker (Bates, 1976).

Imaginative monologue, which appears to include synpractic monologue as far as the sample studied here affords some evidence, might best be regarded as a hybrid form half socialized, half individualized. In the first place, it is possible that, by the age of three or four at least, the child may need an audience to elaborate his fantasy verbally. More evidence is needed on this, more children must be pursued into solitude by the ubiquitous tape recorder. In any case, the monologues seems to be typical examples of elaborated play in which the experiences of reality are brought in to structure the current activity. This process may take place in play interaction, or it may be exhibited as in these monologues entirely under the control of the child.

If the monologues cited here have precursors in the child's earlier vocal and verbal play, the succession might be something like the following:

(1) motor activity with accompanying vocalization or vocalization with accompanying motor activity depending on the child's focus of attention

(2) motor activity with synchronized verbalization as when a child says run run run while running or bang bang bang while banging. In this the motor action and the verbal gesture have the same content.

(3) motor activity extended by vocalization or verbalization as when a child runs making symbolic noises such as doo-dah doo-dah doodah for an ambulance or neeeeeooown for a diving aeroplane

(4) motor activity structured and transformed by verbalization, as when Rebecca creates a scenario out of putting the wooden toys back in the box.

(5) verbalization with synchronized motor activity, where the verbal creation plays the dominant role

(6) pure verbal creation without accompanying motor acting out.

It is not intended to imply by this that monologue develops on its own pathway, simply to say that once past stage one, everything that happens in the child's communicative development in an environment of social interaction can become an element in the child's own activity outside or alongside such social interaction.

It is not suggested either that each subsequent form of monologue necessarily develops out of or replaces the previous one. The list is a heuristic device only, pending the collection of more information. Rebecca's monologue partakes of both (3) and (4) and in the last section of her monologue verges upon (5). Alpana's monologue falls almost wholly under (5), and so does Michael's. Indeed in Michael's narrative form he is verging on (6). However, in other parts of Michael's protocol he produces monologues very like Rebecca's with the same raised count of nouns, and the same proliferation of locatives. The content of the activity seems to determine the style of the monologue.

How do the monologues cited here relate to the child's thought? They bear witness to a capacity to manipulate experience imaginatively, they present thought as creating its own temporary reality, but creating it out of the permanent realities of experience of the material and social world. This experience has a dual source. The properties of things, their size, weight, ductility, moisture, temperature, can become a part of the child's experienced reality through direct sensory motor experience. The significance of objects and their relation to socialized conceptual systems, however, is given by the place they occupy in shared or interpersonal experience. The child after all is surrounded by objects which are social artifacts, and even the natural objects he meets are encountered in a human or social setting, in farms, zoos, parks, gardens, hedgerows. The child's ideas and rule systems are moulded in exchange with others who are repositories of socialized information, social know-how and social rules. It is, in the main, by dialogue with others that such information is conveyed and the direct impressions of the senses are restructured as part of social knowledge. It is, therefore, likely that it is language as dialogue which has the most important influence on thought. It is by being able to set up an internal dialogue, and divide the self against the self, by arguing for and against, considering differing sources of evidence, and possible objections to them; by weighing alternative views of what ought to be done that we sharpen the ability to think and act. Perhaps it is imaginative monologue where reality is assimilated to the purposes of the individual which gives that individual the ability (and courage) to pursue his purposes in accommodation to reality, fortified by his or her mastery of the world within.

BIBLIOGRAPHY

Aarts, F. G. A. M. (1971) On the distribution of noun-phrase types in English clause structure. Lingua, 26, pp. 281-293.

Bates, E. (1975) Peer relations and the acquisition of language. In M. Lewis and Rosenblum (eds.), Friendship and Peer Relations, New York: Wiley.

Bates, E. (1976) Language and Context, The Acquisition of Pragmatics, New York: Academic Press.

Brazelton, T. B., Koslowski, B., and Main, M. (1974) The origins of reciprocity: The early mother-infant interaction. In M. Lewis and Rosenblum (eds.), The Effect of the Infant on its Caregiver, New York: Wiley.

Bruton, C. J., Candlin, C. N., and Leather, J. H. (1977) Doctor speech functions in casualty consultations--Predictable structures of discourse in a regulated setting. In G. Nickel (ed.), Proceedings of the Fourth International Congress of Applied Linguistics, 1, pp. 297-311.

Bullowa, M. (1975) When infant and adult communicate, how do they synchronise their behavior. In A. Kendon, R. Harris and M. Key (eds.), The Organisation of Behavior in Fact to Face Interaction, The Hague: Mouton.

Dore, J. (1977) Children's illocutionary acts. In R. Freedle (ed.), Discourse Comprehension and Production, Hillsdale, N.J.: Lawrence Erlbaum.

Dore, J., Gearhart, M., and Newman, D. (1977) The structure of nursery school conversation. Mimeo.

Duncan, S. D., Jr. (1974) On signalling that it is your turn to speak. Journal Experiment and Social Psychology, 10(3), pp. 234-247.

Edwards, D. (1978) The social context of early language development. In A. Lock (ed.), Action, Gesture and Symbol: The Emergence of Language, London Academic Press (forthcoming).

French, P. (1977) Personal communication on work on language for self. At School of Education Research Unit. University of Bristol.

Garvey, C. (1976) Some properties of social play. Reprinted in J. S. Bruner, A. Jolly and K. Sylva, Play: Its Role in Development and Evolution, Harmdsworth: Penguin.

Garvey, C. (1977) Play with languages. In B. Tizard (ed.), The Biology of Play, London: William Heineman (Medical Books), pp. 74-100.

Haberman, J. (1970) Toward a theory of communicative competence. In H. P. Dreitzel (ed.), Recent Sociology, 2, New York/London: Collier Macmillan.

Hasan, R., and Halliday, M. A. K. (1976) Cohesion in English, London: Longman.

Hawkins, P. (1968) Social class, the nominal group and reference. Language and Speech, 12(2).

Howe, R. (1976) Encouraging children to talk. Paper presented at the Psychology of Language Conference, Stirling, 1976.

Jefferson, G. (1973) A case of precision timing in ordinary conversation: Overlapped tag positional address terms in closing sequences. Semotica, 9, pp. 47-96.

Keenan, E. (1974) Conversational competence in children. Journal of Children's Language, 1(2), pp. 163-184.

Lee, C. (1975) Towards a cognitive theory of interpersonal development: Importance of peers. In M. Lewis and L. Rosenblum (eds.), Friendship and Peer Relations, New York: Wiley.

Luria, A. R. (1961) The Role of Speech in the Regulation of Behavior, Harmondsworth: Penguin.

Lyons, J. (1975) Deixis as the source of reference. In E. Keenan (ed.), Formal Semantics of Natural Language, Cambrigde: C.U.P.

Piaget. (1926) The Language and Thought of the Child, New York: Harcourt Brace.

Piaget. (1959) The Language and Thought of the Child, (revised and enlarged), London: Routledge and Kegan Paul.

Poyatos, F. (1977) Verbal and non-verbal expression in interaction research; and pedagogical perspectives. In G. Nickel (ed.), Proceedings of the Fourth International Congress of Applied Linguistics, 1, pp. 87-95.

Sacks, H. (1976) Tying techniques (Lecture 11. 1967). In Gazdar and Levinson (eds.), Pragmatics Microfiche, Oxford: Microform Publications.

Sacks, H., Schegloff, E. A. and Jefferson, G. (1974) A simplest systematics for the organising of turntaking for conversation. Language, 50-4 (1), pp. 696-735.

Schegloff, E. A. (1968) Sequencing in conversational openings. In J. Gumperz and D. Hymes (eds.), Directions in Sociolinguistics--The Ethnography of Communication.

Shields, M. M. (1976) Some communicational skills of young children: A study of dialogue in the nursery school. Paper delivered at the Psychology of Language Conference, Stirling.

Shields, M. M. (1977) The implications for psychology of the study of dialogue skills in pre-school children. Paper presented at the Conference of the Committee of Psychological Sciences and the Warsaw University Institute of Psychology at Warsaw.

Shields, M. M. (1978) Construing the social world: The child as psychologist. In A. Lock (ed.), Action, Gesture and Symbol: The Emergence of Language, London: Academic Press.

Sinclair, J. H. and Coulthard, R. M. (1975) Towards an Analysis of Discourse, London: C.U.P.

Tough, J. (1977) The Development of Meaning, London: Unwin.

Trevarthen, C. (1974) Conversations with a two month old. New Scientist, 62(986).

Ure, J. (1971) Lexical density and register differentiation. In G. E. Perren, and J. L. M. Trim (eds.), Applications of Linguistics, London: C.U.P.

Vigotsky, L. (1934) (tr. 1962) Thought and Language, Cambridge: M.I.T.

Vigotsky, L. (1962) Thought and Language, M.I.T. Paperback, Cambridge, Mass.

Weir, R. H. (1970) Language in the Crib, The Hague: Mouton.

Wells, G. (1975) Language Development in Pre-School Children: Transcripts of Boys and Girls Aged 39 Months. Published University of Bristol School of Education, Bristol.

*It's Not Whether You Win or Lose, It's How You Play the Game**

JEFFREY SCHULTZ
University of Cincinnati, School of Education

INTRODUCTION

This paper presents a microethnographic analysis of a game played by a teacher and three of her students during the first week of school. Three issues will be examined: 1) What children need to know in order to make sense of what is going on in the classroom, and thereby learn how to behave appropriately in the classroom; 2) What the teacher needs to know about the students in order to make sense of their actions, and how the teacher makes inferences on the basis of the students' behavior to determine who her students are; and 3) How microethnographic analyses can be used to shed light on 1) and 2).

Earlier studies of person perception and impression formation have treated these processes as static phenomena. (c.f. Asch, 1946 and Tagiuri and Petrullo, 1958) These studies assumed that impressions of persons are based primarily on attributes of persons such as age, sex, and ethnicity, and that these impressions arise independent of social interaction. Ethnomethodology, on the other hand, considers that persons are always making sense of the world around them and that this process of making sense is derived in part from their interactions with others. (c.f. Garfinkel, 1967 and Mehan and Wood, 1975) One of the assumptions behind this research is that the way in which persons make sense of the world and of other persons is a dynamic process, arising in part out of social interaction.

Another assumption of this research is that in order to arrive at a description of how persons make sense of the world, it is necessary to look in detail at what persons are doing and saying. This is the perspective of microanalytic studies of the organization of behavior in face to face interaction, as exemplified by the work of Kendon et. al. (1975), Scheflen (1973), and Erickson (1975a, 1975b).

The approach to the study of social interaction presented in this paper attempts to combine the two perspectives referred to above, in order to arrive at a description of how the three students and their teacher made sense of what was going on in the game by making sense of the behavior of the other participants.

---

*The help of Frederick Erickson, Susan Florio, Don Bremme and Martha Walsh in the preparation of this manuscript is gratefully acknowledged. The results reported here and the opinions expressed in this paper are strictly the responsibility of the author. The research was supported by a postdoctoral fellowship from the National Institute of Mental Health to the author and by a grant from the Spencer Foundation to Frederick Erickson.

Another assumption upon which this research is based is that persons act differently depending upon the situation they are engaged in. Persons "style switch" depending upon what they perceive is required by the situation. (c.f. Blom and Gumperz, 1972) For example, the behavior of members of a family is different at dinner time depending upon whether or not there is a guest present, and their behavior is different depending upon who the guest is: a close friend or the father or mother's boss.

Similarly, the students and the teacher act differently in the classroom depending upon the situation they are engaged in. For example, times when the whole class is assembled in a circle to discuss an issue are different from times when students are working in small groups on a variety of projects. There are different contingencies for how loud one can speak, when one can speak, what one can say, how much one can move, etc. The task faced by children entering school for the first time is therefore to figure out what the appropriate contexts are for interaction (circles as opposed to small group work) and then to figure out what behavior is considered appropriate in each of the different contexts (when one can speak, what one can say, how loud one can speak, when one can move, etc.). One cannot assume that there is one "correct" way to behave in the classroom just as one cannot assume that there is one correct way to behave at home. Students and teachers need to be constantly monitoring what is going on in order to determine what they are supposed to be doing.

In order for students to make sense of what is going on in the classroom, in order for them to be "practical reasoners" (Cook-Gumperz, 1975), they need to discover what the appropriate contexts for interaction are in the classroom and they also need to discover what the appropriate range of behavior is for each of those contexts. At the beginning of school, the teacher needs to find out who her students are. She discovers who they are in part by making sense of their interaction with her. A teacher partly bases her impressions of her students on the time she spends interacting with each of them, and in so doing she has access to only a small range of the behavioral repertoire of each of her students. In other words, a teacher with twenty-four students bases her impression of each of them on their behavior in a limited set of situations in the classroom.

The Classroom

The classroom in which the study was conducted was a combined kindergarten/first grade classroom in a suburb of Boston. The teacher was an experienced teacher who had been teaching in mixed age classrooms for several years. There were fourteen kindergarten students and eleven first grade students in the room. Eight of the eleven first graders had been in kindergarten in the same room with the same teacher the previous year.

There were basically two different kinds of activities in the classroom: 1) activities that occurred while the whole group was assembled on the rug for some kind of joint endeavor. These activities will be referred to as "circles." 2) Activities that occurred while the class was dispersed around the room performing a variety of tasks. These activities will be referred to as "small group periods." A typical day in the classroom was divided into a cycle of circles and small group periods. Circles were used by the teacher for bringing the students together to convey information to them, to discipline them and as a measure of control when things got out of hand in the room. Also, music and other special activities were conducted while the students were sitting in a circle. Small group periods ranged from what was called "work time," when the students were engaged in a variety of different tasks throughout the room, to snack time, when the students either sat alone or in small groups at tables distributed around the room and ate their snacks.

The Activity

This paper will examine the behavior of a kindergarten child (Angie) and her teacher playing a game of tic-tac-toe with two other students during work time on the fourth day of school. This was Angie's fourth day in a classroom. (Angie is not the student's real name.) She had never attended school before, and so she was still in the process of figuring out what the appropriate contexts were in the classroom and subsequently what behaviors were considered appropriate in each of those contexts.

Angie had never played tic-tac-toe before. Also, she had never played a board game with the teacher before. The task for Angie was therefore twofold: 1) first, she had to learn to play the interactional game of when to speak, what to say, how to say it, etc. and, 2) she also had to learn to play the board game.

The analysis of Angie's behavior reported in this paper was performed as a result of the teacher's characterization of Angie as being dependent and not a "leader," two attributes which she does not value highly. In other contexts, at home at dinner and playing with her peers during work time, Angie did not exhibit these attributes in the opinion of the research team. The analysis of Angie's behavior in the presence of the teacher would hopefully show what it was that led the teacher to attribute these qualities to Angie. The research team had also noticed that Angie's behavior was different when she interacted with the teacher than when she interacted with her peers or her family. This analysis was performed as a starting point in documenting the differences between Angie's behavior when in the presence of the teacher and her behavior when she was interacting with peers and relatives. Any statements about Angie's social naivete should be taken as referring to her lack of acculturation into the culture of the classroom. I follow Goodenough (1964, p. 36) in using a cognitive definition of culture. "As I see it, a society's culture consists of whatever it is one has to know or believe in order to operate in a manner acceptable to its members, and do so in any role that they accept for any one of themselves."

Goodenough later refines this notion of culture to include the expectation persons have of the behavior of others. "There are different role-expectations that go with different social relationships and different social situations. Each of these different expectations constitutes a different culture to be learned." (1975, p. 4)

It is in this sense that Angie can be seen as socially naive. By the fourth day of school, she had not learned what was expected of her and what she was supposed to expect of others. In other words, she had not yet been acculturated into the culture of the classroom.

The teacher had asked a first grade child (S1) to play a game with Angie, and then the teacher recruited another first grader (S2) to play the game also. S1 began to draw the crosshatch for a tic-tac-toe game on a piece of paper, but was stopped by the teacher who got out a three dimensional tic-tac-toe game which could be played by three students. (See Appendix for complete transcript) In order to simplify the game even further for the kindergarten student (Angie), the teacher removed the top board of the three board game and restricted play to that board alone. Each board is made up of four rows of four places each.

The three students and the teacher sat down at a table to play. Since it was work time, and the teacher did not have a student teacher yet, several students came over to the table to ask her questions, to try to get involved in the action of the game, or simply to watch. These interruptions occurred during the course of the entire game. The time between when S1 first approached Angie to play the game and the time when the teacher sent Angie away at the end of the game to take a test was slightly over six minutes. The actual playing time of the game was slightly over three minutes.

The identification of the tic-tac-toe game as a significant segment to analyze came after many hours of watching the tapes and looking for an extended period when Angie was involved with the teacher in a focused activity. The tic-tac-toe game provided a continuous strip of activity between Angie and the teacher during which Angie's and the teacher's behavior could be examined in close detail. [Note that the tic-tac-toe game is a slot in the period "work time" which in turn is a slot in the period "class day." Other slots which occur during work time are: "setting-up," when students are choosing what activities they want to be involved with; "play time," when the students are actually involved in an activity; and "clean-up," when students are putting away materials they have just been involved with. These slots can (and frequently do) occur more than once during any given work time, as students frequently engage in more than one activity.]

The initial analysis of the tic-tac-toe game considered the game as a whole. The assumption was that there was a "correct" way to behave during the game, and that this would change very little, if at all, during the course of the game. The question then became "What are the boundaries of the game?" At what point could it be said that the teacher and the three students were involved in the game; and consequently how did Angie behave and how did the teacher evaluate this behavior? The analysis took as an undifferentiated whole the segment beginning with S1's invitation to Angie to play the game until the time the teacher sent Angie off to take her test.

The Players

The three students who participated in the game were very different in terms of their social identity at that point in the year. Angie was the child the study focused on. She was a kindergarten student who had never attended school before, had no siblings and was a true neophyte with respect to school. As was stated earlier, the teacher categorized her as not being a "leader type" after watching her on videotape.

S1 was one of the classroom leaders. She was a first grade student who had been in the same classroom the year before. She was very highly evaluated by the teacher in terms of social skills and the teacher labelled her as being independent, able to follow through on things and aggressive. She was a member of a small group of first grade students who formed the "elite" corps of the classroom.

S2 was a student who later on in the year would become a member of the elite corps. At this point in the year (the fourth day of school) she was very shy and retiring. The teacher attributed her shyness to the fact that S2 had attended a parochial school the preceding year and still had not "come out of her shell." Also, S2 was among the top readers in the classroom and so was highly thought of in an academic sense.

A later section of the paper will examine the teacher's differential treatment of the three students in terms of how she gave advice and complimented them during the game.

Analyses of Verbal and Non-Verbal Behavior

Angie's Verbal Behavior

The first analysis performed on the data was an analysis of Angie's utterances. It was hoped that this analysis would reveal Angie's perception of the game and her role in it. This analysis is followed by an analysis of the teacher's utterances, since an analysis of either Angie's utterances or the teacher's utterances would hopefully reveal the basis for the teacher's evaluation of Angie's performance in the game, in the way she treated Angie as opposed to S1 and S2.

Most studies of classroom interaction and coding schemes for classroom verbal behavior concentrate on these major issues: How teachers ask questions; how teachers give directions and how teachers provide information. They concentrate therefore on the linguistic forms "interrogatives" and "declaratives." No study, with a few exceptions (Mehar, et. al., 1976; McDermott, 1976; Shuy et. al., 1975; Gumperz and Herasinchuk, 1975), treat student behavior to any great extent or as an integral part of what goes on in the classroom. There are no good models for analyzing student behavior in the classroom, so the two categories of utterances chosen to be examined first in Angie's speech were the same as two of the categories chosen in the analysis of teachers' verbal behavior in other studies: interrogatives and declaratives. Specifically, the analysis examined what Angie used questions for, what she demonstrated about her knowledge of the game through her questions, what she asked questions about, why she made declarative utterances, what she talked about, and whom she addressed her statements to.

Table 1 contains a breakdown of Angie's verbal behavior.

TABLE 1 Angie's Verbal Behavior

	Total Number	Self-Initiated	As Part of a Response
Declaratives	11	1	10
Interrogatives	8	4	4

The major point that can be made from the above table is that three times as many of Angie's utterances were said in response to something someone else said as compared to the utterances which she herself initiated. The criterion used for whether or not Angie was responsible for initiating the utterance was whether or not the utterance referred to anything said by one of the other participants in the game or said by anybody else in the classroom within three utterances preceding Angie's utterance.

The fact that in most cases Angie waited for someone to say something before speaking can be seen as evidence supporting the teacher's view of her as being dependent. An analysis of the content of Angie's utterances reveals more about the same issue.

Angie's questions reveal that she:

a) DOES NOT KNOW WHAT TIC-TAC-TOE IS (a board game played by several players):

   1 S1: Angie, you wanna play tic-tac-toe?
   2 Angie: What's tic-tac-toe mean?

b) DOES NOT KNOW WHAT TIC-TAC-TOE LOOKS LIKE (a board game):

   (As the teacher began to set up the three dimensional tic-tac-toe game, Angie asked the following question.)
   11 Angie: What's it called?

c) DOES NOT KNOW WHAT THE GAME PIECES ARE SUPPOSED TO BE USED FOR (a series of turns):

   (The game began and the teacher urged S2 to put down one of her pieces.)
   89 T: Go ahead.
   90 Angie: Where's my one?
   91 T: (To S2) Put it anyplace now, it's OK.

d) DOES NOT KNOW WHAT THE RESULTANT MOVES ARE TO ACCOMPLISH (to relate to the turns of others by "blocking" others who are opponents):

   (As the game progressed, the teacher attempted to help Angie make her next move. The teacher mistakenly called Angie by S2's name, then corrected herself.)
   104 T: It's not your turn, S1! (To Angie) Go ahead, S2. No,
   105 you wanna get four Angie, in a row. If you put one here, it won't be a row.
   106 Angie: Where, where's four?
   107 T: See you're already blocked. This is 1,2,3,4...you gotta
   108 go across. (Angie moves.) This is a hard game for you, I think.

e) DOES NOT KNOW WHAT THE OUTCOME OF THE GAME IS SUPPOSED TO BE (there is only one winner):

   (As Angie was about to make her next move, the teacher warned her of what the consequences of making the wrong move would be.)
   129 T: If she puts one and makes four in a straight row, then she wins.
   130 Angie: And me too?

These questions demonstrate that Angie does not know anything about the successive stages of the game:

a) What the game looks like (visually and strategically) to begin with.
b) What the game looks like in process.
c) What the game is supposed to look like at the end.

There is only one question asked by Angie which demonstrates that she knows what is going on. This occurred in line 103. Seeing S1 moving out of turn, Angie asked "My turn?" She had recognized that S1 had gone out of turn and attempted to demonstrate that it was in fact her turn. However, this question could also be interpreted as showing that Angie did not in fact know what was going on because she could have been wondering whether or not it was her turn, rather than asserting the fact that it was her turn.

One way of looking at Angie's questions is that she asked a series of questions in an attempt to figure out how to play tic-tac-toe. These questions on the part of Angie can be construed as a search for the structure of tic-tac-toe and a search for the appropriate strategies needed to play the game.

Angie's questions, then demonstrate her incompetence in playing tic-tac-toe. From Angie's perspective, she was probably asking the questions in order to find out what was going on. It was the teacher's impression, however, after watching the game on videotape, that Angie had no idea of what was going on in the game, even at the end of the game. Inadvertently, Angie's inquisitive search into the structure of the game was used by the teacher as yet another manifestation of Angie's social naivete.

In direct contrast to her use of questions, and as further evidence of her social naivete, Angie asserted at two different times before and during the game that although (as the teacher had told her) tic-tac-toe was a difficult game, she could do it. As the teacher and Angie were walking over to the table where the game was being played, Angie asked the teacher what tic-tac-toe was.

2 Angie: What's tic-tac-toe mean? (Pause) Wha...What's tic-tac-toe?
3 T: You know how to play tic-tac-toe? IT'S A HARD GAME.
4 Angie: I KNOW, BUT I BET I CAN DO IT.

As the game progressed and the teacher realized that in fact the game as it was being presented at that time was too difficult for Angie to learn, she again commented on this issue.

107 T: See you're already blocked. This is 1,2,3,4...you gotta
108 go across (Angie moves.) THIS IS A HARD GAME FOR YOU, I THINK.
109 Angie: NO IT ISN'T.

Not only did Angie acknowledge that tic-tac-toe was a difficult game, but she enjoyed playing it.

143 T: ...There's too many people playing on this board for any-
144 body to win. THIS IS A HARD GAME. We're going to try something __________
145 S1: I like it.
146 Angie: I LIKE IT TOO.

In another context and uttered by another child, these declarative statements of Angie's about her ability to play the game would be interpreted as signs of agression and independence, both of which are highly valued by the teacher. In the context of this game, and in the context of the kinds of interrogatives that Angie used, these assertions can be seen as further evidence that Angie is naive and socially incompetent.

In the last example from the transcript quoted above, Angie imitated what S1 had just said. This pattern of imitation can be seen as another indication of Angie's potential social incompetence. This pattern was repeated on three other occasions. After the game was set up, the teacher asked Angie to start playing.

63 T: Alright, Angie wanna start?
64 S1: I START HERE (points to corner of top board).
65 T: Shh. Alright.
66 Angie: I START HERE (points to corner of next-to-top board).

The last two instances of imitation occurred as the teacher asked Angie to choose the color she wanted her game pieces to be.

15 T: I can only have three people play--you can watch.
16 What color is your favorite color, Angie?
17 Angie: Um...(Pause) (Shrugs)
18 T: O.K. here's the choice: you can be red,...
19 Angie: Red.
20 T: ...yellow, or blue. Which color do you wanna be?
21 S1: I TAKE BLUE.
22 Angie: BLUE.
23 T: Oh, we have to decide.
24 Angie: I TAKE BLUE.

Although the teacher had told her students on other occasions that when in doubt, they should look around and see what other students are doing, particularly the first graders who had been in the classroom longer and therefore knew what was going on, imitation can be seen as another indication of Angie's social naivete.

Angie's hesitancy about choosing a color and her creation of a potential problem by choosing the same color as S1 can also be seen as additional evidence regarding her social naivete. Angie may not have understood the true intent of the teacher's first question: "What color is your favorite color, Angie?" (line 16). She may not have seen the connection between her favorite color and the playing of tic-tac-toe. Angie responded by first saying the first color the teacher mentioned (red), then changed her response to blue after S1 chose blue. This exchange regarding colors can be seen as evidence that Angie is unable to make decisions on her own and must rely on the judgment of others.

At another point in the interaction, the teacher turned around and yelled at a group of students who were playing with a set of small blocks behind her. She said: "Tony what are you doing?" Angie responded to this by saying "He...they're playing with the big blocks." (Lines 147-149) Angie interpreted what the teacher apparently meant as a reprimand as a question which required an answer. Her answer was ignored by the teacher who presumably knew very well what the student was doing and was actually asking him to stop. Not knowing the illucutionary force of this utterance in question form (reprimanding, rather than seeking information) also made Angie appear socially naive.

The preceding analysis may be seen as treating Angie too harshly. The analysis is not intended to prove Angie's incompetence. Rather, it is done to demonstrate how the teacher could have formed a judgment of Angie as not being a "leader" type and therefore, in her estimation, not socially competent.

So far, all but one of Angie's utterances before and during the game have been accounted for. It was because of the following utterance that the relationship between appropriate behavior and the segmentation of interaction became highlighted in this analysis.

In line 97, while the teacher was trying to help S2 make her move, Angie looked up at her and said: "I'm going to tell my mommy again." The only response Angie got from the teacher after this utterance was a small grin followed by the teacher continuing her advice to S2. The topic was left hanging and never brought up again. Of Angie's eleven declaratives, this was the only one she initiated. In doing the analysis, the utterance looked out of place. However, it was not an imitation, a response to a question asked by the teacher, nor was it an assertion of her ability to play the game. The utterance seemed out of place at the time when it occurred, but there was no ready explanation for why it should be so.

Approximately one-and-a-half minutes before Angie made the utterance about her mother, the following exchange took place between S1 and the teacher:

52 S1: I saw Kevin's father today.
53 T: Kevin Brown's father?
54 Boy: (Brings in ball of plasticine) Right here?
55 T: (Nods) Make a long snake and then make an S. Draw it.
56 S1: How did you know his name was Kevin Brown? ___
57 T: He's busy, isn't he?

This exchange, along with Angie's utterance about her mother in line 97, make up the only two instances during the entire game when non-game related talk took place. During the remainder of the game, the conversation among the game players (the teacher, S1, S2, and Angie) was concerned with either the process of setting up the game or the actual playing of the game. The two instances cited above stand out as being different from the remainder of the talk that took place during the game.

When S1 brought up the topic of Kevin's father (line 52), the teacher responded to it by asking a question. On that occasion, the topic was discussed by the teacher, and it seemed to be appropriate for the situation. When Angie said "I'm going to tell my mommy again" in line 97, the teacher virtually ignored her and the utterance seemed out of place. Why should it be that talk about acquaintances and relatives seems to be appropriate for one child to talk about, but not another? A simple answer could be that S1 was one of the teacher's favorite students, whereas Angie was not. But that is not enough. The teacher had discussed similar issues with Angie earlier in the day, but did not choose to do so at the point in the playing of the game when Angie brought it up.

The answer seems to lie in timing; that is, the point in the interaction when the topic was brought up. Something seems to have changed in the minute-and-a-half between the time S1 made her utterance and the time Angie made hers. This suggests that there are times to bring up certain topics and times not to. Therefore it is not enough to consider the game as an undifferentiated whole; a further segmentation of the stream of interaction is necessary to account for the situational inappropriateness of this utterance by Angie.

FURTHER SEGMENTATION OF THE TIC-TAC-TOE GAME

In order to understand why Angie's comment to the teacher about her mother seemed inappropriate at the time when it occurred, a further segmentation of the tic-tac-toe game was required. In further examining the game, it appeared that it was made up of three distinct segments: 1) Set-up: This was the time beginning with S1's asking Angie if she wanted to play tic-tac-toe through the point when the teacher told Angie to begin the game. (Lines 1 through 63) 2) Serious Play: This was the time beginning with the first move of the game and ending with the teacher's comment that no one was going to win the game. (Lines 63 through 141) 3) Wind-up: This was the time beginning with the teacher's statement that no one was going to win the game and ending with the teacher sending Angie off to take her test. (Lines 141 through 155)

The exact beginnings and endings of the segments are not perfectly clear. As Pike (1967) has pointed out, in segmenting a stream of ongoing activity, there is an indeterminancy of boundaries or junctures which does not allow the outside observer to determine the precise instant when one segment has ended and another has begun. (Pike, 1967, p. 77) Despite the issue of the indeterminancy of junctures, there is ample behavioral evidence that the three segments of the tic-tac-toe game are in fact distinct from one another, and that they each impose different social constraints--communicative rights and obligations--upon the players in the game. This evidence follows.

Both segment junctures (between segment 1 and segment 2 and segment 3) are marked by distinct behavioral indicators on the part of the teacher. Preceding each of the junctures, the teacher had turned away from the game and then turned back. At the point at which the teacher turned back, the volume of her voice changed, and she made a comment about the playing of the game, a comment about what was going on in the game at that time. (Lines 63 and 141) These meta comments are termed "formulations" by Garfinkel and Sacks (1970).

Erickson (1975b) and Scheflen (1973) and Shultz (1975), among others, have found that changes in body orientation, interpersonal distance, paralinguistic features, and meta communicational features are very good behavioral indicators of junctures between socially salient interaction segments. In the tic-tac-toe game, the teacher performed paralinguistic, body position and metacommunicational shifts at the segment junctures. The behavior of the teacher therefore is a further indicator of the existence of the three segments.

Further evidence of the differences among the three segments may be found in the number of interruptions and attempted interruptions of the teacher which occurred during the three segments. An attempted interruption of the teacher by a student outside the game is defined as an approach by the student to the table where the tic-tac-toe game was being played followed by either a verbal or non-verbal attempt to attract the teacher's attention. If the teacher interacted with the student, the attempt was successful.

In all, there were twelve interruptions or attempted interruptions during the tic-tac-toe game. Seven of these occurred during the first segment, three during the second segment and two during the third segment. Table 2 summarizes the data on interruptions.

TABLE 2 Number of Interruptions
During Different Segments of the Game

	Length (in seconds)	Interruptions	Attempted Interruptions
Segment 1	161	7	0
Segment 2	184	0	2
Segment 3	33	3	0

It can be seen from the above table that segment 2 appears to be quite different from segments 1 and 3 in terms of interruptions. Two attempts are made to interrupt the teacher during segment 2, neither of which was successful. There was one interruption which succeeded that occurred right at the boundary between segment 2 and segment 3, and so it is questionable whether the interruption occurred in segment 2 or in segment 3. This interruption is counted as one of the three successful ones in segment 3. It is interesting to note that all interruptions attempted during segments 1 and 3 were successful. [Note: Although there were only two attempted interruptions during segment 2, several students were seen hovering near the table without actually approaching it. These were not counted as attempted interruptions since it is not possible to know whether or not they intended to interact with the teacher.]

In an attempt to understand the pattern of interruptions across the three segments, an analysis was made of the teacher's posture to see if there were any differences in the way she oriented to the game and to the students outside the game during the three segments.

A rough sketch was made of the teacher's back and head everytime she moved during the course of the game. These sketches were traced from the image on the videotape monitor. (This analysis was begun once the teacher sat down at the table where the game was being played, which occurred during line 11.) The analysis revealed that the teacher had three basic ways of positioning her head and back during the course of the game. These three positions may be illustrated as follow:

Position 1: 

Position 2: 

Position 3: 

The distribution of positions across segments is contained in Table 3.

TABLE 3 Teacher's Posture During
Different Segments of the Game

	# of Instances of Position 1	# of Instances of Position 2	# of Instances of Position 3
Segment 1	3	5	1
Segment 2	0	5	4
Segment 3	2	2	2

It can be seen from table 3 that the teacher never sat up straight (Position 1) during segment 2. Instead, she was always leaning forward, and was always leaning into the game. By not sitting up straight and instead leaning into the game, the teacher was in a sense shutting out the world outside the game and including in her field of interaction only the players of the game. This does not mean to imply that the teacher moved her body consciously or shut out the other students consciously. However, the position of her torso and head may have given students outside the game the impression that the teacher was very deeply engrossed in what she was doing and was therefore not available to be interrupted. As table 2 showed, it was actually more difficult to interrupt the teacher during segment 2 than it was during segments 1 and 3. Her leaning-in posture may have given the game an aura of "seriousness" or "cohesion" among players which was lacking during segments 1 and 3.

S1's posture changed as her involvement in the game changed. After S1 sat down, she leaned into the game as she became more involved in the game. She leaned into the game to get her pieces, then leaned out again. As the teacher started to give the instructions about how to play the game, (in line 72) S1 leaned into the game and did not lean out again until the teacher "reprimanded" her for going out of turn on line 115. From that point on, she only leaned into the game to put her pieces down.

Angie and S2, on the other hand, became fairly locked into a position once they sat down at the game table. They leaned into the game when they were collecting their pieces, putting a piece down, pointing at the board in response to a question by the teacher, or when they were examining the board to see where to put a piece down. Once they had finished what they were doing, they would lean back out of the game into their original position. The only exceptions to this were when Angie leaned towards the teacher to tell her about her mother (line 97), when Angie leaned out of the game to respond to the person who was calling her, (lines 114 and 117) and when Angie leaned out and turned around to look at the disruption at the small blocks. (line 137) These movements by Angie were not connected with the playing of the game, and they all occurred during segment 2. These movements, which neither of the other two students made, were inappropriate at the time, because they could be interpreted as lack of involvement in the game, which was not supposed to happen during segment 2, the serious playing time.

Another indication of the "seriousness" of segment 2 is the amount of talk done by each of the participants in the game during the three segments. These figures are found in table 4.

As can be seen from table 4, the percentage of talk by the different participants varied across the three segments. During segment 1, the students talked more than in either segments 2 or 3. The teacher dominated the conversation during segment 2 to a greater extent than in either segments 1 or 3. Since the teacher is supposed to be the most important person in the classroom, it is assumed that what she has to say is more important than what anybody else says. (This is one of the assumptions made by most coding schemes of classroom verbal interaction. The teacher's language is coded in great detail and what the students say is virtually ignored.) By virtue of her position, the teacher can designate whose turn it is to speak. Although she did not do it explicitly, the teacher appears to have designated segment 2 as her "time," whereas segment 1 was more of a "student's time." This fact, in addition to how the teacher positioned her torso and head, adds to the impression of "seriousness" of segment 2.

TABLE 4 Percentage of Talk for Each Participant During Different Segments of the Game

	Total amount of time when talking occurs	% Time Talking By* Teacher	Angie	S1	S2	Others
Segment 1	121 seconds	65	7	21	0	16
Segment 2	143.5 seconds		12.5	7	0	2
Segment 3	29 seconds		3	7	3	10

* The percentage of talk is computed by dividing the time each participant was speaking by the total amount of time during which speech occurred. Note that the figures add up to more than 100%. This is because there were instances when more than one person was speaking at a time, and so these times are in effect counted twice.

The "seriousness" of segment 2 imposes limitations not only on who can speak but also on what can be said. The focus of segment 2 was the playing of the game. In segment 1, the focus was setting up the game, but other activities could take place while the game was being set up. During segment 1, there was not only a higher tolerance for interruptions by students who were not players in the game, but also a higher tolerance for digressions by student players from the main topic being discussed within the frame of the game. Since segment 2 was more focused than segment 1, the tolerance for digression in topics of discussion was much lower.

In the light of this discussion, the comment Angie made in line 97 (segment 2) can be seen as inappropriate. During this segment--the actual playing of the game--it was inappropriate to attempt to start a discussion about parents or friends. The teacher did not sanction Angie's choice of topic. There was not explicit mention of the fact that the topic was inappropirate for that time. However, the teacher's response, a very short grin in the general direction of Angie, seems to have functioned as an implicit message regarding the inappropriateness of the topic.

Comparison between Angie's Behavior and Behavior of S1 and S2

The only other instance of non-game related talk regarding parents or parents of friends occurred in lines 52 and 57 between S1 and the teacher. (This occurred during segment 1.) As was stated earlier, it was appropriate during segment 1 to discuss topics other than those directly related to the playing of the game. It was therefore appropriate for S1 at this time to initiate a discussion about her friend and her friend's father. While Angie's comment during segment 2 was virtually ignored, the teacher responded to S1's comment, and in fact the discussion of this topic continued for four more lines.

This comparison between Angie's unsuccessful attempt at initiating a non-game related topic and S1's successful venture into the realm of non-game related topics points to a fundamental difference between the performance of Angie in the presence of the teacher and the performance of S1 in the presence of the teacher. From the preceding discussion, it is clear that S1 was more capable of choosing appropriate topics in the presence of the teacher than Angie was. In addition to this, it seems that S1 was a better judge of whose time it was to speak than Angie was. As can be seen in table 4, S1 did 21% of the talking during segment 1, while she did only 7% of the talking during segment 2. Angie, on the other hand, did 7% of the talking during segment 1, and then increased her amount of talking to 12.5% during segment 2. (Part of Angie's talking was done to persons outside the game. Her percentage of talk to persons inside the game was only about 8% or 9%.) S1 appears to have recognized that segment 1 was "student's time," whereas segment 2 was "teacher's time." Angie appears not to have made that distinction.

One further point can be made about differences between Angie's verbal behavior and S1's verbal behavior. As was shown earlier, Angie demonstrated, through her use of questions, that she did not understand what the game of tic-tac-toe was all about. S1, on the other hand, served as the teacher's assistant in teaching the other two students how to play the game. In lines 40-43 and 74-85, S1 demonstrated her knowledge of the game by telling the teacher and the other two students how it was played. S1 therefore demonstrated knowledge not only of social rules, but also of game rules.

It is interesting to note that on two occasions, S1 tried to go out of turn. On both occasions, the teacher "reprimanded" her, using a mock angry tone and pointing her finger at S1. (The teacher's responses are in lines 104 and 115.) Following the second occasion S1 repeated the teacher's words back to the teacher in a mock angry tone, and pointed her finger at the teacher. It seems from the teacher's response to S1's trying to go out of turn, that the teacher did not really believe that S1 thought it was her turn, but rather that S1 was impatient and wanted to put her piece in a strategic location before anyone else could take that spot. Therefore, the teacher's "reprimand" to S1 was not really a reprimand of S1 because she did not know the rules of the game. It was in fact an interactional game between S1 and the teacher, in which both indicated that they knew the rules of the tic-tac-toe game. This kind of camaraderie between the teacher and S1 occurred frequently between the teacher and members of the elite group of students, of which S1 was a part. The teacher would frequently joke with these students, all of whom were first graders, whereas the same kind of interaction did not occur between the teacher and other students in the room. This camaraderie can also be seen in line 7 where S1 calls the teacher silly.

In all fairness to Angie, although S1's behavior in the presence of the teacher could be considered competent, her behavior with Angie alone left a great deal to be desired. At the beginning of the segment under analysis, S1 approached Angie and asked her if she wanted to play tic-tac-toe. When Angie responded by asking her what tic-tac-toe meant, S1 turned away from Angie and walked away, leaving Angie and her question hanging. On other occasions as well, S1 did not respond to questions asked her by Angie and other students. The trick of appearing competent in the classroom is to do the right things while you are in the teacher's presence. When you are not in the teacher's presence, your behavior does not matter as much; all that matters at that time is that you not attract the teacher's attention. What Angie had not learned yet on the fourth day of school was to alter her behavior in front of the teacher in such a way as to appear socially capable, rather than socially naive. (For another treatment of this issue, see Mehan, 1976).

A COMPARISON BETWEEN THE TEACHER'S TREATMENT OF ANGIE AND THE TEACHER'S TREATMENT OF S1 AND S2

The last section ended with a discussion about the teacher's relationship with S1, and how the relationship was manifested in the mock "reprimands" of S1 by the teacher. This section will begin by analyzing the difference between the advice the teacher gave Angie and the advice the teacher gave S2 during the course of the game. S1 did not need any advice and the teacher did not give her any, because S1 already knew how to play the game.

Angie and S2 each made three moves. During the first move, Angie did not receive any advice, while S2 was told by the teacher: "put it anyplace now, it's O.K." (line 91). The advice given for the second move for both students was much more explicit than the advice given for the first move. (The advice to S2 is found in lines 98 to 102, whereas the advice to Angie is found in lines 104 to 108.) The teacher virtually told both students where to put their pieces. The difference in the performance of the two students, however, indicated their differential understandings of the game. Neither student put their piece where the teacher told them to put it. However, S2 put her piece in a place where she blocked Angie's progress (the teacher had suggested she block S1's progress) whereas Angie put her piece in a spot which (to the teacher at least) did not make any sense in terms of the progress of the game. S2, therefore, demonstrated that she knew what she had to do when she put her piece down, whereas Angie did not.

This difference is reflected in the advice the teacher gave to the two students for their third moves. The advice given to S2 was quite implicit: "You better wake up here, S2, and block her or she's gonna win...S1's already got three in a row." (Line 110-112) Although the teacher mentioned that S2 should block S1, there was absolutely no mention of where S2 should put her piece. S2 had to figure that out for herself. S2 actually put her piece where the teacher wanted her to put it, because the teacher complimented her move.

The advice given to Angie before her third move was of a quite different order. The teacher attempted to help Angie understand what was happening in the game. She attempted this by asking a series of seven questions, which were meant to clarify what was happening on the board. (This series of questions is contained in lines 119-131.) In the final analysis, the teacher must have realized that Angie still did not understand what was happening, because on line 133 the teacher said: "Put your man right there and she can't put hers there. Put it right there." While she was saying this, the teacher was pointing to the spot in question.

The basic difference between the advice given to Angie and the advice given to S2 was that the advice given to Angie became more explicit, while the advice given to S2 became more implicit from the second to the third move. Erickson and Shultz (1976) found that the explicit-implicit dimension was a very important indicator of social solidarity between counselor and student in junior college counseling interviews. Giving implicit advice has the social meaning "You know what you're doing so I don't have to spell it out for you in detail," whereas explicit advice carries the social meaning "since you obviously don't know what's going on, I'd better try to make the situation as clear as possible so that you will know what to do." The teacher was indeed acknowledging that in her estimation, S2 could follow what was happening in the game, whereas Angie could not. (The teacher mentioned after she saw the videotape of the game that she thought that Angie did not understand how the game was played even after the game was over.) At this point in the year, S2 was not a member of the elite group of students. However, she was to become a member soon afterward (after she "came out of her shell") and this move was perhaps foreshadowed by the treatment S2 received from the teacher during the tic-tac-toe game.

One final comparison can be made. After the third move of S2 and Angie and the fourth move of S1, the teacher complimented each of them. After S2's third move (the teacher's advice to S2 before she made this move is reported above), the teacher said to S2: "...good girl. Now she can't get any." (lines 112-113) After Angie's third move, in which the teacher actually told her where to put her piece, the teacher said to her: "Now S2 can't put four in a row! So you stopped her. That was good." (lines 134-135) Following her fourth move, S1 said to the teacher: "I put mine in there so she can't go" (gestures to the board). (line 140) S1 filled in the context of her move, so all the teacher had left to say was "That's good." (line 141)

There seems to be an inverse relationship between the ability of the child to play the game (in the teacher's eyes) and the compliment the child received after making a good move: the greater the presumed ability of the child, the less elaborate the compliment. Therefore, the least able child, Angie, received the most elaborate compliment, while the most capable child, S1, received the least elaborate compliment. Erickson (1968) and Shultz (1975) found an inverse relationship between the amount of elaboration of speech and the amount of social solidarity among speakers; that is, persons with higher social solidarity used less words per speaking turn than persons with lower social solidarity. The kind of compliment given each child by the teacher can therefore be used as another indicator of her relationship with the child: S1 was regarded the highest by the teacher at that time, followed by S2, and finally Angie.

CONCLUSIONS

This paper has attempted to describe the relationship between a student's social performance and a teacher's judgments about the child's abilities. Given the teacher's negative evaluation of Angie, the aim of the paper was to show what it was about Angie's behavior that might lead the teacher to evaluate Angie the way she did.

Several aspects of Angie's behavior were identified as possible bases for the teacher's judgment: Angie's lack of knowledge about tic-tac-toe as revealed by the kinds of questions she asked; her imitations of other students; her lack of initiative in introducing new topics; and most importantly, her inability to notice the interactional juncture between setting the game up and the actual play of the game. Not being able to identify the juncture between interactional contexts can lead to the production of situationally inappropriate behavior (Erickson and Shultz, 1977). This appears to be what happened when Angie said "I'm going to tell my mommy again." There is further evidence that Angie "missed" other junctures between interactional contexts during the first two weeks of the school year. Until she learned what those interactional contexts were, when they occurred, and the behavior appropriate to each of them, she ran the risk of continuing to be identified as socially incompetent. Fortunately, for Angie, by December of that year, she had figured out what constituted appropriate behavior in this classroom.

The short length of the segment under analysis precludes the formulation of any broad generalizations about the nature of classroom interaction. That was not the purpose of the paper. Rather, the purpose was to demonstrate methods for doing microethnographic analyses of classroom activities which will eventually add to our understanding of the social organization of classrooms. (For reports of work done on other aspects of this classroom, see Bremme, 1976; and Florio, 1978.)

The kind of information provided by this type of research can be very beneficial to teachers. The teacher in the classroom described in this paper reports that she has gained a better understanding of the patterns of interaction between students and teachers from the findings of this and other work on her classroom and from interaction with the research team. She has also been able to identify the kind of information she uses to make inferences about children's abilities by attempting to separate her perception of children's social performance from their performance on cognitive tasks.

Much more work needs to be done in this area. It is hoped that the findings reported here, as well as those coming from similar research being done elsewhere, will stimulate further work on the social organization of classrooms that will lead to a further understanding of what really goes on in schools.

BIBLIOGRAPHY

Asch, S. E. (1946) Forming impressions of personality. Journal of Abnormal and Social Psychology, 41: 258-290.

Blom, J. P., and Gumperz, J. (1972) Social meaning in linguistic structures. In J. Gumperz and D. Hymes (eds.), Directions in Sociolinguistics, New York: Holt, Rinehart and Winston.

Bremme, D. W. (1976) Accomplishing a classroom event: A microethnography of first circle. Working Paper #3, Newton Classroom Interaction Project, Harvard University.

Cook-Gumperz, J. (1975) The child as practical reasoner. In M. Sanches and B. G. Blount (eds.), Sociocultural Dimensions of Language Use, New York: Academic Press.

Erickson, F. (1968) Discussion behavior in the black ghetto and in white suburbia: A comparison of language style and inquiry style. Northwestern University, Unpublished Dissertation.

Erickson, F. (1975a) Gatekeeping and the melting pot. Harvard Educational Review, 45: 1, 44-70.

Erickson, F. (1975b) One function of proxemic shifts in face-to-face interaction. In A. Kendon, R. Harris and M. R. Key (eds.), Organization of Behavior in Face-to-Face Interaction, The Hague: Mouton.

Erickson, F. and Shultz, J. (1976) Social solidarity and indexical repair: Contexts, forms and functions of a speech act. Unpublished paper.

Erickson, F. and Shultz, J. (1977) When is a context? Some issues and methods in the analysis of social competence. The Quarterly Newsletter of the Institute for Comparative Human Development, 1 (2):5-10.

Florio, S. (1978) Learning how to go to school: an ethnography of interaction in a kindergarten/first grade classroom. Harvard Graduate School of Education, Unpublished Dissertation.

Garfinkel, H. (1967) Studies in Ethnomethodology, Englewood Cliffs, N.J.: Prentice Hall.

Garfinkel, H. and Sacks, H. (1970) The formal properties of practical actions. In J. C. McKinney and E. A. Tiryakian (eds.), Theoretical Sociology, New York: Appleton, Century, Crofts.

Goodenough, W. H. (1964) Cultural anthropology and linguistics. In D. Hymes (ed.), Theoretical Sociology, New York: Appleton, Century, Crofts.

Goodenough, W. R. (1975) Multiculturalism as the normal human experience. Paper presented at the Annual Meeting of the American Anthropological Association, San Francisco.

Gumperz, J. and Herasimchuck, E. (1975) The conversational analysis of social meaning: a study of classroom interaction. In M. Sanches and B. G. Blount (eds.), Sociocultural Dimensions of Language Use, New York: Academic Press.

Kendon, A. (1975) Introduction. In A. Kendon, R. Harris and M. R. Key (eds.), Organization of Behavior in Face-to-Face Interaction, The Hague: Mouton.

Kendon, A., Harris, R. M. and Key, M. R. (1975) Organization of Behavior in Face-to-Face Interaction, The Hague: Mouton.

McDermott, R. P. (1976) Kids make sense: an ethnographic account of the interactional management of success and failure in the first-grade classroom. Stanford University, Unpublished Dissertation.

Mehan, H. (1976) Ethnomethodological reflections on socialization in education. Paper presented at the Annual Meeting of the American Educational Research Association, San Francisco.

Mehan, H., Fisher, S., and Maroules, N. (1976) The social organization of classroom lessons. A Technical Report submitted to the Ford Foundation under auspices of Ford Foundation Grant 740-0420.

Mehan, H., and Wood, H. (1975) The Reality of Ethnomethodology, New York: Wiley-Interscience.

Pike, K. L. (1967) Language in Relation to a Unified Theory of the Structure of Human Behavior, The Hague: Mouton.

Scheflen, A. E. (1973) Communicational Structure: Analysis of a Psychotherapy Transaction, Bloomington: Indiana University Press.

Shultz, J. (1975) The search for potential co-membership: an analysis of conversations among strangers. Harvard University, Unpublished Dissertation.

Shuy, R., Griffin, M., and Cahir, S. (1975) Project to study children's functional language and education in the early years. Proposal submitted to the Carnegie Corporation of New York.

Tagiuri, R., and Petrullo, L. (1958) Person Perception and Interpersonal Behavior, Stanford: Stanford University Press.

APPENDIX A

Note: This is a transcript of a tic-tac-toe game played by a teacher and three students in a kindergarten/first grade classroom. Other students are engaged in other activities in the room at the same time. Angie is in kindergarten; S1 and S2 are in first grade. A = Angie, T = teacher.

S1: Angie, you wanna play tic-tac-toe?
A: What's tic-tac-toe mean? (Pause) Wha...What's tic-tac-toe?
T: You know how to play tic-tac-toe? It's a hard game.
A: I know, but I bet I can do it.
T: O.K. I'll go get the game--you stay right here S2 will play with you too.
S1: I'm drawing it, silly.
T: You're drawing it? Oh. You're going to play that kind? I have a harder kind to play S1. Let me get one here. Judy! who else is gonna play? How many people do we have to play?
A: What's it called?
S1: I'm gonna play
T: O.K., I'll show you--it's hard. You can try.
Boy: I wanna play that game.
T: I can only have three people play--you can watch. What color is your favorite color, Angie?
A: Um... (Pause) (Shrugs)
T: O.K. here's the choice: you can be red, ...
A: Red.
T: ...yellow, or blue. Which color do you wanna be?
S1: I take blue.
A: Blue.
T: Oh, we have to decide.
A: I take blue.
S1: And I pick red.
T: (Aside to Boy)
A: This color (points to piece on table).
S1: That's red.
T: What's this color?
Boy: It isn't. This is a mushroom.
T: That's a nice mushroom. Can you make it stand up? Try to fix it. Alright. If you wanna be red ...Angie, ...
A: Red.
T: ...take all the red pieces out for you.
S1: And I get blue.
T: S2, you're gonna have to be yellow. And all the blue ones ...take all the red ones outta here and put 'em in a pile.
S1: I know how to play
T: Sh...
S1: Um, if I'm like a here ...
T: We have to sort all the colors out first.
S1: If I'm here, right?--then if she, right?, Angie, puts her man here, then I don't get a tic-tac-toe. I don't getta...
Boy: Miss T...(repeated 4 times)
T: Joey, I can't understand you if you don't talk to me. Come over here so I can see you.
Boy: I wanna play I wanna play with the earphones.

T: You have to wait 'til there's room for you. How about if you go and play with the plasticene. Make me something--a snake. Go make an S in the plasticene. Let me see you make an S for me, Joey, out of the plasticene.
S1: I saw Kevin's father today.
T: Kevin Brown's father?
Boy: (Brings in ball of plasticene) Right here?
T: (Nods) Make a long snake and then make an S. Draw it.
S1: How did you know his name was Kevin Brown?
T: He's busy, isn't he?
Boy: Miss T.
T: What?
Boy: Miss T.
T: What? We're busy.
S1: O.K. I put one right here. (To Angie:) Your turn, your turn.
T: Alright, Angie wanna start.
S1: I start here (points to corner of top board).
T: Shh. Alright.
A: I start here (points to corner of next-to-top board).
T: No-no-no-no. Wait a minute. Just let me tell you. We're gonna use just one lane, O.K., S1...let's do it this way to start out with.
It's gonna take too much if we play the whole game. We'll start making it easier to start with. (Removes top board and sets rest of board aside.) O.K., here's what we're gonna play on. You wanna get 1,2,3,4,--you wanna have four of your color in a row, O.K.? (Looks at Angie who nods yes.) Or four of your color this way (Looks at S2) You know how to play tic-tac-toe?--you know how to play?--or four that way.
S1: Or four...
T: But if...
S1: ...or four...
T: ...somebody...
S1: or four, or four that way.
T: But if somebody blocks you...
S1: ...you can't go...
T: ...you can't have your row, can you?
S1: And you can't take the men away.
T: No. So S1, alright S1's gone. Now it's your turn. You have to get four in a row someplace
S1: Four.
T: Go ahead.
A: Where's my one?
T: (To S2) Put it anyplace now, it's O.K.
Girl: You can take them off.
T: (S2 moves) Good for you. O.K. now Angie. (Angie moves) alright. (S1 moves) Now it's S2's turn.
S1: You wanna try to get four in a row.
Girl: What is youse playing?
A: I'm gonna tell my mommy again (addressed to T.)
T: You have to block each other though, you know. It won't work if you don't block. (Pause) No, you can't get in a row there, S2. You wanna get four this way, or four that way (Pause). I'd put it over there and you'd block her. Oh you'll block Angie there, O.K.

A: My turn? (S1 starts to move.)

T: It's not your turn, S1! (To Angie) Go ahead, S2. No, you wanna get four, Angie in a row. If you put one here, it won't be a row.

A: Where, where's four?

T: See you're already blocked. This is 1,2,3,4,...you gotta go across. (Angie moves) This is a hard game for you, I think.

A: No, it isn't.

T: You better wake up here, S2, and block her or she's gonna win.

A: What? (To call from person in background.)

T: S1's already got three in a row (S2 makes move)..good girl. Now she can't get any.

A: Wait a second. (In response to outside call.)

T: (To S1) It's not your turn. Come on, Angie.

A: (To person in previous two turns) Wait a second, I'm playing a game.

T: Can you see where S2 can get...Wait a minute. Can you see where S2 can get four in a row?

A: (Shrugs.)

T: Look. O.K., she has three in one row. Let's see where are the three that are in a row? (Pause) (Angie points at board) No, three yellow ones. Where do you see three yellow ones? (Angie points at board) Are they in a straight row, almost?

S1: Yeah.

T: Do you see where another one goes?

S1: She's gonna win...

T: If she puts one and makes four in a straight row, then she wins.

A: And me too?

T: Can you stop her? Can you stop her from winning?

S1: Yeah, she can put her man...

T: Put your man right there and she can't put her's there. Put it right there. (Angie moves) Now S2 can't put four in a row! (Angie smiles) So you stopped her. That was good.

Girl: Can I have a magic marker?

T: (to game players) O.K. (Pause) (T turns around) Tony, what are you doing?

A: He...They're playing with the blocks.

S1: I put mine in there so she can't go...(points at board)

T: That's good. I don't think anybody's gonna win this game...

Girl: Can you get this off for me?

T: ...There's too many people playing on this board for anybody to win. This is a hard game. We're going to try something____

S1: I like it.

A: I like it too.

S2: Four in a row?

S1: It's easy.

T: Wanna play the real way and I'll help Angie? (Pause) (to other girls) Sure. (to game players) Alright, we'll play so you can really win this time, and I'll help Angie...'cause you two can win, you know how to play.

Girl: She wants her.

T: (to girl) Tell her to take somebody else first. Alright. O.K. Angie how about you going with Mrs.______. You can come back.

Author Index

Subject Index